The Obamas and a (Post) Racial America?

Series in Political Psychology

Series Editor
John T. Jost

Image Bite Politics: News and the Visual Framing of Elections
Maria E. Grabe and Erik P. Bucy

Social and Psychological Bases of Ideology and System Justification
John T. Jost, Aaron C. Kay, and Hulda Thorisdottir

The Political Psychology of Democratic Citizenship
Eugene Borgida, Christopher Federico, and John Sullivan

On Behalf of Others: The Psychology of Care in a Global World
Sarah Scuzzarello, Catarina Kinnvall, and Kristen Renwick Monroe

The Obamas and a (Post) Racial America?
Gregory S. Parks and Matthew W. Hughey

Forthcoming books in the series:

Ideology, Psychology, and Law
Jon Hanson

The Competent Voter
Paul Goren

The Ambivalent Partisan: How Critical Loyalty Promotes Democracy
Howard Lavine and Marco Steenbergen

The Obamas and a (Post) Racial America?

Edited by

Gregory S. Parks and Matthew W. Hughey

OXFORD
UNIVERSITY PRESS
2011

OXFORD

UNIVERSITY PRESS

Oxford University Press, Inc., publishes works that further
Oxford University's objective of excellence
in research, scholarship, and education.

Oxford   New York
Auckland   Cape Town   Dar es Salaam   Hong Kong   Karachi
Kuala Lumpur   Madrid   Melbourne   Mexico City   Nairobi
New Delhi   Shanghai   Taipei   Toronto

With offices in
Argentina   Austria   Brazil   Chile   Czech Republic   France   Greece
Guatemala   Hungary   Italy   Japan   Poland   Portugal   Singapore
South Korea   Switzerland   Thailand   Turkey   Ukraine   Vietnam

Copyright © 2011 by Oxford University Press, Inc.

Published by Oxford University Press, Inc.
198 Madison Avenue, New York, New York 10016

www.oup.com

Library of Congress Cataloging-in-Publication Data
The Obamas and a (post) racial America?/edited by Gregory S. Parks and
Matthew W. Hughey.
   p. cm. – (Series in political psychology)
   Includes bibliographical references and index.
   ISBN 978-0-19-973520-4 (hardcover : acid-free paper) 1. United States–Race
relations. 2. African Americans–Social conditions–21st century.
3. Racism–United States. 4. Post-racialism–United States. 5. Obama,
Barack–Influence. 6. Obama, Michelle, 1964—Influence. I. Parks,
Gregory, 1974- II. Hughey, Matthew W. (Matthew Windust)
   E185.615.O27 2010
   973.932092–dc22   2010022024

Printed in the United States of America
on acid-free paper

Foreword

THE OBAMA I KNOW

Barack Obama matters to America not just as a politician—not even just as a president—but as a person. A strikingly large proportion of the unprecedented torrent of books and other media published about President Obama in the past several years appear to be as much about personality as politics. In addition to openly biographical works such as *New Yorker* editor David Remnick's *The Bridge: The Life and Rise of Barack Obama* or journalist David Mendell's *Obama: From Promise to Power*, political commentary on the current administration displays a deep fascination with Barack Obama and his family. The dust jacket of *Newsweek* columnist Jonathan Alter's *The Promise: President Obama, Year One* proposes to answer the question, "What is the president really like, on the job and off-hours?" Less charitably, Aaron Klein's *The Manchurian President* dedicates a chapter to "Unmasking the Mysterious College Years." Perhaps most straightforwardly, the subtitle of David Bergen Brophy's biography, *Michelle Obama*, invites young readers to "Meet the First Lady."

It comes as no surprise to me that there is such a clamor to know the first family. They are wonderful people, well worth knowing. I first met Barack and Michelle separately, over twenty years ago, when they were students at Harvard Law School. Over the years I have been privileged to know the Obamas not only as a professor but also as a mentor, an advisor, and a friend. I am pleased to share a few of the impressions I have formed over the past two decades and to compare the Obamas I know with the image of the first family that has emerged over the past few years.

When I first encountered Barack Obama, I thought he was a Republican. That Obama, a man even then deeply committed to progressive values, could be mistaken for a conservative was, I think, an early indication of his exceptional personal thoughtfulness and inclusiveness as a leader. Obama was always uniquely capable not only of seeing both sides of a legal or political argument, but also of making participants on opposite sides of that argument feel like he respected and even agreed with them. As a law student he managed to be a unifying, mediating force even on the thorniest of racial issues.[1] For this reason friends even then found him "hard to pin down," as Obama's classmate and my colleague Lawrence Mack put it.[2]

Far from keeping his head down at HLS, though, Obama marched into the political fray. Speaking to issues from faculty diversity to affirmative action, he somehow managed to find allies on both sides of what then seemed irreconcilable ideological divides. He did this not by politicking or talking out of both sides of his mouth, but by being perfectly fair and sincere. Rather than playing both sides, Barack "walks between two worlds," as his half-sister, Maya Soetoro-Ng, once put it.[3]

As a candidate for the presidency of the Harvard Law Review, Obama succeeded not by elbowing others out of his way—a skill he reserved for fierce competitions on the basketball court—but by taking that path between left and right that others could scarcely see, let alone walk down. After he became president of the Law Review, Obama expertly charted a course through a time of ideological turmoil that somehow kept the left and right wings of the Law Review unified even as the school's faculty became so deeply divided that faculty hiring virtually froze.

As long as I have known him, Obama has always been a powerful unifier. He is inclusive, sometimes to a fault, and is able to bring out inclusive sentiments in those fortunate enough to be around him. This remarkable talent for bringing people together was clearly visible during the 2008 campaign, which inspired people of all races to vote in record numbers.[4] It is still visible today in the standing and respect that the United States now enjoys around the world, in the relationships President Obama has fostered with countries that had grown apart from the US in the past decade. Approval ratings for the United States are much higher now then they were under the previous administration, and even as citizens of other countries express dissatisfaction with their own government's treatment of the economic crisis, they continue to express enthusiasm for Obama's leadership.[5]

But the reach of Obama's inclusiveness, which at one time unified the Harvard Law Review and now embraces much of the world, somehow does not include over half of the American people.[6] Beyond these poll numbers, which are not much different from those of other recent presidents,[7] there is an unprecedented level of personal animosity directed at Obama that cannot be explained simply as political disagreement with the president. Indeed, incidents such as Joe Wilson's shouting "You lie!" at Obama's speech on health care and Justice Alito's mouthing the words "not true" at the 2010 State of the Union address are unprecedented in the modern history of presidential speeches.

Respect for the office has always trumped disagreement with the man currently occupying it—until now.

Many of Obama's actions since taking office have, for good reason, been politically controversial. In a year and a half he has overhauled health care, orchestrated a major financial bailout, instituted an economic recovery plan, and revamped banking regulation all while managing two wars overseas. As dramatic as these actions are in the short term, the full force of their impact will be felt not in the coming months but in the coming decades, as major societal structures shift in response to the new legal rules. The desirability of these overhauls is up for debate, and it is for the American people, now and in the years to come, to judge Obama on the basis of his already substantial record as president.

What concerns me, though, is that the anger and hostility of a noticeable portion of the American people is not a response to the political and economic reforms that Obama has presided over, but to Obama himself. What I see isn't simple racism, an open rejection of Obama because he is black. Instead, it is Obama's unique capacity to "walk between worlds"—the very thing that makes him such an exceptional and inclusive leader—that has made him vulnerable to attack. Rather than seeing the president's position as one that embraces both the left and right, many have chosen to paint him as "other," an outsider (and not one of those good populist "Washington outsiders"). This effort to delegitimize Obama's unifying capacity, to exclude him from the communion of "us" on the basis of his inclusiveness of all of us, is emblematic of this country's continuing and unresolved racial problems.

While there have been moments when Obama's race has been used overtly to cast him as an oddity, an outsider, the deeper problems are more veiled. The song "Barack the Magic Negro" may have played well with Rush Limbaugh's audience during the presidential campaign, but its later use by Chip Saltsman quickly derailed his campaign for the chair of the RNC. Tea party references to Obama as "professor," though not explicitly about race, also traffic in the idea that "he's not one of us," that he has these ideas that are left wing, that are socialist, that he's palling around with terrorists. Behind these buzzwords, the reality is that these tea partiers look at this president as an African American who is out of place.[8]

Even as Obama appears to some out of place as an African American in the White House—an "uppity" black man not playing the proper racial role— much of the country also sees him as stepping out of line in his role as occupant of the White House when he ventures into the subject of race. Obama's comments regarding the arrest of my friend and fellow Harvard professor Skip Gates for breaking into his own home met with general criticism. The "beer summit" that followed managed to put the story to rest, but the meeting on the White House lawn was hardly the successful resolution of racial tensions that Obama accomplished as president of the Harvard Law Review. America is perhaps not ready for such a resolution, and white America is at the moment not interested in having a black president who is going to address race issues on a national level.

At the same time, Obama is also open to criticism from black Americans. Though President Obama has recognized the systemic inequities that continue to place black people in America at a disadvantage, he has yet to enact policies addressing the disproportionately harsh impact the recession has had on black Americans because of these structural disadvantages. But as support for Obama among black Americans remains strong and his approval ratings among whites falters, Obama may not be in a political position where addressing such disparities is a viable priority. More, he may be less able to promote such policies than a white president would have been.

This is all to say that the race of the Obamas, and race in the age of Obama, is very complicated, and having any productive discussion about it is complicated further by a national attention span that is limited to what can be contained in a sound byte or a single news cycle. Nowhere is this clearer than in the case of Shirley Sherrod. Sherrod told a long story of halting, painful racial reconciliation that pointed towards a future free from bias against farmers of any race. What we heard, and what we responded to, talked about, and drew battle lines over, was a seconds-long clip, decontextualized to the point of meaninglessness. In the clamor to decide whether Sherrod is a racist, the far more important problem of impersonal structural racism and subconscious bias—the problems addressed in Sherrod's speech—disappeared.[9]

This collection is an important counterweight to the gross simplifications and resistance to nuance that mark the current national discussions of race. By looking closely at the persistent problems of bias that lie even beneath the level of conscious thought, this book helps to explain how and why Barack Obama has become both a symbol of hope for an inclusive, "post-racial" future and the epitome of excluded "otherness."

Charles J. Ogletree
Jesse Climenko Professor of Law
Harvard Law School
Cambridge, Massachusetts

NOTES

1 Jodi Kantor, *In Law School Obama Found Political Voice*, THE NEW YORK TIMES (January 28, 2007). Available at http://www.nytimes.com/2007/01/28/us/politics/28obama.html?pagewanted=print

2 *Id.*

3 Sharon Cohen, *Barack Obama, Walking between Worlds*, THE ASSOCIATED PRESS (June 24, 2008). Available at http://www.cbc.ca/world/story/2008/06/04/f-obama- biography.html.

4 *National Voter Turnout in Federal Elections: 1960–2008*. Available at http://www.infoplease.com/ipa/A0781453.html

5 *Obama More Popular Abroad Than At Home, Global Image of U.S. Continues to Benefit*, PEW RESEARCH CENTER (June 17, 2010). Available at http://pewglobal.org/2010/06/17/obama-more-popular-abroad-than-at-home/.

6 *Obama Averages 47.3% Approval in Sixth Quarter*, GALLUP (July 20, 2010). Available at http://www.gallup.com/poll/141461/Obama-Averages-Approval-Sixth-Quarter.aspx. Obama's approval ratings have fallen below 50% in 2010. The Pew study similarly shows a 50/50 split regarding Obama's leadership in the economic crisis.

7 *Id.*

8 *See,* Jack Stripling, *Professor in Chief,* Inside Higher Education (February 10, 2010). Available at http://www.insidehighered.com/news/2010/02/10/obama.

9 *See,* Charles J. Ogletree Jr. and Johanna Wald, *After Shirley Sherrod, We All Need to Slow Down and Listen,* THE WALL STREET JOURNAL (July 25, 2010). Available at http://www.washingtonpost.com/wp-dyn/content/article/2010/07/23/AR2010072304583.html.

Acknowledgments

We thank Stephen Wrinn at the University Press of Kentucky and Eduardo Bonilla-Silva of Duke University for encouraging us to tackle such a project. Thank you to John Jost (Political Psychology series editor) and Lori Handelman (acquisitions editor) at Oxford University Press for reaching out and taking interest in this project. We also thank Lori and her assistants for shuttling this project along and keeping us as close to our deadlines as possible.

We thank Professor Charles Ogletree for taking time out of his very busy schedule to write the Foreword to this book. We were quite humbled that he was willing to do it.

Thank you to all of the contributing authors: Leslie Ashburn-Nardo, Meghan G. Bean, Tamara L. Brown, George Ciccariello-Maher, Geoffrey L. Cohen, Nilanjana Dasgupta, Thierry Devos, John F. Dovidio, Samuel L. Gaertner, Eric Hehman, John T. Jost, Kristin A. Lane, Robert W. Livingston, Clarenda M. Phillips, Valerie Purdie-Vaughns, Shanette C. Porter, Jennifer A. Richeson, Tamar Saguy, Donald A. Saucier, Rachel Sumner, Joshua Waytz, Russell J. Webster, and Kumar Yogeeswaran. We know we pressed you all hard to submit well-researched, well-written articles on some tough deadlines. We appreciate all of your hard work on great chapters.

Thank you to all of the commentators, those individuals who took the respective chapters and helped to expound on the arguments made therein: Ian Ayres, Lawrence D. Bobo, Farai Chideya, Michael C. Dawson, Jenée Desmond-Harris, Eddie Glaude, Jr., Melissa Harris-Lacewell, Marc Lamont Hill, Richard O. Lempert, Kenneth Mack, Julianne Malveaux, and Marc H. Morial.

Contents

Contributors

Leslie Ashburn-Nardo
Department of Psychology
Indiana University—Purdue
  University Indianapolis

Meghan G. Bean
Department of Psychology
Northwestern University

Tamara L. Brown
Department of Psychology
University of Kentucky

George Ciccariello-Maher
Department of History and Politics
Drexel University

Geoffrey L. Cohen
School of Education & Department
  of Psychology
Stanford University

Nilanjana Dasgupta
Department of Psychology
University of Massachusetts,
  Amherst

Thierry Devos
Department of Psychology
San Diego State University

John F. Dovidio
Department of Psychology
Yale University

Samuel L. Gaertner
Department of Psychology
University of Delaware

Eric Hehman
Department of Psychology
University of Deleware

Matthew W. Hughey
Department of Sociology
Mississippi State University

John T. Jost
Department of Psychology
New York University

Kristin A. Lane
Department of Psychology
Bard College

Robert W. Livingston
Kellogg School of Management
Northwestern University

Gregory S. Parks
Law School
Cornell University

Clarenda M. Phillips
Department of Sociology, Social
    Work, and Criminology
Morehead State University

Shanette C. Porter
Department of Psychology
Northwestern University

Valerie Purdie-Vaughns
Department of Psychology
Columbia University

Jennifer A. Richeson
Department of Psychology
Northwestern University

Tamar Saguy
School of Psychology
Interdisciplinary Center,
    Herzliya

Donald A. Saucier
Department of Psychology
Kansas State University

Rachel Sumner
Department of Human
    Development
Cornell University

Joshua Waytz
Department of Psychology
Northwestern University

Russell J. Webster
Department of Psychology
Kansas State University

Kumar Yogeeswaran
Department of Psychology
University of Massachusetts,
    Amherst

Introduction

On January 3, 2008, then-Senator Barack Obama gave his Iowa Caucus victory speech and—in the cadence of a Black Baptist preacher, or civil rights leader, or both—stated, "You know they said . . . this day would never come." In the context of his speech, Obama was clearly talking about the commentators', critics', and pundits' doubts about his ability to be a viable candidate in the 2008 presidential election. But in the larger narrative of Black people in the United States, it is hard to believe that he did not also intend for those opening words to mean that there have long been doubters as to whether a Black person could ever be a viable candidate for, let alone win, the presidency. But that day had arrived. Many months later, on the evening of November 4, 2008, "The Obamas" (Barack, Michelle, Sasha, and Malia) took the stage in Chicago's Grant Park, clad in their black and burgundy as 44th President-Elect, the soon-to-be First Lady, and First Family. It was a striking image of a Black man ascending to the position of being the most powerful person in the world, with his family by his side. But that image, in many respects, paled in comparison to that of him taking his oath of office, again with his family by his side, and millions of people in attendance to witness "change" in America.

The rise of Barack Obama and the ascension of the Obama family as the all-American, if not quintessentially American, family has evoked the word "post-racial" in the American lexicon. But when we think of that word, do we mean it as a statement or a question? For many, the sheer fact that Obama was elected President bespeaks how far this country has come with regard to race relations, particularly as it relates to Blacks in America. And, to some degree, this assessment is accurate. Everything, however, is not as it seems—even when it comes to racial progress.

In this book, we interrogate the notion that President Obama's election places America within a post-racial era. We move beyond the debates about the degree to which Americans are "racist" in the explicit sense and even to the degree to which racism continues to perpetuate structural inequalities between people of different racial groups. Rather, we employ advances in the way that contemporary cognitive and social psychology are used as a means to understand racial prejudice. Specifically, the contributors to this volume draw from research on implicit, automatic race bias to illustrate that (1) people often fail to articulate those racial attitudes that they are fully aware of for a host of reasons; (2) even individuals who harbor explicit, egalitarian racial views may also harbor "unconscious" race bias against certain categories of people; and (3) these attitudes influence behavior. Generally, we make two points in this book: First, despite the fact that the United States has made tremendous strides in the area of race relations, the metric used for that progress is outdated and ineffective. By employing the metric of implicit bias, we see that implicit anti-Black bias is prevalent even in the age of the Obamas and in many ways influences Whites' perceptions of, attitudes about, and interaction with Blacks in many ways. Second, the prominence of the Obamas would seem to bode well for racial progress, because positive Black exemplars may help to racially debias individuals even at the implicit level.

CHAPTER 1

Measuring Racial Progress in America: The Tangled Path

Matthew W. Hughey

> I understand there may be a temptation among some to think that discrimination is no longer a problem in 2009. . . . But make no mistake: the pain of discrimination is still felt in America. . . . But we also know that prejudice and discrimination are not even the steepest barriers to opportunity today. The most difficult barriers include structural inequalities that our nation's legacy of discrimination has left behind; inequalities still plaguing too many communities and too often the object of national neglect. . . . Yes, if you're African American, the odds of growing up amid crime and gangs are higher. Yes, if you live in a poor neighborhood, you will face challenges that someone in a wealthy suburb does not. But that's not a reason to get bad grades, that's not a reason to cut class, that's not a reason to give up on your education and drop out of school. No one has written your destiny for you. Your destiny is in your hands—and don't you forget that.
>
> *—President Barack Obama, address to the NAACP*
> *centennial convention, July 19, 2009*

On the morning I sat down to begin writing this chapter, my phone rang. "Did you hear?" the voice on the other end of the phone exclaimed, "Obama was awarded the Nobel Peace Prize!" As I quickly searched for more information, I ran across the headline, "I did not realize the Nobel Peace Prize had an affirmative action quota . . ." (Erickson, 2009). In the following days, discourse reached a fevered pitch, as talk of the Nobel became intertwined with discussions regarding health-care reform and cries of "socialism," the radical-fringe "birther" movement, secret service reports on the unprecedented amount of death threats against the president (The Public Record, 2009; Zeleny & Rutenberg, 2009, p. A30), and "tea-bagger" protests.

Such conversation does not represent a simple cacophony of differing opinions and passionate invective regarding the role of race in the age of Obama. Rather, these debates and stories possess a set of ideological assumptions that propel them in the public sphere. That structure is particularly Janus-faced. There is, as Lawrence Bobo and Camille Charles (2009, p. 244) write, "a tendency in lay discourse and much social science work to rely on simple phrases or sweeping characterizations, 'racist America' versus 'the end of racism.'" Such binary discourse remains a cornerstone of social structures and a roadmap for the navigation of everyday life.

Aside from die-hard adherents on the extremes, most have found a way to meld these two positions into a unique worldview. As evidenced by Obama's words in the epigraph, we ritually begin with the idea that "structural inequalities" exist and that the United States possesses a "legacy of discrimination," and we close that thought with the admonition that none of that *really* matters in the end—that instead "your destiny is in your hands." Obama's words illumine how supposedly apparent, plain, and opposed positions actually mask a cohesive strategy for speaking about race. These two strands represent a double-helix of sorts—an intertwined narrative of race embedded in the nation's DNA. Such a structure remains both pernicious and seductive. It melds aspects of our bifurcated and antagonistic view of race and racism as either omnipresent or absent so as to satisfy both constituencies, but it does not address reality.

What is the reality of race? It is, in a word, complex. Some measures of racial equality indicate improvement, others decline, and still others show a stubborn stagnancy over the past half-century. Sociologist Orlando Patterson (1989, p. 480) argues that such data represent the "homeostatic principle of the entire system of racial domination"—racial domination decreases in one location only to increase in another. To provide a brief glimpse of this voluminous data, I present a three-pronged approach. First, I survey the common ways in which people admit racial inequality while minimalizing both its effects and social causes. Second, I chronicle the zigzag path of racial progress through key moments of legal battles. Third, I provide a cursory view of five key social arenas: attitudes, housing, education, wealth, and incarceration. Although the data represent quite a mixed bag, I unapologetically demonstrate and argue, despite our discourse of a "post-racial America" in the age of Obama, that racial inequality is neither natural nor predestined but remains well-entrenched and tethered to the promotion of White supremacy.

RACED WAYS OF SEEING: BAD APPLES, GENOMES, AND CULTURE, OH MY!

Part of the burden that saddles the sociologist of race and ethnicity is that most everyone thinks they are a sociologist. Simply because one holds an opinion about race, had an encounter with "racism," or spoke to someone of a different race, the layperson proclaims that their view is both sociologically well-informed and little more than "common sense." As freelance journalist Kate Ledger (2009, p. 49) wrote:

> It doesn't take a sociologist to know that American society has long been plagued by problems of race and inequality. But knowing race is a problem and knowing how to think about that problem (much less what to do about it) are two very different things.

In this vein, it is important to sociologically critique the three dominant "raced ways of seeing."

Bad Apples

In *The Political Mind*, George Lakoff notes that we consistently employ the "bad apple" framework: "All you have to do is find the bad apples in the organization and get rid of them. The organization is redeemed. There was never anything wrong with it. The problem was the bad apples" (2008, pp. 163–164). Taking this work as a point of departure, most readily admit the presence of racism when they hear outbursts from Mel Gibson, Michael Richards (a.k.a. *Seinfeld*'s "Kramer"), and shock-jock Donald Imus.[1] Most will confess there was racism afoot when the White nationalist James W. Von Brunn walked into the Washington, D.C., Holocaust museum in 2009 and began shooting. A few others will admit that recent political protests portraying Barack Obama as a monkey were based on well-established racist caricatures.

Yet despite the regular and patterned repetition of these actions, they are often cavalierly dismissed as "bad apples." To compound the matter, attempts to draw attention to the patterned and systemic nature of racism in today's world, often results in a willful blindness toward racial inequality. This dynamic was recently epitomized by "Katrina Fatigue"; after blatant examples of housing segregation, environmental racism, and intersection of race and poverty were exposed by NPR, NBC News, CNN and *The New York Times*, many media outlets reported that their listeners and readers tired of hearing about race. "Enough already. Nobody cares," one NPR listener wrote (Feeney, 2007). As a consequence, racism is not revealed as a tradition that "weighs like a nightmare on the brains of the living" (Marx, 1852/1978, p. 595) but is framed more like the pipedreams of elitist intellectuals, the product of people that "take things too seriously," or the result of non-Whites who "play the race card."

Genomics and the Mismeasure of Man

Recent advances in molecular biology, genetics, and the mapping of "the" human genome have enabled the expedient study of population differences. Although many scientists explicitly examine *human* variation, some have begun to frame their findings in terms of *racial* differences. As such, some conflate the concepts "race," "ethnicity," "ancestry," "geographic region," and "nationality," confuse individual with population difference, and assume that *inter*-"racial" differences are greater than observable *intra*-"racial" differences. As scholars remarked in a recent special issue of the *Social Studies of Science*:

> In the context of American race politics, folk-understandings of race, and the history of racist scientific investigations in the USA, it is not surprising that members of the media and other public groups read the genetics of difference as the genetics of race. (Fujimura, Duster, & Rajagopalan, 2008, p. 644)

Such conflation has led to a resurgence of the idea that a biological reality underlies "race." For example, pushed by pharmaceutical and capital interests, several companies have marketed drugs aimed at specific non-White populations.[2] Although the effectiveness of these drugs has been questioned, the usage of "race" or "ethnicity" as a proxy for genetic similarities serves as a simplistic and seductive way to attract consumers. As a recent report in *Clinical Pharmacology & Therapeutics* concludes, "[Intra-racial] differences underscore the importance of personalized genomics over a race-based approach to medicine" (Ng, Zhao, Levy, Strausberg, &Venter, 2008, p. 306). Phenotypical similarities between individuals (e.g., skin color and hair texture) that we use to demarcate "race" do not match with genetic similarities between individuals (Begley, 2008).

Accordingly, if one divides humanity by variations of certain DNA structures, then equatorial Africans, Italians, and Greeks fall into the "sickle-cell race;" Swedes and South Africa's Xhosas are a part of the "healthy-hemoglobin race;" those within the "epicanthic eye fold race" include *Kung San* (Bushmen), Japanese, and Chinese; and those within the "pro-lactase race" include the majority of Norwegians, Arabians, and north Indians. Yet, through sound bites, talking heads, and snippets of published research, the notion of a biological racial reality has trickled down to the public sphere.

The Culture of Poverty, Reloaded

As a bookend to biological arguments, the concept of "culture" is often invoked to explain racial inequality and disparities in outcomes. Defined as an abstract set of values, norms, and beliefs, and piggybacking off the work of Oscar Lewis and Daniel P. Moynihan, "culture" became the inspiration for the controversial "culture of poverty" standpoint in the 1960s. It was readily accepted that a "tangle of pathology" pervaded poor, urban, non-White communities.

On the flip side of the argument, specific racial and ethnic communities were lauded for their supposed ability to defer gratification, embrace hard work, and value education. Jews, certain Asian communities, and Northeastern U.S. White Anglo-Saxon Protestants (WASPs), were particularly singled out as possessive of a "culture of success." Such academic renderings eventually saturated everyday life and even transcended traditional political antagonisms. The term *model minority* (first used by sociologist William Peterson in 1966) became an accepted widespread moniker for Asians by the 1980s and 1990s, gracing the pages of *Newsweek, The New Republic, Fortune, Time, and Parade*,[3] and Presidents Reagan and Clinton evoked images of "Black welfare queens" as the rationale for welfare reform.

The problems with this line of reasoning are twofold. First, culture as an abstract and cognitive-only process is a myopic definition that excludes material practices, objects, and resources. Second, it assumes the existence of objectively "good" and "bad" cultures that transcend context. For example, many today would remark that racially unequal levels of wealth accumulation are the result of Blacks' and Latinos' possession of "bad," "deficient," and "dysfunctional" cultural traits that predispose their "wrong" choices. Yet, what may be wrong or right in one context may not translate in another. As Sandra Smith argued in *Lone Pursuit* (2007), many poor, non-White people do not use available social networks to find employment because of a strong sense of moral individualism that dictates a Horatio Algers-like tale of individual, meritocratic uplift. Hence, their lower social positioning and reluctance to use available social connections to obtain work was neither the result of "bad" values nor their placement in a "tangle of pathology" but was influenced and reproduced by both a lack of material resources and the usage of a what many consider to be the "right" type of attitude: an individualist and meritocratic work ethic. Moreover, both Edin and Kefalas' *Promises I Can Keep: Why Poor Women Put Motherhood Before Marriage* (2005) and Anderson's *Code of the Street: Decency, Violence, and the Moral Life of the Inner City* (2000) show that recent attempts among policymakers to convince the underclass to value marriage are based on woefully misguided assumptions. Namely, many presuppose that unmarried, lower-class women of color have higher birth rates than their middle-class, White counterparts because they do not value marriage. On the contrary, evidence shows that underclass women hold marriage in such high esteem that they delay marriage until they believe they and their partners are financially prepared to support the institution.

Much of the aforementioned work flies in the face of both layperson understandings of culture, as well in the face of then-candidate Barack Obama's campaign and policy rhetoric. Speaking to a predominantly Black church in Chicago in June, 2008, Obama said:

> Too many fathers are M.I.A, too many fathers are AWOL, missing from too many lives and too many homes . . . They have abandoned their responsibilities, acting like boys instead of men. And the foundations of our families are weaker because of it. (Bosman, 2008)

As Small, Harding, and Lamont wrote in "Reconsidering Culture and Poverty," "Then-candidate Obama gave little ground to those who countered that poverty undermined fatherhood—he was firm in his belief that fathers needed to change their (cultural) attitudes about parenting: "Most give little ground because this type of rhetoric and argumentation feeds our established and dominant "raced ways of seeing."

THE TANGLED PATH OF RACIAL PROGRESS

As the late historian Ronald Takaki (1993) wrote, "Much of the America's past . . . has been riddled with racism. At the same time, . . . people offer hope, affirming the struggle for equality as a center theme in our country's history. . . . Americans have been constantly redefining their national identity from the moment of first contact on the Virginia shore." Just a cursory glance at key measures of legal and legislative action present us with a critical cartography of the contested terrain of race.

The Legal-National Formation of Race and Racial Inequality

The 55 White men who met for the Philadelphia Constitutional Convention of 1787 legally enshrined several crucial mechanisms that reproduced racial inequality: it gave Congress the authority to suppress slave insurrections, it prevented the abolishment of the slave trade, it exempted slave-made goods from export duties, and it marked the beginning of the "three-fifths" formula (also termed the "federal ratio") by which three-fifths of all enslaved Blacks were counted for the purpose of expanding White political representation from slave states. Such counting of the population began in 1790, when the first U.S. Census also created the first legal racial categories ("White," "Black," and "Other").

The three-fifths compromise set into motion a pageant of future events. As sociologist Joe Feagin wrote (2010, pp. 30–31):

> [Without the compromise] Thomas Jefferson would not have become the third president . . . the extra twelve or so votes that he got in the electoral college because of the white electors who were there only because of the three-fifths counting of enslaved black Americans in southern states. . . .

Slavery would have been banned in the new state of Missouri, the slave-holding President Andrew Jackson would have failed to pass his extreme 1830 Indian Removal Act and the Kansas-Nebraska bill allowing residents to choose slavery in these Midwestern areas would not have become law.

The philosopher Charles Mills (1997) argues that the United States began not with a neutral, Rousseau-esque "social contract" but a "racial contract" in which peoples' identities, rights, and opportunities were undemocratically set in motion by way of a race-based system of stratifying people and resources.

The Office of Indian Affairs, Manifest Destiny, and the Question of Slavery

Although the Office of Indian Affairs was officially formed in 1824, official government relations with Native peoples fell under the jurisdiction of the War Department beginning in 1789. From 1796 to 1822, the office of superintendent of Indian trade became responsible for the operation of the "factory trading system"—a process instituted by the Indian Intercourse Acts (1790), which foresaw the Native concession of extensive territory in exchange for trading posts. Yet in 1824, Secretary of War John C. Calhoun abolished the factory system and created, without Congressional authorization, the Bureau of Indian Affairs. The Bureau moved from a policy of forced trade and assimilation to one of direct military expansion and "Indian removal." Just 6 years later (in 1830), the Indian Removal Act was signed into law by President Andrew Jackson and authorized the United States to forcibly remove Indians to lands west of the Mississippi River, an action that led to several "Indian wars" lasting until the late 1840s. So also, Indian removal facilitated the zeitgeist of Manifest Destiny and Westward expansion, and conflicts over resources occurred between Whites, Indians and Mexicans. As a result, both local statutes and federal policies systematically disenfranchised Mexican Americans and Indians. Moreover, after Texas won independence from Mexico in 1836, the state legalized slavery, and free Blacks and mulattoes were forbidden from entering Texas. This reversed the course of migration, as Mexico had previously abolished slavery in the territory in 1829, making Texas a former refuge for runaways. In addition, by 1850, a second Fugitive Slave Act was passed, which enabled the federal government to enforce the capture of slaves in "free states," effectively extending slavery beyond the official "slave states."

The Dred Scott Case and the Beginnings of the Civil War

One of the major obstacles to ending slavery was the landmark case of *Dred Scott v. Sandford* (1857). The *Scott* case, vis-á-vis Chief Justice Roger B. Taney's words that "the Negro has no rights that a white man is bound to respect," found both that Black slaves were not citizens (and thus could not bring suit to court) and that Congress was powerless to regulate slavery in U.S. territories (thus overturning the Missouri Compromise of 1820). Such a decision would cement the foundation for the Civil War (1861–1865). Shortly into the war, on June 19, 1862, Congress passed an act that prohibited slavery in U.S. territories but not states. This was landmark legislation in that it stood in opposition to the *Scott* case (1857). Moreover, under the hope that the loss of enslaved labor amidst the confederacy would damage the rebel economy, the 1862 House of Representatives leadership called for the total emancipation of slaves. By July 1862, Congress passed the "Second Confiscation Act," which liberated slaves held by confederates.

The Emancipation Proclamation

Despite these measures and increasing pressure among activists to "free the slaves," President Lincoln proved hesitant and contradictory. In August 1862, after *New York Tribune* editor Horace Greeley accused Lincoln of being weak on the question of slavery, Lincoln responded, "My paramount object in this struggle *is* to save the Union, and is *not* to save or to destroy slavery. If I could save the Union without freeing *any* slave I would do it, and if I could save it by freeing *all* the slaves I would do it" (Striner, 2006, pp. 175–176). Little more a month later, Lincoln would issue the first of two "emancipation proclamations" during the U.S. Civil War. The first, issued September 22, 1862, declared the freedom of all slaves in any state of the Confederate States of America that did not return to Union control by 1863. However, as the proclamation was not *carte blanche*, a second executive order, issued January 1, 1863, named specific areas where the proclamation would and would not apply and did not challenge the legality of slavery left intact in the Constitution.

The "Reconstruction Amendments" and White Backlash

It was not until passage of the 13th Amendment to the U.S. Constitution on December 18, 1865, that slavery, "except as a punishment for crime," was abolished. This amendment, along with the 14th (1868) and 15th (1870), were known as the "reconstruction amendments." At first, the court seemed to evince weighty support for these amendments, yet in just a few short years the court would reverse tack. For example, the *Civil Rights Cases* of 1883 invalidated the 1875 Civil Rights Act that required equal public accommodations without regard to race. Amidst a rising White backlash that saw the formation of the Ku Klux Klan (1865) and other organizations like the White League (1874) and the Red Shirts (1875), legal attempts to achieve equality were—much like today—framed as either "anti-White" or as "special rights." Such logic was also manifest in the numerous anti-Chinese riots in California in the 1870s and the lynching and expulsions of Chinese immigrants that were rampant until the passage of the Chinese Exclusion Act (1882) (McKenzie, 1928; Miller 1969; Pfaelzer, 2007).

Plessy v. Ferguson and the Jim Crow Era

In what eerily predicted the "separate-but-equal" logic of Plessy v. Ferguson (1896), Supreme Court Justice Bradley privately wrote, ". . . what are the essentials to the enjoyment of citizenship?. . . Is the white man's carriage or railroad car [my emphasis] such an essential, if the colored man has a suitable car provided for him?" (Fairman, 1987, p. 564). These words would find tangible expression in the question of Louisiana's 1890 Jim Crow statute that required White and "colored" people to sit in separate railroad cars after Homer Plessy (a light-skinned Black man) declined to sit in the "colored" car. Plessy based his case on the 13th and 14th amendments, to which Justice Henry Billings Brown replied in the majority opinion:

> We consider the underlying fallacy of the plaintiff's argument to consist in the assumption that the enforced separation of the two races stamps the colored race with a badge of inferiority [my emphasis]. If this be so, it is not by reason of anything found in the act, but solely because the colored race chooses to put that construction upon it.

In other words, racial segregation was understood as equal, and if non-Whites thought otherwise, it was the result of non-Whites' incorrect view of their social conditions as inferior.

Separate but Equal and the Race of Citizenship

The logic of separate but equal was applied broadly, and the increasing legislation in the wake of Plessy (1890) necessitated a legal definition of racial categories. Hence, law not only regulated race relations, it assisted in the creation of "race" itself. For example, the Naturalization Act of 1906 provided that only White persons and persons of African descent or African nativity were eligible for citizenship. Hence, in 1922 the case of Takao Ozawa v. United States was decided on the basis of current scientific—particularly anthropological—evidence. The Court found that Ozawa, a light-skinned native of Japan, could not be counted as White. Because "Whiteness" was the equivalent of "Caucasian," Ozawa was understood as belonging to the "Asian" race; he was scientifically disqualified from Whiteness. Yet, in United States v. Bhagat Singh Thind (1923), the Court found that eastern Asians were not "free White men" entitled to citizenship, although scientific opinion at the time indicated that eastern Asians were a part of the "Caucasian" race. As legal scholar Ian Haney-Lopez (1996, pp. 119–120) writes:

> Ostensibly the Court refused to naturalize Thind because he was not White. Yet, it was in large part the judicial determination that Thind could not become a citizen that rendered him non-White. Had the Court admitted Thind to citizenship in accord with the substantial body of precedent, the Whiteness of Thind would have been clear. Thind's exclusion from the American polity established rather than reflected his race; the condition of being a permanent alien coded Thind with a non-White racial identity.

Thus, in the *Thind* case, the Court contradicted itself and its prior utilization of anthropological evidence in the *Ozawa* ruling, revealing not a dedication to neutral precedent or objectivity but White supremacist logic. The Court did not find Thind to be "White," although he was part of the "Causasian" race, because in the words of Justice George Sutherland, such a finding would not "be interpreted in accordance with the understanding of the common man" (*United States v. Bhagat Singh Thind*, 1923).

Dawn of the Civil Rights Era

Long before the recognition of the formal "Civil Rights Movement" (1955–1968), several cases were instrumental in providing a justification for closer and intense federal scrutiny of racial equality. For example, the *Scottsboro Cases* (1932, 1935) by which the Supreme Court commuted death sentences against eight Black men accused of rape because they were denied effective counsel in prior court proceedings. Other examples included the legal backlash after the Supreme Court confirmed the World War II-era exclusion orders and internment camps against Japanese-Americans in *Hirabayashi v. United States* (1943) and *Korematsu v. United States* (1944). And perhaps most importantly, the NAACP's twenty-some odd-year fight against *Plessy* birthed the likes of Thurgood Marshall and William Henry Hastie from the tutelage of Howard Law School's Charles Hamilton Houston. As Louis H. Pollak writes:

> . . . in *Smith v. Allwright* [1944], Hastie and Marshall persuaded the Court that the so-called white primary, under which the Democratic Party maintained whites-only hegemony throughout the one-party South, unconstitutionally excluded blacks from effective participation it the political process (2005, p. 38).

Brown v. Board of Education and Bolling v. Sharpe

Despite many of the aforementioned challenges to legalized White supremacy, *Plessy* remained in place until the *Brown v. Board of Education* (1954) and

Bolling v. Sharpe (1954) decisions that found, ". . . in the field of public educa-tion the doctrine of "separate but equal" has no place" (*Bolling v. Sharpe*, 1954). Although those decisions and successive verdicts regarding segregation in other public areas were landmark victories for desegregation, the Court made a critical error in the logic it employed. The misstep took place in the Court's reluctance or unwillingness—given that Judge Warren felt it an imperative to deliver an unanimous decision—to deal with White supremacy. Although the Court reversed *Plessy* because "the basis of segregation and "separate-but-equal" rests upon a concept of the inherent inferiority of the colored race" (Patterson, 2001, p. 64), the problem of the imputed and inherent superiority of Whites remained untouched. Segregation was seen as the crucial issue rather than a symptom of the real problem—the promotion of White suprem-acy and re-creation of Whiteness as the dialectic of non-Whiteness. As Cheryl Harris wrote in the *Harvard Law Review*:

> The Supreme Court's rejection of affirmative action programs on the grounds that race-conscious remedial measures are unconstitutional under the Equal Protection Clause of the Fourteenth Amendment—the very con-stitutional measure designed to guarantee equality for blacks—is based on the Court's chronic refusal to dismantle the institutional protection of ben-efits for whites that have been based on white supremacy and maintained at the expense of blacks. As a result, *the parameters of appropriate remedies are not dictated by the scope of the injury to the subjugated, but by the extent of the infringement on settled expectations of whites* [my emphasis]. . . . Thus under this assumption, it is not only the interests of individual whites who chal-lenge affirmative action that are protected; the interests of whites as whites are enshrined and institutionalized as a property interest that accords them a higher status than any individual claim to relief.

My intention here is to demonstrate—by sympathizing with the verdict but holding skeptical to the rationale—that the Court's *Brown* decision left wide open the door that would effectively promote an ironically disastrous "color-blind" approach that would find expression in a series of future deci-sions that would chip away at laws and policies designed to bring about racial equality and fight segregation.

Beginnings of a Backlash

Desegregation and racial equality is often treated as if they were accomplished after the *Brown* and *Bolling* decisions. Yet, more legislation in subsequent years was required. The Civil Rights Act of 1964 sought to eliminate continued racial segregation, especially in the labor market and education. Signed by President Johnson in 1965, the Voting Rights Act was passed to ensure the 15th Amendment (of 1870) was applied in all states. That same year, various racist immigration laws were struck down, and just after the assassination of Dr. King in 1968, Congress enacted the Open Housing Act, which banned racial housing discrimination.

Yet over the next 30 years, racial segregation and discrimination in public areas waxed and waned. For example, the last positive legislation for desegregation was the Emergency School Aid Act (1972) and the *Keyes* decision (1973). In 1980, the Supreme Court heard *Fullilove v. Klutznick*, a case that arose as a suit against the enforcement of provisions in a 1977 spending bill that required 10% of federal funds in public works programs to go to minority-owned companies. The Court held that Congress could constitutionally use its spending power to remedy past discrimination, yet 15 years later (in 1995), *Fullilove v. Klutnick* was overruled by *Adarand Constructors, Inc. v. Pena*. By the 1990s, the Supreme Court decisions of *Board of Education of Oklahoma City v. Dowell* (1991), *Freeman v. Pitts* (1992), and *Missouri v. Jenkins* (1995) effectively limited prior desegregation efforts.

Gratz, Grutter, and Meredith

The Court recently demonstrated that proved violations arising from a history of segregation and inequality can justify race-based judicial remedies, but only for a limited time. Furthermore, a judge can dissolve a desegregation plan and order if the judge believes the district has done enough to provide equality for a number of years—what the Court calls "unitary status." Orfield and Lee (2007, p. 7) explain that under this framework:

> . . . actions that would have been illegal under the court order, such as creating a highly segregated neighborhood school system that leaves most whiles in good middle class schools and most nonwhites in segregated high poverty schools failing to meet federal standards, become legal. At the same time, remedies which were required under the court orders as essential element of desegregation become illegal and forbidden as soon as the court order is lifted. Unitary status implies that the desegregation plan has eliminated the continuing effects of the history of segregation and that this district treats all students equally, but researchers examining what happens in districts after such orders often see very serious separation and inequality continuing and, often, intensifying.

For example, in 2003 the Supreme Court rendered a decision in *Gratz v. Bollinger* (2003), which found the University of Michigan law school's use of race in its admissions process was unconstitutional because its system was too mechanistic and did not afford enough attention to individual merit. In the corollary case of *Grutter v. Bollinger* (2003), the Court upheld the affirmative action admissions policy of the University of Michigan. These cases marked the first time the Court examined race and student admissions under the

Equal Protection Clause of the 14th amendment since *Regents of the University of California v. Bakke* (1978). In the latter *Grutter v. Bollinger* case, the Court drew upon *Bakke to* argue that student body *diversity* rather than *inequality* is a compelling governmental interest that validates the use of race as a "plus" factor in admissions. These two decisions, albeit with different results, illuminate a similar logic.

> The Court's use of race-neutral criteria, such as diversity and individuali-
> zation, in the analysis of "compelling government interest" and "narrowly
> tailored" in its recent decisions on affirmative action allow the Justices to
> sidestep a larger social problem—namely, the ongoing need for race-
> conscious admissions policies because of the persistence of a racial gap in
> education. (Walsh, 2004, pp. 455–456)

When the topic of power vis-á-vis racial discrimination and inequality is taken out of the affirmative action debate, the impetus for such a program is lost. Diversity *qua* diversity appears as the end goal and obfuscates the reasoning behind implementation of race-specific programs—to begin to achieve racial equality and equal protection.

The logic employed in both *Gratz* and *Grutter*—to forbid most race-conscious desegregation efforts unless there is a case for "diversity" rather than equality—found expression again in *Meredith v. Jefferson County Board of Education* (2007). Although the majority of the divided Court said the goal of integrated schools remained a compelling interest, it decided that the means to achieve integration were unconstitutional and that schools must either develop other plans or abandon their efforts to maintain integrated schools. In so doing, the Court:

> reversed nearly four decades of decisions and regulations which had per-
> mitted and even required that race be taken into account because of the
> earlier failure of desegregation plans that did not do that. . . . The Court's
> basic conclusion, that it was unconstitutional to take race into account in
> order to end segregation represented a dramatic reversal of the rulings of
> the civil rights era which held that race must be taken into account to the
> extent necessary to end racial separation. (Orfield & Lee, 2007, p. 3)

MEASURING RACIAL PROGRESS: FIVE KEY AREAS

Racial Attitudes

On face value, Americans' attitudes appear to be moving toward a genuinely "color-blind" society. Among Whites, fewer today than in years past readily endorse statements that Blacks and Latinos are less intelligent and hardworking than themselves. In many ways, these attitudes have "caught up" with non-White attitudes that have historically favored equality of access, opportunity, and behavior. Yet, Whites continue to lag behind non-White attitudes regarding key issues such as integration in housing and inter-racial marriage. In this vein, many scholars contend that the greatest shift in White attitudes concerns the most public and impersonal areas of social life (Bobo, Kluegel, & Smith, 1997).

Although survey data reveal a sweeping shift among Whites, these findings must be tempered with other data. On the one hand, the declining use of stereotypes among Whites demonstrates that Whites remain less willing (in survey interview formats) to draw sharp distinctions between racial groups on the traits of intelligence and laziness. In fact, there has been no real decline in White progressive attitudes on racial inclusivity and equality since the 1950s. On the other hand, evidence shows that stereotypes continue to shape how Whites think about race and racial groups. Today, even with improvements over the years, 25% of Whites agree that Blacks as a group are less intelligent than Whites, and 40% of Whites endorse the belief that Blacks hold weaker "commitment to their families" than Whites (Krysan & Faison, 2008). Accordingly, "politically correct" answers and expected social norms, rather than changes in actual levels of racial bias, seem to be at play (Schuman, Steeh, Bobo, & Krysan, 1997). As Feagin and Picca found in *Two-Faced Racism: Whites in the Backstage and Frontstage* (2007), Whites have become particularly savvy in expressing public racial-tolerance while engaging in hateful racist invective in areas in which they feel to be private and safe. Hence, many Whites have shifted expression of racial attitudes "underground" where stereotypical assertions and prejudices can be shared unchecked.

Housing

With the passage of the "Fair Housing Act" in 1968, *de jure* practices of housing discrimination such as red-lining and restrictive covenants became illegal, and many believed that antidiscrimination legislation would mark the gradual demise of residential segregation. Yet, by the 1970s, racial segregation remained, especially in urban Black areas. Fast forward thirty-some years to 2006 and we witness the largest amount of housing discrimination complaints on record at more than 10,000 (Goodloe, 2007). As Bobo and Charles wrote of a housing segregation study in 1989: "Geographic steering was also quite common: for every four visits to a real estate agent, black and Latino home-seekers were steered away from predominantly White areas 40 and 28 percent of the time, respectively" (2009, p. 250). By 1999, Blacks were being steered away from White communities at greater rates than years prior (Turner, Ross, Galster, & Yinger, 2002). Other studies have estimated that race-based housing discrimination may occur at a rate of 3.7 million times per year but is largely unrecognized and unreported (McKoy & Vincent, 1993, p. 200).

Although the overall population is not as segregated in housing as it was in the late 1960s, Blacks and Whites are "hypersegregated" from one another. By 1990, 29 U.S. metropolitan areas held 40% of the entire U.S. Black population in "extreme segregation" (Denton, 1994, p. 49). According to the 2000 census, Whites are most likely to be segregated than any other group, have the largest suburban presence, and are most likely to own their homes. In contrast, Latinos and Asians are only moderately segregated, although their levels of segregation are increasing largely because of high-volume immigration.

Education

According to the Department of Education, almost one-half of Whites believe that Blacks have attained education levels equivalent to their own. Yet, only 16% of all Black adults are college-educated, as opposed to 28% of adult Whites (Kao & Thompson, 2003). Although college enrollment for White and some Asian groups are very high, the rates of Blacks and Latinos lag far behind (Kao & Thompson, 2003, p. 428). And although Black and Latino college enrollment has increased over time, the trend significantly slowed in the 1980s. Additionally, not all colleges and universities are equal; the types of postsecondary institutions vary significantly by racial make-up (Karen, 2002). In fact, "inequalities persist or even increase at the postsecondary level as groups become more equal at lower levels of education" (Kao & Thompson, 2003, p. 430). Blacks remain the least likely racial group to attend the nation's highest-ranked public institutions (University of Virginia or UC-Berkeley) as well as highest-ranked private institutions (Harvard, Chicago, or Yale). This effect remains even when controlling for test scores, grades, expectations, and co-curricular activities (Karen, 2002). Although Asian-Americans are found in somewhat more prestigious universities than other racial groups, there is wide variation within the racial category (e.g., among those aged 25–29 years, 26% of Japanese, 37% of Chinese, and 52% of Asian Indians had completed 4 years or more of college in 1980, whereas only 6% of Laotians, 3% of Hmong, 13% of Vietnamese, 10% of Native Hawaiians, 11% of Melanesians, and 7% of Samoans did the same) (Camburn, 1990).

Yet, even if the above educational completion pipeline was equalized, we have to account for the related aspect of both unequal educational resources and racial stereotypes. Compared to the average White student, the average Black student attends a school with twice as many lower income students (Blau, 2003, p. 48). Moreover, compared with schools that are predominantly White, predominantly non-White schools are more than 1000% more likely to have concentrated levels of poverty among their students (Orfield, Eaton, & Jones, 2006). Even Black students from families with much higher incomes than Whites are more likely to attend schools with higher concentrations of poverty (Massey & Denton, 1993, p. 153). By the turn of the millennium, the percentage of Black children who attended an integrated public school was at its lowest level since 1968 (Kozol, 2005). The trend worsened in the first decade of the 21st century. "The country's rapidly growing population of Latino and black students is more segregated than they have been since the 1960s and we are going backward faster in the areas where integration was most far-reaching" (Orfield & Lee, 2007, p. 4).

Both differing secondary schools, and the racial groups within them, are stratified into specialties and "tracks." Low-income, urban schools do not offer the same range and level of courses as their affluent and suburban counterparts (which may offer three times as many advanced placement courses) (Orfield, Eaton, & Jones, 2006). Accordingly, urban schools are less likely to offer advanced courses or gifted and talented programs (Garibaldi, 1998). With such a setting, education is less the great equalizer and more the reproducer of existing hierarchies of domination. So also, there exist great intra-school differences. "Numerous studies have shown that poor children and racial and ethnic minorities are disproportionately placed in low-ability groups early in their educational careers and in non-college-bound groupings in junior high and high school" (Kao & Thompson, 2003, p. 423). Research indicates that teachers do not expect Black and Latino children to achieve at levels comparable to Whites and Asians (Ferguson, 2003). Teachers may convey this belief in their instruction of children and that this expectation both lowers and raises differently raced students' cognitive test scores.

Although there is some debate regarding the underpinning of tracking mechanisms, recent studies reveal that once academic achievement is controlled, racial and ethnic differences in tracking decrease but do not disappear (Hallinan, 1994). In this vein, differences in tracking may be caused by robust stereotypes on the part of educators and families (Immerwahr & Foleno, 2000). Since Stanford psychologist Claude Steele found evidence of "stereotype threat" (1997), social scientists have discovered repeated evidence that perceptions of one's identity directly affects performance on seemingly "objective" metrics such as IQ tests, grades, and other testing devices. In specific, Steele found that when a person's social identity (especially race or gender) became attached to a negative stereotype (e.g., "Blacks are intellectually inferior to Whites" or "Girls are bad at math"), that person would perform in a manner more consistent with the stereotype.

Wealth

Currently, the United States is witnessing the greatest wealth and income inequality in its history. The top 1% takes in just over 25% of all income in the United States. This rate surpasses the percentage just before the Great

Depression (23%) and is twelve times the income of the bottom fifth of the population (Mishel, Berstein, & Shierholz, 2007). When race is added to the equation, the results are even bleaker. In 2006, the Black and Latino poverty rate was 24% and 21%, respectively, compared to a 10% poverty rate among Whites (U.S. Census, 2009). So also, in 2006, the median household income for Whites was $61,280, whereas it was $38,269 for Blacks and $40,000 for Latinos (Rivera, Huezo, Kasica, & Muhammad, 2009). Moreover, this rate has not improved over recent years. From 2000 to 2006, the Black median income fell by nearly 3%, and Latinos saw nearly a 1% drop (Saxton, 2008).

The typical family of color has only 18 cents for every dollar Whites have (Lui, Robles, & Leondar-Wright, 2006). The Black–White wage gap has decreased over the past 70 years but has leveled off in recent years. In 1940, the average Black male worker earned only 43% as much as the average White male worker, but nearly 60 years later in 1999, Black men made nearly 81% as much as White men. Yet of late, the wage gap has actually increased, reaching almost 30% by 2009 (the gap for White women remains close to 25%, nearly 40% for Black women, and almost 50% for Latinas). Over the past 40 years, wages of Latino men have decreased almost 25% compared with those of White men. Scholars have found that Latino assimilation may be losing momentum and even reversing so that

> . . . children and grandchildren of immigrants may lose ground economi-
> cally, disengage politically, and end up with poorer health, higher rates of
> crime, or greater family instability than their ancestors or counterparts in
> the native country. (Hochschild, 2005, p. 74)

Historically, the United States has demonstrated racially stratified unemployment rates. Although these rates have varied over the past 35 years, the racial gaps have remained relatively consistent: Black rates varied from 13.1% (1974) to 14.3% (1992) to 15.4% (2009). Latino rates varied from 9.1% (1974) to 11.5% (1992) to 13.1% (2009). White rates varied 6.4% (1974) to 6.5% (1992) to 9.5% (2009) (U.S. Bureau of Labor Statistics, 2009). This trend has increased, although over the last 40 years, U.S. residents have begun working longer and longer hours per year. In that time span, the hours worked per year by the average White family grew by 11%, compared to the average Latino family (increase of 14%) and the average Black family (increase of 15%). "By 2000, middle income black families actually worked the equivalent of nearly 12 full-time weeks more than white families to maintain the same income level" (Rivera, Huezo, & Kasica, 2009, p. 20).

These trends did not occur by happenstance. Rather, in so long as government policies are laws are structured to benefit large businesses, the higher educated, and the upper class—all strata dominated by Whites—these trends are likely to remain stable if not exacerbate. In consideration of tax breaks enacted from 2000 to 2008, the top 1% (making more than $545,845 annually) of the population saw an average $487,751 tax reduction (a 23.5% share of the total tax cut), whereas the lowest 25% (making less than $18,347) saw an average $817 tax reduction (a 1.3% share of the total tax cut) (Johnson, 2009, P. F1).

Incarceration

Since the 1970s there has been more than a 600% rise in the number of people incarcerated in U.S. prisons and jails, resulting in a total of 2.3 million people behind bars in 2007 (Mauer & King, 2007; Pager, 2003). In fact, the current United States has the highest documented incarceration rate and the highest total documented prison population in the world (Walmsley, 2007). By the end of 2008, 7.2 million people were behind bars, on probation, or on parole. Moreover, the United States ranks fourth in historical incarceration rates (738 per 100,000), falling behind only the Cambodian Khmer Rouge of the 1970s (60,000 per 100,000), the Russian Gulag of the 1930s (3,000 per 100,000), and Nazi Germany from 1933 to 1945 (793 per 100,000). The United States comprises 5% of the world's population and 23.6% of the world's prison population (Walmsley, 2007).

"In 1964, just three years after Barack Obama was born, about two thirds of all persons locked up in the nation's jails and prisons were white, while a third were persons of color, mostly African American" (Wise, 2009, p. 56). If we move forward to Obama's election as president, we find an odd reversal: approximately 65% of those locked up are people of color. Of the total 2.3 million people behind bars in 2007, approximately 950,000 are Black and 450,000 are Latino (Mauer & King, 2007). As the Bureau of Justice Statistics documents, one in six Black men have been incarcerated as of 2001. If the current trend continues, one in three Black males and one in six Latino males born today can expect to spend time in prison during his lifetime (Mauer & King, 2007). Overall, rates of incarceration are (per 100,000): Blacks (2,290), Latinos (742), and Whites (412).

As shown, the expansion of the prison population has been particularly consequential for people of color, especially Black men.

> Young black men today have a 28% likelihood of incarceration during their lifetime . . . a figure that rises above 50% among young black high school dropouts . . . These vast numbers of inmates translate into a large and increasing population of black exoffenders returning to communities and searching for work. (Pager, 2003, p. 937)

Accordingly, recidivism rates and employment are compounded by the Janus-face of racial and criminal stigma. Across an array of settings, a robust

White supremacist bias works against men of color's attempts to obtain employment (Pager, 2007a, 2005). To isolate the effect, pairs of young, well-groomed, college men with nearly identical résumés were sent to apply for entry-level jobs. Results showed that employers were more likely to call Whites *with* a criminal record than Blacks *without* a criminal record. And while having a criminal background hurt all applicants' chances of getting an interview, Blacks with a nonviolent offense faced particularly dismal employment prospects. "Being black in America today is just about the same as having a felony conviction in terms of one's chances of finding a job" (Pager, 2007b).

OBAMA: A LIGHT IN THE DARKNESS OR THE BLACKFACE OF EMPIRE?

The 2008 election was a stage set for a drama of racial transcendence. Despite a large lead in polls, Barack Obama lost to Hillary Clinton in the New Hampshire primary, a result that signaled the possible resurgence of the "Bradley effect." And with the injection of race into the campaign via Geraldine Ferraro and Bill Clinton's less-than-polite remarks, the flap over Reverend Jeremiah Wright and "black liberation theology," and Obama's own remarks on race in his "A More Perfect Union" speech of March 2008, an Obama victory seemed a Sisyphean feat.

Given this background, the wake of the 2008 election propelled scholars, laypersons, and talking media heads to frame the event as the penultimate triumph over the color line. "Racial Barrier Falls in Decisive Victory," proclaimed the front page of *The New York Times*. Writing on the "Obama Effect," scholars noted, "The unprecedented drop in implicit bias observed in our studies indicates that the impact of Obama's historic campaign went beyond him winning the election. It appears to have produced a fundamental change in at least the minds of the American public" (Plant et al., 2009, p. 961). Actor Will Smith stated, "African-American excuses have been removed. There's no white man trying to keep you down, because if he were really trying to keep you down, he would have done everything he could to keep Obama down" (Smith, 2009). Representative James Clyburn of South Carolina, the majority whip, stated that the election of Obama means: "Every child has lost every excuse." George Will praised the election and Obama for "taking America beyond an utterly exhausted narrative about race relations in the United States" (Younge, 2008), one that "subscribe[s] to a racial narrative of strife and oppression [and denies] fifty years of stunning progress" (Will, 2008). Bill Bennett, the former Secretary of Education under Ronald Reagan stated:

> "Obama has taught the black community you don't have to act like Jesse Jackson, you don't have to act like Al Sharpton. You can talk the issues.

Great dignity. And this is a breakthrough. . . . [Obama] never brings race into it. He never plays the race card" (Media Matters, 2008). And the day after the election, the *Wall Street Journal* editorial page declared, "One promise of his victory is that perhaps we can put to rest the myth of racism as a barrier to achievement in this splendid country."

Note the common thread amidst the "age of no excuses" rhetoric—racism and racial inequality is not the real issue, rather the politically correct evocation of "race" is an opportunist ploy devoid of merit and dignity—racism is simply an ill-conceived "myth." These aforementioned moments of collective self-congratulation and denial fail to take into account that Obama's ability to navigate around *racial discourse*, rather than engage with *racism and racial inequalities*, remains at the heart of faulty evidence for a "post-racial" nation. Obama's capacity, or rather his obligation, not to disturb the mirage of a post-Civil Rights utopian landscape is, in and of itself, a monument to how far we have not moved past race. As Stephen Steinberg noted in *Turning Back: The Retreat from Racial Justice in American Thought and Policy* (1995, pp. 149–150):

> It may well be that blacks who have acquired the "right" status character-
> istics are exempted from stereotypes and behaviors that continue to be
> directed at less privileged blacks. . . . there is nothing new in this phenom-
> enon. Even in the worst days of Jim Crow, there were blacks who owned
> land, received favored treatment from whites and were held forth as
> "success stories" to prove that lower-class blacks had only themselves to
> blame for their destitution . . . The existence of this black elite did not prove
> that racism was abating (though illusions to this effect were common even
> among blacks). On the contrary, the black elite itself was a vital part of the
> system of [racial] oppression, serving as a buffer between the [ruling white]
> oppressor and [most truly black] oppressed and furthering the illusion
> that blacks could surmount their difficulties if only they had the exemplary
> qualities of the black elite.

In so long as the metric for a post-racial society remains predicated on cherry-picking Black examples-as-exceptions—in the vein of canonizing the existence of Oprah Winfrey, Condoleezza Rice, and Colin Powell—we shall remain stuck in the age of denial.

Still, many claim that despite rampant racial inequality, the United States reached a critical turning point with the election of Barack Obama. Some remark, social science evidence and theory aside, that the election of Obama is a landmark signal we have moved beyond Whites' near-universal support for racial equality in the abstract and their stubborn opposition to efforts to ensure that equality (Krysan, 2000). However, when we empirically observe the election, we find that White support for Obama was not historically high. Although

Obama received 53% of the votes cast, he received only 43% of the White vote. Examine the following White voting patterns from 1996 to 2008: In 1996 (43% Democrat and 46% Republican), in 2000 (42% Democrat and 54% Republican), in 2004 (41% Democrat and 58% Republican) and in 2008 (43% Democrat and 55% Republican) (Hutchings, 2009). Obama's victory resulted from a perfect storm rather than a "fundamental change . . . in the minds of the American public" (Hutchings, 2009). His election was the product of a widely unpopular lame duck president, serious gaffes by McCain and Palin, out-of-favor wars in Iraq and Afghanistan, severe economic downturn, and a technologically savvy and culturally attuned campaign by the Democratic Party to create high turnout among the young and Blacks (95% of the vote), Latinos and Hispanics (67% of the vote), and Asians (62% of the vote). It is difficult to read these numbers as the transcendence of race and the culmination, or even beginning, of color-blind attitudes.

Still, concepts like hope and change can take on a commanding presence in everyday life. "Yes we can" was powerful currency in the 2008 election— just as it was when Dolores Huerta and Cesar Chavez of the United Farm Workers made "Sí se puede" their motto 36 years before the Obama campaign appropriated it, translated it, and blunted much of its critical edge in the interests of the Democratic Party and the White racial framing of the American empire. Yet, a belief in change, motivated by hope, and contextualized by the election of Barack Obama, could not have happened without certain steps of racial progress that the United States has attained. That is a reality that should not be discounted, even as it is contextualized and the myth of a post-racial society debunked.

Although we cannot dismiss the meaning of 232 years of struggle to elect the first Black president, we have limited public outlets to admit and analyze the historically driven cultural contradictions of our modern era. Events like the fundamental abandonment of (and nationwide commitment to forget) post-Katrina New Orleans, the retrenchment of Arab and Middle-Eastern stereotypes and discrimination in the wake of 9/11, the White backlash against Affirmative Action and Equal Rights legislation, the strengthening of Nativist and White Nationalist movements for anti-immigration, the resumption of U.S.-controlled colonial projects in darker-skinned nations on the global periphery (most notably seen in policies toward, and violent conflicts in, the Middle East, South-Eastern Asia, and South America), the juggernaut of the increasing incarceration of Black and brown bodies, the arrest of Harvard professor Dr. Henry Louis Gates, Jr., and Obama's own contradictory prose that urges acknowledgment of "structural inequalities" alongside the belief that your "destiny is in your hands" together represent the indispensable centrality of racial inequality in today's world.

NOTES

1 For a more detailed discussion, *see*: Hughey, Matthew W. (July 2007). "It's Much More Than Imus! The Industrial, Textual, and Cultural Facets of Media Racism." *Society for the Study of Social Problems, Racial and Ethnic Minority Division News*, 4–5.

2 NitroMed's "BiDil" was approved by the Federal Drug Administration (FDA) as the first "ethnic specific" drug based on clinical trials in African-American subjects, leading some to claim that the social constructionist point of view is erroneous. However, the drug's supposed race-specific efficacy has been questioned because it has not been established that it is ineffective in other ethnic or racial groups.

3 *c.f.*: "Asian Americans: 'A Model Minority'," *Newsweek* (1982); "The Drive to Excel," *Newsweek* (April 1984); "America's Greatest Success Story: The Triumph of Asian Americans," *The New Republic* (July 1985); "America's Super Minority," *Fortune* (November 1986); "The New Whiz Kids," *Time* (August 1987); "Why They Excel," *Parade* (1990).

REFERENCES

Anderson, E. (2000). *Code of the Street: Decency, Violence, and the Moral Life of the Inner City*. New York, NY: W. W. Norton.

Begley, S. (August 19, 2008). Racial Medicine: Not So Fast. *Newsweek Lab Notes*. Retrieved from http://blog.newsweek.com/blogs/labnotes/archive/2008/08/19/racial-medicine-not-so-fast.aspx, last accessed January 20, 2010.

Blau, Judith R. (2003). *Race in the Schools: Perpetuating White Dominance?* Boulder, CO: Lynne Rienner Press.

Bobo, L. & Charles, C. Z. (2009). Race in the American Mind: From the Moynihan Report to the Obama Candidacy. *The ANNALS of the American Academy of Political and Social Science, 621(1)*, 243–259.

Bobo, L., Kluegel, J. R., & Smith, R. A. (1997). Laissez-Faire Racism: The Crystallization of a "Kindler, Gentler" Anti-black Ideology. In S. A. Tuch and J. K. Martin (Eds) *Racial Attitudes in the 1990s: Continuity and Change*. Westport, CT: Praeger.

Bosman, J. (June 16, 2008). Obama Sharply Assails Absent Black Fathers. *The New York Times*. Retrieved from http://www.nytimes.com/2008/06/16/us/politics/15cnd-obama.html, last accessed January 23, 2010.

Camburn, E. M. (1990). College Completion Among Students from High Schools Located in Large Metropolitan Areas. *American Journal of Education 98*, 551–569.

Denton, N. A. (1994). Are African Americans Still Hypersegregated? In R. Bullard, C. Lee, and J. E. Grigsbgy (Eds) *Residential Apartheid: The American Legacy*, edited by R Bullard, C Lee, JE Grigsby. Los Angeles, CA: Center for African American Studies, 49–79.

Edin, K. & Kefalas, M. (2005). *Promises I Can Keep: Why Poor Women Put Motherhood Before Marriage*. Berkeley, CA: University of California Press.

Erickson, E. (October 9, 2009). Barack Obama Wins Nobel Peace Prize: He's Becoming Jimmy Carter Faster Than Jimmy Carter Did. Retrieved from http://www.redstate.com/erick/2009/10/09/barack-obama-wins-nobel-peace-prize/, last accessed January 23, 2010.

Fairman, C. (1987). *Reconstruction and Reunion, 1864–88*, vol. 2. New York, NY: Macmillan.

Feagin, J. (2010). The White Racial Frame: Centuries of Racial Framing and Counterframing. New York, NY: Routledge.

Feeney, S. (2007). Katrina Fatigue: Listeners Say They've Heard Enough. *Nieman Reports: Neiman Foundation for Journalism at Harvard University*. Retrieved from http://www.nieman.harvard.edu/reportsitem.aspx?id=100163, last accessed January 28, 2010.

Ferguson, R. F. (2003). Teachers' Perceptions and Expectations and the Black-White Test Score Gap. *Urban Education 38(4)*, 460–507.

Fujimura, J. H., Duster, T. & Rajagopalan, R. (2008). Race, Genetics, and Disease: Questions of Evidence, Matters of Consequence. *Social Studies of Science 38(5)*, 643–656.

Garibaldi, A. M. (1998). Four Decades of Progress and Decline: An Assessment of African American Educational Attainment. *Journal of Negro Education 66(2)*, 105–120.

Goodloe, S. (April 3, 2007). Housing Discrimination Complaints at an All-time High. US Department of Housing and Urban Development. Retrieved from http://www.hud.gov/news/release.cfm?content=pr07-032.cfm, last accessed January 20, 2010.

Hallinan, M. T. (1994). Tracking: From Theory to Practice." *Sociology of Education 67(2)*, 79–84.

Haney-Lopez, I. (1996). *White By Law: The Legal Construction of Race*. New York, NY: New York University Press.

Harris, C. I. (1993). Whiteness as Property. *Harvard Law Review, 106(8)*, 1707–1791.

Hochschild, J. L. (Winter 2005). "Looking Ahead: Racial Trends in the United States." *Daedalus*, 70–81.

Hutchings, V. L. (20-March 21, 2009). The Role of Race in the 2008 Election: Change or More of the Same? Presentation for "Still Two Nations? The Resilience of the Color Line: A conference honoring John Hope Franklin" Goodson Chapel, Duke University, Durham, NC.

Immerwahr, J. & Foleno, T. (2000). Great Expectation: How the Public and Parents "White, African American, and Hispanic" View Higher Education. *National Center for Public Policy and Higher Education Public Agenda Consortium for Policy Research*, Retrieved http://www.highereducation.org/reports/expectations/expectations.shtml, last accessed January 28, 2010.

Johnson, D. C. (October 29, 2009). Easing the Impact of a Tax Rise. *The New York Times*, F1.

Kao, G. & Thompson, J. S. (2003). Racial and Ethnic Stratification in Educational Achievement and Attainment. *Annual Review of Sociology 29*, 417–442.

Karen, D. (2002). Changes in Access to Higher Education in the United States: 1980–1992. *Sociology of Education 75(3)*, 191–210.

Kozol, J. (2005). *The Shame of the Nation: The Restoration of Apartheid Schooling in America*. New York, NY: Random House.

Krysan, M. (2000). Prejudice, Politics, and Public Opinion: Understanding the Sources of Racial Policy Attitudes. *Annual Review of Sociology 26*, 135–168.

Krysan, M. & Faison, N. (2008). Racial Attitudes in America: A Brief Summary of the Updated Data. An update and website to complement *Racial Attitudes in America: Trends and Interpretations, Revised Edition*, H. Schuman, C. Steeh, L. Bobo, and M. Krysan, 1997. Harvard University Press. Retrieved from http:// www.igpa.uillinois.edu/programs/racial-attitudes/, last accessed January 20, 2010.

Lakoff, G. (2008). *The Political Mind: Why you can't understand 21st-century American politics with an 18th-century brain*. New York, NY: Penguin Books.

Ledger, K. (Fall 2009). The Moynihan Report, A Retrospective. *Contexts*, 49–52.

Lui, M., Robles, B. & Leondar-Wright, B. (2006). *The Color of Wealth: The Story Behind the U.S. Racial Wealth Divide*. New York, NY: United for a Fair Economy/ The New Press.

Marx, K. (1978). In R. Tucker (Ed, Trans), *The Marx-Engels Reader* (2nd ed) New York, NY: W. W. Norton & Company.

Massey, D. & Denton, N. (1993). *American Apartheid: Segregation and the Making of the Underclass*. Cambridge, MA: Harvard University Press.

Mauer, M. & King, R. S. (July 2007). Uneven Justice: State Rates of Incarceration by Race and Ethnicity. The Sentencing Project. Retrieved from http://www. sentencingproject.org/doc/publications/rd_stateratesofincbyraceandethnicity. pdf, last accessed January 27, 2010.

McKenzie, R. D. (1928). *Oriental Exclusion: Effect of American immigration laws, regulations, and judicial decisions upon the Chinese and Japanese on the American Pacific coast*. Chicago, IL: University of Chicago Press.

McKoy, D. L. & Vincent, J. M. (1993). "Housing and Education: The Inextricable Link," in *Segregation: The Rising Costs for America*, edited by J. H. Carr and N. K. Kutty. New York, NY: Routledge

Media Matters. (2008). "CNN's Bennett: Barack Hussein Obama Has Taught the Black Community You Don't Have to Act like Jesse Jackson." Retrieved from http://mediamatters.org/items/200801040004, last accessed January 28, 2010.

Miller, S. C. (1969). *The Unwelcome Immigrant*: The American Image of the Chinese, 1785-1882. Berkeley, CA: University of California Press.

Mills, C. (1997). *The Racial Contract*. Ithica, NY: Cornell University Press.

Mishel, L., Bernstein, J. & Shierholz, H. (2007). *State of Working America 2006/2007*, Economic Policy Institute. Ithaca, NY: Cornell University Press.

Orfield, G. & Lee, C. (2007). Historic Reversals, Accelerating Resegregation, and the Need for New Integration Strategies. UCLA, A report of the Civil Rights Project/*Proyecto Derechos Civiles*, 77–91.

Orfield, G., Eaton, S. E., & Jones, E. R. (2006). *Dismantling Desegregation: The Quiet Reversal of Brown v. Board of Education.* New York, NY: The New Press.

Orfield, G., Bachmeier, M. D., James, D. R. & Eitle, T. (1997). Deepening Segregation in American Public Schools: A Special Report from the Harvard Porject on School Desegregation. *Equity and Excellence in Education 20*, 5–24.

Pager, Devah. (2007a). *Marked: Race, Crime, and Finding Work in an Era of Mass Incarceration.* Chicago, IL: University of Chicago Press.

Pager, Devah. (2007b). Is Racial Discrimination a Thing of the Past? Retrieved from blog.aapss.org/index.cfm?date=1/2007, last accessed January 28, 2010.

Pager, Devah. (2005). Walking the Talk: What Employers Say Versus What They Do. *American Sociological Review 70(3)*, 355–380.

Pager, Devah. (March 2003). The Mark of a Criminal Record. *American Journal of Sociology 108(5)*, 937–975.

Patterson, J. T. (2001). *Brown v. Board of Education: A Civil Rights Milestone and Its Troubled Legacy.* New York, NY: Oxford University Press.

Patterson, O. (Fall 1989). Toward a Study of Black America. *Dissent*, 476–486.

Peterson, W. (January 9, 1996). "Success Story: Japanese American Style." *New York Times Magazine.*

Picca, Leslie Houts and Joe R. Feagin. (2007). *Two-Faced Racism: Whites in the Backstage and Frontstage.* New York, NY: Routledge.

Pfaelzer, J. (2007). *Driven Out: The Forgotten War Against Chinese Americans.* Berkeley, CA: University of California Press.

Plant, E., Ashby, P. G., Devine, W.T.L., Cox, C. C., Miller, S. L., Goplen, S & Peruche, B. M. (July 2009). The Obama effect: Decreasing Implicit Prejudice and Stereotyping. *Journal of Experimental Social Psychology 45(4)*, 961–964.

Pollak, L. H. (Winter 2005). Race, Law, & History: The Supreme Court from "Dred Scott" to "Grutter v. Bollinger." *Daedalus*, 29–41.

Public Record, The. (August 28, 2009). "CNN: Death Threats Against Obama Increase by 400 Percent." Retrieved from http://pubrecord.org/multimedia/4273/during-sermon-arizona-pastor-tells/comment-page-1/, last accessed January 18, 2010.

Rivera, A., Huezo, J., Kasica, C. & Muhammad, D. (January 2009). The Silent Depression: State of the Dream 2009. United for a Fair Economy.

Saxton, J. (2008). United States Congress, *Employment Numbers as Recession Indicators.* Washington, DC: Joint Economic Committee. Retrieved from http://www.house.gov/jec/studies/2008/Employment%20Numbers%20as%20Recession%20Indicators.pdf, last accessed January 18, 2010.

Schuman, H., Steeh, C., Bobo, L., & Krysan, M. (1997). *Racial Attitudes in America: Trends and Interpretations.* Cambridge, MA: Harvard University Press.

Small, N. L., Harding, D. J. & Lamont, M. (2009). Introduction: Reconsidering Culture and Poverty. Forthcoming in a special issue of the *Annals of the American Academy of Political and Social Science.* Retrieved from http://www.wjh.harvard.edu/soc/faculty/lamont/publications/Small-Harding-Lamont_Introduction-Reconsidering-Culture-and-Poverty.pdf, last accessed January 19, 2010.

Smith, S. S. (2007). *Lone Pursuit*. New York, NY: Russell Sage.

Smith, W. (January 1, 2009). Personal Reflections on a Historic Moment. *USA Today*. Retrieved from http://www.usatoday.com/news/opinion/personal-reflections.htm, last accessed January 20, 2010.

Steele, C. M. (1997). A Threat in the Air: How stereotypes shape the intellectual identities and performance of women and African-Americans. *American Psychologist, 52*, 613–629.

Steinberg, S. (1995). *Turning Back: The Retreat from Racial Justice in American Thought and Policy*. Boston, MA: Beacon.

Striner, R. (2006). *Father Abraham: Lincoln's Relentless Struggle to End Slavery*. New York, NY: Oxford University Press.

Takaki, R. (1993). *A Different Mirror: A History of Multicultural America*. Boston, MA: Back Bay Books.

Turner, M. A., Ross, S.L., Galster, G.C., & Yinger, J. (2002). *Discrimination in Metropolitan Housing Markets: National Results from Phase I HDS 2000*. Washington, DC: U.S. Department of Housing and Urban Development.

U.S. Bureau of Labor Statistics. (2009). U.S. Unemployment Rates by Race, 1974-Latest. Retrieved from http://verifiable.com/charts/1361, last accessed January 25, 2010.

U.S. Census Bureau. (2009). *The National Data Book: 2009 Statistical Abstract*. Retrieved from http://www.census.gov/compendia/statab/tables/09s0691.pdf, last accessed January 21, 2010.

Walmsley, R. (2007). Word Prison Population List. International Centre for Prison Studies. School of Law, King's College London. Retrieved from http://www.kcl.ac.uk/depsta/law/research/icps/downloads/world-prison-pop-seventh.pdf, last accessed January 20, 2010.

Walsh, K. R. (2003/2004). Color-Blind Racism in *Grutter and Gratz*. *Boston College Third World Law Journal*. Retrieved from http://www.bc.edu/schools/law/lawreviews/meta-elements/journals/bctwj/24_2/07_FMS.htm, last accessed January 25, 2010.

Will, G. (January 14, 2008). The GOP - Grand Old Pulpit. *Newsweek*. Retrieved from http://www.newsweek.com/id/84534, last accessed January 25, 2010.

Wise, T. (2009). *Between Barack and a Hard Place: Racism and White Denial in the Age of Obama*. San Francisco, CA: City Lights Books.

Younge, G. (January 7, 2008). An Obama Victory Would Symbolize A Great Deal and Change Very Little. *The Guardian*.

Zeleny, J. & Rutenberg, J. (December 5, 2009). Threats Against Obama Spiked Early. *The New York Times*. p. A30.

Constraint and Freedom in the "Age of Obama"

Kenneth W. Mack

Structure and agency, constraint and freedom, or, to use the older terminology, determinism and free will. Matthew Hughey is surely right to deploy both as ways of viewing the racial politics of a post-civil rights, if demonstrably not post-racial, America. Some contend that continuing Black–White racial inequality (the type that gets most of our interest, although there are others) is the product of a long history of structurally entrenched legal, economic, and social inequality that cannot be erased in one generation. Others point to the undeniable revolution in law, policy, and racial attitudes since the 1960s and argue that racial inequality persists because many African-Americans do not grasp for the freedom that is readily available. Hughey's thesis is that most people, President Obama included, seem to believe in some combination of both explanations. They concede the long history of entrenched racial inequality that lies behind us but nonetheless contend that at this particular juncture we have the freedom to overcome it. Hughey lodges himself comfortably in the area of "cultural contradictions"—we live in an age of paradoxes, with our confused rhetoric of race just a symptom of a deeper malady.

At the outset, I should point out that there are actually two types of structural explanations for racial inequality, just as there are two argumentative styles for freedom. Conservative structuralists sometimes lodge their explanations in a "culture of poverty" that permits inequality to be inherited from generation to generation. The modern roots of this argument lie in the provocative 1960s-era work of Nathan Glazer and Daniel Patrick Moynihan (Glazer & Moynihan, 1963; U.S. Department of Labor, 1965). More controversially, some conservatives also focus on the inheritability of intelligence, with its most famous recent incarnation being Hernstein and Murray's *Bell Curve*. Its historical roots are lodged in the invention of modern intelligence testing in the early twentieth century, which put the imprimatur of science behind the idea there was racial differentiation among White Americans and that Eastern and Southern European immigrants possessed inherent mental defects (Painter, 2010; Gould, 1996). Liberal to left structuralists, by contrast, tend to make arguments like those presented in the second part of Hughey's paper—that centuries of racial inequality backed by law, economic exploitation, and raw White racism continue to make their effects felt in the present. The roots of this argument go back to the Great Depression, when left intellectuals began to describe race as a product of wealth inequality, and to the late 1950s and 60s, when nascent Black power theorists began to describe what, by 1967, would be called *institutional racism* (Holloway, 2002; López, 2000).[1]

A popular form of the conservative argument for freedom calls attention to markets as a corrective for racial prejudice or to the desirability of leaving social actors free to make their own choices, good or bad. In either case, race relations are characterized by freedom, and we are all better off for it (Epstein, 1992). A classic liberal argument for freedom was captured by Los Angeles civil rights lawyer Loren Miller's statement, offered somewhat dismissively in 1962, that the "liberal outlook on the race question . . . contemplates the ultimate elimination of all racial distinctions in every phase of American life" (Miller, 1962, p. 235). Political liberals once predicted that if African-Americans could be freed from explicit race discrimination, racial inequality would be placed on the road to extinction. Some left-liberal groups crafted audacious uses of this idea, such as in the short-lived Freedom Now political movement of the early 1960s, which envisioned a "Negro-led, Negro-officered, army [marching] under the banner of Freedom Now" (Miller, 1962, p. 238). By 1965, however, even President Johnson would concede that "freedom is not enough" in his famous Howard University address. For differing reasons, both White liberals and Black radicals began to focus on entrenched racial inequality in the late 1960s, although they offered contrasting explanations for the phenomenon.

Yet there are reasons to think more deeply about liberal freedom in what Hughey calls "the age of Obama." If this is the proper name for our historic juncture, it suggests that left-liberal structural explanations for race inequality are bound to remain prophetic, speaking more to an imagined future than a possible present. The age of Obama is also likely to be the age of pragmatism, as that is the type of politics that resulted in the election of a Black man to the presidency, and that is how the present administration tends to govern. The tendency of Americans to believe in freedom-oriented explanations for racial inequality is itself evidence that there is likely to be little political will for structuralist solutions in the near future. Liberal visions of freedom once tapped into a deep-seated, and very American, need to imagine that freedom would lead, ineluctably, to equality. Between World War II and the 1960s, such visions helped generate research agendas for social scientists, policy proposals, and, ultimately, political coalitions.

The choice between prophetic visions of the future and pragmatic programs for the present is a personal one. Given the entrenched forms of inequality that the subsequent contributors to this volume will, no doubt, demonstrate, many readers will conclude that a pragmatic politics of freedom is neither desirable nor possible. But it is, at least, worthwhile imagining.

NOTE

1 I am indebted to Cornel West's formulation of the distinction between conservative and liberal-left structuralism, although I formulate it slightly differently here. See West, C. (1994). Nihilism in Black America, in *Race Matters*. New York: Vintage Books, Random House.

REFERENCES

Epstein, E. (1992). *Forbidden Grounds: The Case Against Employment Discrimination Laws*. Cambridge: Harvard University Press.

Glazer, N. & Moynihan, D.P. (1963). *Beyond the Melting Pot: The Negroes, Puerto Ricans, Jews, Italians, and Irish of New York City*. Cambridge: Harvard University Press.

Gould, S.J. (1996). *The Mismeasure of a Man*. New York: W.W. Norton.

Holloway, J.S. (2002). *Confronting the Veil: Abram Harris, Jr., E. Franklin Frazier, and Ralph Bunche, 1919-1941*. Chapel Hill: University of North Carolina Press.

López, I.F.H. (2000). Institutional Racism: Judicial Conduct and a New Theory of Racial Discrimination. *Yale Law Journal 109*, 1717–1884.

Miller, L. (October 20, 1962). Farewell to Liberals: A Negro View. *The Nation*, p. 235.

Painter, N.I. (2010). *The History of White People*. New York: W.W. Norton.

United States Department of Labor (1965). *The Negro Family: The Case for National Action*. Washington: U.S. Government Printing Office, 1965.

CHAPTER 2

Implicit Bias: A Better Metric for Racial Progress?

Leslie Ashburn-Nardo, Robert W. Livingston, and Joshua Waytz

With the election of the United States' first African American president, Barack Obama, many people believe that the country has finally overcome its long history of racial tension. For example, a New York Times headline proclaimed on the day of the historic election, "Obama Elected as Racial Barrier Falls" (Nagourney, November 5, 2008). The article went on to quote Obama's opponent, Senator John McCain:

> This is a historic election, and I recognize the significance it has for African Americans and for the special pride that must be theirs tonight. We both realize that we have come a long way from the injustices that once stained our nation's reputation.

Similarly, Senator Bob Casey expressed in the article:

> I always thought there was a potential prejudice factor in the state. I hope this means we washed that away.

Research corroborates these initial reactions to the 2008 Presidential election. In a longitudinal study of college students, beliefs that America has made great progress toward racial equality improved significantly post-election from their pre-election levels (Kaiser, Drury, Spalding, Cheryan, & O'Brien, 2009).

Even before Election Day, in the midst of his campaign, then-Senator Obama indicated that his candidacy underscored the United States' racial progress and that denying such progress would "dishonor the memories of all those who fought for our civil rights throughout the generations" (CNN, October 1, 2007). He further stated:

> My belief is that we have changed sufficiently in this country that it is possible for a large number of whites to vote for an African American candidate. If I did not believe that, I would not be running.

Given America's tumultuous racial past—particularly the fact that it was only 40 years prior to Obama's election that the nation's icon of hope for racial equality, Dr. Martin Luther King, Jr., was assassinated—it is easy to understand why many perceive Obama's election to signify a "post-racial" America. Few could have imagined that there would ever come a day in which a non-White—and especially an African American—candidate would be elected to the nation's highest office. To many, such an historic milestone surely means that we have put our prejudices behind us.

But not everyone is as optimistic about America's racial progress. For example, according to a survey conducted during the 2008 election, 38% of African Americans believed that discrimination was a "serious problem." This number increased to 55% in a 2009 survey conducted by the same organization (CNN, July 20, 2009). Such numbers do little to suggest that Obama's election has had a positive impact on race relations in the United States.

Further illustrating beliefs about the persistence of racism, and in light of unprecedented hostile remarks conveyed directly to a U.S. President in a public forum, former President Jimmy Carter expressed to NBC Nightly News, "I think an overwhelming portion of the intensely demonstrated animosity toward President Barack Obama is based on the fact that he is a black man, that he is African American" (NBC News and News Services, September 16, 2009). Consistent with President Carter's statements about race-based reactance to Obama's presidency, participants in a longitudinal study expressed significantly less support for policies that address racial inequality (e.g., affirmative action programs, desegregated schools) and perceived significantly less need for further efforts at achieving racial progress in the United States *following* the 2008 election than they did before the election (Kaiser et al., 2009).

Collectively, these divergent views about race relations in America underscore a challenge for social scientists: finding an appropriate metric for racial progress. Several decades of social psychological research suggest that finding a way to measure racial biases proves to be a bigger challenge than one might imagine. Certainly, researchers can ask people to report their racial attitudes and beliefs via questionnaire or interview, but are such self-reports always the most valid tool for understanding racial biases? Given normative pressure to appear nonprejudiced, people are sometimes unwilling to express their honest opinions about African Americans. Furthermore, because racial attitudes and stereotypes originate at an early age and are shaped by a variety of experiences over the lifespan, people often have poor insight into their own racial biases. Consequently, social scientists have looked for ways to assess racial attitudes and stereotypes that minimize both socially desirable responses and responses that rely on conscious access. We refer to such measures as *implicit* measures.

In the present chapter, we provide an overview of implicit social cognitive methodology, and we review the growing literature on implicit racial bias. In particular, we distinguish implicit from explicit biases; describe how implicit biases are measured; and discuss the predictive utility of implicit measures of racial bias, with an eye toward circumstances in which implicit bias is a better predictor than explicit, self-reported bias. We then summarize several studies investigating the role of implicit versus explicit racial biases in the 2008 Presidential election and discuss whether there is evidence of racial progress in light of recent findings.

WHAT IS IMPLICIT RACIAL BIAS?

The origins of the terms *implicit* and *explicit* to refer to social cognitive constructs such as attitudes, biases, and stereotypes can be traced to cognitive psychology, where the terms were employed to describe memory systems. An implicit memory was said to occur when a participant demonstrated a behavioral outcome that was the direct result of a prior event that occurred, for which they had no conscious recollection or awareness (*see* Richardson-Klavehn & Bjork, 1988; Roediger, 1990; Schacter, 1987; for reviews). Greenwald and Banaji (1995) later adapted cognitive psychology's definition of an implicit memory to describe implicit social cognitions. They suggested:

> A template for definitions of specific categories of implicit cognition is: *An implicit C is the introspectively unidentified (or inaccurately identified) trace of past experience that mediates R.* In this template, *C* is the label for a construct (such as attitude), and *R* names the category of responses (such as object-evaluative judgments) assumed to be influenced by that construct (p. 5).

Because of individuals' inability to identify (accurately) the experience driving the social cognition, their review called for more indirect measures.

Fazio and Olson (2003) further argued that individuals may be simply unwilling (rather than unable) to report certain attitudes (e.g., prejudice) because of social desirability concerns, again highlighting the need for *implicit measures* that provide an estimate of (in this case) racial attitudes or stereotypes without the utilization of explicit self-report. In this chapter, we refer to the outcome of implicit measures as implicit racial biases, thus broadly referring both to implicit racial attitudes (i.e., evaluations implicitly associated with racial groups) and stereotypes (i.e., traits and characteristics implicitly associated with racial groups).

According to Aversive Racism Theory, implicit racial biases are the result of an inner psychological conflict. The theory suggests that contemporary prejudice is characterized by the paradoxical combination of egalitarian values and anti-Black affect (Dovidio & Gaertner, 1996; Gaertner & Dovidio, 1986). That is, many people believe it is important to treat others fairly and consistently, they consider themselves to be nonprejudiced individuals, and yet they harbor some negative feelings toward Blacks. To cope with threats to the nonprejudiced self-concept posed by this inherent contradiction, aversive racists push their negative feelings into the subconscious and only discriminate when their behaviors can be readily attributed to some factor other than race. For example, in their review of studies regarding employment selection decisions over a 10-year period, Dovidio and Gaertner (2000) found evidence of discrimination against African American job candidates only when their qualifications were ambiguous—not when they were undeniably strong or weak. When candidates' credentials were clear, discrimination would be obvious, both to others as well as to participants themselves. Only when candidates' qualifications were mixed could participants "afford" to discriminate and simultaneously maintain their egalitarian self-image.

Much empirical support exists for aversive racism theory, but the theory does not directly address the origins of anti-Black affect. From whence do such unacknowledged negative feelings toward African Americans come? One possibility is that mechanisms underlying the formation of general affective associations (e.g., classical conditioning) also govern the formation of implicit racial biases. Consistent with this idea, research has shown that conditioning processes are closely tied to the genesis of implicit racial attitudes (Olson & Fazio, 2001, 2006; Olsson, Ebert, Banaji, & Phelps, 2005). Moreover, individual differences in susceptibility to evaluative conditioning can predict who is implicitly racially biased toward Blacks and who is not (Livingston & Drwecki, 2007), such that individuals who are susceptible to the acquisition of negative affective associations in general are also more prone to develop implicit racial biases toward Blacks.

HOW ARE IMPLICIT RACIAL BIASES MEASURED?

Although there are dozens of different types of implicit measures, nearly all of them fall into one of three broad categories: (1) reaction time measures (Fazio, Jackson, Dunton, & Williams, 1995; Greenwald, McGhee, & Schwarz, 1998; Payne et al., 2005); (2) language measures (Maas et al., 1997; Semin & Fiedler, 1988; Vargas, Sekaquaptewa, & von Hippel, , 1997); and (3) psychophysiological measures (Phelps et al., 2000; Vanman et al., 1997). Although a detailed discussion of all of these implicit measures is beyond the scope of this chapter, we briefly describe three of the most common methods of measuring implicit racial bias, all of which rely on reaction times. (For a comprehensive review, *see* Wittenbrink & Schwarz, 2007.)

Fazio et al.'s (1995) "bona-fide pipeline" task is a sequential priming task that measures participants' reaction time to judge target words as "good" or "bad" as a function of whether the target words are preceded by the brief presentation of a Black or White facial prime. The underlying assumption, based on spreading activation theory (Neely, 1977), is that the presentation of an attitude object (e.g., an African American face) will automatically activate associated evaluations from memory, which in turn facilitate (speed up) responses to evaluatively congruent words and inhibit (slow down) response times to evaluatively incongruent words following the prime. For someone high in implicit racial bias, the brief presentation of a Black facial prime on a computer screen should facilitate responses to negative words (e.g., evil) following the facial prime while slowing down response times to positive words (e.g., happiness) following the prime. The presentation of a White face, on the other hand, should facilitate response times to positive target words and inhibit response times to negative target words. These differences (measured in milliseconds) in response times to positive versus negative words as a function of whether the prime preceding it is a Black or White face are used to compute an index of implicit racial bias (*see* Fazio et al., 1995).

Another popular measure of implicit racial bias is the Implicit Association Test or "IAT" (Greenwald et al., 1998). The IAT is a response competition task that involves the classification of race concepts (i.e., Black or White faces or proper names [e.g., Tyrone vs. Adam]) and evaluative attributes (i.e., pleasant or unpleasant words [e.g., flower or garbage]) using two computer keys. Participants first practice this task by classifying only race concepts by pressing keys labeled as "Black" or "White," then only evaluative words by pressing keys labeled as "pleasant" or "unpleasant." In the critical trials, the two judgment tasks are combined such that one of the concept categories (e.g., "Black") is paired with one of the attribute categories (e.g., "unpleasant") using the same key, with the other race concept and attribute category paired on the other key. The underlying assumption is that racially biased participants should be faster to complete blocks involving "compatible" pairings (i.e., Black-unpleasant, White-pleasant) compared with blocks involving "incompatible" pairings (i.e., Black-pleasant, White-unpleasant). Participants' average overall reaction time to classify words and names in the compatible block is subtracted from their reaction time to classify words in the incompatible block (for a more thorough description of the IAT scoring algorithm, *see* Greenwald, Nosek, & Banaji, 2003). This score serves as the index of implicit racial bias (visit the IAT website at www.implicit.harvard.edu for a test demonstration).

Finally, the Affective Misattribution Procedure (AMP; Payne et al., 2005) taps implicit racial bias using the logic of projective tests and priming techniques. Participants are first primed with attitude objects (e.g., a Black face) follow by a neutral or ambiguous object (e.g., a Chinese ideograph, which, for most participants in Western cultures, has no inherent meaning). The measure of interest is the extent to which evaluation of the neutral object is influenced by its pairing with a Black or White face. If negative affect is "transferred" from the primed object to the ambiguous object (similar to the logic of evaluative conditioning), then participants are presumed to hold a negative attitude toward the primed object. The technique provides an unobtrusive means to test implicit racial bias toward Blacks.

WHAT DO IMPLICIT RACIAL BIASES PREDICT?

With the increasing use of implicit measures in the stereotyping and prejudice literature, as well as in the social cognitive literature more broadly, researchers have begun to examine several key questions to shed light on their utility. First, to what extent are implicit and explicit measures related? Second, how do implicit measures fare in terms of predictive validity? And finally, do implicit measures do a better job predicting behavior than explicit measures and, if so, under what circumstances? Some may find it disappointing, but perhaps not surprising, to learn that there is no straightforward answer to any of these questions.

With regard to whether implicit and explicit measures are related, the best answer appears to be "it depends" (*see* Greenwald & Nosek, 2008). Under some circumstances, implicit measures are highly correlated with explicit measures. For example, Nosek (2005) found strong relationships between implicit and explicit measures of preferences related to certain social issues (e.g., whether one identifies as pro-choice vs. pro-life), political leanings (e.g., support for Gore vs. Bush), and taste in soda (e.g., Coke vs. Pepsi). Correlations between implicit and explicit measures of racial bias, however, are often more modest (for reviews, *see* Blair, 2001; Dovidio, Kawakami, & Beach, 2001; Greenwald, Poehlman, Uhlmann, & Banaji, 2009).

Proposed explanations for the concordance versus discordance of implicit and explicit measures vary as well. Some theorists suggest that implicit and explicit biases are the result of distinct cognitive processes (e.g., Gawronski & Bodenhausen, 2006) or even separate memory systems (e.g., Smith & DeCoster, 2000; Wilson et al., 2000). Others maintain that implicit and explicit biases stem from a single representation in memory, with greater likelihood of a match when motivation and opportunity to consider one's response are low (e.g., Fazio, 1990; Fazio & Olson, 2003).

What is clear is that implicit biases do predict certain theoretically relevant outcomes and behaviors. This is especially true in the domain of intergroup relations. Indeed, a recent meta-analysis revealed that a measure of implicit racial bias (in this case, the IAT) actually outperformed self-report measures in predicting interracial behavior involving Whites and Blacks (Greenwald, Poehlman et al., 2009). Although a complete review of studies assessing the relationship between implicit racial bias and behavior is beyond the scope of this chapter, we highlight here the sheer variety of intergroup behaviors that implicit measures do predict. For example, implicit racial biases predict non-verbal behavior (e.g., signs of discomfort, unfriendliness) toward Blacks (e.g., Dovidio, Kawakami, & Gaertner, 2002; Dovidio et al., 1997; Fazio et al., 1995; McConnell & Leibold, 2001); seating distance from Blacks (Sargent & Theil, 2001); negative evaluations of Blacks (e.g., Amodio & Devine, 2006; Rudman & Lee, 2000); and lack of support for policies and resource allocations favoring Blacks (e.g., Rudman & Ashmore, 2007). Such findings are not limited to White participants. Under some circumstances, even Blacks more positively evaluate Whites over Blacks to the extent that they are implicitly biased in favor of Whites (Ashburn-Nardo & Johnson, 2008; Ashburn-Nardo, Knowles, & Monteith, 2003; Livingston, 2002).

One might be tempted to conclude that implicit racial biases predict intergroup behavior only in rather innocuous situations. But, in fact, they predict decisions and behaviors of great consequence, such as harsher criminal sentencing (Livingston, 2001), disparate treatment in medical settings (Green et al., 2007), job discrimination (Ziegert & Hanges, 2005), misidentification of benign objects as weapons when primed with Black faces (Payne, 2001), and even a propensity to "shoot" African American targets in a video game-like police simulation (Correll, Park, Judd, & Wittenbrink, 2002; Glaser & Knowles, 2008). Most would agree that such behavioral outcomes are of real import, even related to matters of life or death.

Not only do implicit racial biases predict important outcomes, but they also demonstrate incremental validity over explicit measures or at least offer differential prediction from explicit measures. For example, research employing the IAT with African American samples has demonstrated the unique contribution of implicit racial bias—above and beyond that of explicit measures—to judgments of Blacks versus Whites (Ashburn-Nardo et al., 2003) and to self-reported psychological well-being (Ashburn-Nardo, Monteith, Arthur, & Bain, 2007). Other research, conducted with not only with the IAT but also with sequential priming tasks, has shown that although explicit measures are often better predictors of verbal behaviors, implicit measures are often better predictors of nonverbal behaviors (e.g., Dovidio et al., 2002; McConnell & Leibold, 2001).

In short, implicit and explicit measures of racial bias are often independent of one another, and they often uniquely predict different types of behavior. Is one type of measure "better" than the other? We believe the answer is, "no." In fact, in tests of incremental validity, both types of measures capture variance above and beyond the other, suggesting that both types of measures contribute to our understanding of intergroup judgments and behavior (Greenwald, Poehlman et al., 2009).

OBAMA'S ELECTION AND IMPLICIT VERSUS EXPLICIT RACIAL BIASES

The 2008 Presidential election offered a unique opportunity for social scientists who investigate racial biases—both implicit and explicit. First, researchers could examine the ability of implicit and explicit measures of racial bias to predict voter behavior. In addition, one could argue that Obama's election served as a race-relations "intervention," with the potential for changing biases at both the implicit and explicit levels. Thus, researchers have also assessed the ways in which Obama's presidency has affected both implicit and explicit racial biases.

In terms of predicting voter behavior—a behavior that is effortful, under conscious control, and has significant implications—one might expect a straightforward relationship between explicit racial biases and anti-Obama sentiment, with greater bias predicting lack of support for Obama. Indeed, several studies found that the higher participants were in explicit, self-reported anti-Black prejudice, the more likely they were to intend to (Greenwald, Smith, Sriram, Bar-Anan, & Nosek, 2009) or actually vote for (Payne et al., 2009) McCain, the non-Black candidate. Payne et al. (2009) further found that the higher participants were in explicit racial bias, the less likely they were to vote for Obama.

But it is interesting to note that self-reported racial bias does not exclusively predict a vote against Obama. In fact, one study found that explicit anti-egalitarian attitudes predicted *support* for Obama but only among participants who believed that an Obama victory meant the end of racism in the United States (Knowles, Lowery, & Schaumberg, 2009). In other words, a subset of voters who consciously endorsed modern racism and anti-egalitarian ideology willingly voted for an African American candidate to justify the assertion that a post-racial America exists and perhaps consequently, to deny the continued need for social policy to remedy racial inequality (*see* Kaiser et al., 2009).

Independent of explicit racial biases, implicit racial biases also predicted voting intentions (Greenwald, Smith et al., 2009) and actual behavior

(Payne et al., 2009) in the 2008 election. Greenwald and colleagues found that both the IAT and AMP predicted voter intentions, such that the higher participants were in implicit racial bias the greater their intent to vote for McCain. Payne and colleagues' findings in particular illustrate the complexity of the relationship between implicit racial bias and voting. In their data, they coded separately whether participants indicated a vote for Obama (or not) or a vote for McCain (or not), thus recognizing that some voters might vote for a third-party candidate or abstain altogether. They found that when controlling for explicit racial bias, the higher voters were in implicit anti-Black bias, the less likely they were to vote for Obama. However, implicit anti-Black bias did not predict a vote *for* McCain. Instead, the higher participants were in implicit anti-Black bias, the more likely they were to vote for a third-party candidate or not vote at all. Thus, both implicit and explicit racial biases played some role in the 2008 U.S. Presidential election.

Has Obama's election had an impact on implicit and/or explicit racial biases? Given the recent occurrence of the election, only a few studies have addressed this question. Two studies have examined the effect of Obama's presidency on explicit, self-reported racial biases, and they have shown that having a Black president can actually *increase* racial bias. Effron, Cameron, and Monin (2009) demonstrated that after endorsing Barack Obama, participants were more likely to favor a White person for a job over a Black person. In addition, after indicating support for Obama, participants allocated more hypothetical funds to a group that supported Whites at the expense of a group that supported Blacks. The authors call this effect *moral credentialing* (*see* Monin & Miller, 2001). That is, people are willing to act in discriminatory ways if their previous behavior—in this case, supporting a Black presidential candidate—established their lack of bias.

Kaiser and her colleagues obtained similarly counterintuitive results using explicit measures. Before and after the election, they asked participants questions regarding the degree to which they supported policies that address racial inequality and their beliefs about how much further the United States needs to go to achieve racial equality. Consistent with the idea that electing President Obama might provide a license to express prejudice explicitly, participants showed decreased support for policies that addressed racial inequality after the election. They also were less inclined to believe that the United States needs to continue efforts to achieve racial equality (Kaiser et al., 2009). This post-election backlash occurred despite the fact that Blacks, compared with Whites, have almost double the unemployment rate and are 30% more likely to die from heart disease and cancer resulting from health disparities (Blow, 2009; Kaiser et al., 2009).

Obama seems to have had an impact on implicit racial biases as well. The most direct evidence comes from a study conducted by Plant and her colleagues. They compared IAT scores obtained after the election to those recorded before the election, albeit in successive independent samples rather than following a single sample longitudinally. Compared with pre-election results reported in the literature, Plant et al. (2009) found less evidence of implicit anti-Black bias and stereotyping following the election. Their follow-up studies suggested that this decrease in implicit racial bias had to do with the fact that exposure to Obama, a counter-stereotypical Black individual, positively changed underlying associations with African Americans.

These results underscore the complex nature of President Obama's effect on race relations. Implicitly, Obama has had a positive effect, appearing to reduce racial bias as measured by the IAT. However, explicitly, the salience of Obama has caused certain anti-egalitarian beliefs and ideologies to change in a negative manner, decreasing support for social policies that would benefit African Americans.

CONCLUSIONS

In this chapter, we have reviewed the literature on implicit racial bias, comparing such biases with those that are measured explicitly via self-report. We provided a brief overview of some of the most popular methods used to assess implicit racial bias, and we discussed evidence establishing the predictive validity of such measures. We then described the extant literature regarding the roles of implicit and explicit racial biases in the 2008 Presidential election. In light of all the evidence, can we conclude with certainty that implicit racial bias is a better metric for racial progress?

One certainty about the literature on implicit racial bias is the speed with which it has grown. Circa 1980, researchers relied on inferences made from behavioral observation to estimate unobtrusive racial bias. For example, the fact that Whites were more likely to deny help to African Americans in remote situations rather than face-to-face situations was taken as evidence of implicit racial bias (e.g., Crosby, 1980). Such unobtrusive measures only hinted at the measurement options researchers have today. Devine's (1989) seminal paper on the automatic and controlled components of racial bias brought an explosion of reaction time measures similar to those employed in research today. But in Devine's research, stimuli were presented with a cumbersome tachistoscope, making it virtually impossible to collect data outside the laboratory. Today, with the near omnipresence of personal computers and the Internet, it is much easier to collect reaction time data and, therefore, to move outside the confines of the lab and beyond the exclusive use of college samples that some would argue is problematic for the study of racial bias (Henry, 2008). In short, in only a few decades, the use of implicit measures to assess racial bias has changed dramatically and increased exponentially.

Another certainty is that implicit measures of racial bias have contributed to our knowledge of intergroup behavior more generally and to our understanding of voting behavior in the 2008 election more specifically, as illustrated by the studies we reviewed herein as well as countless others. Although more theory is needed to decipher exactly *what* is being captured by implicit versus explicit measures (*see* Fazio & Olson, 2003; Greenwald & Nosek, 2008), the fact remains that they each capture unique variance in judgments and behavior.

However, we certainly cannot conclude that implicit measures are a *better* metric of racial progress than explicit. As Payne et al. (2009) eloquently stated, "Although modern theories of prejudice often emphasize subtle implicit forms of bias, old-fashioned explicit prejudice should not be underestimated" (p. 7). Indeed, our advice to researchers based on our review of the extant literature is to employ both types of measures whenever possible to account for maximum variance in race-related outcomes.

We also cannot conclude that the election of Barack Obama symbolizes the beginning of a "post-racial" America. Although his salience in the media as a leader, an orator, and a political groundbreaker seems to have decreased implicit racial bias (Plant et al., 2009) and perhaps increased the accessibility of positive characteristics associated with African Americans, Obama's presidency also has served as a threat to the status quo, thus incurring backlash (Effron et al., 2009; Kaiser et al., 2009). We hope that the evidence described in our chapter and others in this volume will serve as a reminder that although America made some racial progress with the election of Barack Obama, it is by no means post-racial.

REFERENCES

Amodio, D. M, & Devine, P. G. (2006). Stereotyping and evaluation in implicit race bias: Evidence for independent constructs and unique effects on behavior. *Journal of Personality and Social Psychology, 91*, 652–661.

Ashburn-Nardo, L., & Johnson, N. J. (2008). Implicit outgroup favoritism and intergroup judgment: The moderating role of stereotypic context. *Social Justice Research, 21*, 490–508.

Ashburn-Nardo, L., Knowles, M. L., & Monteith, M. J. (2003). Black Americans' implicit racial associations and their implications for intergroup judgment. *Social Cognition, 21*, 61–87.

Ashburn-Nardo, L., Monteith, M. J., Arthur, S. A., & Bain, A. (2007). Race and the psychological health of African Americans. *Group Processes and Intergroup Relations, 10*, 471–491.

Blair, I. V. (2001). Implicit stereotypes and prejudice. In G. B. Moskowitz (Ed.), *Cognitive social psychology: The Princeton Symposium on the Legacy and Future of Social Cognition* (pp. 359–374). Mahwah, NJ: Lawrence Erlbaum Associates.

Blow, C. (2009, December 4). Black in the age of Obama. *New York Times,* Editorial.

Correll, J., Park, B., Judd, C. M., & Wittenbrink, B. (2002). The police officer's dilemma: Using ethnicity to disambiguate potentially threatening individuals. *Journal of Personality and Social Psychology, 83*, 1314–1329.

CNN (2007, October 1). Obama: Candidacy a sign of racial progress. <http://www.cnn.com/2007/POLITICS/09/28/martin.obama/index.html>Accessed January 5, 2010.

CNN (July 2009, 20). Blacks in survey say race relations no better with Obama. <http://www.cnn.com/2009/POLITICS/06/25/obama.poll/index.html#cnnSTCOther1> Accessed January 5, 2010.

Crosby, F., Bromley, S., & Saxe, L. (1980). Recent unobtrusive studies of Black and White discrimination and prejudice: A literature review. *Psychological Bulletin, 87*, 546–563.

Devine, P. G. (1989). Stereotypes and prejudice: Their automatic and controlled components. *Journal of Personality and Social Psychology, 56*, 5–18.

Dovidio, J. F., & Gaertner, S. L. (1996). Affirmative action, unintentional racial biases, and intergroup relations. *Journal of Social Issues, 52*, 51–76.

Dovidio, J. F., & Gaertner, S. L. (2000). Aversive racism and selection decisions: 1989 and 1999. *Psychological Science, 11*, 315–319.

Dovidio, J. F., Kawakami, K., & Beach, K. R. (2001). Implicit and explicit attitudes: Examination of the relationship between measures of intergroup bias. In R. Brown, & S. L. Gaertner (Eds.), *Blackwell handbook of social psychology: Intergroup processes* (pp. 175–197). Malden, MA: Blackwell.

Dovidio, J. F., Kawakami, K., & Gaertner, S. L. (2002). Implicit and explicit prejudice and interracial interactions. *Journal of Personality and Social Psychology, 82*, 62–68.

Dovidio, J. F., Kawakami, K., Johnson, C., Johnson, B., & Howard, A. (1997). On the nature of prejudice: Automatic and controlled processes. *Journal of Experimental Social Psychology, 33*, 510–540.

Effron, D.A, Cameron, J.S, & Monin, B. (2009) Endorsing Obama licenses favoring Whites. *Journal of Experimental Social Psychology, 45*, 590–593.

Fazio, R. H. (1990). Multiple processes by which attitudes guide behavior: The MODE model as an integrative framework. In M. P. Zanna (Ed.), *Advances in experimental social psychology* (Vol. 23, pp. 75–109). New York: Academic Press.

Fazio, R. H., Jackson, J. R., Dunton, B. C., & Williams, C. J. (1995). Variability in automatic activation as an unobtrusive measure of racial attitudes: A bona fide pipeline? *Journal of Personality and Social Psychology, 69*, 1013–1027.

Fazio, R. H., & Olson, M. A. (2003). Implicit measures in social cognition: Their meaning and use. *Annual Review of Psychology, 54*, 297–327.

Gaertner, S. L., & Dovidio, J. F. (1986). An aversive form of racism. In J. F. Dovidio & S. L. Gaertner (Eds.), *Prejudice, discrimination, and racism* (pp. 61–89). New York: Academic Press.

Gawronski, B., & Bodenhausen, G. V. (2006). Associative and propositional processes in evaluation: An integrative review of implicit and explicit attitude change. *Psychological Bulletin, 132,* 692–731.

Glaser, J. & Knowles, E. D. (2008). Implicit motivation to control prejudice. *Journal of Experimental Social Psychology, 44,* 164–172.

Green, A. R., Carney, D. R., Pallin, D. J., Ngo, L. H., Raymond, K. L., Iezzoni, L., & Banaji, M. R. (2007). Implicit bias among physicians and its prediction of thrombolysis decisions for black and white patients. *Journal of General Internal Medicine, 22,* 1231–1238.

Greenwald, A. G., & Banaji, M. R. (1995). Implicit social cognition: Attitudes, self-esteem, and stereotypes. *Psychological Review, 102,* 4–27.

Greenwald, A. G., McGhee, D. E., & Schwartz, J. L. K. (1998). Measuring individual differences in implicit cognition: The Implicit Association Test. *Journal of Personality and Social Psychology, 74,* 1464–1480.

Greenwald, A. G., & Nosek, B. A. (2008). Attitudinal dissociation: What does it mean? In R. Petty, R. H. Fazio, & P. Briñol (Eds.), *Attitudes: Insights from the new implicit measures* (pp. 65–82). Hillsdale, NJ: Erlbaum.

Greenwald, A. G., Nosek, B. A., & Banaji, M. R. (2003). Understanding and using the Implicit Association Test: I. An improved scoring algorithm. *Journal of Personality & Social Psychology, 85,* 197–216.

Greenwald, A. G., Poehlman, T. A., Uhlmann, E. L., & Banaji, M. R. (2009). Understanding and using the Implicit Association Test: III. Meta-analysis of predictive validity. *Journal of Personality and Social Psychology, 97,* 17–41.

Greenwald, A. G., Smith, C. T., Sriram, N., Bar-Anan, Y., & Nosek, B. A. (2009). Implicit race attitudes predicted vote in the 2008 U.S. Presidential election. *Analyses of Social Issues and Public Policy, 9,* 241–253.

Henry, P. J. (2008). College sophomores in the laboratory redux: Influences of a narrow data base on social psychology's view of the nature of prejudice. *Psychological Inquiry, 19,* 49–71.

Kaiser, C. R., Drury, B. J., Spalding, K. E., Cheryan, S., & O'Brien, L. T. (2009). The ironic consequences of Obama's election: Decreased support for social justice. *Journal of Experimental Social Psychology, 45,* 556–559.

Knowles, E. D., Lowery, B. S., & Schaumberg, R. L. (2009). Anti-egalitarians for Obama? Group-dominance motivation and the Obama vote. *Journal of Experimental Social Psychology, 45,* 965–969.

Livingston, R. W. (2001). *Bias in the absence of malice: The phenomenon of unintentional discrimination.* Unpublished doctoral dissertation, The Ohio State University, Columbus, Ohio.

Livingston, R. W. (2002). Perceived negativity as a moderator of African Americans' implicit and explicit racial attitudes. *Journal of Experimental Social Psychology, 38,* 405–413.

Livingston, R. W. & Brewer, M. B. (2002). What are we really priming? Cue-based versus category-based processing of facial stimuli. *Journal of Personality and Social Psychology, 82*, 5–18.

Livingston, R. W. & Drwecki, B. B. (2007). Why are some individuals not racially biased? Susceptibility to affective conditioning predicts nonprejudice toward Blacks. *Psychological Science, 18*, 816–823.

McConnell, A. R. & Leibold, J. M. (2001). Relations among the Implicit Association Test, discriminatory behavior, and explicit measures of racial attitudes. *Journal of Experimental Social Psychology, 37*, 435–442.

Maass, A. Ceccarelli, R. & Rudin, S. (1996).Linguistic intergroup bias: evidence for in-group protective motivation. *Journal of Personality and Social Psychology, 17*, 512–526

Monin, B. & Miller, D. T. (2001). Moral credentials and the expression of prejudice. *Journal of Personality and Social Psychology, 81*, 33–43.

Nagourney, A. (2008, November 5). Obama elected President as racial barrier falls. *The New York Times*.

Neely, J. H. (1977). Semantic priming and retrieval from lexical memory: Roles of inhibitionless spreading activation and limited-capacity attention. *Journal of Experimental Psychology: General, 106*, 226–254.

NBC News and News Services. (September 2009, 16). White House disputes Carter's analysis. <http://www.msnbc.com/id/32869276/> Accessed January 5, 2010.

Nosek, B. A. (2005). Moderators of the relationship between implicit and explicit evaluation. *Journal of Experimental Psychology: General, 134*, 565–584.

Olson, M. A., & Fazio, R. H. (2001). Implicit attitude formation through classical conditioning. *Psychological Science, 12*, 413–417.

Olson, M. A., & Fazio, R. H. (2006). Reducing automatically activated racial prejudice through implicit evaluative conditioning. *Personality and Social Psychology Bulletin, 32*, 421–433.

Olsson, A., Ebert, J. P., Banaji, M. R., & Phelps, L. (2005). The role of social groups in the persistence of learned fear. *Science, 309*, 785–787.

Payne, B. K. (2001). Prejudice and perception: The role of automatic and controlledprocesses in misperceiving a weapon. *Journal of Personality and Social Psychology, 81*, 181–192.

Payne, B. K., Cheng, C. M., Govorun, O., & Stewart, B. (2005). An inkblot for attitudes:Affect misattribution as implicit measurement. *Journal of Personality and SocialPsychology, 89*, 277–293.

Payne, B. K., Krosnick, J. A., Pasek, J., Lelkes, Y., Akhtar, O., & Tompson, T. (2009). Implicit and explicit prejudice in the 2008 American presidential election. *Journal of Experimental Social Psychology*. Advance online publication. doi:10.1016/j.jesp.2009.11.001

Phelps, E., O'Connor, K., Cunningham, W., Funayama, E., Gatenby, J., Gore, J., & Banaji, M. R. (2000). Performance on indirect measures of race evaluation predicts amygdala activation. *Journal of Cognitive Neuroscience, 12*(5), 729–738.

Plant, E. A., Devine, P. G., Cox, W. T. L, Columb, C., Miller, S. L., Goplen, J., & Peruche, G. M. (2009). The Obama effect: Decreasing implicit prejudice and stereotyping. *Journal of Experimental Social Psychology. 45*, 961–964

Richardson-Klavehn, A., Bjork, R. A. (1988). Measures of memory. *Annual Review of Psychology, 39*, 475–543

Roediger, H. L. (1990). Implicit memory: retention without remembering. *American Psychologist, 45*, 1043–1056

Rudman, L. A., & Ashmore, R. D. (2007). Discrimination and the Implicit Association Test. *Group Processes and Intergroup Relations, 10(3)*, 359–372.

Rudman, L. A., & Lee, M. R. (2002). Implicit and explicit consequences of exposure to violent and misogynous rap music. *Group Processes and Intergroup Relations, 5*, 133–150.

Sargent, M. J., & Theil, A. (2001). When do implicit racial attitudes predict behavior? On the moderating role of attributional ambiguity. Unpublished Manuscript.

Schacter, D. L. (1987). Implicit memory: history and current status. *Journal of Experimental Psychology*, Learning, Memory, and Cognition, *13*, 501–518.

Semin, G. R., & Fiedler, K. (1988). The cognitive functions of linguistic categories in describing persons: Social cognition and language. *Journal of Personality and Social Psychology, 54*, 558–568

Smith, E. R., & DeCoster, J. (2000). Dual-process models in social and cognitive psychology: Conceptual integration and links to underlying memory systems. *Personality and Social Psychology Review, 4*, 108–131.

Vanman, E. J., Paul, B. Y., Ito, T. A., & Miller, N. (1997). The modern face of prejudice and structural features that moderate the effect of cooperation on affect. *Journal of Personality and Social Psychology, 73*, 941–959.

Vargas, P., Sekaquaptewa, D., & von Hippel, W. (2007). Armed only with paper and pencil: "Low-tech" measures of implicit attitudes. In B. Wittenbrink & N. Schwarz (Eds.), *Implicit measures of attitudes* (pp. 103–124). New York: Guilford Press.

Wilson, T., Lindsey, S., & Schooler, T. Y. (2000). A model of dual attitudes. *Psychological Review, 107*, 101–126.

Wittenbrink, B., & Schwarz, N. (Eds.). (2007). *Implicit measures of attitudes*. New York: Guilford Press.

Ziegert, J. C., & Hanges, P. J. (2005). Employment discrimination: The role of implicit attitudes, motivation, and a climate for racial bias. *Journal of Applied Psychology, 90*, 554–562.

The Erasure of the Affirmative Action Debate in the Age of Obama

Ian Ayres

After hearing Barack Obama's 2010 State of the Union address, MSNBC commentator Chris Matthews reflected:

> It's interesting. He is post-racial, by all appearances. You know, I forgot he was black tonight for an hour. You know, he's gone a long way to become a leader of this country and past so much history in just a year or two. I mean, it's something we don't even think about. I was watching and I said, "wait a minute, he's an African-American guy in front of a bunch of other white people and there he is, President of the United States, and we've completely forgotten that tonight." (Talmazan, January 28, 2010)

Matthews's ability to not consciously think about our president's race for an hour and the controversy that his claim engendered are intimately tied to the complicated currents explored by Ashburn-Nardo, Livingston, and Waytz's far-ranging overview of the implicit bias literature and the 2008 election's impact on implicit views about race. The chapter does an admirable job, particularly in summing up the ways in which measures of implicit bias have been shown across several studies to predict a variety of behaviors. But a weakness of the chapter is that it does not fully take on the growing criticism of both the interpretation and the methodology of the implicit bias research (Blanton et al., 2009). The chapter would have been stronger if it had included reactions to the more critical assessments of the literature.

Another lens through which to assess the impact of Obama's election on racial perception is to look at what used to be one of our nation's most contentious policy issues—the appropriate role of government-sponsored affirmative action. On the very day of Obama's election (November 4, 2008), the Court of Appeals for the Federal Circuit struck down as unconstitutional one of our nation's most important affirmative action laws, Section 1207, which countenanced the use of 10% bidding credits for firms "owned and controlled by socially and economically disadvantaged individuals" if necessary to reach an overall procurement goal of directing 5% of "contract dollars to businesses owned by socially and economically disadvantaged businesses."[1] The decision found that Congress did not have a sufficiently current disparity study to support the 2006 reauthorization of the program. (The Bush Administration had failed to follow the Clinton Administration's regulatory directives, which called for periodic disparity studies by the Commerce Department to assess whether continued racial preferences were necessary and would pass constitutional muster.) Somewhat surprisingly, the Federal Circuit's decision received very little coverage.[2]

In a very short time, affirmative action has changed from being a hot-button issue to a non-issue. In the past, presidential candidates had to answer questions about affirmative action. Along with abortion and, more recently, gay rights, affirmative action was a highly charged, contentious issue that aroused deep-seated voter emotions. But in 2008, not a single question was asked on affirmative action at any of the three McCain/Obama debates or at the single Biden/Palin debate. Only one of the dozens of Democratic primary debates featured a serious question on affirmative action.[3] It is as though the political parties and the media have agreed to take the issue off the table.

The nation seems to have tacitly agreed to move beyond debates about government-sponsored affirmative action. Affirmative action preferences in college admissions will be tolerated (at least for the next 25 years) as long as the racial preferences are merely an amorphous plus factor (Ayres & Foster, 2006). But there seems to be a growing political consensus to forego discussions of using racial preferences in government procurement. To my knowledge, the Obama Administration has not asked the Commerce Department to undertake a new disparity study to assess whether federal minority contractors are underutilized relative to their capacity in particular markets. Congress (after having re-enacted the 10% Department of Defense bidding credit in 1989, 1992, 1999, 2003, and 2006) made no effort to reauthorize the Section 1207 program, so that in the very first year of our nation having an African-American president, the most important federal affirmative action program in procurement expired of its own accord at the end of 2009. When it comes to federal procurement, we seem to be headed, without discussion, toward a post-racial world.

NOTES

1 *Rothe Development Corporation v. U.S. Department of Defense*, 545 F.3d 1023 (Fed. Cir. 2008) ("*Rothe VII*"). I was a "narrow tailoring" expert for the government. *See* Wainwright, J. & Holt, C. (2009). *The Limited Impact of Rothe VII on M/W/DBE Programs* (NERA Economic Consulting), http://www.nera.com/image/PUB_ Rothe_Impact_0609.pdf.

2 *But see* Brady, J. (November 28, 2008). Minority Contractors Lose Preference At Pentagon, http://www.npr.org/templates/story/story.php?storyId=97591671.

3 In the waning moments of the Philadelphia debate on April 16, 2008, George Stephanopoulos asked Obama: "How specifically would you recommend changing affirmative action policies so that affluent African Americans are not given advantages, and poor, less affluent whites are?" Then-Senator Obama responded:

Well, I think that the basic principle that should guide discussions not just on affirmative action but how we are admitting young people to college generally is, how do we make sure that we're providing ladders of opportunity for people? How do we make sure that every child in America has a decent shot in pursuing their dreams?

And race is still a factor in our society. And I think that for universities and other institutions to say, you know, we're going to take into account the hardships that somebody has experienced because they're black or Latino or because they're women –

MR. STEPHANOPOULOS: Even if they're wealthy?

SENATOR OBAMA: I think that's something that they can take into account, but it can only be in the context of looking at the whole situation of the young person. So if they look at my child and they say, you know, Malia and Sasha, they've had a pretty good deal, then that shouldn't be factored in. On the other hand, if there's a young white person who has been working hard, struggling, and has overcome great odds, that's something that should be taken into account.

So I still believe in affirmative action as a means of overcoming both historic and potentially current discrimination, but I think that it can't be a quota system and it can't be something that is simply applied without looking at the whole person, whether that person is black or white or Hispanic, male or female. What we want to do is make sure that people who have been locked out of opportunity are going to be able to walk through those doors of opportunity in the future.

Transcript of the Debate, http://www.nytimes.com/2008/04/16/us/politics/16text-debate.html?pagewanted=print

REFERENCES

Ayres, I., Foster, S. (2006). Don't Tell, Don't Ask: Narrow Tailoring After *Grutter*, *Gratz. Texas Law Review* 85, 517–583.

Blanton, H. (2009). Strong Claims and Weak Evidence: Reassessing the Predictive Ability of the IAT. *Journal of Applied Psychology* 94, 567–582.

Talmazan, Y. (January 28, 2010). Chris Matthews 'Forgot He Was Black': Obama's State Of The Union. *NowPublic*, http://www.nowpublic.com/world/chris-matthews-forgot-he-was-black-obamas-state-union-2565209.html, last accessed July 31, 2010.

CHAPTER 3

Black Man in the White House: Ideology and Implicit Racial Bias in the Age of Obama

Kristin A. Lane and John T. Jost[1]

> "We cannot help but believe that the old hatreds shall someday pass; that the lines of tribe shall soon dissolve."
> —*Barack H. Obama, Inaugural Address, January 20, 2009*

The election of Barack Obama—a man of mixed-race ancestry who identifies himself as, and is generally regarded as, Black—to the United States presidency on November 4, 2008, was understandably heralded as a pivotal moment in the complex, sometimes calamitous trajectory of race relations in the United States. The *New York Times* proclaimed "Obama Elected President as Racial Barrier Falls" (Nagourney, 2008), and Anna Quindlen (2008) noted in *Newsweek* that it is "impossible to overstate what that means to this nation." To be sure, Obama's candidacy and election to the nation's highest political office were possible only because of tremendous national changes that have taken place during his own lifetime. For example, it was 4 years *after* Obama's birth that the United States Supreme Court ruled in *Loving v. Virginia* that anti-miscegenation statutes were unconstitutional. That the son of a White Kansan woman and a Black Kenyan man—who could have been legally prevented from marrying in several regions of the United States—was ultimately elected to the presidency reflects a remarkable, if not seismic, shift in American racial attitudes and policies (e.g., Bobo & Dawson, 2009).

To a number of observers, Obama's election marked the dawn of a new "post-racial" era in which "America is now officially beyond racism" (Steele, 2008; *see also* Crowley, 2008; Tierney, 2008). A Google search for "Obama" and "post-racial" (or "post racial" or "postracial") in November 2009 yielded more than 400,000 search results. Commentators opined, "We are supposed to be living in post-racial times" (Givhan, 2008) and "For many people in America, Obama's election ushered in a post-racial era that was expected to push race to the back burner of our national consciousness" (Wickham, 2009). Such conclusions were probably hubristic from the start. For one thing, the overwhelming majority of Obama's support came from the politically liberal—that is,

least authoritarian and racially biased—segment of the United States population (e.g., *see* Jost, 2006; Jost, West, & Gosling, 2009; Nosek, Banaji, & Jost, 2009;
Reyna, Henry, Korfmacher, & Tucker, 2006; Sears, Van Laar, Carrillo, &
Kosterman, 2004; Sidanius, Pratto, & Bobo, 1996). Moreover, the election of
one Black man to high public office with the votes of less than 25% of
the country's adult population (http://www.cnn.com/ELECTION/2008/
results/president/), following a campaign that was itself far from post-racial
(http://www.guardian.co.uk/world/2008/aug/01/barackobama.uselections
2008), hardly satisfies the logical criteria for the existence of a tectonic shift in
Americans' racial attitudes. Still, it would be an important historical achievement if even half of the voting public were accurately said to inhabit a truly
"post-racial" world.[2]

In this chapter, we explore what Obama's election does—and, just as
importantly, does *not*—mean for understanding racial attitudes and intergroup relations in the contemporary United States. In so doing, we highlight
findings from the social sciences (especially experimental social psychology)
pertaining to the existence of robust and pervasive racial bias at an implicit
(i.e., relatively nonconscious and uncontrollable) level of awareness (*see also*
Jost, Rudman et al., 2009). We start by assessing the notion that Obama's election reflects a sea change in racial sentiment. Does it really mean that race-
based animus has been eliminated or even subdued? We summarize findings
from several large-scale survey and experimental studies on implicit and
explicit racial attitudes. These studies suggest that not only is the United States
still quite some distance from becoming a "post-racial" society but also that
implicit and explicit racial bias *did* play a significant role in the 2008 election
and in reactions to Obama's first year in the White House.

Furthermore, we contend that the relationship between Obama's presidency and racial attitudes is likely to be dynamic rather than static. His
election provides some insight into Americans' opinions about racial matters
in late 2008, but his tenure as president may well affect attitudes toward
African-Americans in ensuing years, for better or worse. One of the key
contributions social psychology can make is to highlight the analytic distinction between individuals' implicit or automatic evaluations and the explicit
attitudes and behaviors they exhibit because of, or in spite of, these evaluations. Research on the psychology of prejudice suggests that much "post-
racial" behavior represents not an absence of bias but rather an active attempt
to control it (e.g., Dunton & Fazio, 1997; Glaser & Knowles, 2008; Plant &
Devine, 1998).

Indeed, in keeping with past research on motivation to control racism,
some evidence suggests that Obama's presidency could ironically *worsen* race
relations in the United States, to the extent that it encourages people to dismiss

evidence of racial discrimination and stop striving for egalitarian goals (e.g., Effron, Cameron, & Monin, 2009; Kaiser, Drury, Spalding, Cheryan, & O'Brien, 2009). Near the end of the chapter, we review the first few studies to investigate whether Obama's election vanquishes or excuses racial prejudice; the evidence at this point is mixed. In a very real sense, the social psychological jury is still "out" when it comes to knowing whether the Obama presidency will help or hurt the cause of reducing racial prejudice at home and abroad. Any transformative effects that come from having a Black president may well be apparent only much later, as a result of comparative or historical analysis or by examining changes in implicit bias over time (e.g., Schmidt & Nosek, 2010). At the time of writing, Obama has completed only a year and a half in office; because we lack the crystal ball that would enable sound prognostication about the future of race relations in the United States, our remarks are necessarily speculative. Nevertheless, social psychological theories and methods may prove useful for understanding the long-term effects of having an African-American president on both implicit and explicit attitudes.

EVALUATING THE POST-RACIAL CLAIM

We are by no means alone in exploring racial attitudes and behaviors in light of Obama's electoral success (e.g., *see* the 2009 special issues of the *DuBois Review* and *Journal of Experimental Social Psychology*). In an especially brash dismissal of the notion that race continues to matter in American politics, one *New York Times* editorialist asked provocatively, "Where Have all the Bigots Gone?" only a few days after the election. In this article, Tierney (2008) wondered how to reconcile social scientific data showing persistent negativity toward Blacks with the election of a Black president. He asked: "After Mr. Obama's victory, should social scientists reconsider their research—and their image of the bigoted American?" Crowley (2008) raised similar questions in *The New Republic*, claiming (quite mistakenly, in retrospect) that "even white supremacists don't hate Obama."

As behavioral scientists, we are reticent to draw any general conclusion on the basis of a single event—no matter how important or extraordinary. Rather, what is needed is systematic study and careful observation of the thoughts, feelings, and behaviors of large numbers of individuals using multiple, converging methods of analysis. Furthermore, the question "Can an African-American be elected President?" is and always was the wrong criterion for determining whether the United States has entered a "post-racial" phase. As Mahzarin Banaji (2008) noted, did anyone seriously believe that sexism ceased to exist in Great Britain the moment that Margaret Thatcher was elected Prime Minister?

It is likewise perilous to try to draw conclusions about the attitudes of an entire nation. Nevertheless, if one is determined to identify some kind of national litmus test, we would propose this: "Would a Black candidate and a White candidate, who are equivalent in all respects other than race, be judged and evaluated in the same way(s) for the identical position (elected or otherwise)?" Of course, Obama and his opponent in the general election, John McCain, differed on many dimensions—not only in terms of their race but also age, experience, background, political ideology, party affiliation, and support for specific policy positions. Knowing only the outcome of the election, it is impossible to distinguish between two possibilities: *(1)* anti-Black racial bias played no role in the 2008 election, and *(2)* the degree of anti-Black bias, although substantial, was not great enough among his potential supporters to trump all of the other factors that determined the election's result. In other words, Obama might have been elected *despite* continued racial bias. Only by creating an Obama doppelgänger, who is 100% White but otherwise identical to the original, could one directly compare votes garnered by two candidates who differ only in terms of race.[3] Because this is ethically and technologically out of the question, we draw on established social scientific methodologies to gauge the role of race in electoral politics and in contemporary American culture more generally. Fortunately, these techniques provide ways of isolating the effects of racial categorization on human judgment and decision making (e.g., see Dovidio, Glick, & Rudman, 2005; Schneider, 2004; Stangor, 2000).

Racial Attitudes, Beliefs, and Opinions

Americans report increasingly tolerant and egalitarian attitudes. In the decades since the Civil Rights movement and the end of Jim Crow segregation, Americans have generally reported more positive racial attitudes and beliefs. Overt racism and support for anti-Black discrimination have markedly declined (Bobo & Dawson, 2009; Schuman, Steeh, Bobo, & Krysan, 1997; Sniderman & Carmines, 1997). Although 55% of White survey respondents in 1954 supported the notion that White job candidates should have "the first chance at any kind of job," by 1972 97% of White respondents rejected this policy (Schuman, Steeh, Bobo, & Krysan, 1997). Moreover, White Americans' professed willingness to vote for a Black presidential candidate also shifted considerably. Whereas 53% of respondents stated that they would vote for a qualified Black presidential candidate from their own party in a 1953 Gallup poll, 94% reported a willingness to do so in 2007 (Jones, 2007). The trend toward increasing racial egalitarianism appeared first among political liberals; over time, conservatives came to hold more positive explicit attitudes toward African-Americans as well (e.g., *see* Nosek et al., 2009).

Less conscious bias persists. At the same time, an abundance of scientific evidence from social and cognitive psychology makes clear that much (if not most) of social thought takes place outside of conscious awareness (e.g., Bargh & Williams, 2006; Greenwald & Banaji, 1995). For many decades, psychologists have known that memory and perception are subject to *explicit* (i.e., more deliberative, conscious) processes that can be articulated and reflected upon as well as *implicit* (i.e., less conscious) processes that are relatively inaccessible but can nonetheless have important consequences for behavior. It was hardly a gigantic conceptual leap, then, when social psychologists began to demonstrate that social sentiments—attitudes, stereotypes, and prejudices—similarly operate at both implicit and explicit levels of awareness (e.g., Devine, 1989; Fazio, Jackson, Dunton, & Williams, 1995; Fazio, Sanbonmatsu, Powell, & Kardes, 1986; Greenwald & Banaji, 1995). Explicit preferences correspond to lay definitions of "attitudes"—that is, what individuals say when they are asked how much they like opera, the Boston Red Sox, Apple computers, Mexican-Americans, Democrats, or a given presidential candidate. At the same time, individuals hold *implicit* or automatic evaluative responses toward the same attitude objects, and these implicit responses may or may not be consistent with their verbal self-reports (e.g., Greenwald & Banaji, 1995; Wilson, Lindsey, & Schooler, 2000; Wittenbrink & Schwarz, 2007).

Although many specific research paradigms have been developed to assess implicit attitudes and evaluations (including stereotypes and prejudices), the largest class relies on response latency measures—that is, estimating the length of time it takes to perform various mental operations (*see* Jost, Rudman et al., 2009, for a primer). The logic of this method is rooted in several decades of research in cognitive psychology establishing that response latency (i.e., reaction time) indexes the strength of associations between different concepts. For example, people respond more quickly to the word "robin" than "arm" after having been exposed briefly to the word "bird" (Neely, 1977). Eventually, work of this kind on *semantic priming* was extended to social domains through the use of *evaluative priming* techniques (e.g., Fazio et al., 1986, 1995). These latter techniques measure the relative strength of associations between concepts such as "Americans" and value-laden judgments such as "good" and "bad."

The Implicit Association Test. The Implicit Association Test (or IAT) is simply another method of using reaction time to gauge implicit evaluations by measuring how quickly people associate positively (vs. negatively) valenced words with White (vs. Black) faces or names, respectively (Greenwald, McGhee, & Schwartz, 1998; Lane, Banaji, Nosek, & Greenwald, 2007; Nosek, Greenwald, & Banaji, 2007). A summary of more than 2.5 million IATs completed at a public website (http://implicit.harvard.edu) provides several clear conclusions (Nosek, Smyth et al., 2007). First, on average, people exhibit marked implicit preferences for socially advantaged (or high status) groups over disadvantaged (or low status) groups (e.g., White over Black, light-skinned over dark-skinned people, and straight people over gays and lesbians).[4] Second, many individuals also show robust and pervasive implicit stereotypical associations linking, for example, Black men with weapons or men (more than women) with science (Nosek, Smyth et al., 2007). Third, implicit biases against members of stigmatized or disadvantaged groups (including African-Americans) are frequently more pronounced than explicit biases, suggesting that people may be unaware of some of their social preferences or are reluctant to admit to them.

Research reveals that implicit evaluations and stereotypes are only modestly correlated with explicit evaluations and stereotypes at the individual level of analysis (*see* Hofmann, Gawronski, Gschwender, Le, & Schmitt, 2005, for a meta-analytic review). Such evidence is typically taken to indicate that implicit and explicit evaluations capture unique or distinctive aspects of one's overall attitudinal system (e.g., Banaji & Heiphetz, 2010). If this is true, it is essential to consider both implicit and explicit attitudes when evaluating the claim that the United States has entered a "post-racial" era. Unfortunately, the results from the largest study conducted to date do not provide grounds for optimism. Schmidt and Nosek (2010) examined implicit racial attitudes among more than 470,000 visitors to the Project Implicit website prior to the moment that Obama announced his presidential candidacy, throughout the campaign, and even into his first few months in office. Average levels of implicit racial bias remained virtually unchanged among members of every demographic group tested during the 2.5-year period. The results were unambiguous: Moderate levels of implicit racial bias persisted before, during, and after Barack Obama's election.

Do milliseconds matter? Still, one might wonder, as did Chugh (2004), whether "milliseconds matter." Does knowing a person's score on an implicit measure of bias really help us to predict his or her behavior? Some critics claim that it does not (e.g., Tetlock & Mitchell, 2008, 2009), but the scientific consensus on this question is a resounding "yes." A meta-analysis of dozens of studies reveals that implicit stereotypes and prejudices are, in fact, *better* predictors of some forms of behavior (including discriminatory behavior) than are explicit attitudes (Greenwald, Poehlman, Uhlmann, & Banaji, 2009). A comprehensive detailing of this research literature, which clearly establishes the predictive utility of implicit measures, is well beyond the scope of the present chapter (for reviews, *see* Hardin & Banaji, in press; Jost, Rudman et al., 2009; Lane et al., 2007; Nosek, Smyth et al., 2007). Here we describe just a few representative findings to convey a sense of the literature as a whole.

One of the earliest studies in this tradition revealed that implicit anti-Black attitudes (as measured with an evaluative priming technique) predicted less friendly behavior toward a Black experimenter (Fazio et al., 1995). Subsequent work has shown that anti-Black bias (estimated by other implicit measures) is associated with negative nonverbal behavior directed at a Black partner, including the decision to sit farther away from him or her (e.g., Amodio & Devine, 2006). Similarly, participants who hold stronger anti-fat attitudes at an implicit level maintain greater social distance from an overweight inter-action partner (Bessenoff & Sherman, 2000). Finally, White college students who harbor more negative implicit racial attitudes are less likely to be living with their Black roommates at the end of the school year, as compared to those White students who exhibit more positive implicit racial attitudes (Towles-Schwen & Fazio, 2003).

Tetlock and Mitchell (2009), among others, have questioned whether laboratory and field demonstrations such as these speak to the existence of implicit bias "in the real world." In response, Jost, Rudman, and colleagues (2009) identified and summarized the results of 10 studies that employed diverse (including several nonstudent) samples and/or measured behavioral outcomes with clear and significant consequences for societal and organiza-tional functioning. For example, a study by Rooth (2007) revealed that profes-sional recruiters in Sweden who received equally qualified resumes from job applicants possessing either Swedish or Arabic last names were 3.3 times more likely to offer interviews to those applicants with Swedish names. On average, these recruiters exhibited strong implicit, but not explicit, stereotypes associating Swedish men with "high productivity" (and Arab Muslim men with "low productivity"). Moreover, recruiters' implicit bias scores predicted the likelihood that they would make discriminatory judgments. The more recruiters exhibited implicit stereotypes, the less likely they were to interview a candidate with an Arab-sounding name. Approximately half of the statisti-cal variability in callback rates resulting from ethnicity could be accounted for by implicit bias.

Rudman and Ashmore (2007) found that White student-participants who scored higher on various measures of implicit bias against racial and ethnic outgroups were significantly more likely to report engaging in verbal slurs, social exclusion, and acts of physical harm against members of minority groups and their property, even after statistically adjusting for their explicit racial attitudes. Those who exhibited greater implicit bias were also more likely to recommend cutting university funding for Jewish, Asian, and Black (vs. other) student associations to resolve a budgetary shortfall. Other studies reveal that significant proportions of police officers, judges, and medical pro-fessionals exhibit implicit racial biases that affect their professional judgment, especially under circumstances of ambiguity and time pressure (e.g., Correll, Park, Judd, Wittenbrink, Sadler, & Keesee, 2007; Eberhardt, Goff, Purdie, & Davies, 2004; Green, Carney, Pallin, Ngo, Raymond, Iezzoni, & Banaji, 2007; Plant & Peruche, 2005; Rachlinski, Johnson, Wistrich, & Guthrie, 2009; von Hippel, Brener, & von Hippel, 2008).

Implicit processes in voting behavior. Even these behaviors, however, might seem too distant from what goes on in the voting booth to answer questions about implicit bias in the age of Obama. Months of media coverage, debates, political advertisements, and direct campaign outreach activities all shape voters' perceptions and evaluations of candidates. Research suggests that even behaviors that are as consequential as voting are affected by seemingly irrelevant factors. For example, Todorov, Mandisodza, Goren, and Hall (2005) showed pictures of pairs of candidates for United States congressional seats to people who were unfamiliar with the candidates. These naïve viewers made quick judgments of the candidates' competence levels, and these judgments were remarkably concordant with the election results. Specifically, candidates who were perceived as more competent by naïve judges won 71.6% of the Senate and 66.8% of the House of Representative races. These data suggest, among other things, that voting decisions are not merely the product of conscious and deliberative reflection.

More direct investigations establish the relationship between implicit attitudes and voting behavior (e.g., *see* Roccato & Zogmaister, 2010). For example, implicit attitudes predicted self-reported voting behavior in the 2002 German parliamentary election, even after adjusting for participants' self-reported attitudes toward the political parties (Friese, Bluemke, & Wänke, 2007). In another study, implicit candidate preferences predicted eventual voting patterns in a local Italian election for both decided and undecided voters (Arcuri, Castelli, Galdi, Zogmaister, & Amadori, 2008). Galdi, Arcuri, and Gawronski (2008) found that for undecided voters, implicit attitudes predicted citizens' (future) voting behavior *better* than explicit attitudes with regard to an important matter of public policy (expansion of an American military base in Vicenza, Italy). (Among decided voters, explicit attitudes were better predictors than implicit attitudes of voting behavior.)

Findings such as these led Wilson and Bar-Anan (2008) to suggest that so-called "undecided" voters "may have already made up their minds at an implicit level" (p. 1047). Although the precise mechanisms by which implicit social psychological processes influence voting behaviors have not yet been identified, it seems likely that implicit attitudes and stereotypes affect the ways in which political information obtained from the media and elsewhere is processed and interpreted. Similarly, media coverage (e.g., of political scandals) has the capacity to influence implicit (as well as explicit) attitudes. To the extent that incoming information both affects and is affected by one's implicit beliefs, assumptions, and motivations, one would expect that (over time) the relationship between implicit and explicit attitudes (and, ultimately, their relationship to voting behaviors) would be strengthened, especially for those who are interested in politics (e.g., *see* Nosek, 2005).

Implicit bias and Obama's election. The studies of implicit preferences among initially undecided voters—taken in conjunction with the vast literature demonstrating that implicit group preferences predict behavioral outcomes, such as quality of treatment of ingroup and outgroup members (Greenwald et al., 2009; Jost, Rudman et al., 2009)—make a reasonably strong *prima facie* case that implicit attitudes (i.e., racial bias) played some role in the 2008 election. However, this possibility was roundly dismissed by Philip Tetlock, who was quoted in Tierney's (2008) *New York Times* article as claiming:

> Obama's candidacy is in itself a major embarrassment for the unconscious-bias crowd. . . . [P]eople did not seize on these [non-racial] rationales in anywhere near the numbers they should have if unconscious bias were as pervasive and potent as typically implied.

This is a sweeping conclusion that fails to withstand critical scrutiny, as we show in this chapter.

For one thing, the election outcome shows that political liberals and some moderates were willing to send a Black man to the White House, but it says nothing at all about the willingness of conservatives to do so (cf. Jost, West, & Gosling, 2009). In fact, the outcome itself does not even establish that liberals are unbiased; it might suggest instead that they were simply successful in *controlling* implicit bias (e.g., Glaser & Knowles, 2008). Still, the evidence remains that conservatives are significantly more racially biased than liberals when it comes to implicit attitudes (e.g., Greenwald, Smith, Sriram, Bar-Anan, & Nosek, 2009; Jost et al., 2004; Nosek et al., 2009; Schmidt & Nosek, 2010).

Of course, race was but one of many factors that differentiated Obama from his opponents in the Democratic primary and general election. The real question, as we noted above, is what the outcome would have been if Obama's White doppelgänger had headed the Democratic (or, more to the point, Republican) ticket. Unless and until we know the answer to questions such as these, we can only conclude that Obama's racial background was not a substantial *enough* negative factor to overcome all of the other factors (including Bush fatigue) that led voters to support him. Purely as a matter of logic, it is fallacious to conclude, as some have, that the election of Barack Obama in 2008 in and of itself signifies that racial bias—whether implicit or explicit— exerted little or no influence during the campaign or that it plays no appreciable role in society at large. As we shall see, the evidence shows clearly that racial bias affected perceptions and evaluations of Obama.

Explicit racial bias and support for Obama. Several studies have explored the influence of explicit (i.e., self-reported) racial bias on voting in the 2008 election. For example, a survey of 781 Americans in October 2008 revealed, unsurprisingly, that more negative attitudes about Blacks were associated with less favorable evaluations of Obama (Dwyer, Stevens, Sullivan, & Allen, 2009). The authors concluded that racism, but not sexism, affected voting behavior in 2008. Piston (in press) found that participants in the 2008 American National Election Studies (ANES) who believed that Blacks are lazier or less intelligent than Whites also rated Obama less favorably. By contrast, the endorsement of racial stereotypes was unrelated to the degree of support for Hillary Clinton (Obama's main competitor in the Democratic primary) or Joseph Biden (Obama's vice presidential nominee). Mas and Moretti (2009) found no evidence that Obama was more likely to underperform (relative to White Democratic candidates) in racially intolerant (vs. tolerant) electoral districts, but they cautioned that their conclusions were "not definitive, in particular because [they did] not have microdata on race attitudes and on how people actually voted in the 2008 election" (pp. 328–329).[5]

Implicit racial bias and support for Obama. There are at least three published articles that answer Mas and Moretti's (2009) call for individual-level "microdata" and, in so doing, directly adddress the provocative claim that the United States has entered a "post-racial" phase with the election of Barack Obama. As it happens, these articles also address the skeptical claim that implicit attitudes fail to predict meaningful or consequential forms of social behavior (e.g., Tetlock & Mitchell, 2009), insofar as one assumes that voting behavior is meaningful and consequential. Importantly, the studies reported in these three articles made use of very different measures of implicit and explicit racial attitudes (Greenwald, Smith et al., 2009; Knowles, Lowery, & Schaumberg, 2009; Payne et al., 2010), but they arrived at the same conclusion: *People with more negative implicit and explicit anti-Black attitudes were indeed less likely to vote for Obama.*

Greenwald, Smith, and their colleagues (2009) assessed the implicit and explicit attitudes of approximately 1,000 visitors to a public website in the week prior to the 2008 election. Participants completed a brief version of the IAT and another well-validated implicit measure, the Affect Misattribution Procedure (AMP; Payne, Cheng, Covorun, & Stewart, 2005). They also reported their explicit attitudes (i.e., feelings of warmth) toward Black and White people, their degree of explicit preference for Blacks vs. Whites, and their voting intentions. Finally, participants completed a 4-item explicit measure of modern or symbolic racism (Sears & Henry, 2005). The researchers found that political conservatism was significantly correlated with implicit and explicit measures of pro-White/anti-Black racial preferences, replicating and extending previous research (e.g., Jost et al., 2004; Nosek et al., 2009; Reyna et al., 2006; Sears et al., 2004; Sidanius et al., 1996). Nevertheless, even after statistically adjusting for political orientation, Greenwald and colleagues observed that implicit and explicit racial preferences contributed independently and significantly to voting intentions; as expected, people who exhibited more negative implicit and explicit racial attitudes were less likely to support Obama.

Payne, Krosnick, and their colleagues (2010) conducted three studies involving nationally representative probability samples of the United States population (ranging in size from 1056 to 1933). Participants completed the AMP as well as various explicit measures of racial bias between the end of August 2008 and the day preceding the election. After the election, participants indicated whom they had voted for. As in the Greenwald et al. (2009) study, people who scored higher in explicit racial bias were more likely to have voted for McCain and less likely to have voted for Obama, even after adjusting for political orientation and, in this case, a host of other demographic variables. Implicit attitudes also predicted voting behavior (as well as expressed feelings of discomfort with a Black president), and these effects were statistically mediated by explicit attitudes in all three samples. That is, greater implicit negativity toward Blacks was associated with greater explicit prejudice, which, in turn, was associated with an increased tendency to vote for McCain, a decreased tendency to vote for Obama, and an increase in self-reported discomfort with having a Black president. Even after adjusting for levels of explicit prejudice, implicit prejudice predicted a reluctance to vote for Obama (and discomfort in response to a Black president), although it did not predict an increased willingness to vote for McCain. Based on these findings, Payne and his colleagues concluded, "Mr. Obama was not elected because of an absence of prejudice, but despite its continuing presence" (p. 373).

Knowles, Lowery, and Schaumberg (2009) conducted a study in which implicit bias was assessed using the Go/No-go Association Test (GNAT; Nosek & Banaji, 2001), which provides an index of attitudes toward a single group rather than relative preferences, as measured by the IAT. They found that individuals who exhibited greater implicit racial bias in late October 2008 were less likely to report (after the election) that they had voted for Obama. The effect of implicit bias was considerable: An increase of 1 standard deviation in implicit bias from the mean (i.e., moving from the 50th to the 66th percentile) was associated with a 42.5% drop in likelihood of voting for Obama. Furthermore, Knowles et al. demonstrated that implicit bias scores predicted opposition to a health-care plan when it was represented as Obama's plan but not when it was represented as Bill Clinton's plan. These findings suggest that implicit bias not only played some role in the 2008 election but also that it has likely influenced the first year or more of Obama's presidency.

Taken in conjunction, the five studies reported in these three articles included data based on well over 5,000 participants and were conducted by scientists working in independent laboratories and employing diverse means of estimating implicit and explicit bias. These methodological differences across studies render their empirical convergence all the more striking. The studies show quite conclusively that both implicit and explicit forms of racial bias predicted voting intentions to a statistically significant extent in the 2008 presidential election. It seems premature, then, to celebrate the nation's graduation to the status of a "post-racial" society. Rather, the available evidence—especially from the study by Knowles et al. (2009)—is more consistent with the notorious observation made by former President Jimmy Carter early in the Obama presidency: "I think an overwhelming portion of the intensely demonstrated animosity toward President Barack Obama is based on the fact that he is a black man" (Blow, 2009).

Research conducted by Caruso, Mead, and Balcetis (2009) suggests that political ideology and racial bias can affect fairly basic perceptual processes as well as behavioral outcomes such as voting. In a pair of studies conducted prior to the 2008 election, participants were asked to indicate which of several photographs of Barack Obama were most representative of him and captured his "true essence." Unbeknownst to the participants, Obama's skin tone had been digitally altered to appear lighter or darker in some of the photographs. In both studies, political conservatives were more likely than liberals to believe that the darkened photos were more representative of Obama, whereas liberals were more likely than conservatives to believe that the lightened photos were more representative. (Among conservatives [but not liberals], anti-Black IAT scores were significantly correlated with the tendency to see the darkened photographs as more representative.) Furthermore, even after adjusting for the significant effects of political orientation, participants who judged the darkened (vs. lightened) photos to be more representative were far less likely to support Obama.

CONSEQUENCES OF OBAMA'S ELECTION

Quite independent of the question of whether Obama's election in and of itself signifies that racial prejudice in the United States became purely vestigial in November 2008 is the question of how his election will affect racial attitudes going forward. Kaiser et al. (2009) have staked out a pessimistic position, arguing that "Obama's election could produce ironic consequences in the form of decreased support for policies aimed at mitigating racial injustice" (p. 556). Consistent with this general notion, Kaiser and colleagues found that, compared to college students just prior to Obama's election, students sampled right after the election were more likely to endorse the *system-justifying* beliefs that hard work is always rewarded in our society, that we have made great strides in terms of racial progress, and that there is less of a need for additional racial progress. Post-election respondents also reported less willingness to support programs designed to reduce racial inequality, such as affirmative action, school desegregation, and attempts to ensure equal access to health care across ethnic groups.

This work suggests that some people may have seen the election as reflecting *all* Americans' racial attitudes and concluded that if the country elected a Black president, it must not be as prejudiced as they had previously assumed. Indeed, this is how Tetlock (2008), Tierney (2008), and many others seem to have interpreted Obama's election. The 2008 election also may have assuaged some individuals' concerns that they themselves were biased. The mere act of voting for Obama may have offered a kind of dispensation of prejudice that diminished concern among Obama supporters about acting in a discriminatory fashion. Research on *moral credentialing* suggests that after people express condemnation of prejudice and discrimination—and therefore establish their egalitarian qualifications—they tend to exhibit more bias (Monin & Miller, 2001). In three studies conducted prior to the 2008 election by Effron, Cameron, and Monin (2009), one group of Obama supporters was given the chance to convey their voting intentions, whereas another equivalent (control) group either made no such report (Study 1) or indicated which candidate they supported in the 2004 presidential election (Studies 2 and 3). After declaring their support for Obama, participants were more likely to favor a White over a Black applicant for a job on a police force that was described as having racial tensions. Participants were also more likely to recommend allocating funds to a community organization that served a mostly White (vs. Black) population. That is, publicly expressing one's support for Obama appeared to ease any potential concerns about being or appearing prejudiced, thereby triggering increases in racially biased judgments. Not all studies, however, paint such a bleak picture of the consequences of Obama's election.

Consequences of Obama's election for implicit racial bias. The social psychological literature suggests that positive role models can attenuate implicit bias. For example, exposure to admirable Black Americans (and contemptible White Americans) reduces implicit anti-Black negativity both immediately and even 24 hours later (Dasgupta & Greenwald, 2001). Dasgupta and

Asgari (2004) found, furthermore, that although women enrolled in co-educational and all-female colleges started with similar implicit stereotypes associating "male" with "leader," this stereotypical association was eliminated after 1 year for women studying in the single-sex college, but it grew stronger for women at the co-educational college. It appears that greater exposure to female professors at the single-sex school caused the reduction in bias.

President Obama and his wife, Michelle, have been referred to as "role model[s]-in-chief" (e.g., Bellantoni, 2009; Jamieson, 2009). Consistent with this designation, Plant et al. (2009) reported a serendipitous finding—namely, that research participants in fall, 2008 were not showing the (generally robust) implicit preference for Whites over Blacks. The researchers conducted additional studies to explore the possibility that this sudden disappearance of racial bias resulted from Obama's influence. They observed that the ease with which positive Black exemplars came to mind attenuated implicit bias. Specifically, participants listed the first 5 thoughts that came to their minds or were likely to come to others' minds about Black people. People who spontaneously generated the name of a celebrated Black individual (i.e., listed one such person in the "top 5" on either list) exhibited less implicit bias than did those whose lists included no such exemplars. Additionally, the stronger a given individual's association between the concepts "Black people" and "government," the less likely he or she was to exhibit implicit racial bias.

Findings such as these suggest that it is plausible that repeated exposure to President Obama could mitigate the otherwise pervasive display of implicit racial preference, at least for some citizens. However, as noted above, Schmidt and Nosek (2010) observed stable, moderate levels of implicit racial bias (on average) before, during, and even after Obama's election. Still, the possibility that positive role models can at least temporarily reduce implicit bias should not be discarded, given previous evidence (e.g., Blair, 2001; Dasgupta & Greenwald, 2001; Gawronski & Bodenhausen, 2006).

Is there an "Obama effect" on stereotype threat? Thus far, we have focused on what social psychologists call *perceiver effects*—that is, attitudes and beliefs *about* African-Americans held by voters and other members of society. But racial inequality also leaves psychological marks on African-Americans themselves (i.e., "target effects"). For example, negative cultural stereotypes about one's group can create *stereotype threat*—that is, a performance decrement presumably caused by a fear of confirming those stereotypes (Steele & Aronson, 1995). Such impairments can occur even when individuals explicitly reject the stereotypes. For example, compared to White students, Black students underperform on academic tests (adjusting for prior academic performance) when race is made salient (Steele & Aronson, 1995) or the test is described as diagnostic of innate ability (Brown & Day, 2006; Steele & Aronson, 1995).

By contrast, students from both groups perform equally well when the tests are administered in a race-neutral situation or described simply as puzzles rather than tests.

Because of Obama's intellectual capacities and accomplishments, as well as prior work showing that positive role models attenuate stereotype threat effects (e.g., Blanton, Crocker, & Miller, 2000; Marx & Roman, 2002; Marx, Stapel, & Muller, 2005), researchers have considered whether exposure to Obama might diminish the occurrence of stereotype threat among Black Americans. Marx, Ko, and Friendman (2009) found some support for this hypothesis using a quasi-experimental design. After adjusting for participants' education levels, White test-takers outperformed Black test-takers during periods in which Obama's success was somewhat low in salience (e.g., a week before Obama was officially nominated at the Democratic convention and halfway between the convention and the election itself). However, Black and White participants performed equally well immediately following the election, when thoughts about Obama were likely very high in salience.

In a more direct test, Aronson, Jannone, McGlone, and Johnson-Campbell (2009) randomly assigned Black and White students during the summer of 2008 to think about the positive qualities of Obama, McCain, or an unnamed political candidate (and a fourth group did not think about political figures at all). Unfortunately, thinking about Obama failed to diminish the disparity in academic performance between White and Black students. Although the elimination of stereotype threat in the Marx et al. (2009) study generates some basis for optimism, the more carefully controlled experiment by Aronson et al. (2009), especially when taken in conjunction with the findings of Schmidt and Nosek (2010) from the very large sample at the Project Implicit website, indicates that Obama's election has not yet managed to counteract the long-standing effects of culturally entrenched stereotypes and biases (e.g., *see also* Allport, 1954/1979; Jost & Hamilton, 2005). In retrospect at least, it was probably unrealistic to expect that it could.

CONCLUDING REMARKS

In this chapter, we have sought to distill and describe the most relevant insights from social psychological research concerning the significance of Barack Obama's extraordinary election to the presidency of the United States. Specifically, we have brought data to bear on the most optimistic remarks about the disappearance of racial prejudice in the nation. Unfortunately, the results indicate that Obama's election does not in itself signify that the United States has entered a truly "post-racial" phase of historical development. Nor has sending a Black man to the White House proven to be a racial panacea when it comes to implicit bias and stereotype threat. However, there are glimmers of hope, as detected in several independent studies. None of this, we suspect, would surprise the President himself. After all, he declared in March, 2008, "Contrary to the claims of some of my critics, black and white, I have never been so naïve as to believe that we can get beyond our racial divisions in a single election cycle, or with a single candidacy—particularly a candidacy as imperfect as my own." At the same time, it is somehow fitting to end this chapter, at least for now, on the more hopeful words that Obama chose to follow this sober admission: "I have asserted a firm conviction . . . that working together we can move beyond some of our old racial wounds, and that in fact we have no choice if we are to continue on the path of a more perfect union."

NOTES

1 We thank Jeff Ebert, Erin Hennes, Anesu Mandisodza, Artur Nilsson, Andrew Shipley, Jojanneke van der Toorn, and Ian Weiss for extremely helpful comments on an earlier version of this chapter.

2 The reader might also recall the concerns of some conservative pundits and strategists regarding a potential *pro*-Black racial bias among liberal and minority voters. Although we acknowledge these claims, we do not address them in this chapter, because the "post-racial" perspective (Steele, 2008; *see also* Crowley, 2008; Tierney, 2008) has focused on the presence vs. absence of anti-Black (rather than pro-Black) bias. Moreover, data on voter turnout as a function of demographic group membership are best interpreted by political scientists; we focus here on the ways in which *social psychological* research on racial attitudes may inform our understanding of Obama's presidency and its impact.

3 Of course, a White doppelgänger would not actually be "otherwise identical" to Obama, because of cultural and other factors (e.g., differential treatment of Black and White children, etc.). The thought experiment is raised in part to illustrate the impossibility of truly knowing the role that race played in the 2008 presidential election.

4 These implicit preferences for advantaged over disadvantaged groups are consistently stronger among political conservatives than liberals or moderates (e.g., Greenwald, Smith, Sriram, Bar-Anan, & Nosek, 2009; Jost, Banaji, & Nosek, 2004; Nosek et al., 2009; Schmidt & Nosek, 2010).

5 The use of a single item to measure racial attitudes is also potentially problematic, especially given that it tapped support for vs. opposition to an outdated and unconstitutional policy—namely, the prohibition of inter-racial marriage.

REFERENCES

Amodio, D. M., & Devine, P. G. (2006). Stereotyping and evaluation in implicit race bias: Evidence for independent constructs and unique effects on behavior. *Journal of Personality and Social Psychology, 91,* 652–661.

Allport, G. W. (1954/1979). *The Nature of Prejudice* (25th Anniversary Edition). Cambridge, Massachusetts: Perseus Books.

Arcuri, L., Castelli, L., Galdi, S., Zogmaister, C., & Amadori, A. (2008). Predicting the vote: Implicit attitudes as predictors of the future behavior of decided and undecided voters. *Political Psychology, 29,* 369–387.

Aronson, J., Jannone, S., McGlone, M., & Johnson-Campbell, T. (2009). The Obama effect: An experimental test. *Journal of Experimental Social Psychology, 45,* 957–960.

Banaji, M. (personal communication, November, 2008).

Banaji, M. R. & Heiphetz, L. (2010). Attitudes. In S. T. Fiske, D. T. Gilbert, & G. Lindzey (Eds.), *Handbook of Social Psychology* (pp. 348–388). New York: John Wiley & Sons.

Bargh, J. A., & Williams, E. L. (2006). The automaticity of social life. *Current Directions in Psychological Science, 15,* 1–4.

Bedard, P. (2009). Clinton rejects Carter's claim on racism against Obama. From http://www.usnews.com/mobile/articles_mobile/clinton-rejects-carters-claim-on-racism-against-obama/index.html. Last accessed July 25, 2010.

Bellantoni, C. (2009). Michelle Obama settling as a role model. *The Washington Times.*

Bessenoff, G. R., & Sherman, J. W. (2000). Automatic and controlled components of prejudice toward fat people: Evaluation versus stereotype activation. *Social Cognition, 18,* 329–353.

Blair, I. V. (2001). The malleability of automatic stereotypes and prejudice. *Personality and Social Psychology Review, 6,* 242–261.

Blanton, H., Crocker, J., & Miller, D. T. (2000). The effects of in-group versus out-group social comparison on self-esteem in the context of a negative stereotype. *Journal of Experimental Social Psychology, 36,* 519–530.

Blow, C. M. (2009). Here we go again. *New York Times.*

Bobo, L. D., & Dawson, M. C. (Eds.). (2009). Obama's path [Special issue]. *DuBois Review, 6*(1).

Brown, R. P., & Day, E. A. (2006). The difference isn't black and white: Stereotype threat and the race gap on Raven's Advanced Progressive matrices. *Journal of Applied Psychology, 91,* 979–985.

Caruso, E. M., Mead, N. L., & Balcetis, E. (2009). Political partisanship influences perception of biracial candidates' skin tone. *Proceedings of the National Academy of Sciences, 106,* 20168–20173.

Chugh, D. (2004). Societal and managerial implications of implicit social cognition: Why milliseconds matter. *Social Justice Research, 17,* 203–222.

Correll, J., Park, B., Judd, C. M., Wittenbrink, B., Sadler, M. S., & Keesee, T. (2007). Across the thin blue line: Police officers and racial bias in the decision to shoot. *Journal of Personality and Social Psychology, 92,* 1006–1023.

Crowley, M. (March 12, 2008). Post-racial: Even white supremacists don't hate Obama. *New Republic.*

Dasgupta, N., & Asgari, S. (2004). Seeing is believing: Exposure to counterstereo-typic women leaders and its effect on the malleability of automatic gender stereotyping. *Journal of Experimental Social Psychology, 40*, 642–658.

Dasgupta, N., & Greenwald, A. G. (2001). On the malleability of automatic atti-tudes: Combating automatic prejudice with images of admired and disliked individuals. *Journal of Personality and Social Psychology, 81*, 800–814.

Devine, P. G. (1989). Stereotype and prejudice: Their automatic and controlled components. *Journal of Personality & Social Psychology, 56*, 5–18.

Dovidio, J. F., Glick, P., & Rudman, L. (Eds.) (2005). *On the nature of prejudice: Fifty years after Allport*. Malden, MA: Blackwell.

Dunton, B. C., & Fazio, R. H. (1997). An individual difference measure of motiva-tion to control prejudiced reactions. *Personality and Social Psychology Bulletin, 23*, 316–326.

Dwyer, C. E., Stevens, D., Sullivan, J. L., & Allen, B. (2009). Racism, sexism, and candidate evaluations in the 2008 U.S. presidential election. *Analyses of Social Issues and Public Policy, 9*, 223–240.

Eberhardt, J. L., Goff, P. A., Purdie, V. J., & Davies, P. G. (2004). Seeing black: Race, crime, and visual processing. *Journal of Personality and Social Psychology, 87*, 876–893.

Effron, D. A., Cameron, J. S., & Monin, B. (2009). Endorsing Obama licenses favor-ing whites. *Journal of Experimental Social Psychology, 45*, 590–593.

Fazio, R. H. (1986). How do attitudes guide behavior? In R. M. Sorrentino & E. T. Higgins (Eds.), *Handbook of motivation and cognition: Foundations of social behavior* (pp. 204–243). Guilford Press.

Fazio, R. H., Jackson, J. R., Dunton, B. C., & Williams, C. J. (1995). Variability in automatic activation as an unobtrusive measure of racial attitudes: A bona fide pipeline? *Journal of Personality and Social Psychology, 69*, 1013–1027.

Fazio, R. H., Sanbonmatsu, D. M., Powell, M. C., & Kardes, F. R. (1986). On the automatic activation of attitudes. *Journal of Personality and Social Psychology, 50*, 229–238.

Friese, M., Bluemke, M., & Wänke, M. (2007). Predicting voting behavior with implicit attitude measures: The 2002 German parliamentary election. *Experimental Psychology, 54*, 247–255.

Galdi, S., Arcuri, L., & Gawronski, B. (2008). Automatic mental associations pre-dict future choices of undecided decision-makers. *Science, 321*, 1100–1102.

Gawronski, B., & Bodenhausen, G. V. (2006). Associative and propositional proc-esses in evaluation: An integrative review of implicit and explicit attitude change. *Psychological Bulletin, 132*, 692–731.

Givhan, R. (2008). Edging (at times clumsily) toward a post-racial America. *The Washington Post*.

Glaser, J., & Knowles, E. D. (2008). Implicit motivation to control prejudice. *Journal of Experimental Social Psychology, 44*, 164–172.

Green, A., Carney, D. C., Pallin, D. J., Ngo, L. H., Raymond, K. L., Iezzoni, L. I., et al. (2007). Implicit bias among physicians and its prediction of thrombolysis decisions for black and white patients. *Society of General Internal Medicine 22*, 1231–1238.

Greenwald, A. G., & Banaji, M. R. (1995). Implicit social cognition: Attitudes, self-esteem, and stereotypes. *Psychological Review, 102*, 4–27.

Greenwald, A. G., McGhee, D. E., & Schwartz, J. L. K. (1998). Measuring individual differences in implicit cognition: The Implicit Association Test. *Journal of Personality and Social Psychology, 74*, 1464–1480.

Greenwald, A. G., Poehlman, T., Uhlmann, E., & Banaji, M. (2009). Understanding and using the Implicit Association Test: III. *Meta-analysis of predictive validity. Journal of Personality and Social Psychology, 97*, 17–41.

Greenwald, A. G., Smith, C. T., Sriram, N., Bar-Anan, Y., & Nosek, B. A. (2009). Race attitude measures predicted vote in the 2008 U.S. Presidential Election. *Analyses of Social Issues and Public Policy, 9*, 241–253.

Hardin, C. D., & Banaji, M. R. (in press). The nature of implicit prejudice: Implications for personal and public policy. In E. Shafir (Ed.), *The behavioral foundations of policy*.

Hofmann, H. G., Gawronski, B., Gschwender, T., Le, H., & Schmitt, M. (2005). A meta-analysis on the correlation between the Implicit Association Test and explicit self-report measures. *Personality and Social Psychology Bulletin, 31*, 1369–1385.

Jamieson, A. (2009). Barack Obama denies racism is driving opposition to health care plans. *The Daily Telegraph*.

Jones, J. M. (2007). Some Americans reluctant to vote for Mormon, 72-year old presidential candidates. *Gallup Daily News*, from http://www.gallup.com/poll/26611/some-americans-reluctant-vote-mormon-72yearold-presidential-candidates.aspx. Last accessed July 25, 2010.

Jost, J. T. (2006). The end of the end of ideology. *American Psychologist, 61*, 651–670.

Jost, J. T., Banaji, M. R., & Nosek, B. A. (2004). A decade of system justification theory: Accumulated evidence of conscious and unconscious bolstering of the status quo. *Political Psychology, 25*, 881–919.

Jost, J. T., & Hamilton, D. L. (2005). Stereotypes in our culture. In J. F. Dovidio (Ed.), *On the nature of prejudice: Fifty years after Allport* (pp. 208–224). Malden Blackwell Publishing.

Jost, J. T., Rudman, L. A., Blair, I. V., Carney, D. R., Dasgupta, N., Glaser, J., et al. (2009). The existence of implicit bias is beyond reasonable doubt: A refutation of ideological and methodological objections and executive summary of ten studies that no manager should ignore. *Research in Organizational Behavior, 29*, 39–69.

Jost, J. T., West, T. V., & Gosling, S. D. (2009). Personality and ideology as determinants of candidate preferences and "Obama conversion" in the 2008 U.S. presidential election. *Du Bois Review, 6*, 103–124.

Kaiser, C. R., Drury, B. J., Spalding, K. E., Cheryan, S., & O'Brien, L. T. (2009). The ironic consequences of Obama's election: Decreased support for social justice. *Journal of Experimental Social Psychology, 45*, 556–559.

Knowles, E. D., Lowery, B. S., & Schaumberg, R. L. (2009). Racial prejudice predicts opposition to Obama and his health care reform plan. *Journal of Experimental Social Psychology, 46,* 420–423.

Lane, K., Banaji, M., Nosek, B. A., & Greenwald, A. (2007). Understanding and using the Implicit Association Test: IV: What we know (so far) about the method. In B. Wittenbrink & N. Schwartz (Eds.), *Implicit measures of attitudes* (pp. 59–102). New York: The Guilford Press.

Marx, D. M., Ko, S. J., & Friedman, R. A. (2009). The "Obama Effect": How a salient role model reduces race-based performance differences. *Journal of Experimental Social Psychology, 45,* 953–956.

Marx, D. M., & Roman, J. S. (2002). Female role models: Protecting women's math test performance. *Personality and Social Psychology Bulletin, 28,* 1183–1193.

Marx, D. M., Stapel, D. A., & Muller, D. (2005). We can do it: The interplay of a collective self-construal orientation and social comparisons under threat. *Journal of Personality and Social Psychology, 88,* 432–446.

Mas, A., & Moretti, E. (2009). Racial bias in the 2008 presidential election. *American Economic Review, 99,* 323–329.

McConnell, A. R., & Leibold, J. M. (2001). Relations among the implicit associations test, discriminatory behavior, and explicit measures of racial attitudes. *Journal of Experimental Social Psychology, 37,* 435–442.

Monin, B., & Miller, D. T. (2001). Moral credentials and the expression of prejudice. *Journal of Personality and Social Psychology, 81,* 33–43.

Nagourney, A. (2008, November 5, 2008). Obama elected president as racial barrier falls. *New York Times.*

Neely, J. H. (1977). Semantic priming and retrieval from lexical memory: Roles of inhibitionless spreading activation and limited-capacity attention. *Journal of Experimental Psychology: General, 106,* 226–254.

Nosek, B. A. (2005). Moderators of the relationship between implicit and explicit evaluation. *Journal of Experimental Psychology: General, 134,* 565–584.

Nosek, B. A., & Banaji, M. R. (2001). The Go/No-go Association Task. *Social Cognition, 19,* 625–666.

Nosek, B. A., Banaji, M. R., & Jost, J. T. (2009). The politics of intergroup attitudes. In J. T. Jost, A. C. Kay, & H. Thorisdottir (Eds.), *Social and psychological bases of ideology and system justification* (pp. 480–506). New York: Oxford University Press.

Nosek, B. A., Greenwald, A. G., & Banaji, M. R. (2007). The Implicit Association Test at age 7: A methodological and conceptual review. In J. A. Bargh (Ed.), *Social psychology and the unconscious: The automaticity of higher mental processes* (pp. 265–292). New York: Psychology Press.

Nosek, B. A., Smyth, F. L., Hansen, J. J., Devos, T., Lindner, N. M., Ranganath, K. A., et al. (2007). Pervasiveness and correlates of implicit attitudes and stereotypes. *European Review of Social Psychology, 18,* 1–53.

Palfai, T. P., & Ostafin, B. D. (2003). Alcohol-related motivational tendencies in hazardous drinkers: Assessing implicit response tendencies using the modified-IAT. *Behaviour Research and Therapy, 41,* 1149–1162.

Payne, B. K., Cheng, C. M., Govorun, O., & Stewart, B. (2005). An inkblot for attitudes: Affect misattribution as implicit measurement. *Journal of Personality and Social Psychology, 89,* 277–293.

Payne, B. K., Krosnick, J. A., Pasek, J., Lelkes, Y., Akhtar, O., & Tompson, T. (2010). Implicit and explicit prejudice in the 2008 American presidential election *Journal of Experimental Social Psychology, 46,* 367–374.

Piston, S. (in press). How explicit racial prejudice hurt Obama in the 2008 election. *Political Behavior.*

Plant, E.A., & Devine, P.G. (1998). Internal and external motivation to respond without prejudice. *Journal of Personality and Social Psychology, 75,* 811–832.

Plant, E.A., Devine, P.G., Cox, W., Columb, C., Miller, S. M., Goplen, J., et al. (2009). The Obama effect: Decreasing implicit prejudice and stereotyping. *Journal of Experimental Social Psychology, 45,* 961–964.

Plant, E.A., & Peruche, B. M. (2005). The consequences of race for police officers' responses to criminal suspects. *Psychological Science, 16,* 180–183.

Quindlen, A. (November 17, 2008). Living history. *Newsweek.*

Rachlinski, J. J., Johnson, S., Wistrich, A. J., & Guthrie, C. (2009). Does unconscious bias affect trial judges? *Notre Dame Law Review, 84,* 1195–1246.

Reyna, C., Henry, P. J., Korfmacher, W., & Tucker, A. (2006). Examining the principles in principled conservatism: The role of responsibility stereotypes as cues for deservingness in racial policy decisions. *Journal of Personality and Social Psychology, 90,* 109–128.

Roccato, M., & Zogmaister, C. (2010). Predicting the vote through implicit and explicit attitudes: A field research. *Political Psychology, 31,* 249–274.

Rooth, D. (2007). Implicit discrimination in hiring: Real world evidence. *IZA Discussion Paper No. 2764. Forschungsinstitut zur Zukunft der Arbeit (Institute for the Study of Labor),* Bonn, Germany.

Rudman, L. A., & Ashmore, R.D. (2007). Discrimination and the Implicit Association Test. *Group Processes & Intergroup Relations, 10,* 359–372.

Schmidt, K., & Nosek, B. A. (2010). Implicit (and explicit) racial attitudes barely changed during Barack Obama's presidential campaign and early presidency. *Journal of Experimental Social Psychology, 46,* 308–314.

Schneider, D. J. (2004). *The psychology of stereotyping.* New York: Guilford.

Schuman, H., Steeh, C., Bobo, L., & Krysan, M. (1997). *Racial attitudes in America: Trends and interpretations* Revised edition. Cambridge: Harvard University Press.

Sears, D. O, & Henry, P. J. (2005). Over thirty years later: A contemporary look at symbolic racism and its critics. *Advances in Experimental Social Psychology, 37,* 95–150.

Sears, D. O., Laar, C. V., Carrillo, M., & Kosterman, R. (1997). Is it really racism? The origins of White Americans' opposition to race-targeted policies. *Public Opinion Quarterly, 26,* 16–53.

Sidanius, J., Pratto, F., & Bobo, L. (1996). Racism, conservatism, affirmative action, and intellectual sophistication: A matter of principled conservatism or group dominance? *Journal of Personality and Social Psychology, 70,* 476–490.

Sniderman, P. M., & Carmines, E. G. (1997). Reaching beyond race. *Political Science and Politics, 30,* 466–471.

Stangor, C. (Ed.) (2000). *Stereotypes and prejudice: Key readings.* New York: Psychology Press.

Steele, C. M., & Aronson, J. (1995). Stereotype threat and the intellectual test performance of African Americans. *Journal of Personality and Social Psychology, 69,* 797–811.

Steele, S. (2008, November 5, 2008). Obama's post-racial promise. *Los Angeles Times.*

Tetlock, P. E., & Mitchell, G. (2008). Calibrating prejudice in milliseconds. *Social Psychology Quarterly, 71,* 12–16.

Tetlock, P. E., & Mitchell, G. (2009). Implicit bias and accountability systems: What must organizations do to prevent discrimination? *Research in Organizational Behavior, 29,* 3–38.

Tierney, J. (2008, November 7, 2008). Where have all the bigots gone? *New York Times.*

Todorov, A., Mandisodza, A., Goren, A., & Hall, C. (2005). Inferences of competence from faces predict election outcomes. *Science, 308,* 1623–1626.

Towles-Schwen, T., & Fazio, R. H. (2003). Choosing social situations: The relation between automatically activated racial attitudes and anticipated comfort interacting with African Americans. *Personality and Social Psychology Bulletin, 29,* 170–182.

Truth about health care: A trifecta of storms: Ana, Bill and Claudette; Japan's economy rebounding?; Human smuggling in Mexcio; Losing a child to violence. (2009, August 16). CNN Newsroom. [Television News Program]. Retrieved fromhttp://www.cnnstudentnews.cnn.com/TRANSCRIPTS/0908/16/cnr.05. html . Last accessed July 25, 2010.

von Hippel, W., Brener, L., & von Hippel, C. (2008). Implicit prejudice toward injecting drug users predicts intentions to change jobs among drug and alcohol nurses. *Psychological Science, 19,* 7–11.

Wickham, D. (2009). Black expatriates not ready to return home. *Opinion, 2009,* from   http://content.usatoday.com/topics/post/USA+TODAY+editorial/ 66374353.blog/1, Last accessed July 25, 2010.

Wilson, T. D., & Bar-Anan, Y. (2008). The unseen mind. *Science, 321,* 1046–1047.

Wilson, T. D., Lindsey, S., & Schooler, T. Y. (2000). A model of dual attitudes. *Psychological Review, 107,* 101–126.

Wittenbrink, B., & Schwarz, N. (2007). *Implicit measures of attitudes.* New York: Guilford.

Black Man in the White House

Marc H. Morial

The question of whether Barack Obama's election to the U.S. presidency is evidence of a post-racial society is perhaps and even more relevant now, more than a year into his term, than it was at the time of his election. The rise of the so-called "Tea Party" movement sheds as much light on racial attitudes in contemporary America as Obama's election itself.

The racial attitudes of "Tea Partiers" are worth examining in terms of implicit bias, as discussed in Chapter 3. In some respects, the Tea Party movement is nothing more than virulent racism barely disguised as legitimate political dissent. It is perhaps true—and the research presented in Chapter 3 supports the idea—that some of those active in the Tea Party movement may not be aware of their own implicit racial biases. Particularly striking is the experiment described in Chapter 3 in which the subjects' responses to a legislative health-care proposal were contrasted when it was presented as President Obama's plan versus President Clinton's plan.

The contrast is similarly evident in the issues that Tea Party members claim are the motivations of their activism. The purported objects of their ire—for example, taxes or deficit spending—somehow failed to rouse them under a White president. To paraphrase an old stand-up comedy routine, you might be a racist if a particular fiscal policy irritates you when proposed by a Black president and delights you when proposed by a White president.

Of course, we need not examine subconscious attitudes through laboratory experiments to uncover racial bias in contemporary America. During the recent health-care debate, racial slurs were hurled at African-American Congress members. Many of the signs and slogans displayed at Tea Party rallies are blatantly racist, and even candidates for public office have been caught relaying racist jokes through e-mail. We often invoke Dr. Martin Luther King Jr.'s comment about the arc of justice to remind ourselves that it bends toward freedom. But incidents like these remind us that it is long.

The more interesting and relevant question addressed in Chapter 3 is not whether racial attitudes influenced Obama's election, but whether Obama's election is influencing racial attitudes. During President Obama's first State of the Union address, one of the television commentators drew attention by remarking that he "forgot" the President was Black during the speech. His comment reveals two things borne out by the research presented in Chapter 3: that we haven't come so far in America that we forget to notice racial differences most of the time, but that we also are beginning to "forget" how much they are supposed to matter.

CHAPTER 4

Obama-Nation? Implicit Beliefs about American Nationality and the Possibility of Redefining Who Counts as "Truly" American

Nilanjana Dasgupta and Kumar Yogeeswaran

The 14th Amendment of the U.S. Constitution defines American citizenship by stating that *"All persons born or naturalized in the United States, and subject to the jurisdiction thereof, are citizens of the United States and of the State wherein they reside."* Although this legal definition draws a bright line separating who is American from who is not, the psychological boundary defining nationality is considerably fuzzier—driven by stereotypes, social norms, the context in which the question is asked, and who is answering the question. Indeed, psychological research suggests that Americans' perceptions of who belongs in the country are often driven by subjective perceptions of who seems to be prototypical or representative of the country based on dimensions such as race. As such, people grant American identity to Whites more easily than to Blacks, Asians, and Latinos even if they were born and raised in the United States.

The 2008 campaign for the U.S. presidency offers an excellent illustration of this point: throughout the campaign season, many questioned Barack Obama's patriotism as a "true" American. Newspaper and magazine articles, TV reports, and Internet blogs were agog with stories about the absence of a flag pin on his lapel, rumors about his religion, his middle name, and quotes from everyday citizens who stated, "I just don't feel he's a true American" (Todd, Murray & Montanaro, 2008). In other words, Obama's hybrid ethnicity, his unusual name, Muslim middle name, internationally traveled childhood, and family tree spanning three continents were perceived by many to be far too different from the typical Anglo-Protestant American, which cast doubt on his patriotism. Using the 2008 Presidential election as the backdrop, the present chapter has four broad goals.

First, we will present social psychological evidence showing that doubts about ethnic minorities' patriotism and national belongingness is not limited to Barack Obama. Rather, Americans hold strong implicit (and sometimes explicit) assumptions that link authentic American identity with Whiteness while excluding other ethnic minority groups from being seen as "truly" American. These implicit beliefs exist despite the widespread societal endorsement of multiculturalism that embraces the idea that there are multiple ways of being American without having to look the same and assimilate into mainstream society.

Second, we will describe a series of studies from our laboratory showing that implicit race-based assumptions about nationality are not simply private beliefs that remain confined to people's minds; rather they influence people's actions, especially in contexts where national security and patriotism are salient, producing job discrimination and opposition to public policies endorsed by American minorities.

Third, we will identify what it might take to change implicit assumptions about national belonging and under what conditions these implicit beliefs become more inclusive vs. more exclusive. We will describe a series of studies revealing that people's beliefs of who is American become more racially inclusive when they are exposed to ethnic minorities who appear ethnically assimilated and whose work benefits the national good. However, when the same individuals appear ethnically identified and their contributions only benefit their local community (e.g., work place, city, or state), people's beliefs about nationality become racially restrictive. We apply these findings to the Presidential election by arguing that two critical ingredients may have helped Obama's victory: his self-presentation as a fairly assimilated American who was not "too Black" and his ability to highlight his professional work as benefiting fellow Americans.

We conclude by projecting into the future and ask several questions about what might happen now that Barack Obama is the President of the United States. Will his presence change people's perceptions of who is American and who is foreign? Will it affect people's racial attitudes and support for social policies promoting intergroup equality?

THE IMPLICIT ASSUMPTION THAT THE AUTHENTIC AMERICAN IS WHITE

The United States has a unique history and immigration policy that has created a population that changes in demographics relatively rapidly across generations (Roberts, 2009). It is a country comprised of multiple immigrant groups (with the obvious exception of the original people of the land, Native Americans) whose national origins are various but whose commonality lies in shared belief in democracy, civic institutions, political and religious freedom, and economic opportunity. Although multi-ethnic, specific groups vary in their length of immersion in mainstream American culture, their immigration history, their size and visibility, and socioeconomic and political power. As a result of these dimensions of difference between ethnic and racial groups that comprise the United States, the last half-century has witnessed great debate about the most appropriate way to be American. What are the qualities essential to be truly American? Is there only one way to be American, or are there multiple ways to express one's national identity? How can one balance national unity with strong allegiances to specific ethnic groups?

Some have argued that people can preserve their identification with ethnic groups and at the same time feel identified with a larger superordinate national group. Others have argued that these two types of identities are difficult to maintain simultaneously—thus, individuals should shed (or at least relegate to secondary status) their ethnic identity and prioritize their national identity as a way of fitting into mainstream American society and also of preserving national unity. These two opinions are captured by two popular sociocultural ideologies: assimilation and multiculturalism. Assimilation argues that people belonging to all ethnic or cultural groups that co-exist within a larger superordinate nation state should embrace a common set of cultural practices, values, language, ways of dressing, and so forth that represent the national group. Moreover, it posits that the only way to do so is by discarding or downplaying one's ethnic identity along with the values, cultural practices, and languages that come with it (Gordon, 1964; Hirschman, 1983; Schlesinger, 1992; Schmidt, 1997). Multiculturalism, on the other hand, eschews these expectations by assuming that ethnic identities are not disposable but, in fact, fundamental to one's self-concept (Hornsey & Hogg, 2000). Multiculturalism, therefore, argues that group differences should not only be acknowledged but also celebrated so that people can preserve important aspects of their own identity while co-existing with other ethnic groups (Berry, Kalin & Taylor, 1977; Foster & Herzog, 1994; Moghaddam, 2008; Takaki, 1993; Taylor, 1991; Yinger, 1994).

Although multiculturalism has become the desired ideal in many parts of the United States and in many American institutions (e.g., schools, colleges, universities, businesses), empirical research reveals a great divide between the abstract endorsement of multiculturalism as a principle versus the actual practice of evaluating individuals of different ethnicities, deciding whether or not to include them within the national fold or trust them in positions of power. Recent research has found the image that spontaneously comes to mind when people think of someone who is American is that of individuals who are White—not Black, Asian, Latino, Native American, or multiracial (Devos & Banaji, 2005; Devos & Ma, 2008; Devos, Gavin, & Quintana, 2010; Yogeeswaran & Dasgupta, 2010; Yogeeswaran, Dasgupta & Gomez, 2010a).

This finding emerges both when people are asked to self-report who looks more American (Cheryan & Monin, 2005) and emerges even more strongly when their *implicit or unconscious* beliefs are assessed by measuring how quickly they group together images of individuals of various races with all-American symbols like the American flag, White House, Mt. Rushmore, bald eagle, and so forth. The logic is that if people automatically consider people of all races to be equally American, then they ought to be equally fast at grouping together faces of all races with American symbols. However, if they implicitly assume that Americans are White, then they ought to be faster at grouping American symbols with White faces compared to faces of any other ethnicity. Results from multiple studies confirm that most Americans automatically associate American symbols with Whites more than with any other ethnic group.

For White Americans, the stronger their national identification, the more they project their own ethnic characteristics onto the definition of the whole nation (i.e., the more they think American equals White; Devos et al., 2010). However, priming greater equality in American society reduces the tendency to define the nation exclusively in terms of one's own ethnic group, especially among Whites who feel strong national identification. In other words, when participants were made to think about the reduction of race-based status inequality in American society, their own national identification became unrelated to implicit assumptions of who is American. But when they were not made to think about social equality, Whites with stronger national identity expressed stronger implicit beliefs that the prototypical American was White.

Interestingly, members of some ethnic minority groups (Latinos and Asian-Americans) seem to have internalized the implicit belief that their ethnic ingroup isn't quite as authentically American as Whites (Cheryan & Monin, 2005; Devos & Banaji, 2005; Devos et al., 2010). African-Americans are the exception here: African American individuals implicitly consider their ethnic group to be as American as Whites; however, they view other minority groups to be less American. Importantly, even ethnic minorities who have internalized the notion that their ethnic ingroup as a whole is less American than Whites consider *themselves* to be very much American (Cheryan & Monin, 2005). In fact, when their own national belongingness is questioned by others, they experience negative emotions and assert their cultural credentials to reclaim their American identity (Cheryan & Monin, 2005).

How Implicit Assumptions about National Identity Affected Public Opinion about Barack Obama

The public discourse about Barack Obama during the 2008 Presidential election is an excellent case in point that illustrates how the misperception that non-White individuals are somehow less American than their White peers affects American politics. Before the election, Barack Obama did not fit most Americans' implicit idea of an authentic American, a true patriot in whose hands could rest the responsibility and national security of the land. Research conducted during the 2008 election season revealed Americans' doubts about Obama's patriotism and national belongingness; people found it easier to associate all-American symbols with White politicians who were American (Hillary Clinton) or even European (Tony Blair) than with Obama (Devos, Ma, & Gafud, 2008). The difference in the degree to which Americanness was automatically associated with Clinton over Obama was greater when their race difference was made salient rather than when their gender difference was made salient. Along the same lines, the perception that Obama was foreign rather than American was significantly stronger when people's attention was focused on his race rather than his individuality (Devos & Ma, 2008; Devos et al., 2008). Importantly, participants who implicitly viewed Obama as less American than Clinton were significantly less willing to say they would vote for him or support his campaign compared to others who did not distinguish the two candidates in terms of national identity.

These findings suggest that Obama's race aroused doubts about patriotism which in turn reduced support for his candidacy as president. More directly to this issue, another series of studies found that when American citizens were primed with an American flag they showed more implicit and explicit prejudice against African-Americans in general and greater reluctance to vote for Barack Obama as president compared to a condition in which the American flag was absent (Porter, Ferguson, Hassin, & Balcetis, 2010). However, the presence versus absence of the flag either had no effect (or even an opposite effect) on people's willingness to vote for White presidential candidates (Porter et al., 2010). These data taken together with the finding that stronger national identification is correlated with stronger implicit assumptions that American-is-White (Devos et al., 2010) suggest that before the election, priming patriotism decreased support for Barack Obama because his race raised implicit doubts about his status as "truly" American.

We argue that doubts about "Americanness" were *not solely* caused by Obama's race but, rather, because he seemed too different from most Americans on *several dimensions*: his hybrid ethnicity, his unusual name, his Muslim middle name, his internationally traveled childhood, and his family tree spanning three continents, all of which were perceived to be too different from the typical Anglo-Protestant American. Research shows that although race is implicitly salient in people's definition of who is authentically American, religion is equally salient, both implicitly and explicitly. One of the primary characteristics that Americans view as important to their definition of American (in addition to love for one's country and civic engagement) is faith in god, especially a Christian god (Carvalho & Butz, 2010; Citrin, Reingold & Green, 1990; Devos & Banaji, 2005; Schildkraut, 2007). Perhaps more importantly, the more people consider America to be a Christian nation the more resources they allocate to Christian organizations compared to other religious organizations on a university campus (Carvalho & Butz, 2010). Applying these findings to the 2008 Presidential election, we propose that Obama's Muslim middle name and the fact that some of his family members are Muslim cast doubt on his *Christian* faith. In fact, during the Presidential campaign, several conservative media commentators repeatedly emphasized Obama's middle name to subtly suggest he is not sufficiently American. As a case in point, in introducing John McCain during a campaign rally, Bill Cunningham, a conservative talk show host, repeatedly referred to McCain's opponent as "Barack Hussein Obama" with emphasis on the middle name (Lou, 2008) to prime the audience to think of him as Muslim and, by extension, to subtly encourage the conclusion that a Muslim Obama cannot be a loyal American.

There were many other instances during the long election season when doubts about Obama's patriotism bubbled to the surface. For example, during the primaries, a rumor circulated that Obama allegedly refused to recite the pledge of allegiance, which was not true (MacGillis, 2008; PBS, 2008; Politifact, 2007). Later, he was criticized for not putting his hand on his heart in customary pose while reciting the pledge during a campaign rally (MacGillis, 2008; Politifact, 2007). Keeping with the same theme, when most politicians were wearing lapel pins with the American flag to highlight their patriotism, Obama was not; he argued that wearing a flag pin paid lip service and was not the hallmark of true patriotism (Wright & Miller, 2007; Zeleny, 2007). When confronted with a barrage of criticism, however, Obama started to wear the obligatory flag pin and surround himself with American flags during campaign events to offset suspicion about his alleged lack of patriotism (Newton-Small, 2008). Finally, one persistent rumor that started during the Presidential campaign and continues to this day is the perception that Barack Obama was not born in the United States and thus cannot legitimately be the country's president (Associated Press, 2009; Nakaso, 2009; Stein, 2009). Even now, post-election, less than half of Republicans (42%) believe that Obama was born in the United States, as reported by a public opinion poll conducted by the liberal website Daily Kos in July 2009; 28% believe that Obama was foreign-born and the remaining 30% of Republicans said they were not sure. This false belief seems to be regionally based. In the South, only 47% of respondents believe Obama is American-born (the rest believe he is foreign-born or are not sure), whereas in the Northeast and Midwest, more than 90% of respondents believe he is American-born. These false rumors about Obama's birthplace and news stories about the flag pin and pledge of allegiance represent a constellation of instances that question the authenticity of Obama's American identity and patriotism, and research suggests that these doubts may be driven by his race and perceived religion.

ASSUMPTIONS ABOUT RACE AND NATIONALITY PRODUCE DISCRIMINATORY BEHAVIOR

Although past research has shown that people view Whites as more authentically American than ethnic minorities, one may ask, what effect do these beliefs have on people's behaviors and decisions? Do these beliefs help preserve or even exacerbate structural inequalities? If Barack Obama is an instantiation of these biased beliefs, one might argue the fact that Obama won the election illustrates that even if people have doubts about ethnic minorities' "Americanness" in terms of their beliefs, these doubts do not translate into biased behavior (e.g., voting). In response, we propose that Obama's example suggests that he had a higher hurdle to cross compared to White presidential candidates to convince the American public of his patriotism and to encourage them to vote for him. His electoral victory depended on his ability to allay these doubts. Put differently, Obama's victory may be interpreted to mean that a Presidential candidate who is an ethnic minority has to outperform his or her White competitors *several times over* to win. Putting aside the specific example of President Obama, one might also ask how do implicit beliefs about nationality affect actions toward, and decisions about, ethnic minorities in general besides the specific case of the 2008 election? Do biases in beliefs encourage discriminatory action and decisions?

In the past decade, numerous social psychological studies have examined whether implicit attitudes and stereotypes that are not fully available to conscious awareness impact behavior and judgments. Collectively, these studies converge on a consistent message; implicit thoughts and evaluations of social groups impact a range of behaviors and judgments including resource allocation, voting preferences, nonverbal behavior, and even medical decisions made by doctors (for a review, *see* Greenwald, Poehlman, Uhlmann, & Banaji, 2009). For example, people's implicit attitudes toward negatively stereotyped groups (e.g., African-Americans, gay men) predict spontaneous nonverbal behavior such as smiling, eye contact, and friendliness when people interact with someone who is Black or gay (Dasgupta & Rivera, 2006; Dovidio, Kawakami & Gaertner, 2002; Fazio, Jackson, Dunton, & Williams, 1995; McConnell & Leibold, 2001). Similarly, implicit racial stereotypes affect the type of questions people ask Black compared to White job candidates during a job interview (Sekaquaptewa, Espinoza, Thompson, & Vargas, 2003). With regard to resource allocation, implicit stereotypes about Asian-Americans,

Jewish-Americans, and African-Americans influence people's willingness to allocate financial resources to Asian, Jewish, and Black cultural organizations (Rudman & Ashmore, 2007). And finally, implicit political preferences have been found to predict individuals' future voting behavior, even among voters who call themselves "undecided" before an election (Arcuri, Castelli, Galdi, Zogmaister & Amadori, 2008; Galdi, Arcuri & Gawronski, 2008).

Recent work from our lab has extended these findings to the domain of nationality to test whether implicit assumptions about the link between race and nationality translate into discriminatory actions and judgments against ethnic minorities. Our research has found that the more people implicitly envision the prototypical American as White, the less willing they are to hire qualified Americans who are ethnic minorities for a job in national security. However, these implicit beliefs do not influence people's willingness to hire the same individuals in a corporate job with an identical job title and type of work (Yogeeswaran & Dasgupta, 2010). In other words, situations that highlight national loyalty are the ones where implicit assumptions about nationality elicit discriminatory hiring decisions, whereas situations where national loyalty is irrelevant are ones where assumptions about nationality have no effect. Our data confirmed that greater suspicion about ethnic minorities' loyalty and patriotism was the underlying reason driving the association between implicit American-White beliefs and biased hiring decisions (Yogeeswaran & Dasgupta, 2010). These findings suggest that implicit assumptions linking American with White do not lead to generalized racial discrimination against ethnic minorities but instead lead to discrimination *only* in contexts where loyalty to the country is important.

In another study, we found that the more people implicitly envision the prototypical American to be White, the more negatively they evaluate an immigration policy when it is proposed by a policy-writer who is an ethnic minority but not when the same policy is proposed by a White American policy-writer (Yogeeswaran & Dasgupta, 2010). Once again, this effect was found to occur because of greater suspicions about the national loyalty and patriotism of ethnic minorities. Additionally, based on recent research showing that political conservatives are more likely than liberals to place importance on ingroup loyalty and establishing group boundaries (Graham, Haidt & Nosek, 2009; Haidt & Graham, 2007; Janoff-Bulman, 2009), we tested whether individual differences in political ideology would influence the link between implicit assumptions about nationality and policy evaluations. We found that for political conservatives (but not liberals), stronger implicit assumptions that authentic Americans are White produced more negative evaluations of an immigration policy proposed by an ethnic minority but not when the same policy was proposed by a White American. Moreover, as before, we confirmed that this effect occurred because political conservatives' implicit assumption that American-is-White influenced their doubts about non-Whites' national loyalty, and these doubts in turn fueled their opposition to an immigration policy proposed by a minority individual (Yogeeswaran & Dasgupta, 2010). These findings suggest that although political liberals and conservatives may both possess implicit cognitions that authentic Americans are White, these thoughts are more likely to translate into action for conservatives who place more emphasis on national loyalty and the maintenance of clear group boundaries.

Mapping these findings to Barack Obama's presidency, these data suggest that people's unconscious tendency to perceive authentic Americans as White may influence the degree to which they support versus oppose Obama's policies concerning national borders. People who implicitly believe that American-is-White may be more opposed to policies proposed by the Obama Administration that have to do with national borders (e.g., immigration, terrorism) than others who don't believe American-is-White. Such opposition may be fueled, at least in part, by concerns about President Obama's patriotism.

In a very direct test of whether Obama's candidacy was hindered by people's tendencies to perceive authentic Americans as White, Devos and colleagues (2008) found that the less people implicitly and explicitly granted American identity to Barack Obama (compared to Hillary Clinton), the less willing they were to vote for Obama, donate money to his campaign, and rally for him. Interestingly, this pattern emerged even when Barack Obama was compared to a politician who was clearly not American—the former British Prime Minister Tony Blair—such that the less people implicitly and explicitly viewed Obama (compared to Blair) as American, the less willing they were to vote for Obama and support his candidacy for President of the United States. These studies demonstrate that beyond racial prejudice, which was at the center of media discussion during Obama's election and even today, people's unconscious and conscious beliefs about who counts as "truly" American (which is different from racial prejudice) may have also contributed toward people's willingness to support Barack Obama and his policies.

HOW TO OVERCOME ASSUMPTIONS ABOUT AMERICAN NATIONALITY

How might we make people's implicit beliefs about who is authentically American become more inclusive to encompass the multi-ethnic population of the United States? This question is closely related to the larger research literature in social psychology that attempts to understand when and how implicit bias changes. Over the last decade, several studies have examined the conditions under which people's implicit stereotypes and prejudice change. These studies have identified a number of factors that are beneficial—the most relevant of which in the present context is the benefit of being exposed to admired members of stereotyped groups (for reviews, *see* Blair, 2002; Dasgupta, 2009). For example, research has shown that exposure to highly admired and counterstereotypical individuals via media exposure and real contact (i.e., admired African-Americans, female leaders, famous gay individuals) decrease implicit stereotyping and prejudice against the corresponding groups (Dasgupta & Greenwald, 2001; Dasgupta & Asgari, 2004; Dasgupta & Rivera, 2008). Moreover, the benefit of such positive exposure on reduced implicit bias endures beyond the immediate experimental setting (Dasgupta & Greenwald, 2001; Dasgupta & Asgari, 2004).

We have extended this line of research to the domain of nationality to identify what factors might increase the inclusion of ethnic minorities as being authentically American. Our research focused on two factors: *(1)* how prominent and noticeable individuals' ethnic identification is to others; and *(2)* how much their work contributes to the national good. In several experiments, we systematically varied these factors by presenting participants with biographies of admired Americans of various ethnic minority groups who: *(1)* either appeared to be strongly identified with their ethnicity or not particularly identified, and *(2)* either engaged in professional work that clearly benefited the national good or benefited the local good. We then measured participants' implicit and explicit beliefs about race and American nationality. Our results showed that exposing participants to highly accomplished ethnic minorities whose work benefited the national good made their implicit and explicit beliefs about who was truly American more inclusive of ethnic minorities. However, this benefit emerged *only* when the ethnic identity of individuals portrayed in the biographies was downplayed (i.e., these individuals appeared ethnically assimilated; Yogeeswaran et al., 2010a). The opposite result was obtained when ethnic minorities appeared strongly ethnically identified *and* their professional work was geared toward the local (not national) good; exposure to such individuals exacerbated implicit and explicit beliefs that American-is-White.

We also examined the impact of exposing people to admired individuals who were White Americans whose ethnic identity (e.g., Polish, German) was made prominent versus not prominent in biographies. Interestingly, results showed that making White individuals appear very ethnically identified did not reduce their ethnic group's inclusion as American, whereas the equivalent manipulation had a negative effect on ethnic minorities' inclusion as American (Yogeeswaran et al., 2010a).

Why does the definition of American become more inclusive when people see ethnically assimilated minorities whose admirable accomplishments benefit the national good? We tested this question and found that learning about such outstanding ethnic minorities bolstered belief in American exceptionalism (the idea that the U.S. has a special place among nations because it is an immigrant nation), which in turn expanded the boundaries of who is American to include the outstanding individuals participants saw and the ethnic groups to which they belong.

Similarly, one might ask: Why does exposure to ethnic minorities who appear ethnically identified and whose accomplishments don't focus on the national good restrict people's definition of who counts as American? Our results revealed that reading about such ethnic minorities increased people's fear that non-European cultural practices are contaminating American society and threatening the distinctiveness of what it means to be American; this fear and perceived threat was in turn responsible for people restricting the definition of who counts as American (Yogeeswaran et al., 2010a).

In the context of Barack Obama's historic race for the Presidency, our findings suggest that Obama's ability to downplay his ethnic identification while emphasizing his public service and contributions to the nation increased the likelihood that voters would view him as authentically American. During his campaign, Obama was able to present himself as a mainstream candidate who would represent the voice of every Americans and avoid a perception that he was, as an African-American candidate, representing only his ethnic group (Bobo & Dawson, 2009). Clearly, he walked a tightrope in terms of how much to discuss race. If he played up his bi-racial or Black identity, he may have appeared not American enough in the eyes of many voters, which in turn would have reduced their support. However, if he played down his Black identity too much, then he may have alienated Black voters. Moreover, he also had to address race-related issues when they erupted during the campaign (e.g., his March 18th, 2008 speech on race after the Jeremiah Wright controversy). Obama's racial dilemma was (and continues to be) real and supported by our research, which has found that public expression of one's ethnic identity is detrimental for ethnic minority individuals because it enhances Whites' perceptions that these individuals are not American enough (Yogeeswaran, Dasgupta, Adelman, Eccleston & Parker, 2010b). Our studies suggest that Americans are more accepting of ethnic identity provided it is expressed in private spaces (e.g., at home) but not when it is expressed in public spaces (e.g., at a mall, on the street) (Yogeeswaran et al., 2010b). These findings suggest that Obama's ability to present himself as a bi-racial or Black candidate who maintained a connection to his ethnic heritage privately while emphasizing his public and national service increased his probability of being seen as authentically American and contributed to his electoral success.

WHAT THE OBAMA PRESIDENCY MIGHT MEAN FOR THE FUTURE

Based on the historical election of the 44th American President who identifies as African-American, who has an extended family that is multiracial, multireligious, and international, one might ask: Will Obama's presidency transform the definition of who counts as "truly" American to make it more racially inclusive? By extension, will his presence change people's racial attitudes and support for policies promoting equality? The psychological evidence thus far suggests that the answer is a proverbial mixed bag.

THE GOOD NEWS

On the optimistic side, there is good reason to believe that implicit biases are malleable (Blair, 2002; Dasgupta, 2009); they change when people are faced with highly admired members of disadvantaged groups who are clearly counterstereotypical (Dasgupta & Asgari, 2004; Dasgupta & Greenwald, 2001; Dasgupta & Rivera, 2008). For example, we have found that exposure to media profiles of highly admired African-Americans decreases implicit anti-Black prejudice and the reduction in race bias endures for at least the 24 hours after which the testing is done (Dasgupta & Greenwald, 2001). This finding has been replicated for other types of disadvantaged groups and extended to show that exposure to admired individuals from disadvantaged groups also makes people more willing to support civil rights policies that promote equality for the disadvantaged group to which they have been exposed (Dasgupta & Rivera, 2008). Applying these findings to the present situation, one can reasonably predict that prolonged positive media exposure to a counterstereotypical Black president will decrease implicit race bias against African-Americans as a group and, assuming that media exposure will continue to be positive, also promote a stable reduction in implicit prejudice.

Consistent with this prediction, Plant and colleagues (2009) recently reported that at the peak of the election season when coverage of Obama was high, American students at their institution showed no implicit race prejudice or stereotyping, although similar students at the same institution had shown considerably stronger bias a couple of years earlier. Moreover, participants who exhibited less implicit prejudice and stereotyping were significantly more likely to spontaneously generate names of admired Black individuals including Barack Obama when asked to mention the first five thoughts that popped into mind when they thought of African-Americans. Moreover, positive qualities associated with Obama in particular (words like president, intelligent, politician, and government) generalized to his ethnic group as a whole, thereby attenuating the negative stereotypes typically associated with African-Americans as a group (e.g., lazy, criminality and violence). Finally, those who implicitly associated new presidential attributes with African-Americans as a group also showed significantly less implicit negativity against this group (Plant et al., 2009; but see Schmidt & Nosek, 2010).

Although the aforementioned research on the malleability of implicit attitudes is specifically focused on changes in global evaluations of, or stereotypes about, an ethnic group, one can reasonably generalize these findings to predict that having a Black president might also change people's implicit construals of who seems American. In support of this conjecture, data from our lab presented earlier (Yogeeswaran et al., 2010a) suggest that media exposure to members of ethnic minority groups who work for the betterment of the country expands the definition of who counts as American by increasing the inclusion of ethnic minorities in the national category compared to when such media exposure is absent. Seeing a Black president's picture in all federal buildings, courthouses, embassies, the Capitol, and so forth is likely to have an incremental effect by strengthening the link between Black and America (see Wittenbrink, Judd, & Park, 2001) and, perhaps by extension, also strengthen the link between "brown" and America. Other work has also shown that exposure to simply positive or admired ethnic minorities can increase the extent to which their ethnic group is perceived to be American. This suggests that media representations of Obama as an admired or positive role model may increase the extent to which African-Americans as a whole are perceived to be American (Rydell, Hamilton, & Devos, 2010).

THE BAD NEWS

On the pessimistic side, considerable research on subtyping indicates that people are cognitive misers; when faced with outgroup members who appear to be too counterstereotypical compared to the rest of their group, they are likely to subtype them as an "exception to the rule" and preserve their existing group-based beliefs because that requires less cognitive effort than changing their original beliefs (for a review, see Richards & Hewstone, 2001). However, the data suggest that although subtyping can prevent people's explicit beliefs about a group from changing, it does not seem to do so for their implicit beliefs (Dasgupta & Greenwald, 2001; Dasgupta & Asgari, 2004). Applying these data to the present case, it is entirely possible that given Obama's personality and stature (e.g., intelligent, articulate, president, calm, upper-middle class) is so different from negative Black stereotypes (e.g., unintelligent, lazy, criminal, aggressive, poor), he may be the textbook case of a subtype who will not change the people's conscious attitudes about African-Americans in general (see Bobo & Charles, 2009).

Other evidence points to a different pessimistic prediction: the election of Barack Obama as president may make many Americans believe that racism is now history and racial equality has been achieved; as a result, they may express less support for future public policies that seek to address injustice. Specifically, Kaiser and colleagues (2009) compared Americans' opinions about racial issues before and after the 2008 Presidential election. They found that after Obama's election, participants concluded that racism was less of a problem, that anyone can achieve success through effort and perseverance, less needs to be done to achieve racial equality, and they expressed less support for policies that address group-based inequality such as affirmative action, school desegregation, and diversity. In other words, ironically, Obama's victory may represent a setback for remedying structural racial injustice.

Relatedly, expressing support for Barack Obama gives people "moral credentials" as unbiased individuals and makes them feel comfortable favoring Whites over Blacks in subsequent decisions (Effron, Cameron, & Monin, 2009). Specifically, once people were given the opportunity to express support for Obama over his competitors, they were more willing to *(1)* describe a job as better suited for Whites in general than Blacks with no good reason and *(2)* decrease the amount of money allocated to an organization serving Blacks at the expense of another organization serving Whites (but this only occurred among high prejudiced participants). Like Kaiser and colleagues' work, these data suggest that endorsement of President Obama may have unintended negative consequences—it may increase race bias against African-Americans in general.

More evidence has found that Barack Obama's new role as American president has not erased subtle race bias. In a recent article, Knowles, Lowery, and Schaumberg (2010) reported that those who harbored implicit race bias before the Presidential election in November 2008 were significantly less willing to support Obama's health-care policy a year later in October 2009. This relation between implicit race bias and policy opposition was mediated by negative attitudes toward President Obama himself. To rule out the possibility that policy opposition may be driven by factors other than race bias (e.g. principled conservatism, etc.), the authors conducted a follow-up experiment testing whether the relation between implicit racial attitudes and support for the health-care policy would change if the policy was attributed to past President Clinton versus current President Obama. Results showed that greater implicit race bias significantly influenced policy opposition *only* when the policy was attributed to Obama not Clinton, clearly suggesting that opposition to the current health-care proposal is, to some degree (but of course not entirely), colored by Americans' attitudes toward African-Americans.

Note that all these post-election studies focus on the impact that having President Obama in office has on Americans' attitudes toward race, tendency to discriminate or not, and support for public policies seeking racial equality. None of the post-election studies have explored whether having this president in office is changing people's perception of *American nationality* (i.e., who is seen as authentically American); whether it is shifting people's support for public policies to allow multiple ways of being American (e.g., in public schools, communities, in the workplace); and whether it is erasing doubts about the patriotism of ethnic minorities when they serve in roles critical to national security. These are the next generation of questions that beg exploration because they get to the heart of the historical promise of this country as a land of immigrants.

REFERENCES

Arcuri, L., Castelli, L., Galdi, S., Zogmaister, C., Amadori, A. (2008). Predicting the vote: Implicit attitudes as predictors of the future behavior of decided and undecided voters. *Political Psychology, 29,* 369–387.

Associated Press (2009, July 28). Hawaii reasserts Obama "natural-born" citizen. *Associated Press.* Retrieved from http://www.msnbc.msn.com/id/32180625/ns/politics-white_house/, last retrieved on 24 July, 2010.

Berry, J., Kalin, R., & Taylor, D. (1977). Multiculturalism and ethnic attitudes in Canada. Ottawa: Minister of Supply and Services.

Blair, I. (2002). The malleability of automatic stereotypes and prejudice. *Personality and Social Psychology Review, 6,* 242–261.

Bobo, L., & Charles, C. (2009). Race in the American mind: From the Moynihan report to the Obama candidacy. *The Annals of the American Academy of Political and Social Science, 621,* 243–259.

Bobo, L., & Dawson, M. (2009). A change has come: Race, politics, and the path to the Obama Presidency. *Du Bois Review, 6,* 1–14.

Carvalho, J., & Butz, D. (2010, January). Examining the separation of church and state: The American = Christian effect. Poster presented at the Annual Meeting of the Society for Personality and Social Psychology, Las Vegas, NV.

Cheryan, S. & Monin, B. (2005). "Where are you really from?" Asian-Americans and identity denial. *Journal of Personality and Social Psychology, 89,* 717–730.

Citrin, J., Reingold, B., & Green, D. (1990). American identity and the politics of ethnic change. *Journal of Politics, 52,* 1124–1154.

Dasgupta, N. (2009). Mechanisms underlying the malleability of implicit prejudice and stereotypes: The role of automaticity and cognitive control. *Handbook of prejudice, stereotyping, and discrimination* (pp. 267–284). New York, NY: Psychology Press.

Dasgupta, N., & Asgari, S. (2004). Seeing is believing: Exposure to counterstereotypic women leaders and its effect on the malleability of automatic gender stereotyping. *Journal of Experimental Social Psychology, 40,* 642–658.

Dasgupta, N., & Greenwald, A. (2001). On the malleability of automatic attitudes: Combating automatic prejudice with images of admired and disliked individuals. *Journal of Personality and Social Psychology, 81,* 800–814.

Dasgupta, N., & Rivera, L. (2006). From automatic antigay prejudice to behavior: The moderating role of conscious beliefs about gender and behavioral control. *Journal of Personality and Social Psychology, 91,* 268–280.

Dasgupta, N., & Rivera, L. (2008). When social context matters: The influence of long-term contact and short-term exposure to admired outgroup members on implicit attitudes and behavioral intentions. *Social Cognition, 26,* 112–123.

Devos, T. & Banaji, M. (2005). American = White? *Journal of Personality and Social Psychology, 88,* 447–466.

Devos, T. & Ma, D. (2008). Is Kate Winslet more American than Lucy Liu? The impact of construal processes on the implicit ascription of a national identity. *British Journal of Social Psychology, 47,* 191–215.

Devos, T., Gavin, K., & Quintana, F. (2010). Say "Adios" to the American dream? The interplay between ethnic and national identity among Latino and Caucasian Americans. *Cultural Diversity and Ethnic Minority Psychology, 16,* 37–49.

Devos, T., Ma, D., & Gaffud, T. (2008, January). Is Barack Obama American enough to be the next President? The role of ethnicity and national identity in American politics. Poster presented at the Annual Meeting of the Society of Personality and Social Psychology, Albuquerque, NM.

Dovidio, J., Kawakami, K., & Gaertner, S. (2002). Implicit and explicit prejudice and interracial interaction. *Journal of Personality and Social Psychology, 82,* 62–68.

Effron, D., Cameron, J., & Monin, B. (2009). Endorsing Obama licenses favoring Whites. *Journal of Experimental Social Psychology, 45,* 590–593.

Fazio, R., Jackson, J., Dunton, B., & Williams, C. (1995). Variability in automatic activation as an unobstrusive measure of racial attitudes: A bona fide pipeline? *Journal of Personality and Social Psychology, 69,* 1013–1027.

Foster, L., & Herzog, P. (1994). *Defending diversity: Contemporary philosophical perspectives on pluralism and multiculturalism.* Amherst, MA: University of Massachusetts Press.

Galdi, S., Arcuri, L., & Gawronski, B. (2008). Automatic mental associations predict future choices of undecided decision-makers. *Science, 321,* 1100–1102.

Graham, J., Haidt, J., & Nosek, B. (2009). Liberals and conservatives rely on different sets of moral foundations. *Journal of Personality and Social Psychology, 96,* 1029–1046.

Greenwald, A., Poehlman, A., Uhlmann, E., & Banaji, M. (2009). Understanding and using the Implicit Association Test: III. Meta-analysis of predictive validity. *Journal of Personality and Social Psychology, 97*, 17–41.

Gordon, M. (1964). *Assimilation in American life*. New York: Oxford University Press.

Haidt, J., & Graham, J. (2007). When morality opposes justice: Conservatives have moral intuitions that liberals may not recognize. *Social Justice Research, 20*, 98–116.

Hornsey, M., & Hogg, M. (2000). Assimilation and diversity: An integrative model of subgroup relations. *Personality and Social Psychology Review, 4*, 143–156.

Hirschman, C. (1983). America's melting pot reconsidered. *Annual Review of Sociology, 9*, 393–423.

Janoff-Bulman, R. (2009). To provide or protect: Motivational bases of political liberalism and conservatism. *Psychological Inquiry, 20*, 120–128.

Kaiser, C., Drury, B., Spalding, K., Cheryan, S., & O'Brien, L. (2009). The ironic consequences of Obama's election: Decreased support for social justice. *Journal of Experimental Social Psychology, 45*, 556–559.

Knowles, E.D., Lowery, B.S., & Schaumberg, R.L. (2010). Racial prejudice predicts opposition to Obama and his health care reform plan. *Journal of Experimental Social Psychology, 46*, 420–423.

Lou, M. (2008, February 27). A host disparages Obama, and McCain quickly apologizes. *The New York Times*. Retrieved from http://www.nytimes.com/2008/02/27/us/politics/27name.html, last retrieved on 24 July, 2010.

MacGillis, A. (2008, May 4). Obama faces test in asserting his own brand of patriotism. *The Washington Post*. Retrieved from http://www.washingtonpost.com/wp-dyn/content/story/2008/05/03/ST2008050302296.html?hpid=topnews last retrieved on 24 July, 2010.

McConnell, A., & Leibold, J. (2001). Relations among the Implicit Association Test, discriminatory behavior, and explicit measures of racial attitudes. *Journal of Experimental Social Psychology, 37*, 435–442.

Moghaddam, F. (2008). *Multiculturalism and intergroup relations: Psychological implications for democracy in global context*. Washington, D.C.: American Psychological Association.

Nakaso, D. (2009, July 28). Hawaii: Obama birth certificate is real. USA Today. Retrieved from http://www.usatoday.com/news/nation/2009-07-27-obama-hawaii_N.htm?POE=click-refer, last retrieved on 24 July, 2010.

Newton-Small, J. (2008, May 14). Obama's flag pin flip-flop? *TIME*. Retrieved from http://www.time.com/time/politics/article/0,8599,1779544,00.html, last retrieved on 24 July, 2010.

PBS (2008, January 4). Anatomy of a smear. *PBS Now*. Retrieved from http://www.pbs.org/now/shows/401/political-smears.html, last retrieved on 24 July, 2010.

Politifact (2007, November 8). Photo was taken during anthem, not pledge. PolitiFact.com. Retrieved from http://www.politifact.com/truth-o-meter/statements/169/, last retrieved on 24 July, 2010.

Plant, A., Devine, P., Cox, W., Columb, C., Miller, S., Goplen, J., & Peruche, M. (2009). The Obama effect: Decreasing implicit prejudice and stereotyping. *Journal of Experimental Social Psychology, 45,* 961–964.

Porter, S., Ferguson, M., Hassin, R., & Balcetis, E. (2010). *Unintended American bias: American cues implicitly increase prejudice.* Manuscript in preparation.

Richards, Z., & Hewstone, M. (2001). Subtyping and subgrouping: Processes for the prevention and promotion of stereotype change. *Personality and Social Psychology Review, 5,* 52–73.

Roberts, S. (2009, December 17). Projections put Whites in minority in U.S. by 2050. *The New York Times.* Retrieved from http://www.nytimes.com/2009/12/18/us/18census.html?hp, last retrieved on 24 July, 2010.

Rudman, L., & Ashmore, R. (2007). Discrimination and the Implicit Association Test. *Group Processes and Intergroup Relations, 10,* 359–372.

Rydell, R., Hamilton, D., & Devos, T. (2010). Now they are American, now they are not: Valence as a determinant of the inclusion of African Americans in the American identity. *Social Cognition, 28,* 161–179.

Schildkraut, D. (2007). Defining American identity in the twenty-first century: How much "there" is there? *The Journal of Politics, 69,* 597–615.

Schlesinger, A. (1992). *The Disuniting of America. Reflections on a Multicultural Society.* New York: W. W. Norton & Co.

Schmidt, A. (1997). The Menace of Multiculturalism: Trojan Horse in America. Westport, CT: Praeger Publishers.

Schmidt, K., & Nosek, B. (2010). Implicit (and explicit) racial attitudes barely changed during Barack Obama's presidential campaign and early presidency. *Journal of Experimental Social Psychology, 46,* 208–314.

Sekaquaptewa, D., Espinoza, P., Thompson, M., Vargas, P., & von Hippel, W. (2003). Stereotypic explanatory bias: Implicit stereotyping as a predictor of discrimination. *Journal of Experimental Social Psychology, 39,* 75–82.

Stein, S. (2009, July 31). New poll: Less than half of republicans believe Obama was born in the U.S. Retrieved from http://www.huffingtonpost.com/2009/07/31/new-poll-less-than-half-o_n_248470.html, last retrieved on 24 July, 2010.

Takaki, R. (1993). *A different mirror: A history of multicultural America.* Boston: Little.

Taylor, D. (1991). The social psychology of racial and cultural diversity: Issues of assimilation and multiculturalism. In A. Reynolds (Ed.). *Bilingualism Multiculturalism, and Second Language Learning* (pp. 1–19). Hillsdale, NJ: Lawrence Erlbaum.

Todd, C., Murray, M., & Montanaro, D. (2008, June 25). First thoughts: A focus group in York. *MSNBC.* Retrieved from http://firstread.msnbc.msn.com/archive/2008/06/25/1166068.aspx, last retrieved on 24 July, 2010.

Wittenbrink, B., Judd, C., & Park, B. (2001). Spontaneous prejudice in context: Variability in automatically activated attitudes. *Journal of Personality and Social Psychology, 81,* 815–827.

Wright, D., & Miller, S. (2007, October 4). Obama dropped flag pin in war statement. *ABC News.* Retrieved from http://abcnews.go.com/Politics/story?id=3690000&page=1, last retrieved on 24 July, 2010.

Yinger, J. (1994). *Ethnicity: Source of strength? Source of conflict?* Albany, NY: State University of New York Press.

Yogeeswaran, K., & Dasgupta, N. (2010). Will the "real" American please stand up? The effect of implicit national prototypes on discriminatory behavior and judgments. *Personality and Social Psychology Bulletin, 36*(10), 1332–1345.

Yogeeswaran, K., Dasgupta, N., & Gomez, C. (2010a). *A new American dilemma: The effect of ethnic identification and public service on the construal of ethnic groups as American.* Manuscript under review.

Yogeeswaran, K., Dasgupta, N., Adelman, L., Eccleston, A., & Parker, M. (2010b). *To be or not to be: The hidden cost of ethnic identification for Americans of European and Non-European origin.* Manuscript in preparation.

Zeleny, J. (2007, October 5). The politician and the absent American flag pin. *The New York Times.* Retrieved from http://www.nytimes.com/2007/10/05/us/politics/05obama.html, last retrieved on 24 July, 2010.

As American as Barack Obama

Lawrence D. Bobo

By early March, 2008, Arizona Senator John McCain had wrapped up the Republican nomination for president. At the end of the month, he launched his first campaign ads of the general election featuring the slogan: "The American President Americans have been waiting for." On the one hand, the ad could be viewed as politics as usual. Appeals to patriotism are often a prominent element of Republican political rhetoric. On the other hand, the slogan took on a deeper, implicit cultural meaning. It seemed to raise a question about whether the leading contender for the then undecided Democratic presidential nomination, Illinois Senator Barack Obama, really counted as an "American." Some commentators viewed the ad, in fact, as another sophisticated manipulation of the "race card," in a subtle way activating latent racial bias against a Black candidate. *Mother Jones* magazine's blog went so far as to denounce the ad as "vulgar and creepy" in the way it seemed to question not just Obama's patriotism but his fundamental "Americanness."

Of course, this particular McCain ad was but one of many ways that racial misunderstanding, tension, and division emerged during the campaign and after Obama's election as the 44th President and first African-American President of the United States. One hardly knows where to begin. Obama was variously characterized as no different than Jesse Jackson in successfully winning the South Carolina campaign, mounting a "fairy tale" effort to secure the presidency, unprepared to answer the phone in the White House at "3 a.m. in the morning," giving good speeches like Martin Luther King but not able to legislate like an LBJ, nothing more than an affirmative action candidate, and as tied to a hopelessly anti-White minister in the Reverend Jeremiah Wright. And, bear in mind, all of these variously racialized digs at Obama came from the camp of his main Democratic challenger! The deluge of racist imagery we have seen since he took the Oath of Office, from postcards featuring watermelons on the White House lawn, through a cartoon of police officers shooting a berserk chimp and leaving a nation in need of "Someone else to write the next stimulus bill," to pictures of Obama as a loin-cloth-clad witch doctor with a bone through his nose promoting "Obama Care: Coming Soon to a Clinic Near You," underscores the enduring power of overt anti-black racial stereotypes in America.

If we raise our sights beyond the specifics of the campaign itself and more recent legislative debates, three larger and arguably nested questions suggest themselves: First, how should we understand Obama's electoral success in the light of still apparently widespread negative perceptions about African-Americans and their loyalty to the United States; second, will African-Americans, like Obama, ever be seen as fully American by their White fellow citizens; and third, does the election of Obama signal the arrival, or at least the near-term onset, of a post-racial America?

Dasgupta and Yogeeswaran review and specify how their research as well as that of others on racial attitudes shed light on Obama's victory, the challenges he currently faces, and the likelihood that his presidency will fundamentally redefine conceptions of who is American. Although they give us few absolute answers to these key questions, they illuminate well how research on implicit beliefs factor into the modern politics of race.

Among the first points Dasgupta and Yogeeswaran establish is that Blacks are not at the top of the list of those who are viewed at present as constituting the image of a patriotic American. Indeed, despite growing talk of diversity and a rhetoric of multiculturalism, they point to numerous ways in which America is understood first and foremost as White. Rather than embracing an understanding of Americanness that reflects a fusion or a mosaic of peoples and cultures, the common assumption, they suggest, is that people become American by undergoing, in the language of sociologists, a process of Anglo-conformity.

This assumption about who is American, when viewed in light of the persistence of negative stereotypes about African-Americans, they argue, suggests that candidate Obama had a very high and distinct set of challenges to overcome. In effect, they suggest, Obama faced special pressure to escape both specific negative images of Blacks and an expectation that Blacks are less patriotic than White Americans. Given these conditions, the mechanism or strategy for success, they argue, is to allay voter doubts on stereotype relevant dimensions and to outperform one's rivals. In numerous ways, in hindsight, we can now say that the Obama campaign cleared these hurdles.

Perhaps the most provocative part of Dasgupta and Yogeeswaran's essay comes in their speculations on whether Obama's election will produce a broadened conception of who is American. They take a somewhat ambivalent position. At one level, they suggest that the malleability of stereotypes and the re-framing power of counterstereotypical examples like Obama point to a meaningful potential for substantial positive change. At another level, however, they are acutely mindful of the potential for, to borrow Gordon W. Allport's phrase for it, "fence mending." That is, to the extent Obama is successful and seen as rising above the stereotypes, he may come to be seen as the exception that proves the rule. He is allowed to "escape" through a hole in the fence of anti-Black racial stereotypes, a hole that is swiftly and neatly repaired once Obama, the individual case, is allowed through to the other side.

At this stage I still believe, to borrow a phrase, in the audacity of hope. In the historic Philadelphia speech on race, Obama said: "I have never been so naïve as to believe that we can get beyond our racial divisions in a single election cycle, or with a single candidacy." Change is a process and Obama's electoral success has not only crystallized the potential for racial progress extant in a particular moment (i.e., electing a Black president) but has nudged us a little farther down the road of deeper racial healing (i.e., broadening the definition of who fundamentally is understood as American).

To be sure, as the review by Dasgupta and Yogeeswaran reminds us, at present it is unclear whether Obama's success will permanently broaden who is seen as truly American or whether he will come to be seen as a quite special exception, with little bearing on the deeper cultural and social roots of racial division in America. My own inclination is to suggest that we eschew the most cynical and pessimistic analyses in favor of guarded optimism. We do have a uniquely propitious confluence of circumstances at present. Enormous positive change in racial attitudes and relations has occurred in the United States, and these are not superficial changes. There are ample grounds—particularly in the light of his intelligence, skill, and character—to expect Obama will prove to be an adroit politician able to sustain a high level of voter support. Thus, despite today's evidence of quite real racial division and tension and of other short-term political setbacks of the moment, I still think it fair to say that Obama's America remains pointed in the direction of laying down the burdens of race, although we have a long, long way yet to go.

CHAPTER 5

Does Black and Male Still = Threat in the Age of Obama?

Jennifer A. Richeson and Meghan G. Bean

The election and inauguration of Barack Obama as the first Black President of the United States was a watershed moment in our nation's history. Although some herald it as evidence that people were able to overcome racial stereotypes regarding Black Americans broadly, and Black men specifically, others suggest that it is Obama's presidency that will provide a new, public image of Black men that will, in turn, help to eradicate racial stereotypes and racism. Given the importance and potentially deleterious consequences of what we've termed the "Black male = threat" stereotype, it is important to consider whether Barack Obama's presidency can indeed have an attenuating effect on this pernicious association. Will frequent exposure to a counterstereotypical, high-status Black man encourage individuals to form new associations with Black men (e.g., intelligent, successful)? Or, rather, is the "Black male = threat" stereotype so strong and pervasive that Obama's presidency will have little to no attenuating effect on it and, instead, be viewed through and, perhaps, limited by the stereotype?

To address these questions, in this chapter we will first review the extant social science evidence that there is a pervasive stereotypical association between Black men and threat in the minds (and brains) of most social perceivers. Specifically, we will present data suggesting that Black men are stereotyped as threatening, dangerous, and criminal both implicitly as well as explicitly. Next, we will consider whether Obama, by virtue of his position of power, prestige, and authority, may be undermining the stereotype and, thus, changing the collective American consciousness (and unconscious). Specifically, we will present research that examines the malleability of the "Black male = threat" association and consider whether the Obama presidency may trigger cognitive processes that are likely to reduce the strength of the association for most Americans. Finally, we will end the chapter with a discussion of how the "Black male = threat" stereotype may have affected Obama's presidential bid and, furthermore, consider evidence that reactions to his first year in office may result from, at least in part, the operation of this stereotype.

THE "BLACK MALE = THREAT" STEREOTYPE

Research examining Whites' perceptions of Black Americans has shown that members of this group, and young Black males specifically, are perceived as more dangerous and threatening than members of numerous other racial and ethnic groups. Research by St. John and Heald-Moore (1995), for example, found that Whites report greater feelings of fear when imagining an interaction with a Black stranger than when imagining an interaction with a White stranger. Further, White participants' fear of Black strangers in this study was moderated by the age and gender of the stranger they were asked to imagine—young Black men were feared more than older Black male targets or Black females of any age. Work by Cottrell and Neuberg (2005) also suggests that White individuals fear Black Americans more than other racial minority groups (in this case, Asian-Americans and Native Americans), and further, these individuals report believing that Black Americans pose a greater threat to their physical safety and property than do other racial minority groups. In a survey of residents of Los Angeles County, Zubrinsky and Bobo (1996) found that a majority of White and Asian-Americans in a wealthy community reported that they would be upset if a Black family moved into their neighborhood. The authors contend that these feelings resulted, in part, from the fact that individuals feared for the safety of their families and property.

In addition to these findings indicating that Black men are explicitly perceived—if not also evaluated—as threatening and criminal, a great deal of psychological research has found that these stereotypes between Black men and threat are also held implicitly and, thus, can be activated in the minds of most Americans automatically and possibly also unconsciously. Said differently, a number of studies have examined whether Whites' perceptions of Black men as threatening affect their cognition and judgments, even without individuals becoming aware that these processes have occurred. One line of research that has illuminated the implicit association between Black men and threat has examined the extent to which anger—a threat-related emotion—is more readily associated with Black, compared with White, males. In one set of studies by Hugenberg and Bodenhausen (2003), White participants watched videos of White and Black male faces that slowly transitioned from a neutral facial expression to an angry facial expression (Study 1) or from an angry facial expression to a neutral facial expression (Study 2). Participants' task was to press a button when the facial expression changed from angry to neutral or visa versa. Results revealed that the more racially biased participants were (assessed by an unobtrusive measure of anti-black bias), the faster they were to detect the onset of anger (Study 1) and the slower they were to detect the offset of anger (Study 2) in Black, compared with White, faces. In other words, participants who were more racially biased in general also tended to over-perceive anger in Black, but not White, male faces.

Building on this work, Maner and colleagues (2005) found that inducing White individuals to feel fearful and anxious leads them to misperceive anger on the faces of Black males, but not on Black female or White faces of either gender, despite the fact that all the faces were actually displaying neutral expressions. Research has also found, furthermore, that perceivers are more likely to categorize racially ambiguous faces (morphs of Black and White male faces) as Black (rather than White) when those faces are expressing anger (Hugenberg & Bodenhausen, 2004; Hutchings & Haddock, 2008). Overall, this line of work suggests that the association between Black men and threat is sufficiently strong so as to bias White Americans' perception of the facial affect of Black men.

The perniciousness of the "Black male = threat" stereotype has been documented further by research testing whether social perceivers automatically respond to Black men in a manner similar to how people automatically react to other stimuli that are thought to be threatening (see Öhman & Mineka, 2001, for a review). This work has primarily drawn upon a line of research demonstrating that people pay greater attention to threatening stimuli than nonthreatening stimuli and are more vigilant in environments in which threats are likely than they are in nonthreatening environments. It has been argued that humans have evolved to detect stimuli in their immediate environments that are likely to be threatening or dangerous quite rapidly and readily. Indeed, a plethora of research has demonstrated that biologically threatening stimuli such as snakes and spiders are attention-"grabbing" (Öhman & Mineka, 2001). Further, research has also found that social threats (e.g., angry facial expressions) can similarly grab and engage attention (e.g., Fox, Russo, & Dutton, 2002; Hansen & Hansen, 1988).

Building on these findings, Trawalter, Todd, Baird, and Richeson (2008) examined whether the "Black male = threat" stereotype is sufficiently insidious and ingrained in the American subconscious so as to lead to patterns of selective visual attention in White perceivers similar to those found for other threatening stimuli. To that end, they employed a task called the dot-probe detection task (MacLoed, Mathews, & Tata, 1986) in which two facial photographs—one of a White male, the other of a Black male—were displayed very rapidly (approximately 33 ms) and then one of the photos was replaced with a small gray dot. The participants' job was to press a button on a computer keyboard as quickly and accurately as possible to indicate where the dot appeared. The logic of the task is that participants whose attention had already been captured (unconsciously and automatically) by one of the faces found the dot faster when it appeared in the same location as the face to which they were attending. Hence, a pattern of finding the dot faster when it appeared in the same location as the Black face compared to when it appeared in the location of the White face reflected an attentional bias toward Black faces—that is, the Black male faces captured participants' attention more than the White faces. Indeed, this is the pattern that was observed in the Trawalter et al. (2008) study. A study by Donders, Correll, and Wittenbrink (2008) using a similar measure of attentional bias found, further, that the stronger an association participants held between Black men and danger, the more likely they were to reveal an attentional bias toward Black male faces.

The pervasive, automatic association between Black men and threat in the minds of most American social perceivers has also been demonstrated by research employing methodology from the field of cognitive neuroscience to examine brain activity in response to Black, compared with White, individuals. Most of this work has used functional magnetic resonance imaging (fMRI) and found differential activity in the amygdala—a brain region selectively responsive to potential threat (Whalen, 1998)—in response to Black, compared with White, male targets (Hart et al., 2000), especially among White individuals with relatively high levels of racial bias (measured unobtrusively; Cunningham et al., 2004; Phelps et al., 2000). These differential patterns of amygdala activity could reflect automatic threat responses to Black male targets. Bolstering this possibility, reducing the threat signal of these Black faces (e.g., by limiting the salience and importance of the racial category membership; Van Bavel, Packer, & Cunningham, 2008; Wheeler & Fiske, 2005) has been found to attenuate the amygdala response. Considered in tandem with the behavioral research reviewed previously, this research suggests that Black men are rapidly, readily, and, regularly appraised as threatening.

Although the research documenting the "Black male = threat" stereotype reviewed thus far is compelling, some of the most profound work examining this pervasive association has considered it within the context of the criminal justice system (e.g., Eberhardt, Davies, Purdie-Vaughns, & Johnson, 2006; Mauer & Huling, 1995). Graham and Lowery (2004) found, for example, that both police and probation officers who were unconsciously primed with the category "Black" rated a hypothetical juvenile defendant more negatively (e.g., as more hostile) and considered him more culpable than did officers who were primed with a race-neutral concept. The automatic and perhaps unconscious association between Blacks and crime/danger has also been demonstrated in a number of studies finding that fast and/or subliminal presentation of faces of Black males facilitates the identification of crime-related objects (i.e., weapons). For example, Eberhardt, Goff, Purdie, and Davies (2004) first primed participants with photographs of either Black male individuals or of White male individuals and then asked them to identify degraded images of weapons or neutral objects. Results revealed that participants in the Black prime condition were better able to discern what the degraded crime-related images were but not what the degraded neutral objects were compared with participants in the White prime condition. Eberhardt and colleagues (2004) also found that priming individuals with Black faces led them to notice crime-related objects faster than neutral objects. Similarly, Payne (2001) found that White perceivers were more likely to mistakenly identify "neutral" objects, like tools, as weapons when they were primed with Black male compared with White male faces.

In addition to the aforementioned work finding that priming "Black" makes crime-related objects more accessible in the minds of most White Americans, recent research also suggests that such priming may contribute to the all too frequent shooting of unarmed Black men. In work by Correll, Park, Judd, and Wittenbrink (2002), non-Black participants were asked to play a video game task in which they were presented with White and Black male targets who were holding either guns (i.e., "criminal" targets) or harmless everyday objects like cell phones (i.e., "civilian" targets). Participants were asked to "shoot" armed criminals and to ignore unarmed civilians. Results of these studies and others using similar methodological paradigms have shown that participants are significantly more likely to shoot in error unarmed Black civilians than unarmed White civilians (*see also* Correll, Park, Judd, Wittenbrink, Sadler, & Keesee, 2007; Plant & Peruche, 2005). Needless to say, the implications of these findings are profound. Not only are Black men associated with threat in the minds of most social perceivers, but the effects of these associations on individuals' judgments and behavior toward Black men can and do have deleterious consequences.

In sum, the research reviewed in this section suggests that Black men are strongly associated with threat-related concepts such as anger, danger, and criminality. Further, these stereotypical associations are apparent in both explicit and more implicit or subconscious judgments and evaluations of Black men. The question we consider in the rest of this chapter, then, is how Obama's presidency might affect these negative associations and, further, how these associations may affect evaluations of President Obama. In the next section, we review psychological research that suggests avenues through which Obama's presidency may attenuate the "Black male = threat" stereotype and obstacles that may limit such a de-biasing effect. After, we turn the tables and review how reactions to Barack Obama's election (and presidency) may be shaped by this pervasive stereotype.

Obama and the Attenuation of the "Black Male = Threat" Stereotype

As mentioned previously, extant research has shown that many social perceivers display automatic threat reactions toward Black men that can be observed in neural activity (e.g., Cunningham et al., 2004), patterns of selective attention (e.g., Trawalter et al., 2008), facilitation of the perception of crime-related objects (e.g., Eberhardt et al., 2004), and judgments of perceived facial anger (Maner et al., 2005) among many other implicit and explicit reactions (Zubrinsky & Bobo, 1996). So, how could Barack Obama possibly counter these varied effects? In this section, we first consider processes through which Obama's presidency may serve to undermine both the "Black male = threat" stereotype as well as improve stereotypes and prejudice against Black Americans in general. After, we consider evidence suggesting that these de-biasing effects may indeed be limited. Finally, we explore the role of important individual differences that are likely to shape for whom Obama's presidency is likely to improve racial stereotypes regarding Black men and, quite ironically, for whom it may increase negative stereotypes and evaluations.

Avenues Toward Obama's De-Biasing Effect

Obama's potential to transcend race and America's racial divisions was a primary contributor to the hope engendered by his campaign. Indeed, many point to the multiracial coalition that led to his election (Bobo & Dawson, 2009) as evidence for the new, post-racial America. The question we pose in this chapter, however, is to what extent can Obama lead to a *post-racist* America? Consistent with this possibility, a recent series of studies found that non-Black individuals revealed significantly lower levels of automatic anti-Black bias during the Fall of 2008 (between Obama's nomination in August and election in November) than found in prior periods (Plant et al., 2009). Specifically, roughly 51% of participants revealed a pro-White, anti-Black automatic racial bias during this Fall 2008 period compared with close to 80% of participants during other periods. These findings suggest, in other words, that Obama's ability to attenuate negative racial stereotypes and attitudes about Blacks may have already begun.

So, what processes may account for this de-biasing effect? The most likely mechanism underlying this change is the effect of exposure to positive, counterstereotypical exemplars on even unconscious, automatic forms of bias. For example, Dasgupta and Greenwald (2001) found that exposure to images of admired Black figures (e.g., Martin Luther King, Jr.) and disliked White figures (e.g., Jeffrey Dahmer) decreased Whites' tendency to automatically associate Blacks with negativity more rapidly than with positivity (and Whites more rapidly with positivity than with negativity). Similarly, Barden, Maddux, Petty, and Brewer (2004) presented participants with images of Black men who were depicted either as inmates or lawyers and found that those who viewed the Black male targets as lawyers (i.e., counter-stereotypical exemplars) subsequently associated Black Americans with negative concepts less readily (and associated them with positive concepts more readily) than participants who viewed them as inmates. In other words, viewing images of Black men in a positive, counterstereotypical social role decreased the negativity that is typically automatically associated with Black people in general and Black men in particular (*see also* Maddux, Barden, Brewer, & Petty, 2005; Richeson & Ambady, 2003; Wittenbrink, Judd, & Park, 2001).

Taken together, this research suggests an important and powerful avenue through which Obama's presidency can reduce the extent to which negative concepts come to mind more readily than positive concepts when individuals are exposed to or encounter Black men. To the extent that individuals admire Obama, even if for no other reason than his ascendance to the Presidency, consistent exposure (e.g., through media coverage) to him should reduce their automatic racial bias. That is, consistent exposure to a Black male who is both counterstereotypical in many ways and in a position of authority may serve to decrease Americans' automatic negative reactions to and evaluations of Black men more generally.

Obstacles to Obama's De-Biasing Effect

Despite these promising findings, there is also evidence that negative stereo-types regarding Black men may persist despite Barack Obama's presidency. Some of our own work has shown, for example, that Black male authority figures (e.g., police officers) may actually be perceived more negatively and engender more severe threat reactions than Black men of lower status (Bean & Richeson, 2010). Specifically, in one study we showed White participants images of Black and White male civilians (e.g., individuals in normal street clothing) and police officers, all of whom were displaying neutral facial expressions, and asked them to rate how much anger they thought each individual was experiencing. Results revealed that although participants tended to perceive less anger on the faces of White male police officers compared with White male civilians, this was not the case for perceptions of anger on the faces of Black male civilians and police officers. Instead, Black male police officers were perceived as somewhat angrier than Black male civilians, and not surprisingly, they were also perceived to be angrier than White male police officers.

To explore this seemingly exaggerated threat reaction to Black males in positions of power (i.e., police officers) further, in a second study we used a less overt measure of threat perception—facilitation of behavioral approach and avoidance tendencies. Previous research has shown that approach and avoidance behavioral tendencies are facilitated when responding to liked (and ostensibly safe) or disliked (and ostensibly feared) stimuli, respectively (Paladino & Castelli, 2008). Building on this work, we presented participants images of Black and White male civilians and police officers, then gave them an instruction either to approach or avoid the computer screen using a standard handheld joystick. We then recorded how quickly participants were able to follow the approach or avoidance instruction as a function of which image preceded it—that is, a Black or White male civilian or police officer. In addition to making approach movements faster after the White police officer images than after the Black police officer images, similarly to our previous results, we also found that participants were somewhat faster to make approach movements after the Black male civilian images compared with after the Black male police officer images, suggesting that Black male police officers were perceived as more threatening to these White participants than Black male civilians. Taken together, the results of these two studies suggest that Black men in a position of status and authority continue to be perceived more negatively than White men in similar positions of status of power, and interestingly, they may also be perceived more negatively than Black men who are not known to hold high-status or powerful positions.

This pattern of results is consistent with research that has found a backlash against women who attempt to assume powerful, high-status roles (Rudman & Glick, 2001; Rudman & Phelan, 2008). Specifically, a number of studies have shown that women must prove that they are independent and competent to be considered for high-status, leadership roles, but then they often pay a price for such "agentic" displays in the form of low evaluations likeability and warmth. Specifically, women who are perceived to be competent enough to assume high-status, leadership roles are often perceived as being cold, domineering, and intimidating and, subsequently, are rejected for such powerful, leadership positions. It is possible that Blacks who attain positions of authority and leadership, like Obama, may engender a similar backlash, resulting in perceptions that they are overly aggressive and domineering—consistent with the epithet that is familiar to many Blacks in high-status positions—namely, "uppity." Further empirical research is needed to examine the extent to which Black men in high-status, powerful roles do indeed encounter such a backlash, but it is clear that such processes would do little to mitigate the perception that Black men are threatening.

Another factor that may limit Obama's ability to generate more positive attitudes toward Black men stems from research noting that it is individuals' motives, not characteristics of the Black individuals themselves, that often shape reactions to even positive, counterstereotypical Blacks. In an elegant series of studies, Sinclair and Kunda (1999) found that reactions to Black professionals depend on the extent to which White perceivers are motivated to evaluate them positively or negatively. For example, participants who received negative feedback from a Black male doctor were more likely to categorize him as Black and reveal activation of negative associations with Black people (e.g., crime) than to categorize him as a doctor and reveal activation of positive "doctor" associations (e.g., health). Participants who received positive feedback from the Black doctor, however, revealed the opposite pattern; positive doctor associations were more accessible for these participants than were negative Black stereotypes, which participants actually suppressed. Sinclair and Kunda (1999) argued that participants' motivation either to accept or discount the feedback that they received led to their selective perception of the Black doctor as either a reliable (i.e., doctor) or unreliable (i.e., Black) evaluator whose opinion could subsequently be accepted or ignored, respectively. Drawing upon this work, it is possible that those individuals who feel that Obama's policies and/or political ideology are a threat to their self-image may continue to evaluate him according to negative stereotypes of Black men, and thus, exposure to Obama may actually serve to increase the extent to which Black men are perceived negatively.

Sinclair and Kunda's (1999) work also suggests that even people who feel that Obama's policies and/or political ideology affirm their self-image may also fail to show a decrease in racial bias toward Black men. Specifically, such individuals are likely to de-emphasize Obama's race in favor of his social role (e.g., "President"), which is typically associated with competence. Hence, Obama's race may not benefit from the positive evaluations afforded him, and thus, other Black men may be similarly cut off from positive associations with Obama. Similarly, research on subtyping—the cognitive "fencing off" of atypical members of a category from the larger group to preserve group stereotypes—suggests that Obama's ability to attenuate the "Black men = threat" stereotype may be limited (see Richards & Hewstone, 2001, for review). Indeed, people who evaluate president Obama positively, but otherwise hold negative associations between Black men and threat, have readily available subgroups or alternative groups into which to categorize him (e.g., as biracial rather than Black) that will ensure that their attitudes toward and perceptions of Black men are not altered.

In sum, a number of lines of social-psychological research place in doubt President Obama's ability to eliminate the "Black male = threat" stereotype.

Specifically, Black men in high-status roles may be deemed even more threatening than Black men in low-status roles, increasing the negativity associated with Black men more generally. In addition, Obama's assumption of the most powerful leadership role in the country (if not the world) may be perceived as a threat to the societal (racial) status quo, resulting in a backlash against both him and Black men in general. Similarly, individuals who perceive Obama's political win and policies as a threat to their self-image (even as a symbolic threat) are likely to categorize him according to negative racial stereotypes; even Obama's supporters may distance him from his race to enhance their support for him. Although such distancing may lead to more positive attitudes toward Obama himself, it is unlikely to reduce the extent to which negative associations with threat and danger are directed toward other Black men. Consequently, this work suggests little promise for Obama's presidency to attenuate the "Black male = threat" stereotype.

The Role of Race & Political Ideology in Obama's De-Biasing Potential

The previous two subsections of this chapter reviewed research regarding the promise and potential pitfalls, respectively, of the prediction that Barack Obama's presidency will attenuate the pervasive "Black male = threat" stereotype. Indeed, there is social-psychological research to support either the view that Obama is likely to have an attenuating effect on this stereotype or the opposite position that he is not very likely to have a positive effect. One potential way to reconcile these two sets of research findings, however, is to examine the role of chronic, relevant individual differences in shaping reactions to Obama and, thus, his likely effect on perceptions of Black men. Specifically, in this section, we briefly examine the ways in which political orientation (and related social ideologies) and race may affect reactions to Barack Obama, generally, and attitudes toward Black men, specifically.

Political Orientation & Social Ideologies. Because Obama is a political figure, one of the most relevant individual difference factors worthy of consideration is party identification. Specifically, as discussed previously, because Democrats are more likely both to have favorable opinions of Obama and his policies compared with Republicans, Democrats are also more likely to be susceptible to any de-biasing effects that Obama may have. Second, liberals and conservatives tend to differ in other individual difference factors that often shape reactions to members of groups with lower socio-cultural status, such as Black Americans. Specifically, political conservatism is positively correlated with both Social Dominance Orientation (SDO; Sidanius & Pratto, 1999) and Right Wing Authoritarianism (RWA; Altemeyer, 1981)—two social ideologies that are known to predict prejudice toward other socio-cultural groups (Sibley & Duckitt, 2008). Individuals who are high in SDO are primarily concerned about maintaining the relative status arrangements among their own social group (e.g., White men) and members of other, competing groups (e.g., Black men). Hence, successful Black men are likely to be perceived as a threat to high-SDO individuals because they blur and, thus, challenge group status boundaries. Individuals who are high in RWA, on the other hand, are concerned about maintaining the order, norms, and customs of mainstream society and culture. Hence, high-RWA individuals may perceive a Black President as a threat to the "American way of life" (*see* Dasgupta & Yogeeswaran, Chapter 4), insofar as it is perceived as expanding or altering the collective understanding of what and who counts as "American" and represents "American values." In other words, individuals who are higher in these social ideologies are likely to have negative reactions to the election of a Black American president and, thus, are unlikely to have a basis from which to perceive other Black men more positively.

Perceiver Race. Although the "Black male = threat" association may be stronger among non-Black individuals, there is considerable reason to believe that Black Americans also hold this association, at least implicitly (Arkes & Tetlock, 2004; Correll et al., 2007). Hence, it is important to consider whether individuals' racial group memberships may affect the magnitude of any de-biasing effects that Obama may have. Because race predicts both perceptions and evaluations of Obama (Bobo & Dawson, 2009), it is reasonable to expect that it may also affect for whom and to what extent the "Black male = threat" stereotype is reduced (or strengthened) in the so-called "age of Obama." Most notably, Obama's presidency has the potential to affect the self-perception, attitudes, and behavior of young Black men—the very targets of the "Black male = threat" stereotype. Specifically, because most Black Americans view Obama extremely favorably but are also unlikely to distance him from his race, they are particularly poised to benefit from the de-biasing effect of exposure to such a positive, counterstereotypical exemplar (Dasgupta & Greenwald, 2001).

Consistent with this view, a creative field study by Dasgupta and Asgari (2004) found that women who attended a competitive, all-female college were less likely to automatically associate men with leadership more than women in their sophomore year compared with women who attended a similarly competitive co-educational college nearby. Indeed, although the women's automatic gender-leadership beliefs did not differ when they entered the two colleges, the women in the co-educational college expressed a pro-male bias by their second year but not the all-female college students. Of particular relevance to the present examination, exposure to female role models in the form of professors (especially in traditionally male fields) seemed to explain the difference between the automatic gender-leadership beliefs held by the two groups of students. Much like the predicted effect of Obama for Black Americans, in other words, this study revealed the power of exposure to counterstereotypical ingroup members (members of one's own social group) to alter individuals' implicit beliefs and, perhaps also, their aspirations and subsequent life outcomes.

In sum, the extant social-psychological research suggests that there are clear routes through which Obama is likely to serve a de-biasing effect, at least for some Americans. Indeed, important individual differences such as political orientation, social ideology, and race are likely to moderate any effect Obama's Presidency will likely have on the extent to which individuals continue to hold the "Black male = threat" stereotype. It is clear from this research, furthermore, that the real possibility that even individuals who are likely to respond favorably to Obama may not generalize this positivity to Black men in general. Instead, Obama may be subtypes or regroup so as to preserve this very pernicious belief.

THE "BLACK MALE = THREAT" STEREOTYPE & EVALUATIONS OF OBAMA

In addition to the primary purpose of this chapter—to examine whether and how Obama might help attenuate the "Black male = threat" stereotype and its many deleterious consequences, it is also important to consider, in turn, how this pervasive stereotype may have affected individuals' reactions to Obama, both as a presidential candidate and now as president. Although, as noted previously, the "Black male = threat" stereotype is particularly prevalent and powerful, there is some reason to believe that Obama may indeed be buffered from it, at least among his political supporters. Specifically, research suggests that automatic threat reactions to Black men are moderated by any number of competing characteristics that signal low levels of threat, such as averted eye-gaze (Richeson et al., 2008; Trawalter et al., 2008) and smiling facial affect (Richeson & Trawalter, 2008). Most notably, Phelps et al. (2000) found that non-Black perceivers failed to generate greater amygdala activity upon exposure to famous (and liked) Black males (e.g., Denzel Washington) compared with similarly famous and admired White males (e.g., Harrison Ford), unlike the differential amygdala activity typically observed for unknown Black and White males. This research suggests, therefore, that individuals who admire Barack Obama are unlikely to respond to him with feelings of threat.

Similarly, Wheeler and Fiske (2005) revealed that when White participants were induced to individuate Black male targets (i.e., by contemplating which vegetables they may like or dislike), rather than categorize them (i.e., by gender), participants similarly failed to show heightened amygdala activity to Black, compared with White, male faces. Obama's supporters are likely to acquire and make use of individuating information about him more and, thus, rely on his racial group membership less than his political opponents. In the presidential campaign, this divergence was particularly clear with Obama opponents willing to make appeals to the relevance of his race, whereas many of his supporters and his campaign itself actively attempted to downplay his race in favor of more individuating characteristics and the idea of a "post-racial" America (see Bai, 2008, and Kornblut, 2008, for discussions of these patterns). For example, former Democratic Party Vice-Presidential nom-inee Geraldine Ferraro—a supporter of Hillary Clinton in the Democratic primary—directly brought up race to explain Obama's success relative to Clinton. Specifically, she stated, "If Obama was a white man, he would not be in this position" (Farber, 2008). Many of Obama's supporters, by contrast, explicitly attempted to make the case that Obama's race was and should not be an issue. At the election night rally following the South Carolina primary, for example, supporters began to chant, "Race doesn't matter! Race doesn't matter!" (Beckerman, 2008).

This pattern of Obama's supporters distancing him from race and his opponents reconnecting him with his racial group was also observed in a recent set of studies conducted by Caruso and colleagues (2009). Prior to the general election, Caruso et al. exposed participants who said that they supported Obama or McCain to photographs of Obama. Some of the photos had been altered such that his skin tone was darker than it actually is and some had been altered such that his skin tone was lighter than it actually is. Participants' task was to indicate which of the images were most "representa-tive of Obama." That is, they were asked to indicate which photos best reflected Obama. Strikingly, results revealed that individuals who supported Obama tended to select the lightened skin tone images as most representative of him, whereas individuals who supported John McCain tended to select the darkened images (Caruso, Mead, & Balcetis, 2009). Hence, both Obama's sup-porters and opponents tended to perceive his skin tone in a biased manner, suggesting that their views about skin tone (and, perhaps, Blacks) were simi-lar (i.e., the Black/darker skin tone is more negative than White/lighter skin tone), but they differed in the extent to which they assimilated Obama to (or contrasted him from) his racial category and actual skin tone. Taken together, this work suggests that political orientation and/or policy support may be the primary predictor of the extent to which Obama is viewed through the lens of the "Black male = threat" stereotype, perhaps primarily because Obama's supporters may be reluctant to categorize him as "Black" in the first place.

Although it is somewhat beyond the scope of the present chapter, we would be remiss if we did not at least speculate on the extent to which the "Black male = threat" stereotype can explain, at least in part, some of the more volatile reactions to Obama's presidency to date. Indeed, almost immediately after his election as the 44th President of the United States of America, a very vocal minority of political opponents began to engage in a number of behaviors seemingly designed to question Obama's legitimacy. For example, a conspiracy theory that Obama was not a natural born citizen of the United States (a requirement to hold the office of President) gained momentum, the American public witnessed a White male Congressman publicly challenge the President during an address to a joint session of Congress, and many conservatives objected to an address by the President directed to school children. Are these reactions related to one another? Are they related to the "Black male = threat" stereotype? Although we certainly can't make any definitive claims here, it seems likely that these reactions do stem from some form of a threat response to the election of Obama, perhaps, at least in part, because he is Black.

Our analysis in previous sections of this chapter suggests that Obama's election may have been experienced as a self-image threat to people who do not support his policies and as a threat to group hierarchy and/or cohesion to people who are high in SDO and RWA, respectively. In either case, research has found that increased stereotyping, prejudice, and discrimination are the likely outcomes of such perceived threats (Stephan & Stephan, 2000). The recent charges that Obama is "Socialist," "Communist," and generally "UnAmerican," furthermore, are particularly consistent with a perceived symbolic threat to the "American way of life," likely experienced by individuals who are high in RWA. Recall, furthermore, that Bean and Richeson (2010) found that White perceivers revealed somewhat greater automatic threat reactions to Black men who were in a position of authority and power (i.e., police officers) than to Black men with less status and power (i.e., civilians). Although the mediators of this effect are yet unknown, it is possible that the high-status, powerful role held by these Black male targets led participants to perceive them as even more dangerous and threatening than their civilian (i.e., low-status, low-power) counterparts. Moreover, it is quite possible that some of the extreme reactions to President Obama reflect similar processes. Taken together, the research reviewed in this section suggests that Obama's political opponents continue to view him according to at least some form of a "Black male = threat" stereotype, although the type of threat associated with Obama may differ from that associated with Black men more generally.

CONCLUDING THOUGHTS

The election of Barack Obama as the first Black President of the United States is a clear indication of America's racial progress—a landmark even on the country's path to realizing the full inclusion of racial minorities as citizens in the American democratic project. In this chapter, we discussed the ways in which this historic event might affect the pervasiveness of one specific race-related belief—the explicit and implicit associations between Black men and threat. As we explored herein, research suggests that there are indeed ways in which Obama's Presidency might decrease this "Black male = threat" stereo-type. Frequent exposure to an admired and counterstereotypical Black leader like Barack Obama is likely to decrease this pernicious stereotype as well as other automatically activated anti-Black biases, at least among his supporters; recent work by Plant and colleagues (2009) provides evidence that this proc-ess may have already begun. Although Obama's non-Black supporters may indeed become less biased toward Black men as a direct result of exposure to him, it is his potential effect on the beliefs of other Black men that may be most profound and, thus, worthy of further study.

It is important to note, however, that a decrease in bias may not occur for all people, and, in fact, the election of Barack Obama as the nation's first Black president may actually lead some Americans to express attitudes toward Black men that are even more negative. It may be the case, for example, that individuals who feel threatened by Obama—perhaps because his policy posi-tions differ so dramatically from their own—will not exhibit decreases in anti-Black bias in response to his presidency. Additionally, individuals high in SDO and RWA may actually exhibit *more* negative attitudes toward Black men as a result of Obama's election because his election will likely represent for them an unwelcome change in the racial status hierarchy and/or the customs of modern American society. Consequently, such reactions may be of particular concern given the especially insidious nature of the "Black male = threat" stereotype and its many deleterious consequences.

Although we have presented a rather sobering, if not pessimistic, view of Obama's potential to attenuate the "Black male = threat" stereotype, we want to stress that any positive effect that Obama may have is likely to have wide-spread impact. The pervasive association between Black men and threat undermines the health, wealth, and well-being of Black men on a daily basis, limiting access to quality employment and maximizing access to the criminal justice system (Mauer & Huling, 1995; Pager, 2003). We hope that this chapter offers a better understanding of the potential routes through which Obama can have such a de-biasing effect and sheds light on potential roadblocks that may thwart the generalization of positive affect toward and beliefs about Obama to Black men more broadly.

REFERENCES

Altemeyer, B. (1981). *Right wing authoritarianism.* Winnipeg, Canada: University of Manitoba Press.

Arkes, H.R., & Tetlock, P.E. (2004). Attributions of implicit prejudice, or "Would Jesse Jackson 'fail' the implicit association test?" *Psychological Inquiry, 15,* 257–278.

Bai, M. (2008, August 10). Is Obama the end of black politics? *New York Times Magazine,* p. MM34.

Barden, J., Maddux, W.W., Petty, R.E., & Brewer, M.B. (2004). Contextual moderation of racial bias: The impact of social roles on controlled and automatically activated attitudes. *Journal of Personality and Social Psychology, 87,* 5–22.

Bean, M.G., & Richeson, J.A. (2010). *Uniform judgments? Examining the effects of a "safe" social role on perceptions of young black men.* Unpublished Manuscript. Northwestern University. Evanston, IL.

Beckerman, G. (2008). Mass Media Criticism. Obama's fans tell off CNN. Columbia Journalism Review. <http://www.cjr.org/campaign_desk/mass_media_criticism.php> Accessed on December 31, 2009.

Bobo, L.D. & Dawson, M.C. (2009). A change has come. Race, politics, and the path to the Obama Presidency. *Du Bois Review, 6,* 1–14.

Caruso, E.M., Mead, N.L., & Balcetis, E. (2009). Political partisanship influences perception of biracial candidates' skin tone. *Proceedings of the National Academy of Sciences, 106,* 20,168–20,173.

Correll, J.C., Park, B., Judd, C.M., & Wittenbrink, B. (2002). The police officer's dilemma: Using ethnicity to disambiguate potentially threatening individuals. *Journal of Personality and Social Psychology, 83,* 1314–1329.

Correll, J.C., Park, B., Judd, C.M., Wittenbrink, B., Sadler, M.S., & Keesee, T. (2007). Across the thin blue line: Police officer and racial bias in the decision to shoot. *Journal of Personality and Social Psychology, 92,* 1006–1023.

Cottrell, C.A., & Neuberg, S.L. (2005). Different emotional reactions to different groups: A sociofunctional threat-based approach to "prejudice." *Journal of Personality and Social Psychology, 88,* 770–789.

Cunningham, W.A., Johnson, M.K., Raye, C.L., Gatenby, J.C., Gore, J.C., & Banaji, M.R. (2004). Separable neural components in the processing of Black and White faces. *Psychological Science, 15,* 806–813.

Dasgupta, N., & Asgari, S. (2004). Seeing is believing: Exposure to counterstereotypic women leaders and its effect on the malleability of automatic gender stereotyping. *Journal of Experimental Social Psychology, 40,* 642–658.

Dasgupta, N., & Greenwald, A.G. (2001). On the malleability of automatic attitudes: Combating automatic prejudice with images of admired and disliked individuals. *Journal of Personality and Social Psychology, 81,* 800–814.

Donders, N.C., Correll, J., & Wittenbrink, B. (2008). Danger stereotypes predict racially biased attentional allocation. *Journal of Experimental Social Psychology, 44,* 1328–1333.

Eberhardt, J.L., Davies, P.G., Purdie-Vaughns, V.J., & Johnson, S.L. (2006). Looking deathworthy. Perceived stereotypicality of black defendants predicts capital-sentencing outcomes. *Psychological Science, 17*, 383–386.

Eberhardt, J.L., Goff, P.A., Purdie, V.J., & Davies, P.G. (2004). Seeing black: Race, crime and visual processing. *Journal of Personality and Social Psychology, 87*, 876–893.

Farber, J. (2008, March 7). Geraldine Ferraro lets her emotions do the talking. *Daily Breeze.* Retrieved July 22, 2010. Web site: http://www.dailybreeze.com/lifeandculture/ci_8489268

Fox, E., Russo, R., & Dutton, K. (2002). Attentional bias for threat: Evidence for delayed disengagement from emotional faces. *Cognition & Emotion, 16*, 355–379.

Graham, S., & Lowery, B.S. (2004). Priming unconscious racial stereotypes about adolescent offenders. *Law and Human Behavior, 28*, 483–503.

Hansen, C.H., & Hansen, R.D. (1988). Finding the face in the crowd: An anger superiority effect. *Journal of Personality and Social Psychology, 54*, 917–924.

Hart, A.J., Whalen, P.J., Shin, L.M., McInerney, S.C., Fischer, H., & Rauch, S.L. (2000). Differential responses in the human amygdala to racial outgroup vs. ingroup face stimuli. *Neuroreport, 11*, 2351–2355.

Hugenberg, K., & Bodenhausen, G.V. (2003). Facing prejudice: Implicit prejudice and the perception of facial threat. *Psychological Science, 14*, 640–643.

Hugenberg, K., & Bodenhausen, G.V. (2004). Ambiguity in social categorization: The role of prejudice and facial affect in race categorization. *Psychological Science, 15*, 342–345.

Hutchings, P.B., & Haddock, G. (2008). Look Black in anger: The role of implicit prejudice in the categorization and perceived emotional intensity of racially ambiguous faces. *Journal of Experimental Social Psychology, 44*, 1418–1420.

Kornblut, A.E. (2008, October 12). Issue of race creeps into campaign. *Washington Post*, p. A01.

MacLeod, C., Mathews, A., & Tata, P. (1986). Attentional bias in emotional disorders. *Journal of Abnormal Psychology, 95*, 15–20.

Maddux, W.W., Barden, J., Brewer, M.B., & Petty, R.E. (2005). Saying no to negativity: The effects of context and motivation to control prejudice on automatic evaluative responses. *Journal of Experimental Social Psychology, 41*, 19–35.

Maner J.K., Kenrick, D.T., Becker, D.V., et al. (2005). Functional projection: How fundamental social motives can bias interpersonal perception. *Journal of Personality and Social Psychology, 88*, 63–78.

Mauer, M., & Huling T. (1995). *Young Black Americans and the criminal justice system: 5 years later.* Washington, DC: Sentencing Project.

Öhman, A., & Mineka, S. (2001). Fears, phobias, and preparedness: Toward an evolved module of fear and fear learning. *Psychological Review, 108*, 483–522.

Paladino, M-P, & Castelli, L. (2008). On the immediate consequences of intergroup categorization: Activation of approach and avoidance motor behavior toward ingroup and outgroup members. *Personality and Social Psychology Bulletin, 34*, 755–768.

Payne, B.K. (2001). Prejudice and perception: The role of automatic and controlled processes in misperceiving a weapon. *Journal of Personality and Social Psychology, 81*, 181–192.

Phelps, E.A., O'Connor, K.J., Cunningham, W.A., et al. (2000). Performance on indirect measures of race evaluation predicts amygdala activation. *Journal of Cognitive Neuroscience, 12*, 729–738.

Pager, D. (2003). The mark of a criminal record. *American Journal of Sociology, 108*, 937–975.

Plant, E.A., Devine, P.G., Cox, W.T.L., et al. (2009). The Obama effect: Decreasing implicit prejudice and stereotyping. *Journal of Experimental Social Psychology, 45*, 961–964.

Plant, A.E., & Peruche, B.M. (2005). The consequences of race for police officers' responses to criminal suspects. *Psychological Science, 16*, 180–183.

Richards, Z., & Hewstone, M. (2001). Subtyping and subgrouping: Processes for the prevention and promotion of stereotype change. *Personality and Social Psychology Review, 5*, 52–73.

Richeson, J.A., & Ambady, N. (2003). Effects of situational power on automatic racial prejudice. *Journal of Experimental Social Psychology, 39*, 177–183.

Richeson, J.A., Todd, A.R., Trawalter, S., & Baird, A.A. (2008). Eye-gaze direction modulates race-related amygdala activity. *Group Processes & Intergroup Relations, 11*, 233–246.

Richeson, J.A., & Trawalter, S. (2008). The threat of appearing prejudiced and race-based attentional biases. *Psychological Science, 19*, 98–102.

Rudman, L.A., & Glick, P. (2001). Prescriptive gender stereotypes and backlash toward agentic women. *Journal of Social Issues, 57*, 743–762.

Rudman, L.A., & Phelan, J.A. (2008). Backlash effects for disconfirming gender stereotypes in organization. *Research in Organizational Behavior, 28*, 61–79.

Sibley, C.G., & Duckitt, J. (2008). Personality and prejudice: A meta-analysis and theoretical review. *Personality and Social Psychology Review, 12*, 248–279.

Sidanius, J., & Pratto, F. (1999). *Social dominance: An intergroup theory of social hierarchy and oppression.* Cambridge, UK: Cambridge University Press.

Sinclair, L., & Kunda, Z. (1999). Reactions to a black professional: Motivated inhibition and activation of conflicting stereotypes. *Journal of Personality and Social Psychology, 77*, 885–904.

St. John, C., & Heald-Moore, T. (1995). Fear of Black strangers. *Social Science Research, 24*, 262–280.

Stephan, W.G., & Stephan, C.W., (2000). An integrated threat theory of prejudice. In S. Oskamp (Ed.), *Reducing prejudice and discrimination. The Claremont symposium on applies social psychology.* (pp. 24-45). Mahwah, NJ: Erlbaum.

Trawalter, S., Todd, A.R., Baird, A.A., & Richeson, J.A. (2008). Attending to threat: Race-based patterns of selective attention. *Journal of Experimental Social Psychology, 44*, 1322–1327.

Van Bavel, J.J., Packer, D.J. & Cunningham, W.A. (2008). The neural substrates of in-group bias. A functional magnetic resonance imaging investigation. *Psychological Science, 19*, 1131–1139.

Whalen, P.J. (1998). Fear, vigilance, and ambiguity: Initial neuroimaging studies of the human amygdala. *Current Directions in Psychological Science, 7,* 177–188.

Wheeler, M.E., & Fiske, S.T. (2005). Controlling racial prejudice: Social-cognitive goals affect amygdala and stereotype activation. *Psychological Science, 16,* 56–63.

Wittenbrink, B., Judd, C.M., & Park, B. (2001). Spontaneous prejudice in context: Variability in automatically activated attitudes. *Journal of Personality and Social Psychology, 81,* 815–827.

Zubrinksy, C.L., & Bobo, L. (1996). Prismatic metropolis: Race and residential segregation in the city of angels. *Social Science Research, 25,* 335–374.

Threat, Fantasy, and President Obama

Eddie Glaude, Jr.

I watched the inauguration of Barack Obama with my 12-year-old son. I picked him up from school early, because I wanted to share with him this historic moment. As a young man, growing up on the coast of Mississippi, the idea of a Black man becoming the President of the United States was the stuff of fantasy for me. On January 20, 2009, I sat next to my son as he witnessed what I could only believe was the impossible. And, I could not help but sense that the context of his living, his own self-conception as a Black man, would be fundamentally altered.

Richeson and Bean have demonstrated that the symbolic significance of President Obama has tangible consequences. That his very presence would, in fact, impact Black men's implicit beliefs about themselves and about the worlds they inhabit. This seems intuitively right. Black male children now see—no matter their material conditions—the most powerful man in the world as someone who looks, at least at first glance, like them. Such an image ought to affect the scope of their aspirations and the substance of their actions.

But this view presumes, rightly or wrongly, some sense of possession— that President Obama belongs to us. And it is precisely in how we parse this assumption—this sense of "we" and the sorts of loyalties that follow from it— that a fuller picture of the complexities and confusions of our current moment comes into view. It is one thing to revel in the demonstrable symbolic significance of a Black president; it is another to assess the implications of his policies for how "we" live our lives. The very idea of what Michael Dawson refers to as *linked fate*, the notion that *my* individual interests are bound up with those of my racial group, has faltered in the face of Obama's ascendance to the White House. He is not *our* president. He is the president of all Americans. This view carries with it a suspicion of old forms of Black identity politics. Indeed something has been lost: perhaps an older conception of Black solidarity and, with it, the loyalties that once held Black individuals, which gave them support, direction, and a unity of outlook are now disappearing. So, an irony or paradox rests at the heart of Obama's powerful presence: He empowers a new generation of Black men *and* simultaneously enables their invisibility in the public domain.

In 1951, in an essay entitled "Many Thousands Gone," with the voice of a White narrator, James Baldwin wrote:

> Time has made some changes in the Negro face. Nothing has succeeded in making it exactly like our own, though the general desire seems to be to make it blank if one cannot make it white. When it has become blank, the past as thoroughly washed from the black face as it has been from ours, our guilt will be finished.

It would seem that Baldwin had it right. Obama's face has been made blank, and the consequence has been a deepening of our national pathology as some seek to finally "get shut" of the problems of race.[1]

Richeson and Bean note that among White supporters of Obama, views of the Black male = threat stereotype wanes. But this outcome may very well be a result of subtyping or regrouping. Among many of his supporters, Obama does not stand in for Black men as such. He simply isn't one of them. This is not to suggest that views about Black men have not been fundamentally affected by Obama's ascendance. It suggests that those views, altered as they may be, do not portend the dawning of a post-racial/racist age. Race still matters.

As a nation, we find ourselves in a moment of profound transition. And transitions "are always out of something as well as into something; they reveal a past as well as project a future" (Dewey, 1988, p. 53). We stand, however, between a past that offers little help in accounting for the moment and a present too confused and chaotic to give us insight into future direction. What is lost in the confusion is the desperate status of so many African-Americans who have lost their bearings and languish on the underside of American life. The significance of Obama's Presidency should be measured not simply by how his very presence makes us feel but by how he fundamentally transforms the material conditions of those who are too often perceived as a threat.

NOTE

1 Ralph Ellison published in 1970 an insightful essay entitled, "What would America be like without Blacks?" There he rightly rejected any attempt to deny the centrality of African-Americans to this fragile experiment in democracy: our style, our language, indeed our very presence are essential to the distinctiveness of American life. That presence also calls attention to the contradictions that have shadowed our country since its inception, and it is here that the American fantasy takes root: our national effort to rid ourselves of the great scandal of the

United States—that "recurring fantasy of solving one basic problem of American democracy by 'getting shut' of the blacks through various wishful schemes that would banish them from the nation's bloodstream."

REFERENCE

Dewey, J. (1988). Individualism, Old and New, in *John Dewey: The Later Works, vol. 5: 1929–1930*. Carbondale: Southern Illinois University Press.

CHAPTER 6

Michelle Obama: Redefining Images of Black Women

Shanette C. Porter and Gregory S. Parks

By now, Michelle Obama's story is well-known—not just her public image, or her behavior over the last several years as the wife of a politician and current president of the United States, but her life story. Indeed, it seems that as much attention is paid to her past as to her present (Rossi, 2007; Norris, 2007; Mundy, 2008). Perhaps most notable about Obama's background is that it is remarkably ordinary. That is, her childhood closely mirrors that of many of those in the Black community, yet she has gone on to reach goals unattained by most *Americans*. She has two Ivy League degrees, was an accomplished attorney, is a devoted wife and mother, and has managed to do all of these things with a disposition that is not easily pigeon-holed into the derogatory and stereotypical categories set aside for Black women. Michelle Obama's persona is interesting in its own right, and her successes are, to be sure, impressive, but taken in the context of her current reality as the first Black First Lady, they lend themselves to an intriguing question: How will exposure to a prominent Black woman influence opinions about Black women as a group? Although it is clear that Americans like her—her approval ratings have equaled or surpassed those of her husband—it is still unclear what the impact of the emergence of Michelle Obama into the public arena will be for the perceptions of Black women more generally (Jones, 2009).

INTERSECTIONALITY: MICHELLE EQUALS MORE THAN BLACK + WOMAN

Most discrimination research focuses separately on the effects of race or gender, ignoring the possibility that Black women encounter the joint effects of dual minority statuses. This is termed *double jeopardy* (Beale, 1970). Interactive discrimination models utilize the *multiple jeopardy* concept to further account for Black women's unique location at the intersection of multiple status hierarchies (including race, gender, and class). This intersection produces experiences distinct from those of White women and Black men

(King, 1988). Accordingly, many perceptions about Michelle Obama—positive and negative, explicit and implicit—highlight the unique role in which she has been placed.

Other authors in this volume have articulated how, despite the wane in explicit anti-Black attitudes over the decades (Hughey, 2010), implicit anti-Black bias remains prevalent (Ashburn-Nardo, Livingston, & Waytz, 2010; Lane & Jost, 2010). But as we contemplate the unique role that Michelle Obama plays in America's ongoing story about race, we must look not only to her race but also at how it intersects with her gender. Not only do many people harbor implicit race biases, they harbor implicit gender biases as well. People associate "male" with "hierarchical" and "female" with "egalitarian" (Mast, 2004). They misattribute high status more readily to unknown men than to unknown women (Banaji & Greenwald, 1995) and evaluate male authority figures more favorably than their female counterparts (Rudman & Kilianski, 2000). Subliminally priming people to think about dependence or aggression also influences their judgments of men and women. They judge women, but not men, as more dependent while thinking about dependence and judge men, but not women, as more aggressive while thinking about aggression (Banaji, Hardin, & Rothman, 1993). Men also automatically associate maleness with power (Rudman, Greenwald, & McGhee, 2001).

Not surprisingly, these attitudes affect evaluations of potential careers. For example, both men and women automatically associate "male" with "career" and "female" with "family." Among men, this connection is consistent with their explicit statements about gender stereotypes, although ironically, women explicitly reject such connections as inconsistent with their beliefs. People also more closely associate men with science and women with humanities (Nosek, Banaji, & Greenwald, 2001). And they more easily associate "engineer" with men and "elementary school teacher" with women than the opposite pairing (White & White, 2006). In one study, participants primed with words associated with historically male roles (e.g., "doctor") tended to categorize a subsequent gender-neutral pronoun as being male, whereas participants primed with words associated with historically female roles (e.g., "nurse") tended to categorize a subsequent gender-neutral pronoun as being female. Like studies of racial bias, even participants who explicitly reject gender-based stereotypes concerning careers carry these implicit biases (Banaji & Hardin, 1996).

Intersectionality vis-à-vis race and gender has been construed as a functional construct by such institutions as federal appellate courts (Jenkins v. Blue Cross Mutual Hospital Insurance, Inc., 1976; Jeffries v. Harris County Community Action Association, 1980). There has been, however, little work in the social sciences on the degree to which race and gender interact to create a unique construct beyond either of them in isolation. Where researchers have analyzed the effect of race/ethnicity and gender together, the results have been mixed. In their study, Goff and colleagues had three findings. First, they found that intersectionality affects Whites' perception process, which leads to their gender categorization errors for Black women. Consequently, both "blackness" and "maleness" are highly associated for Black males and females. Third, women are deemed as unattractive commensurate with their perceived masculinity, leading Whites to rate Black women as less attractive than other women (Goff, Thomas, & Jackson, 2008). Timberlake and Estes explored the degree to which individuals' beliefs about various attributes of several racial/ ethnic target groups interacted with the sex of target group members. Although they found that that the effects of target group sex interacted with particular racial/ethnic stereotypes to the degree that those stereotypes have been gendered in American culture, they also found that race/ethnicity has more predictive power (Timberlake & Estes, 2007).

The question of whether and to what degree the intersection of race/ gender is an independent construct is a lingering one, one that we will not seek to answer here. But just as others have looked to Michelle Obama as an example of how to think about this intersection (Parks & Roberson, 2009), we look to her national image to discern what it says about Black women. Of interest are several issues. First, how is Michelle Obama viewed by White Americans—that is, does she really defy common stereotypes? Second, and important, even if Michelle Obama is perceived as defying stereotypes, will she be able to disconfirm them or otherwise alter the opinions of White Americans toward other Black women? In the following, we consider the ways in which Michelle Obama has been stereotyped in the past, highlighting recent converging public opinion, which tends to view her as not stereotypical, although perhaps also not atypical—a small, but not insignificant point. Next, this chapter examines how and to what extent Michelle Obama might influence the opinions of White Americans in light of relevant research conducted in psychology over the past decades.

MICHELLE AND THE FIVE ARCHETYPES OF BLACK WOMANHOOD

There are at least four traditional stereotypical images of Black American women (the mammy, the sexual siren, the welfare queen, and the matriarch) and one modern one (the angry Black woman), all of them largely negative and pejorative (e.g., Collins, 1990; Jewell, 1993, Childs, 2005). There is variation in the labels given to these stereotypical categories, but consensus in the content. The first category is commonly labeled the mammy stereotype and refers to Black women who are subservient and loyal to more dominant figures, usually White women and men (Collins, 1990). The mammy is characterized as giving, warm, and loving, particularly toward the White family. She is traditionally middle-aged or elderly, darker in skin tone and buoyant in disposition, although these qualities are not necessary components. The second is the sexual siren, or Jezebel. This category refers to women who are overtly sexual or sexualized, and whose independence and control both appear to be derived from their aggressive sexuality (West, 1995; Collins, 2000). The contemporary version of this stereotype paints Jezebels as promiscuous women who dress provocatively, and who are almost always self-centered and defiant. Third, is the welfare queen, typically described as having multiple children, tending to be unkempt, poor, and perhaps employed at a low-paying job (Collins, 1990). She is viewed as lazy and exploitative. Although Obama clearly fails to meet even a minimal threshold for inclusion in the former three categories of stereotypes, there are at least two stereotypes that have a semblance of applicability: the angry Black woman and the matriarch. And during the 2008 campaign, Obama was variously accused of representing each of these categories.

The angry Black woman stereotype, also known as the Sapphire stereotype, is characterized as no-nonsense, fiery, often unapologetically offensive to others, although often viewed as successful in a particular career (Collins, 1990; Davis, 1981). This angry Black woman stereotype highlights the way in which stereotypical categories evolve to accommodate changes in groups' demographics (Stangor, 2000). According to the stereotype content model, stereotypical categories tend to be organized along the dimensions of warmth and competence (Fiske, Cuddy, Glick, & Xu, 2002). Although one's ingroup is usually perceived as favorable on both dimensions—that is, both highly warm and highly competent—most other social groups (e.g., Blacks) and stereotyped subgroups (e.g., the "angry Black woman") are characterized less positively on one or both dimensions (Fiske, Cuddy, Glick, & Xu, 2002). Thus, an ostensibly positive, warm characterization of an outgroup may be tempered with a simultaneous belief that that outgroup is incompetent (or less competent than one's ingroup). Notably, the previously described "mammy" stereotype was characterized in exactly this manner. With the emergence of professionally successful Black women in recent decades, however, came the birth of a new way of stereotyping; and if the "mammy" was seen as warm, but incompetent, the "angry Black woman" has been seen as competent, but hostile.

The "angry Black woman" stereotype has been levied against Michelle Obama since early in her husband's campaign for the presidency (Powell & Kantor, 2008). For example, she was accused of being sharp-tongued and sarcastic, an apparent reference to her lack of warmth (Zakin, 2007; Langley, 2008;

Wolfe, 2008). The accusations were not always quite so subtle. When Obama made the now infamous statement, "For the first time in my adult lifetime, I'm really proud of my country," she was openly admonished by conservative pundits for being hateful (Malkin, 2008; Oinounou & Kapp, 2008; Hornick, 2008; O'Reilly, Tabacoff, & Sohnen, 2008). Moreover, websites, like www. TheObamaFile.com, increasingly painted Michelle Obama as a woman with a wholly negative disposition. And Bill O'Reilly, on his namesake television show, *The O'Reilly Factor*, used the term outright, stating, "I have a lot of people who call me on the radio and say [Michelle Obama] looks angry and I have to say there is some validity to that. She looks like an angry woman" (O'Reilly, Tabacoff, & Sohnen, 2008). Even if largely promoted only by conservative media outlets, the attempts to portray Obama as angry were widespread. Indeed, many speculated that they were the cause of the prudent manufacturing of a warmer, softer image for the First Lady (Powell & Kantor, 2008; Stanley, 2008; Levinson, 2008). This characterization of Obama as the angry Black woman, however, seems to ignore the basic aspects of the stereotype. For one, the angry Black woman stereotype refers to women who appear to be unjustifiably (and disproportionately) upset given the circumstance or subject matter (for example, interracial dating) (e.g., Childs, 2005). Moreover, the woman is typically characterized as being dispositionally unsettled and negative, presumably resulting in the perceived disparity between the size of an issue and the magnitude of the negative response (Collins, 1990, 2000; Davis, 1981; King, 1988). The angry Black woman is thus emotional, easily moved to hostile words and actions. Obama, although frank, full of energy, and by her own admission, dissatisfied with some of America's racial infrastructure, appears to lack the hostility and reckless disinhibition that are the true hallmarks of this category (e.g., Samuels, 2008). The application of this stereotype to refer to Obama, whether implied or explicit, is at best a distortion of her candor.

The matriarch stereotype has similarly been used to describe Michelle Obama. This stereotype crosses racial boundaries, but when applied to Black women, it specifically refers to a woman who is a wife and mother but also one who typically works outside of the home. She is characterized as aggressive, opinionated, controlling, and lacking femininity—embracing the roles of both mother and father, and emasculating her partner if she has one (Collins, 2000; West, 1995). These qualities, which appear to contribute to the matriarch's success outside the home, are simultaneously viewed as detrimental values to pass on to her children. At first blush, this stereotype seems to capture Obama, and that has not gone unnoticed. Numerous sources have made note of Obama's prominent status in the legal profession, her desire to balance work and home life, and what has perhaps euphemistically been called her independent-mindedness (Komblut, 2007; Mundy, 2008; Newton-Small, 2008; Lightfoot, 2008). A second glance reveals that the stereotype is not all that fitting. As is often the case, the stereotype has been overprescribed; given some superficial similarities between Obama and the matriarch stereotype, attempts have been made to paint her completely within the confines of the stereotype. It may explain why "common knowledge" about aspects of her personality or her beliefs can sometimes be traced to a single comment she once made, perhaps taken out of context. For example, a quip about her husband being a "mere mortal" (meant to humanize him) quickly turned into a claim that she was emasculating her husband—a claim that was perpetuated enough for Obama to eventually directly address it (Dowd, 2007; Keen, 2007; Jaffe, 2008; Wolffe, 2008; Kelley, 2008). Contrary to the matriarch stereotype, however, Obama seemed to find a balance wherein she was both an able professional and a devoted wife and mother on the campaign trail, with little or no legitimate evidence of her attempting to emasculate her husband in the process (Kelley, 2008; Dann, 2008; Bigg, 2008). Since then, she has managed to straddle the line of feminism, individualism, and traditional (conservative) values, proving that these philosophies do not have to be mutually exclusive. She is the woman who worked her way through school to become a successful lawyer, then quit her job to support her husband as he began his journey that would eventually end in the presidency.

In other words, to confine Obama to a stereotype, any stereotype, is to overlook or distort fundamental aspects of her life, personality, and accomplishments. Although many journalists and pundits have attempted to make sense of her statements, beliefs, and behaviors by applying some racialized and gendered stereotype, a notable plurality in the media—that does not fall neatly along political or racial lines—has always tended toward a view of Michelle Obama that defies any known stereotype about Black women (Cole, 2008; Kelley, 2008; Brown & Leiby, 2008; Ellis, 2008; Thompson, 2008). Moreover, post-election there was a shift in perceptions of Obama toward this latter view, even by those who previously viewed her as angry (Romano, 2009). And while it is unclear whether public opinion followed or preceded the media, any number of editorials and opinion pieces suggest that many Americans favor a non-stereotypical view of Obama (Mitchell, 2008; Lubin, 2009; Nelson, 2008; Cadet, 2008; James-Johnson, 2008).

THE IMPACT AND INFLUENCE OF MICHELLE

Almost from the moment she appeared, and certainly since she has become the First Lady, there has been a question about how the presence of Obama in the public arena might single-handedly influence the opinions of Americans about Black women. Several articles have suggested that she will become, if she has not already, a role model for young Black women and a source of pride for Black women more generally (Samuels, 2008; Brown & Leiby, 2008; Lewis, 2009). There has been far less agreement about whether and how Obama might influence White Americans' opinions (Samuels, 2008; Burton & Jones, 2008; Doss & Friery, 2009; Thompson, 2008; Kelley, 2008). Although any actual impact of Michelle Obama on attitudes may remain unknown for years, research in social psychology on attitudes and beliefs provides an informative guide for exploring possible outcomes. In these literatures, attitudes refer to evaluations of objects, places, groups of people, and so on, that range from positive to negative, whereas beliefs refer to ideas and information that are held as true about an object, place, or group of people; for example, a stereotype is a belief (Allport, 1935; Brown, 1998; Eagly & Chaiken, 1993; Fazio, Sanbonmatsu, Powell, & Kardes, 1985; Fishbein, 1963, 1967; Fishbein & Ajzen, 1975; Gilbert & Hixon, 1991; Tajfel, 1982; Weber & Crocker, 1983).

Before considering how Michelle Obama might influence the attitudes of White Americans, it is useful to briefly introduce some basic principles of attitude and beliefs measurement and change. For one, measuring individuals' attitudes toward and beliefs about different social groups can be difficult, given that explicit attitudes and beliefs sometimes fail to coincide with implicit attitudes and beliefs (Greenwald & Banaji, 1995; Bargh, 2007). This discrepancy can result from an unwillingness to openly acknowledge one's known racial attitudes and beliefs or even a lack of awareness of one's racial, gender, or social group attitudes and beliefs (Greenwald & Banaji, 1995; Bargh, 2007; Wilson & Brekke, 1994). Second, both types of attitudes and beliefs can be influenced by any number of sources. Perhaps unsurprisingly, social norms, relevant information, and persuasive messages can all influence individuals' explicit and implicit attitudes and beliefs (Chaiken, Liberman, & Eagly, 1989; Eagly & Chaiken, 1993; Petty & Cacioppo, 1986). More surprising, is that even relatively small bits of information can have large impacts. For example, exposure to a single member of a known group can influence attitudes toward the entire group (e.g., Smith, 1992; Fazio, 1989).

It is possible, then, that the mere presence of Michelle Obama in the American spotlight could influence Whites' attitudes toward Black women. According to research in social psychology, there are at least three possible ways in which Obama might influence Whites' attitudes. The first is that Obama could influence attitudes in a positive way. During the 1990s, Bodenhausen and colleagues conducted research suggesting that successful, positive exemplars of groups increase overall positivity toward those groups. Alternatively, work being done at Cornell University suggests that despite being well-received, Obama's impact on attitudes toward other Black women could be negative. There is a third alternative, of course: she could have no impact on attitudes toward other Black women—and indeed, there is some research that supports this possibility.

Studies done by Kunda and Oleson have found that some people can be seen as so atypical that they are considered exceptions to the rule (Kunda & Oleson, 1997; Kunda & Oleson, 1995). In their work, they found that an individual who was seen as an exception to the rule was not used as a basis for judgments about the group more generally. Thus, any potential influence that an individual Black person (in this case, Michelle Obama) has depends, at least in part, on the typicality of that Black person. To be clear, an argument has been made that Obama transcends stereotypical categories, and that many indeed see her in that light, but not that she is atypical, or rather unrepresentative, of Black Americans. And it is here that Obama's upbringing and even her physical appearance may be important. On the one hand, even in modern times, when there have been increasing numbers of professional Black women, Michelle Obama's accomplishments remain exceptional. On the other hand, Obama grew up perhaps middle class, perhaps lower-middle class. She lived in a one-bedroom apartment. Her father was a city worker and her mother was a secretary. This list of facts could easily describe many Blacks' childhoods. Likewise, much has been made of her brown skin tone. Lighter skin traditionally has been associated with elitism, education, and even the assumption that one's success could have resulted from White ancestors (Hughes & Hertel, 1990; Keith & Herring, 1991). Moreover, light-skinned Blacks are perceived as less representative of Blacks than dark-skinned Blacks (Maddox, 2004). Thus, having darker skin should result in Obama being perceived as more reflective of a typical Black person. Still, perceived typicality is subjective, and predicting whether a person will be perceived as typical versus atypical is not always straightforward (Rothbart & John, 1985; Rothbart & Lewis, 1988). Thus, it is possible that Obama could be viewed as atypical, rendering her emergence into the public largely innocuous. More likely, however, she is viewed as a representative member of the Black community, who happens to have incredible success and be largely stereotype disconfirming, in which case, simply by virtue of being a visible presence, she could have quite a powerful impact.

In 1995, Bodenhausen and colleagues conducted one of the early tests of how exposure to successful—and by most standards, positive—Blacks might influence attitudes toward their group (Bodenhausen, Schwarz, Bless, & Wanke, 1995). Specifically, the researchers measured the impact of exemplars from the contemporary mass media, such as Oprah Winfrey and Michael Jordan, on perceptions of discrimination toward Blacks in society. Perceptions of discrimination in society have been found to correlate with other, more transparent, measures of attitudes toward Blacks (e.g., McConahay, 1986). That is, the more one tends to believe that discrimination toward Blacks is still a problem, the more one also tends to have a favorable attitude toward Blacks. In their study, the researchers found that indeed, White people who were first briefly exposed to successful Blacks on a questionnaire more strongly reported a belief that discrimination was still a problem in the United States than those who were not exposed to those exemplars. Thus, as the researchers reasoned, people apparently used their current feelings toward one or two Blacks to make a judgment about the group as a whole (*see also* Fazio, 1989, for further explication of this sort of heuristic-based judgment). There were two caveats. As one might expect from the work on exceptions to the rule described above, beliefs were only generalized to the group when participants felt that the exemplars were not atypical. In addition, the researchers reported that their findings only applied to well-liked Black exemplars; attitudes toward those who were successful, but not well-liked, did not influence attitudes toward the group. This last finding no doubt offers further reason to believe that Michelle Obama could improve attitudes toward Black women.

Several years after Bodenhausen lab's research was published, another group of researchers examined the impact of positive Black exemplars on implicit, rather than explicit, attitudes. Dasgupta and Greenwald exposed participants in their studies to different types of exemplars of White and Black Americans (Dasgupta & Greenwald, 2001). One group of participants was exposed to disliked Black, and admired White, exemplars, whereas a second group was exposed to disliked White, and admired Black, exemplars. A final group was not exposed to any exemplars. The researchers found that implicit attitudes toward Blacks were more positive after exposure to the admired Black, and disliked White, exemplars. This effect remained 24 hours after the initial exposure, suggesting that these effects may be enduring, and thus, recent exposure may not be necessary. Taken together with Bodenhausen's findings, these studies offer evidence that simple exposure to Michelle Obama, so long as she is well-liked and viewed as representative of Black women, could have a positive, lasting impact on both implicit and explicit attitudes toward Black women and perhaps Blacks more generally.

However, an opposing theory of the effect of affluent Blacks on attitudes toward other Blacks was proposed in the early 1990s. Specifically, Jhally and Lewis suggested that exposure to these types of exemplars might result in a sort of explanatory puzzle for White Americans (Jhally & Lewis, 1992). That is, the very existence of successful Blacks suggests that Blacks *can* be successful, yet many White Americans may have a sense that not many Blacks *are* successful. According to the researchers, this puzzle is usually resolved in one of two ways. White Americans can either attribute their sense of the state of a typical Black American to external conditions (e.g., discrimination could make opportunities less available to Blacks) or not, implying that the state of a typical Black American must have something to do with the typical Black American (e.g., he or she is lazy). To determine which was the more common resolution, Jhally and Lewis conducted focus group interviews in which they solicited White Americans' beliefs about the impact of well-known fictional portrayals of successful Blacks on their attitudes toward real Blacks. They concluded that White Americans tend to make the latter attribution, resulting in what has been termed *enlightened* racism. Note that this is exactly the opposite of what Bodenhausen and his colleagues found. One possible reason for this discrepancy, offered by Bodenhausen, is that focus groups were not the ideal method for approaching this question. That is, although focus groups are a valuable source of information, it is not clear in this case that the people questioned accurately knew the ways in which characters on television have an impact on their beliefs. Other researchers have found, for example, that people often incorrectly report how something influences their attitudes, misidentify what has an impact on their attitudes, as well as miscalculate the degree of impact for accurately identified sources of influence (Nisbett & Wilson, 1977; Wilson & Brekke, 1994).

Until recently, this issue with the methodology used by Jhally and Lewis, as well the lack of further evidence, rendered conclusions based on these studies tenuous, at best. Over the last few years, however, a group of researchers at Cornell University have conducted a more rigorous test of the same question. In two studies, using a method conceptually similar to that used in Bodenhausen's work, Critcher and colleagues exposed some people to a successful, well-liked Black exemplar—in fact, one of the exemplars was Barack Obama—and some were exposed to a comparable White exemplar, such as Ted Kennedy (Critcher, Risen, & Ferguson, 2010). Among other findings, people who were exposed to the successful Black exemplar were more likely to feel that racial discrimination was an excuse, rather than a valid explanation, for Blacks who failed to receive job offers and that a lack of success in Black communities resulted from issues in Black communities, rather than oppression. Again, these findings directly contradict the findings produced in Bodenhausen's lab. One possible explanation for the inconsistency in results is that there has been a real shift in the effect of a positive Black exemplar on White Americans' attitudes. Perhaps now, for example, there are so many positive Black exemplars that prejudice no longer seems a viable or attractive explanation for the perceived state of Black society. Thus, individuals believe that Blacks are to blame if they are not successful, resulting in a negative attitude toward them. Moreover, now that the very pinnacle of success, the presidency, has been achieved by a Black man, racism might hardly seem an issue—particularly because White Americans voted for President Barack Obama, conceivably a quite poignant indication that Whites are no longer prejudiced. Alternatively, the discrepancy in findings might reflect an issue with the interpretation of the survey items, rather than a true discrepancy. That is, one's feelings about racial discrimination may no longer be as closely correlated with one's attitudes toward Blacks as they once were. Thus, a different measure of attitudes could find a positive effect of successful Black exemplars, despite a belief that prejudice is waning, and the Bodenhausen and Critcher findings would not be truly contradictory. This is an easily testable proposition. For now, however, the reasons for the discrepancy between the two labs results, and thus the answer to whether and how Michelle Obama might influence attitudes toward Black women, are still unclear. It is worth noting, however, that recent work on another line of research has yielded results consistent with those of Critcher and colleagues. Namely, research on licensing has found that people store up psychological credit that they can use at a later time (Monin & Miller, 2001). For example, hiring a Black person, being nice to a Black person, perhaps even simply liking a Black person, and certainly voting for a Black person may license individuals to be more negative to Blacks more generally. Note that in this research, it is not clear that an attribution about Blacks is being made, but rather that being positive toward one Black person gives one license to dislike, or hold negative beliefs about, other Black people. Nevertheless, the result is the same: a positive exemplar could be negative for the group more generally.

CONCLUSION

The Obamas' meteoric rise has been astonishing. But part of this was predicted several years ago, at least for President Obama. His life story, accomplishments, and oratory all hinted at the position of power in which he has now found himself. The same cannot be said for Michelle Obama. Maybe she married the man who would become the first Black President and leader of the free world. It was hard work and discipline, however, which lead her from the Southside of Chicago to Princeton, then to Harvard Law School, and on to numerous professional positions. She has defied many odds to be a success in her own right as well as a loving and supportive mother and wife. She defies many of the stereotypes by which Black women often find themselves pigeonholed to become respected for her compassion, intelligence, beauty, and even style. We cannot say for sure what type of impact she will have on Americans and others beyond our shores in how they come to view Black women. The research suggests, however, that there is no guarantee that her position as the first Black First Lady will serve to erode away at implicit assumptions that many people may make about Black women. There remains a monumental possibility, however, that she will do just that. Whether we are at the beginning of something auspicious, only time and hard data will tell.

REFERENCES

Allport, G. W. (1935). Attitudes. In C. Murchison (Ed.), *Handbook of social psychology* (pp. 798–844). Worcester, MA: Clark University Press.

Banaji, M. R. & Greenwald, A. G. (1995). Implicit gender stereotyping in judgments of fame. *Journal of Personality and Social Psychology, 68*, 181–198.

Banaji, M. R. & Hardin, C. D. (1996). Automatic stereotyping. *Psychological Science, 7*, 136–141.

Banaji, M. R., Hardin, C., & Rothman, A. J. (1993). Implicit stereotyping in person judgment. *Journal of Personality and Social Psychology, 65*, 272–281.

Bargh, J. A. (2007). Social psychological approaches to consciousness. In P. Zalazo & M. Moskovitch (Eds.), *The Cambridge handbook of consciousness* (pp. 555–569). New York: Cambridge University Press.

Beale, F. (1970). Double jeopardy: To be Black and female. *The Black Woman: An Anthology*, edited by T. Cade. New York: Signet.

Bigg, M. (2008, November 1) . Michelle Obama softens image for first lady role. *Reuters*. Retrieved from http://www.reuters.com, last accessed February 4, 2010.

Bodenhausen, G. V., Schwarz, N., Bless, H., & Wanke, M. (1995). Effects of atypical exemplars on racial beliefs: Enlightened racism or generalized appraisals? *Journal of Experimental Social Psychology, 31*, 48–63.

Brown, D. L., & Leiby, R. (2008, November 21). Michelle Obama affirms Black women's self image. *The Washington Post*. Retrieved from http://www.washingtonpost.com, last accessed February 4, 2010.

Brown, J. D. (1998). *The self.* New York: McGraw-Hill.

Burton, C., & Jones, S. (2008, November 17). Beautiful Black: Michelle Obama's influence. *ABC News*. Retrieved from http://abclocal.go.com, last accessed February 4, 2010.

Cadet, D. (2008, August 28). Michelle Obama frees Black women form stereotypes. Message posted to http://open.salon.com/blog/crabby_golightly, last accessed February 4, 2010.

Chaiken, S., Liberman, A. & Eagly, A. H. (1989). Heuristic and systematic information processing within and beyond the persuasion context. In Uleman, J. S. & Bargh, J. A. (Eds.), *Unintended thought* (pp. 212–252). New York: Guilford Press.

Childs, E. C. (2005). Behind the stereotypes of the "angry Black woman": An exploration of Black women's responses to interracial relationships. *Gender & Society, 19*, 544–561.

Cole, H. (2008, September). The real Michelle Obama. *Ebony*. Retrieved from http://www.ebonyjet.com, last accessed February 4, 2010.

Collins, P. H. (1990). *Black feminist thought: Knowledge, consciousness, and the politics of empowerment*. New York: Routledge.

Collins, P. H. (2000). *Black feminist thought*. (2nd. Ed). New York: Routledge.

Critcher, C. Risen, J. & Ferguson, M. J. (2010, January). If he can do it, so can they: Exposure to successful Black exemplars unintentionally shifts explanations for racial disparities. Paper presented at the Society of Personality and Social Psychology, Las Vegas, Nevada.

Dann, C. (2008). Michelle Obama talks fatherhood. *MSNBC*. Retrieved from http://www.MSNBC.MSN.com, last accessed February 4, 2010.

Dasgupta, N., & Greenwald, A.G. (2001). On the malleability of automatic attitudes: Combating automatic prejudice with images of likes and disliked individuals. *Journal of Personality and Social Psychology, 81*, 800–814.

Davis, A. Y. (1981). *Women, race and class*. New York: Random House.

Doss, D., & Friery, K. (Producers). (2009). Obama-Clinton Power Duo [Television broadcast]. New York, NY: Time Warner Center studios.

Dowd, Maureen (2007, April 25). She's not buttering him up. *The New York Times*. Retrieved from http://www.nytimes.com, last accessed February 4, 2010.

Eagly, A. H., & Chaiken, S. (1993). *The psychology of attitudes*. Fort Worth, TX: Harcourt, Brace, & Janovich.

Ellis, R. (2008, November). A conversation with Michelle Obama. *Good Housekeeping*. Retrieved from http://www.goodhousekeeping.com, last accessed February 4, 2010.

Fazio, R. H. (1989). On the power and functionality of attitudes: The role of attitude accessibility. In A. R. Pratkanis, S. J. Breckler, & A. G. Greenwald (Eds.), *Attitude structure and function* (pp. 153–180). Mahwah, NJ: Erlbaum.

Fazio, R. H., Sanbonmatsu, D. M., Powell, M. C., & Kardes, F. R. (1986). On the automatic activation of attitudes. *Journal of Personality and Social Psychology, 50*, 229–238.

Fishbein, M. (1963). An investigation of the relationships between beliefs about an object and the attitude toward that object. *Human Relations, 16*, 233–240.

Fishbein, M. (1967). A behavior theory approach to the relation between beliefs about an object and the attitude toward the object. In M. Fishbein (Ed.), *Readings in attitude theory and measurement* (pp. 389–400). New York, John Wiley.

Fishbein, M., & Ajzen, I. (1975). *Belief, attitude, intention, and behavior: An introduction to theory and research*. Reading, MA: Addison-Wesley.

Fiske, S. T., Cuddy, A. J. C., Glick, P., & Xu, J. (2002). A model of (often mixed) stereotype content: Competence and warmth respectively follow from perceived status and competition. *Journal of Personality and Social Psychology, 82*, 878—902.

Gilbert, D. T., & Hixon, J. G. (1991). The trouble of thinking: Activation and application of stereotypic beliefs. *Journal of Personality and Social Psychology, 60*, 509–517.

Givhan, R. (2009, June). Echoes of TV's First Lady: Michelle Obama's last true cultural antecedent is "Cosby's" Clair Huxtable. *The Washington Post*. Retrieved from http://www.washingtonpost.com, last accessed February 4, 2010.

Goff, P. A., Thomas, M. A., & Jackson, M. C. (2008). "Ain't I a woman?": Towards an intersectional approach to person perception and group-based harms. *Sex Roles, 59*, 392–403.

Greenwald, A. G., & Banaji, M. R. (1995). Implicit social cognition: Attitudes, self-esteem, and stereotypes. *Psychological Review, 102*, 4–27.

Hornick, E. (2008, August 25). Michelle Obama looking to pull off a message of unity. *CNN.* Retrieved from http://edition.cnn.com, last accessed February 4, 2010.

Hughes, M., & Hertel, B.R. (1990). The significance of color remains: A study of life chances, mate selection, and ethnic consciousness among Black Americans. *Social Forces, 68*, 1105–1120.

Jaffe, I. (2008, April 18). Michelle Obama: Candor, controversy on the stamp. *NPR.* Retrieved from http://www.npr.org, last accessed February 4, 2010.

James-Johnson, A. (2008, August 28). Michelle Obama didn't fit the stereotype. Message posted to http://weblogs.sun-sentinel.com, last accessed February 4, 2010.

Jeffries v. Harris County Community Action Association, 615 F.2d 1025, 1029 (5th Cir. 1980).

Jenkins v. Blue Cross Mutual Hospital Insurance, Inc., 538 F.2d 164, 165 (7th Cir. 1976).

Jewell, K. S. (1993). *From mammy to Miss America and beyond: Cultural images and the shaping of U.S. social policy.* New York: Routledge.

Jhally, S., & Lewis, J. (1992). *Enlightened racism: The Cosby Show, audiences, and the myth of the American dream.* Boulder, CO: Westview Press.

Jones, J. M. (2009, April 2). Michelle Obama's favorable rating eclipses her husband's. Retrieved from http://www.gallup.com, last accessed February 4, 2010.

Keen, J. (2007, May 11). Michelle Obama: Campaigning her way. *USA Today.* Retrieved from http://www.usatoday.com, last accessed February 4, 2010.

Keith, V. M., & Herring, C. (1991). Skin tone and stratification in the Black community. *American Journal of Sociology, 97*, 760–778.

Kelley, R. (2008, February 28). A real wife, in a real marriage. *Newsweek.* Retrieved from http://www.newsweek.com, last accessed February 4, 2010.

King, D. K. (1988). Multiple jeopardy, multiple consciousness: The context of a black feminist ideology. *Signs, 14*(1), 42–72.

Komblut, A. E. (2007, May 11). Michelle Obama's career timeout: For now, weight shifts in work-family tug or war. *The Washington Post.* Retrieved from http://www.washingtonpost.com, last accessed February 4, 2010.

Kunda, Z., & Oleson, K. C. (1995). Maintaining stereotypes in the face of disconfirmation: Constructing grounds for subtyping deviants. *Journal of Personality and Social Psychology, 68*, 565–579.

Kunda, Z., & Oleson, K. C. (1997). When exceptions prove the rule: How extremity of deviance determines deviants' impact on stereotypes. *Journal of Personality and Social Psychology, 72*, 965–979.

Langley, M. (2008, February 11). Michelle Obama solidifies her role in the election. *The Wall Street Journal*. Retrieved from http://www.online.wsj.com, last accessed February 4, 2010.

Levinson, M. (2008, June 4). Michelle: Barack's bitter or better half? *BBC News*. Retrieved from http://news.bbc.co.uk, last accessed February 4, 2010.

Lewis, K. (2009). *Michelle Obama presents modern image for Black women: Helping families find work-life balance will be one of her causes*. Retrieved from America. gov, last accessed February 4, 2010.

Lightfoot, E. (2008). *Michelle Obama: First Lady of Hope*. Guilford, CT: The Lyons Press.

Lubin, J. (2009, March 18). Michelle Obama: Breaking stereotypes, promoting health. Message posted to http://www.publicsquarecom.com, last accessed February 4, 2010.

Maddox, K. (2004). Perspective on racial phenotypicality bias. *Personality and Social Psychology Review, 8*, 383–401.

Malkin, M. (2008, February 20). Michelle Obama's America—and mine. Message posted to http://michellemalkin.com, last accessed February 4, 2010.

Mast, M. S. (2004). Men are hierarchical, women are egalitarian: An implicit gender stereotype. *Swiss Journal of Psychology, 63*, 107–111.

McConahay, J. B. (1986). Modern racism, ambivalence, and the modern racism scale. In J. F. Dovidio & S. L. Gaertner (Eds.), *Prejudice, discrimination, and racism* (pp. 91–125). Orlando, FL: Academic Press.

Mitchell, M. (2008, June 19). Michelle Obama bitter? Not likely. *Chicago Suntimes*. Retrieved from http://www.suntimes.com, last accessed February 4, 2010.

Monin, B., & Miller, D. T. (2001). Moral credentials and the expression of prejudice. *Journal of Personality and Social Psychology, 81*, 33–43.

Mundy, L. (2008). *Michelle: A biography*. New York, NY: Simon & Schuster.

Nelson, S. A. (2008, July 20). Black. Female. Accomplished. Attacked. *The Washington Post*. Retrieved from http://www.washingtonpost.com, last accessed February 4, 2010.

Newton-Small, J. (2008, January 24). Michelle Obama finds her voice too. *Time*. Retrieved from http://www.time.com, last accessed February 4, 2010.

Nisbett, R. &, Wilson, T. (1977). Telling more than we can know: Verbal reports on mental processes. *Psychological Review, 84*, 231–259.

Norris, M. (2007, July 9). Spouses on the campaign trail: Michelle Obama sees election as test for America. *All Things Considered* NPR.

Nosek, B. A., Banaji, M. & Greenwald, A. G. (2002). Harvesting implicit group attitudes and beliefs from a demonstration web site. *Group Dynamics: Theory, Research and Practice, 6*, 101–115.

O'Reilly, B., Tabacoff, D., & Sohnen, A. (Producers) (2008, February 28). Does Michelle Obama dislike America? *The O'Reilly Factor*. Retrieved from http://www.foxnews.com/oreilly, last accessed February 4, 2010.

O'Reilly, B., Tabacoff, D., & Sohnen, A. (Producers) (2008, September 16). Obama Chronicles. *The O'Reilly Factor*. Retrieved from http://www.foxnews.com/oreilly, last accessed February 4, 2010.

Oinounou, M. & Kapp, B. (2008, February 19). Michelle Obama takes heat for saying she's "proud of my country" for the first time. Retrieved from http://www.foxnews.com, last accessed February 4, 2010.

Parks, G. S. & Roberson, Q. M. (2009). Michelle Obama: Intersectionality, implicit bias, and third-party associative discrimination in the 2008 election. *Hastings Women's Law Journal, 20,* 3–44.

Phillips, C. M., Brown, T. L., & Parks, G. S. (2010). Barack, Michelle and the Complexities of a Black "Love Supreme." *The Obamas and a (Post) Racial America,* edited by G. S. Parks & M. W. Hughey. NY: Oxford University Press.

Petty, R. E., & Cacioppo, J. T. (1986). *Communication and Persuasion: Central and Peripheral Routes to Attitude Change.* New York: Springer-Verlag.

Powell, M., & Kantor, J. (2008). After attacks, Michelle Obama looks for a new introduction. *The New York Times.* Retrieved from http://www.nytimes.com, last accessed February 4, 2010.

Rivera, Z. (2008, December 22). Who is Michelle Obama: Angry Black woman or supportive spouse? Retrieved from http://www.diversityinc.com, last accessed February 4, 2010.

Romano, L. (2009, March 31). Michelle's image: From off-putting to spot-on. *The Washington Post.* Retrieved from http://www.washingtonpost.com, last accessed February 4, 2010.

Rossi, R. (2007, January 20). The woman behind Obama. *Chicago Sun-Times.* Retrieved from http://www.suntimes.com, last accessed February 4, 2010.

Rothbart, M., & John, O.P. (1985). Social categorization and behavioral episodes: A cognitive analysis of the effects of intergroup contact. *Journal of Social Issues, 41,* 81–104.

Rothbart, M., & Lewis, S. (1988). Inferring category attributes from exemplar attributes: Geometric shapes and social categories. *Journal of Personality and Social Psychology, 55,* 861–872.

Rudman, L. A., Greenwald, A. G., & McGhee, D. E. (2001). Implicit self-concept and evaluative implicit gender stereotypes: Self and ingroup share desirable traits. *Personality and Social Psychology Bulletin, 27,* 1164–1178.

Rudman, L. A. & Kilianski, S. E. (2000). Implicit and explicit attitudes toward female authority. *Personality and Social Psychology Bulletin, 26,* 1315–1328.

Samuels, A. (2008, November 1). What Michelle Can Teach Us. *Newsweek.* Retrieved from http://www.newsweek.com, last accessed February 4, 2010.

Smith, E. R. (1992). The role of exemplars in social judgment. In L. L. Martin & A. Tesser (Eds.). *The construction of social judgment* (pp. 107–132). Hillsdale, NY: Erlbaum.

Stangor, C. (Ed.). (2000). *Stereotypes and prejudice: Essential readings.* Philadelphia, PA: Psychology Press.

Stanley, A. (2008, June 19). Michelle Obama shows her warmer side on "The View." *The New York Times.* Retrieved from http://www.nytimes.com, last accessed February 4, 2010.

Tajfel, H. (1982). Social psychology of intergroup relations. *Annual Review of Psychology, 33,* 1–39.

Thompson, K. (2008, July 20). Can Michelle defy stereotypes? Message posted to http://www.newser.com, last accessed February 4, 2010.

Timberlake, J. M. & Estes, S. B. (2007). Do racial and ethnic stereotypes depend on the sex of target group members?: Evidence from a survey-based experiment. *Sociological Quarterly, 48,* 399–433.

Weber, R., & Crocker, J. (1983). Cognitive processes in the revision of stereotypic beliefs. *Journal of Personality and Social Psychology, 45,* 961–977.

West, C. M. (1995). Mammy, Sapphire, and Jezebel: Historical images of Black women and their implications for psychotherapy. *Psychotherapy, 32,* 458–466.

White, M. J. & White, G. B. (2006). Implicit and explicit occupational gender stereotypes. *Sex Roles, 55,* 259–266.

Wilson, T. D., & Brekke, N. (1994). Mental contamination and mental correction: Unwanted influences on judgments and evaluations. *Psychological Bulletin, 116,* 117–142.

Wolfe, R. (2008, February 25). Barack's rock. *Newsweek.* Retrieved from http://www.newseek.com, last accessed February 4, 2010.

Zakin, C. (2007, July 20). Michelle Obama plays unique role in campaign. *MSNBC.* Retrieved from http://www.MSNBC.MSN.com, last accessed February 4, 2010.

First Lady Michelle Obama: Getting Past the Stereotypes

Julianne Malveaux

She is a brown-skinned, "solid" sister, whose warm welcoming smile speaks to her own self-confidence. She is tall, gorgeous, well spoken, and an innovative dresser. She is a nurturer–mother to Sasha and Malia, helpmate to President Barack Obama, and an inspiration to a nation. And she is an ordinary Black woman, our Michelle Obama, a sister whose Chicago working-class roots reflect those of so many African-Americans, a college graduate whose attendance at Princeton was a function of both her own academic achievement and the openness that affirmative action encouraged in the 1970s and 1980s. She is a Harvard-educated lawyer whose commitment to community led her to an influential position in the Chicago hospital system. And still, for far too many, she is a symbol and a stereotype.

Shanette Porter and Gregory Parks wax and wane between embracing Michelle Obama's individuality and placing her in stereotypical context. Their well-researched essay seems to twist a Rubik's Cube, as if they expect that research and exploration will line things up with such consistency that they can crack the code of Michelle Obama. They come closest when they state, "to confine Obama to a stereotype, any stereotype, is to overlook or distort fundamental aspects of her life, personality and accomplishments." With this comment, strategically placed in the middle of the essay, Porter and Parks magnify the complexity of their task to redefine images of Black women by insisting on Michelle Obama's individuality and uniqueness. At the same time, their review of the literature and reprising of a litany of stereotypes suggest that their goal is both to connect Michelle Obama to the stereotypes and to create a space in which she can transcend them.

The Obama presidency has forced our nation to confront a myriad of stereotypes about Black men (note the swagger), Black women (she's not Sapphire), Black families (more than a third of Black children are raised in homes with both their biological parents), and Black identity. The intersection of race, class, and gender has been so rich that the presence and image of Michelle Obama has become a proxy for an angst that is rooted in Black women's history of exclusion. Sisters with hair issues focus on hers; those with ward-robe issues have subjected this first lady to a not-unusual scrutiny of her every wardrobe decision. She has been accused of being too earthy (wearing shorts on Air Force One) and too elegant (gracing magazine covers) at the same time. She is flesh, blood, sister, and woman.

Michelle's cover woman status adds complexity to the scholarship about the marginalization and commoditization of Black women. When we are throwing trump cards on the table, which prevails? First Lady Obama or the latest video vixen? Even the lofty image of First Lady is not sufficient to pro-tect Mrs. Obama from the vitriol of those who have described her in the most ugly and awful racially pejorative terms, even after she and her family moved into the White House. This hate is firmly rooted in both institutional racism and in the stereotypes that often define and constrain Black women. Our First Lady's image and presence both soften and harden attitudes about Black women.

First Lady Michelle Obama allows us the opportunity to consider images of Black women and to redefine them. Beyond the images and stereotypes, however, there is a woman with a fascinating and complex story to share. Let's not let the symbol swallow the sister because, as we learned when Michelle Obama spoke in Denver on August 25, 2008, she is a sister, scholar, lawyer, mother, wife, daughter, a complex woman whose intricacies are far more interesting and important than her connection to historical, and often demeaning, stereotypes of Black women.

As Porter and Parks conclude, "Only time and hard data will tell" the whole story of Michelle Obama's impact on our popular culture. I agree, and I would add that Michelle Obama's presence in the public space has infused an interesting and welcome complexity in the contemporary dialogue. Whatever the permanent impact, in the short run, the Obama effect has been to layer contemporary stereotypes with the current contradiction of an ines-capable and also counter-stereotypical presence of a phenomenal, amazing, and profoundly American woman.

CHAPTER 7

Barack, Michelle, and the Complexities of a Black "Love Supreme"[1]

Clarenda M. Phillips, Tamara L. Brown, and Gregory S. Parks

> So much of what is best in us is bound up in our love of family, that it remains the measure of our stability because it measures our sense of loyalty.
>
> *−Haniel Long*

Raymond Pace Alexander (1897–1974) and his wife Sadie Tanner Mossell Alexander (1898–1989) were luminaries in many ways. Raymond was born into a large working-class family in Philadelphia. His mother died shortly after giving birth to his youngest sibling, which left Raymond self-supporting from age 12. Raymond graduated from the University of Pennsylvania's Wharton School in 1920 and Harvard Law School in 1923. Professionally, he served as an attorney, city council member, and judge on the Court of Common Pleas in Philadelphia. Raymond was also remarkably active in numerous civic, fraternal, professional, and social organizations throughout his life. He was a Mason and a member of Alpha Phi Alpha Fraternity, the first intercollegiate fraternity for African-American men. He also served as an active member and National Vice President of the first fraternity for African-American men—Sigma Pi Phi (The Boulé). He was also a member of such groups as the Association for the Study of Negro Life and History and the Philadelphia Cotillion Society. Raymond was active in World Peace through Law and the National Bar Association—the African-American equivalent of the American Bar Association. Raymond, in fact, was cofounder of the National Bar Journal and its associate editor for 4 years (Canton, 2010; University of Pennsylvania, 2010a).

In 1923, Raymond married the equally accomplished, Sadie Tanner Mossell—his sister's best friend and her sorority sister. Sadie was born in Philadelphia, the youngest of three children and a member of an old and distinguished family. Her maternal grandfather, Benjamin Tanner, was a Bishop in the African Methodist Episcopal Church. Sadie's father, Aaron Mossell, was the first African-American to graduate from the University of

Pennsylvania's Law School. Her uncle, Nathan Mossell, was the first African-American to graduate from the University of Pennsylvania's Medical School. When she reached high school, Sadie moved to Washington, D.C. with her uncle, Dr. Lewis Baxter Moore, dean at Howard University. Dr. Moore had been the first African-American to earn a Ph.D. from the University of Pennsylvania and the fifth in the history of the United States. Sadie attended M Street High School in D.C. and graduated in 1915. She earned her undergraduate degree from the University of Pennsylvania in 1918. In 1921, she earned her Ph.D. in economics from the University of Pennsylvania, making her the first African-American woman to earn a Ph.D. in economics. Sadie went on, in 1927, to become the first African-American woman to earn her law degree from University of Pennsylvania. Thereupon, she joined her husband's law practice. Professionally, she served as Assistant Solicitor for the City of Philadelphia and as a member of President Truman's Committee on Human Rights. Sadie served as the first National President for Delta Sigma Theta Sorority—the second oldest and largest African-American sorority. She also served as secretary of the National Bar Association and held leadership roles on the National Committee of the American Civil Liberties Union and the National Urban League. Raymond and Sadie had two daughters, Mary Elizabeth (1934) and Rae Pace (1937), and lived a long life together (Mack, 2002; Nier, 1998; University of Pennsylvania, 2010b).

The biographies of Raymond and Sadie Alexander are compelling not so much for what they achieved individually and collectively. They are compelling because they are representative of so many healthy African-American marriages and families. When *The Cosby Show* first aired in 1984, some critics decried it. To some, the representation of a positive and progressive Black family where the mother and the father were extremely well-educated and successful was unrealistic (Inniss & Feagin, 1995). Although highly educated, successful, and community-oriented Black families are not as commonplace as one might hope, they exist. And they have existed for decades. This chapter highlights the unique position that the Obamas are in as a couple and family and how that position has the potential, although fraught with complexities, to have a positive impact on contemporary Black families.

IMAGES OF AND DATA ON BLACK MEN AND WOMEN IN RELATIONSHIPS

Moynihan's 1965 report, *The Negro Family: The Case for National Action*, created a national debate among politicians and scholars that is still raging today. This report, now known as the *Moynihan Report*, blamed high rates of African-American unemployment on an African-American matriarchal family structure. The supposed matriarchal structure of African-American families was said to deny African-American men power, which increased female-headed households, illegitimate children, and welfare dependence in successive generations. Described as a "tangle of pathology," the African-American family was said to be the cause of African-American inequality—not racism and discrimination. Therefore, 100 years after the end of slavery African-Americans were still believed to be culturally inferior. Although some may continue to assert that the African-American family is weak and pathological, others view it as resilient and adaptive as it has sustained an entire people group for more than 300 years in an oppressive and racist society.

Even before Moynihan's infamous report, White Americans judged African-Americans by the cultural norms governing their own behavior. For example, by contrasting the disposition of African-American women with the cult of "true" womanhood (i.e., purity, piety, submissiveness, femininity, domesticity), White Americans cast African-Americans as deviant and uncivilized. After all, what civilized group of men would not take on their "natural" roles of provider and protector so that their women could take on their "natural" role as homemaker? Ignoring the racist social structure of the United States, which mitigated more rapid assimilation into White American culture, Whites purported that African-Americans were unable to assimilate because of their cultural deficiencies. Thus, the dominant culture has attempted to define, and therefore control, African-Americans through a carefully constructed racist ideology that linked African-Americans' physical traits to deviant psychological traits. This racist ideology has been most clearly depicted in White American stereotypes about African-Americans. Through stereotypical images, White Americans have justified the racism carried out against African-Americans, limited their access to societal resources, and denied them civil rights.

The most prominent stereotypes that have affected the African-American family include: the lazy, shiftless male (unwilling to work to provide for his family) and Sapphire (the dominant, emasculating female; Jewell, 1993). These contrived images were designed to give Whites social and economic control of African-American women by labeling African-American men as unemployable and African-American women as undesirable or unladylike. When African-American wives entered into (or remained in) the labor force when their husbands were unemployed or underemployed, they were portrayed as taking on the male role rather than as doing what was necessary for family survival.

AFRICAN-AMERICAN FAMILIES: HISTORICAL CONSIDERATIONS

The influence of Africa and America on the organization of the African-American family has been a long-standing debate (*see*, for example, Billingsley,

1968; DuBois, 1969; Frazier, 1966; Herskovitz, 1958; Sudarkasa, 2006). Although a host of varying perspectives has been advanced to explain African-American family organization, three have predominated: the cultural-deviant perspective, the cultural-equivalent perspective, and the cultural-variant perspective. The cultural-deviant perspective contends that African culture was lost during slavery, and therefore, the weak, contemporary African-American family structure is a result of an unwillingness to assimilate to Eurocentric values. Implicit in this view is that for African-Americans to have healthy, strong families, they must become more like White families in their structure and organization. Similarly, the cultural-equivalent perspective recognizes the existence of a distinct culture among African-Americans but asserts that all groups should adopt the White American nuclear family structure to ensure success in the United States. In contrast to these approaches, the cultural-variant perspective affirms that African-American families are products of both a transcendent African culture and an American culture, which allowed African-Americans to adapt to the structural constraints of the United States and create a legitimate family form that helps negotiate in a structurally oppressive society. This last view provides a framework that allows us to understand the forms and functions of the African-American family, including the reliance on an extended family network, values and behaviors, and gender roles.

Whereas White families were patriarchal because of the economic dependence of White women, African-American marriages have been more egalitarian (Staples, 1978). The peculiar way slavery was practiced in the United States did not allow African-American men to take on a superordinate role because African-American women were not dependent on them. As a result, African-American marriages during slavery were the result of cultural, social, and psychological factors—not economic factors.

African families, as all families, have two components for membership. The first is consanguinity, which is kinship based on a biological connection, and the second is conjugality, which is kinship based on a legal connection. African families have traditionally been organized by consanguineal relations where newly married couples moved into an attached dwelling of their extended family. As a result, the consanguineal group was dominant over the conjugal group in most areas. Therefore, the stability of the African family was in the large number of consanguineal members and not in the legal bond between conjugal pairs. Both men and women depended on their extended family networks and spouses for their livelihood (Shimkin & Uchendu, 1978; Sudarkasa, 2006). Although the extended family network was essential for African survival in America, early Africans, enslaved and free, also valued marital unions and committed themselves to these lifelong partnerships.

Although very few accurate records were kept for marriages among enslaved Africans, Billingsley reports that approximately 85% of free Blacks were married in 1798 (Billingsley, 1992).

As the United States has shifted into a post-industrial economy, family forms have also shifted. As divorce rates have increased and single adults delay marriage, the two-parent family is decreasing among all populations. Because African-Americans have been more significantly affected by the structural changes in society, their marriage rates have declined more sharply than the rates of other groups. For example, in 1970, marriage was the primary African-American family form with more than 68% of African American families being headed by a married couple; however, in 2008, only 33% of African-American families were headed by a married couple (U.S. Census). These demographic changes have captured the attention of politicians and scholars, which has resulted in an over-examination of African-American single-parent households and a neglect of African-American two-parent households.

AFRICAN-AMERICAN FAMILY ECONOMIC PATTERNS

Purchased from a Dutch ship in 1619 and forced into indentured servitude and then slavery, African women labored alongside African men in plantation fields across the south. After emancipation, with widespread *de jure* and *de facto* racial segregation in housing, employment, and schooling, African-American women's participation in the paid labor force was essential for group survival and self-determination. Although patriarchy provided privileges to White men and some protection and privilege to White women, African-American men were not allowed to participate fully in the labor market. As a result, African-American men were not able to earn enough income to keep African-American women out of the labor force nor protect them from harsh labor conditions. Therefore, African-American families have historically included two earners.

During slavery, a sexual division of labor was common in some tasks. Plantation owners trained only men the crafts of carpentry, stonemasonry, milling, and shoemaking whereas women were taught spinning and sewing (Matthaei, 1982). Men were also selected to chop wood, clear land, and plow the fields. Women's work involved midwifery, nursing and caring for White children, washing, and performing personal service work for the White mistress. However, this division of labor did not hold in the fields or industrial work where profit was the primary motivator (Jones, 1985). Instead, availability and strength were more important than a slave's sex. Interestingly, although women did engage in men's work, there is little evidence that men engaged in women's work (Matthaei, 1982). The result of African-American women engaging in men's work was a greater sense of independence and equality.

Upon emancipation, in an attempt to combat sexual and economic exploitation, more than one-third of African-American women refused to work for White planters, which created a labor shortage (Matthaei, 1982). Importantly, this allowed African-American women to focus on food and clothing production for their own families. With the development of the sharecropping system, African-American women joined their husbands and other extended family members in the fields (Jones, 1985). In most farm households, men worked the fields while women engaged in the double duty of field and domestic work (Giddings, 1984).

At the beginning of the twentieth century, 41% of African-American women were in the labor force (Weiner, 1985). Because they were excluded from other jobs, the majority was still restricted to jobs in agriculture and domestic service (44%, respectively), with only 1% located in professional occupations (Weiner, 1985). In rural areas, more than half of the single employed women worked as servants in White households, 25% provided personal services like laundering, and 20% worked on farms (Reiff, Dahlin, & Smith, 1993). Ninety percent of African-American women in the urban south were domestic servants.

The employment pattern of African-Americans did not shift until after World War I. With a labor shortage and war production, African-Americans migrated north where European immigrants were given preference over African-Americans. As a result, African-American women continued their tradition of paid work because African-American men did not earn sufficient wages to support a wife and family (Amott & Matthaei, 1996). Relief from the disastrous effects of the Great Depression arrived with the economic stimulation of weapon production for World War II. One-half of the African-American population lived in urban areas as a result of the collapse of tenant farming during the 1930s and increased employment opportunities in urban factories (Harris, 1992). Although there were post-World War II setbacks, African-American women were able to expand on the gains made during the war.

The job growth, political organization, and anti-discrimination legislation of the 1960s bolstered African-American women's numbers in white-collar jobs. Between 1950 and 1970, the percentage of African-American women in clerical positions grew from 5% to 21% (Harris, 1992). Furthermore, affirmative action helped African-American women obtain jobs in local, state, and federal governments (Harris, 1992). Despite occupational mobility, racism and sexism colluded to keep African-American women's wages low (Amott & Matthaei, 1996).

By the mid-1970s, the manufacturing economic boom began to slow. African-Americans as a group were the last to benefit from economic prosperity but the first to suffer in the economic recession. African-Americans were 2.5 times more likely to be unemployed than their White counterparts (Amott & Matthaei, 1996). Higher rates of African-American male unemployment, coupled with low wages, increased the percentage of African-American women in the labor force to 58% by 1988 (Amott & Matthaei, 1996).

Racism continues to impact African-American employment. African-Americans experience higher rates of unemployment today, and their occupational mobility within management and other professions has been limited (Collins, 1997). Furthermore, African-Americans with only high school diplomas have been pushed into low-skilled work and are unable to advance from low-paying jobs (Wilson, 1997). Cannon (1988) asserts that "the persistent obstacles of poverty, gender discrimination, and racial prejudice continue to enslave the Black [families] to hunger, disease, and the highest rate of unemployment since World War II." Given the detrimental impact of employment discrimination, African-Americans have developed their own response to survive in a racially hostile society, a response that has not been without its challenges. One such challenge has been the influence of the strong economic role that African-American women have had in their households on the marital relationship. Unlike White women, African-American women were more economically independent, which allowed many of them to develop attitudes of freedom and equality, attitudes that created tensions in African-American marriages.

AFRICAN-AMERICAN FAMILIES: GENDER ROLES

In addition to the high value placed on family and community, African-Americans have demonstrated a commitment to learning and service to others. As Sadie Turner Mossell's life exemplifies, African-Americans often relied on extended family networks to create educational opportunities for their children. Historically, African-American families have sent their daughters to college because their sons had access to a greater variety of occupations (Staples, 1996). By going to college, African-American females could pursue occupations (e.g., school teacher) other than domestic service.

Furthermore, African-American communities have historically developed oppositional cultures to resist racism, refute stereotypical societal images, and celebrate and maintain their own cultures. Because African-American communities and families are matricentric, rather than matriarchal, the role of women as culture bearers has been critical. Patricia Hill Collins (1990) states, "The power of Black women was the power to make culture, to transmit folkways, norms, and customs as well as build shared ways of seeing the world" (p. 147). This culture of resistance has allowed African-Americans to create communities to ensure survival in an oppressive society. Similarly, Leith Mullings (1996) notes that "community is essential for reconstructing ideology, as it may provide the context and validation for rejecting negative stereotypes and developing new ways of knowing" (p. 121). According to Cannon (1988), the development of community allows African-American women to share their strategies for resisting oppression while purging themselves of the self-hatred generated from racist beliefs.

African-American women developed female-centered networks, which have always played an important role in the African-American community and have effectively functioned to sustain it for centuries. The extended families of slaves were female-centered because slavery mandated that mother–child bonds take precedence over other relationships (Billingsley, 1992). Furthermore, the gendered division of some slave work provided women the opportunity to cultivate their identities separate from slave men (White, 1985). Because female slaves often did work alongside their male counterparts, their feelings of independence and equality were nurtured and strengthened. According to Deborah Gray White, African-American slave women, similar to their African ancestors, became the centers of the family to maintain stability and survival (White, 1985).

The women-centered networks in African-American families are not the result of absent men, as men are actively present in culturally significant roles within both the family and community (Collins, 1990). However, women are considered valuable contributors to the family system and community. Furthermore, Mullings (1997) explains that in the African cultures "from which slaves were removed, the definition of masculinity was not based on the dependence of women . . . men and women frequently had independent arenas and occupations, and men and women had asymmetrical but not necessarily unequal roles in society" (p. 82). Importantly, African-American women have had to play significant roles in the extended family system in the United States because racial discrimination has kept African-American male wages so low that families can only survive if there is economic cooperation between men and women. Likewise, the experiences of slaves and freed women in a society where Black men also live under the brutality of racism have taught African-American women that living without a man is an acceptable option, even when children are involved.

Another strategy African-American women employed involved the pooling of their wages to help those that were suffering. Beginning in the 1700s, African-American women organized their own mutual-aid societies to help impoverished African-Americans (Cash, 2001). With strict membership standards, these mutual-aid societies also created leadership opportunities and safe spaces for the development of gendered race consciousness for African-American women, which they used to fight equally for African-American women's and men's rights. Although White women organized to battle for their own rights, African-American women understood that their livelihood was inextricably tied to that of African-American men.

Males and Masculinity

Psychologists have traditionally defined the masculine role as those character-istics that represent adaptive functioning and socially desirable behaviors for males such as independence, assertiveness, competitiveness, and high achieve-ment. However, this masculine gender role has created a double bind for African-American men because of slavery. According to Harris (1992), slavery was a period of African-American male demasculinization because of the physical and psychological coercion used during slavery to discourage African-American male slaves from expressing conventional forms of mascu-linity. As examples of this, Harris describes how assertiveness was discour-aged, the role of provider was undermined because of the slave owners' assumed primary responsibility for the distribution of material goods within slave households, and African-American males were prevented from protect-ing their wives and children from harm because, at the slave owner's discretion, families were separated and the wives of male slaves were forced to submit to the overseer's wishes. Thus,

> the institution of slavery limited the actual and perceived independence, self-confidence, aggression, power, and even sexual behavior of African American men. . . Ironically, after slavery was abolished, African American men were confronted with expectations from Euro-Americans and the African American community to behave, feel, and think according to traditional masculine norms. . . [But] restricted access to educational and employment opportunities representative of conventional masculine status obstruct the expression of behaviors consistent with Euro-American standards. (Harris, 1992, p. 76)

Consequently, many African-American males have developed alternative ways of proving their manhood and preserving positive feelings about them-selves; they have developed an expressive pattern of behavior—including physical postures, content and flow of speech, styles of walking, and demeanor—that are dynamic and evolve over time in relation to the structural stressors and sociopolitical factors that have existed at different points in his-tory (Harris, 1992). It has been argued that the masculine behavior and expres-sions of some African-American men represent their adaptive attempts to disguise the painful emotions of shame and sadness induced by their frustrations with mainstream society; we call this adaptive because it is a style that exudes energy, activity, and coping rather than defeat, depression, and giving up (Harris, 1992).

The experience of African-American men during slavery and since has had a direct bearing on the African-American family. Despite slavery, the essence of African-American family and community life has been a positive, constructive, and even heroic experience (Marable, 1984). Moreover, as Andrew Billingsley has stated in *Black Families and the Struggle for Survival*, the extended family, racial cooperation, and the collectivist ethos are outgrowths of the unique African heritage that African-Americans still maintain (Billingsley, 1974). Yet, African-American families also bear the scars of slavery and post-slavery discrimination and oppression.

Most of the available research on African-American families focuses on African-American women; the exploration of the role of African-American men in socializing children is almost nonexistent. One exception is the work of John McAdoo (1997), who has suggested that the theoretical model often applied to African-American fathers is the provider role. That is, they are generally only portrayed as playing an instrumental role in the family—namely, protecting the family from the outside world and serving as the conduit of information and resources between the family and the outside world. However, the available data on Black fathers do not support this provider theory, a conceptualization borrowed from research on White fathers. In contrast, McAdoo (1997) reports that the greater the economic security, the more active African-American fathers are in childrearing functions, and they tend to be more actively involved in childrearing than their fathers were with them. Further, McAdoo (1997) reports that African-American fathers play many roles in their families, including provider, decision maker, nurturer, husband, and father, and that these roles inter-relate rather than operate in isolation. In terms of decision-making, middle-class African-American men tend to be more egalitarian with African-American women in childrearing.

Regarding parenting style, McAdoo (1997) says African-American fathers tend to be authoritarian, which means they expect their children to respond immediately to their commands, they almost never allow their children to display anger or throw temper tantrums, and they are moderate to very strict in their parenting attitudes. Authoritarian parents also attempt to shape, control, and evaluate behavior according to set standards, value and expect obedience, believe in forceful and punitive measures to control a child's behavior, and expect children to unquestioningly accept their views. Baumrind (1973) found that this parenting style in White fathers is one that should be changed because it is associated with a host of negative child outcomes, including low overall competence; however, for Black fathers, this parenting style actually benefits children, especially daughters. When Baumrind (1973) compared Black and White daughters of authoritarian fathers, he found the Black daughters to be exceptionally independent and at ease in the nursery setting where his observations occurred.

Unfortunately, very little is known about African-American parent–child relationships or father–child interaction in general because African-American men tend not to be included in research studies. McAdoo (1997) states, "Most researchers doing family relationship studies generally collect data on fathers from mothers and/or wives and focus on the impact of absent fathers" (p. 193). From the limited research available, we learn that African-American middle class fathers are nurturing to their children and are equally nurturing to sons and daughters (McAdoo, 1997).

AFRICAN-AMERICAN MALE AND FEMALE RELATIONSHIPS

So far, we have discussed several factors (e.g., stereotypes, economic factors) and how they have impacted the lives of African-American men and women individually, but these factors have also had profound effects on African-American male and female relationships. Negative stereotypes from the past perpetuated by Whites against African-Americans—most notably the lazy, shiftless male and domineering, emasculating female—continue to plague African-American relationships today, especially among those who have internalized these feelings and brought them into their relationships. According to Chapman (2006), many African-Americans have (consciously and subconsciously) colluded with these myths and the effect has been that African-American men and women struggle with one another rather than unite against the external forces that keep them in turmoil. Chapman (2006) described this struggle well:

> Many women say that Black men cannot be counted on because they have met a few who neglect the needs of their women and children. . . . Black men complain that Black women always want control like the character Sapphire who dominated Kingfish in *Amos 'n' Andy*. . . . Black women complain about the failures of Black men. . . . Black women often feel they bear both the burden and the responsibility for how their partners feel about being committed and loving with them. Black men often feel they are blamed for all the problems that exist in their relationships.

Economic factors have also influenced African-American male and female relationships. Although some African-Americans have made great strides in the economic arena, many have not gained the economic equality they need to take care of their families (Chapman, 2006). For example, in 1991, African-American men earned an average of $12,962 annually compared with $21,395 for White men; Black women earned the lowest income, $8,816 compared with $10,721 for White women.[2] Asks Chapman (2006):

> How can a man feel competent or capable of taking care of responsibilities when he is underemployed or unemployed? This dynamic sets up competition and disloyalty between the sexes, creating polarities that cause a sense of mistrust and disappointment. . . .one of the greatest sources of conflict between Black men and women is the myth that the women are doing so much better economically. In reality, neither gender group is faring very well in this society (p. 276).

Added to these economic issues are unbalanced sex ratios and limited marriageable mate availability. It is estimated that there are 1.5 million more African-American women in the population than African-American men, an estimate that does not include men who are sub-, un-, or underemployed or addicted to drugs (Dixon, 2007). Consequently, some African-American women are unable to find African-American men to marry because there are not enough African-American men to go around, a reality that has direct bearing on marriage rates among African-Americans.

More than just marriage rates, economics, and White stereotypes, social pressures also impinge upon African-American relationships to create a rift between the sexes that begins early in their social development. Although society and family encourage young African-American women to pursue scholastic achievement, these same forces discourage young African-American men from this goal and, instead, urge them to prove their manhood through excelling in sports, music, and hustling, a socialization process that teaches African-American men limited, if not dysfunctional, methods for gaining status (Chapman, 2006). According to Chapman, between 1976 and 1981, the number of African-American women with doctoral degrees rose 29% and the number with first professional degrees increased 71%; however, the number of African-American men with doctoral degrees decreased 10%, the number with first professional degrees dropped 12%, and an estimated 40% of the Black male population was functionally illiterate (Chapman, 2006). How does this reality affect African-American male and female relationships? One consequence is that increasingly large numbers of African-American women are unable to find suitable African-American mates and, thus, they focus on their own education and the acquisition of material goods, and, at the same time, African-American men are confused about how to provide what African-American women want and fear rejection because they do not meet certain standards (Chapman, 2006). Another consequence is that these structural conditions, combined with their perceptions of African-American men as unfaithful, untrustworthy, and transient, communicate to African-American women that they cannot rely on others to meet their material needs, protect them, or create stability in their environments (Burton & Tucker, 2009). This affects African-Americans' relationship formation and leads some African-American women to view marriage as not an option for them, which increases the prominence of permanent singlehood as a normative life-course trajectory for many African-American women.

Many African-American men and women struggle because they do not understand the underlying reasons for the tensions between them (e.g., their subconscious acceptance of negative stereotypes) and this lack of understanding makes change or improvement difficult. Yet these statistics and struggles need not define the future for African-American male and female relationships. Even while she paints the grim picture of the condition of African-American male and female relationships, Chapman (2006) is also hopeful about, and provides good directions for, the future:

> A good friendship forms the basis of a strong, durable relationship. . . . For married couples in the past, friendship was the basis of their commitment to each other. They learned how to understand each other's needs, likes, and dislikes. They learned the process of give-and-take and the ability to be less selfish. There was an acceptance of the total person that allowed patience and endurance in trying times. Black men and women need to relearn some of the 'old ways.'. . . Blacks need to recognize that they still have choices. We need to challenge the awful myth that Black men and women cannot get along. . . . Once Blacks accept total responsibility together, Black women can be relieved of bearing the social burdens alone and Black men can stop feeling undervalued and threatened. . . . Conceptualizing love as based on equality and a more balanced way of sharing power will support more devotion and create realistic love bonds.

Barack and Michelle Obama exemplify this approach to relationship well. It is no wonder their marriage is the focus of so much media attention.

THE OBAMAS: BREAKING THE MOLD

The Obamas are a highly visible role model of what healthy, fulfilling, and long-lasting relationships can look like, sorely needed at a time when divorce rates are high, marriage rates are declining, and hooking up is becoming the norm. More and more young adults are preferring "hooking up" to relationships with emotional connection. What's hooking up? As explained in a December 10, 2009 *The Times* article, hooking up refers to the phenomenon in which two people—who may not know each other well or at all—get together for the express purpose of fooling around, which can range from kissing and heavy petting to oral sex and intercourse.[3] According to the article, the hallmark of a hook-up is that physical involvement precedes an emotional relationship; in the hook-up era, the trend is sex first and dating (maybe) later and experts worry that this approach to social connection robs young adults of the opportunity to learn how to build emotional intimacy and connect with a partner on an intimate level.

Twenty percent of first marriages end in divorce within the first 5 years, 33% end within 10 years, and 43% end within 15 years (Bramlett & Mosher, 2001). Although these rates are high overall, rates are higher for African-Americans than for Whites; whereas 32% of White marriages end within 10 years, 47% of African-American marriages end within this same period (Goodwin, 2003). Added to this is the fact that African-Americans are less likely to get married than Whites. These statistics point to the U.S. need for role models of healthy, satisfying marriages, and the Obamas provide such a role model, especially for those who have grown up (or are growing up) seeing only relationship models characterized by distrust, volatility, instability, and conflict rather than mutual support, respect, and shared vision.

Indeed, it is against the backdrop of high divorce and hooking-up rates that Barack and Michelle's dating experiences, marriage, love, and advice on how to make a relationship work are shown in sharpest relief. They and their marriage embody those elements that make a marriage healthy and satisfying—namely, emotional health, physical health, trust, equity, and closeness to in-laws (Goodwin, 2003). Couples that are emotionally healthy are better able to handle the demands of marriage, and couples that are physically healthy are not only better equipped to take on marital tasks but they also create fewer burdens for the family. Inequitable relationships are those in which one partner feels he or she contributes more but receives less; successful marriages are equitable in the sense that both partners give and take in equitable measure. Trust in relationships is vitally important for all relationships. However, closeness to in-laws, although unrelated to marital success for Whites, is particularly important for African-American families (Goodwin, 2003), which is not surprising given the premium they place on extended family connectedness.

Barack and Michelle speak candidly about their relationship in their interviews with Christopher Andersen in *Barack and Michelle: Portrait of an American Marriage*. Their dating relationship began when they both worked for the law firm Sidley Austin in Chicago (Andersen, 2009). Michelle was already fully entrenched at the firm when Barack came on board, and it was her responsibility, as his advisor, to meet with him when he first arrived and acclimate him to the firm. Although Barack expressed an interest in getting to know Michelle better and would try to flirt with her, "she told Barack in no uncertain terms that she had big plans, was on the fast track, and had no time for distractions—especially men" (Andersen, 2009, p. 121). But Barack gradually wore down Michelle and after impressing her in a speech he delivered at a community organizing event, she agreed to spend a day with him on a "nondate." After that "nondate," Michelle was won over; they both were. She liked his ambition, his ability to take off his suit jacket, roll up his sleeves and relate to the average person, and his open mind and free spirit; and he liked her strength and stability, the trace of vulnerability that shown through despite her tough exterior, and the positive effect she had on him: "Michelle centered me in a sense. She made it possible for me to really concentrate on what was important in life" (Andersen, 2009, p. 135).

Unlike many other presidential families, the Obamas did not come from the top tiers of society nor did they have family wealth they could tap. According to Ackman (2003), writing in *Forbes Magazine*, the vast majority of U.S. presidents have come from the top echelon of society and some have ranked among the super-rich. Ackman (2003) notes that it is difficult to trace and compare the wealth of presidents across generations because most presidential wealth is family money, although many also had substantial personal worth. In terms of presidents in recent memory (i.e., the past five presidents), both Bush presidents came from family wealth and had multimillion-dollar personal wealth as well. In fact, George W. Bush ranks on *Forbes* top-10 list of the richest U.S. presidents (Ackman, 2003). Of all U.S. presidents, Bill Clinton is one of few who was born poor (Andrew Johnson and Barack Obama being the only others; Ackman, 2003); his wealth did not come until after his term in office was over. Owing to profits from his speaking engagements and the sale of his and Hillary's books, they became multimillionaires and reported earnings of $109 million in the years between 2001 and 2007 (Kay, 2008). Both Ronald Reagan and Jimmy Carter were also millionaires.

A significant part of what draws people to Barack and Michelle is the fact that in many ways, despite being the presidential First Family, they are just like the average American family. Take family finances for example. Unlike most other presidents, the Obamas did not have much in the way of personal or family wealth to draw from (prior to Barack's book sales, which took place within the few years immediately preceding his presidency). The *Washington Post*, comparing Barack to the other candidates running against him for president, put it this way:

> Perhaps only one word can be used to describe all of the leading presidential contenders: multimillionaire. . . . The exception: Sen. Barack Obama (D-Ill). As a community organizer-turned-law professor-turned-state senator-turned U.S. senator, the bulk of Obama's wealth has come only in the past few years, with the huge success of his second book, *The Audacity of Hope*. (Goldfarb, 2007)

Barack's parents were students at the University of Hawaii when he was born. Barack's mother, Ann, dropped out of school to devote herself to his care, while Barack Sr. finished up his studies the following June, and then left his wife and son to pursue a master's degree in economics at the New School in New York (Andersen, 2009). Barack Senior ignored his new family, established a relationship with another woman, and moved on with his life; meanwhile, Ann returned to school to finish her degree, received food stamps to make ends meet, had her parents take care of her son, and, at her mother's urging, filed for divorce (Andersen, 2009). Eventually, Ann married an Indonesian man name Lolo and moved her family to Indonesia to live with him. Unfortunately, Lolo's employment situation changed just prior to their arrival, leaving him stuck in a low-paying job and a small home without electricity or indoor plumbing (Andersen 2009). It was in these meager beginnings that Obama's life-long dreams and aspirations were nurtured. In one of the essays he was assigned to write during his first year in Indonesia, which was on the theme "What I Want to Be When I Grow Up," he wrote, "I will become President" (Andersen, 2009).

When Michelle and Barack met, Barack was driving a used Datsun 210 hatchback that was full of rust and had a hole in the door that allowed passengers to watch the pavement zip by as they rode along (Andersen, 2009). When they got married, they lived with Michelle's mother for 6 months and then purchased a two-bedroom apartment on the ground floor of a condominium complex. Jodi Kantor, a Washington correspondent for the *New York Times*, described their apartment as narrow and worn with aging fixtures, a cramped master bedroom, and a dining room table that tilted so much that food sometimes skidded south (Kantor, 2009). They lived modestly but struggled financially because their collective income was not enough to pay off their massive student loan debt and the costs associated with Barack's political ambitions. Thus, the Obama family understands well the economic concerns and challenges of the average American family; they have lived it, and recently.

Barack and Michelle have also been very transparent about the challenges of marriage. They take their responsibility to be the "First Family" very seriously and have provided unprecedented access to their family, a decision that has garnered them criticism from some who have derisively described them as celebrities and considerable praise from others who view their decision as a display of generosity and selflessness that renders them more human and approachable. This letter written to Michelle by Lori Jones, a resident of Bowie, Maryland, is an example of the latter view:

> For all the history you and Barack have and will continue to make, one of the simplest and most treasured is your showing the world the face of

black America; the beautiful, faithful, accomplished, nurturing, caring, loving, smart, strong, and moral face of black America. . . . And what a beautiful portrait of real love you have shown the world. Thank you for showing the world how love between a black man and woman can, and should, look. Through you black men have the opportunity to see the way Barack expresses his love for you; the way he shows his respect for you; the way he communicates with you; the way he allows you to be—to shine. Through you black women see the way you do all of the same things for your husband. Through you, we see how the two of you depend and lean on each other. Thank you. (Nevergold & Brooks-Bertram, 2009, p. 24)

It is obvious Barack and Michelle love one another deeply and have tremendous respect for one another. In *Portrait of an American Marriage*, Michelle says "Barack and I complete each other—as partners, as friends, and as lovers," and Barack says of Michelle, "She is my rock—the one person who keeps it real" (Andersen, 2009). However, they are careful to make it clear that their successful marriage is not magic, that it takes concerted and consistent effort to make it work. In an interview with Jodi Kantor of the *New York Times*, Michelle said, "our ups and downs in our marriage can help young couples realize that good marriages take work . . . The image of a flawless relationship is the last thing we want to project. It's unfair to the institution of marriage, and it's unfair for young people who are trying to build something, to project this perfection that doesn't exist" (Kantor, 2009).

They had the usual family fights over household responsibilities, childrearing, and money. But because both Barack and Michelle were ambitious and high-achieving in their own rights, they also had the added issue of how to manage both their careers so that they supported one another's goals and so that neither one's advancement came at the expense of the other. Despite being brilliant and as accomplished and high-achieving as her husband (perhaps, arguably, more so), Michelle, like so many young working mothers, was expected to bear most of the parenting responsibilities. This became a sore spot between the two. Michelle had expected a more egalitarian parenting arrangement, and she had not expected that Barack would be so willing to put his career ahead of his family, whereas Barack expected a little more understanding of the sacrifices that needed to be made for him to pursue a career that would ultimately benefit his family, an ongoing argument they described this way:

"You only think about yourself," she would say to him again and again in a tone dripping with disdain. "I never thought I'd have to raise a family alone." Barack, convinced that whatever time he devoted to his career would ultimately benefit his wife and daughters, shrugged off the criticism. . . . "Barack just doesn't seem to care *what* I think," a frustrated Michelle complained to her mother, Marian Robinson. "He can be so selfish—and I just can't get through to him that we're supposed to be in this *together.*" Barack believed that his political commitments required him to spend long periods away from home. Those absences were likely to grow even longer, since he was not about to give up a burning ambition to achieve higher office. Michelle's criticisms were "unfair" and "short-sighted" he repeatedly claimed. (Andersen, 2009, pp. 5, 11)

These types of arguments and struggles are not uncommon in healthy families, and all marriages experiences glitches or bumps along the way. What is important in maintaining a healthy marriage is effective communication and "keeping it real." That is, the couples that know how to effectively communicate their needs and listen to one another are the ones able to weather the challenges of marriage and grow closer and stronger as a result of them. Moreover, the couples that deal with the way things are—not the way they wish they were—are the ones able to work through challenges and arrive at mutually agreeable solutions.

The Obamas are masters at both effective communication and keeping it real. In speeches during the campaign, Michelle would jokingly make jabs about Barack's not picking his clothes up around the house and about him being a regular guy. Although these comments led some in the media to describe her as emasculating, Barack certainly did not view them that way; he laughed at them and is often quoted as saying that Michelle is the one person he can count on to keep it real and, as such, she is his rock. Moreover, Michelle's humorous approach to conveying that they are just regular people has been greatly appreciated by the African-American community, as exemplified in this quote from Patricia Hill, a retired educator and president of a civic center in New York:

> The love we see within your family is awesome. We realize no family is perfect, but yours is so close. You and Obama let the world see that people of color have strong family ties, love that is not hidden, faith in God, who guides, and respect for all people. You show this love in the way you look at each other and even the touch of your hands especially the "fist bump." Then you add that touch of humor that makes us smile or even laugh . . . But you know what I truly respect you for? It is that you have let us see your husband as a man, who is not perfect because he is human, like us. Moreover, you are keeping your children grounded by making sure they will still have chores to do. (Nevergold & Brooks-Bertram, 2009, p. 122)

It is without a doubt that in their own right, and certainly against the backdrop of prior presidential families (e.g., Bill Clinton's infidelity, George W. and Laura Bush's cool distance and problems controlling the behavior of their late adolescent children, and comments about whether George Bush, Sr. was married to his mother that were not just about Barbara Bush's age but also about the public face of their marital relationship), the Obamas project a healthy model for American families. Many of the letters that have been written to the Obamas reflect this theme; like this one by Doris Green, a former faculty member at Brooklyn College and Teachers College of Columbia University:

> The joy of seeing the image of a happy Black couple, with their children in the White House, enthralled me. Black people were commonly portrayed as detached people living a life without care and having a welfare mentality. The only positive image we have of the Black family was The Cosby Show, which I welcomed with open arms. For Black people of my generation, it was all about family. The Black family was the norm not the exception. (Nevergold & Brooks-Bertram, p. 93)

Despite the refreshing glimpse of a healthy husband and wife love relationship that Barack and Michelle embody and project, some in the media have maligned their relationship as too loving and too expressive, comments that harken back to negative stereotypes about African-Americans' sexuality that have prevailed since the time of slavery. According to Bernard, in *Marriage and Family Among Negroes*, which traces the marriage and family patterns that were shaped in slavery: "In the 19th century, when frigidity was prized among White women, any degree of responsiveness in a [Negro] woman would seem like ecstatic abandon. Actually there is no reason at all to believe that Negro women are any more 'highly sexed' than other women" (Bernard, 1966). Still today, comments about African-American love relationships are often predicated on stereotypes that either stem from slavery and/or equate difference with deviance.

No doubt these stereotypes were at the root of an October 2, 2009 *Huffington Post* column stating:

> After spending two days nearly 4,000 miles apart, the president and first lady engaged in PDA [public displays of affection] of Olympic proportions during the Chicago 2016 bid presentation at the International Olympic Committee session on Friday. See the photographic evidence below.

Several pictures are included in the article, one showing them standing side-by-side looking at each other, one showing him whispering something to her, another showing them walking across a stage to greet each other, and three others that in succession show what happens when they reach each other on the stage (he whispers something to her, then hugs her, then walks away from her toward the podium); finally, there is a picture of them walking side-by-side up the steps of the airplane with his hand on her lower back. It's hard to see the "Olympic-sized affection" the writer is describing, but it is clear that the Obamas are not frigid toward one another as some other presidential couples have been, and they are not afraid to show emotion toward one another (e.g., smiling, embracing, kissing on the cheek, holding hands, etc.). Certainly, when compared to many couples and the emotional frigidity in their relationships, the Obamas seem consumed by "ecstatic abandon." But what some describe as inappropriate displays of affection, others have hailed as a breath of fresh air and a needed model for the country.

It is the expressiveness that shows their love is genuine—and not just for the media blitz—and it is the expressiveness that makes their relationship a visible role model for others. Attica Georges expressed it this way:

> You exude so much genuine love and respect that it's visible. It is so evident. I had never seen that kind of absolutely authentic, not-for-public-consumption kind of connection between a high profile couple before. The world goes away, and it's just the two of you, knowing all you've been through leading up to those moments. So natural and effortless, you flow together, and that is powerful for us to see. (Nevergold & Brooks-Bertram, 2009, pp. 215–216)

THE OBAMAS, IMPLICIT DEBIASING, AND THE COMPLEXITIES OF "BLACK" LOVE

As articulated by other contributors in this volume, negative representations of African-Americans work to strengthen Whites' implicit, anti-Black biases. Conversely, positive representations of African-Americans work to undermine these very same biases among Whites. Such representations need not be direct. Whites' positive exposure to African-Americans via the media, also serves to undermine Whites' anti-Black prejudice. Many African-Americans, too, harbor implicit anti-Black attitudes (reviewing the literature, see Porter and Parks, 2010). African-American's exposure to positive representations—whether via direct or indirect contact—of African-Americans serves to debias African-Americans at the implicit level in meaningful ways, namely in the area of academic achievement (reviewing the literature, Purdie-Vaughns, 2010). The question is whether and to what degree the Obama's marriage, implicitly and explicitly, alters blacks' attitudes about mate selection, dating, marriage, and ultimately family life. This is particularly so given that, as we have indicated above, there are racialized components to blacks' romantic relationships. Undoubtedly, implicit attitudes influence mate selection and romantic relationships (Cate, Bassett, & Dabbs, 2003; Czopp, Monteith, Zimmerman, & Lynam, 2004; Olsson, Ebert, Banaji, & Phelps, 2005; Rojahn, Komelasky, & Man, 2008; Thomson, Patel, Platek, & Shackelford, 2007).

Needless to say, the Obama marriage is a reaffirming exemplar of traditional African-American family life and provides an aspirational vision of what African-Americans can attain (*see* Inniss & Feagin, 1995), if not the ideal African-American family (*see* Payne, 1994). Their marriage is a great source of hope with respect to romantic relationships for African-Americans, exemplifying the directives Chapman (2006) provides for the future of African-American relationships. At the explicit level, and maybe most fitting African-American women's social networks encourage professional development and community service (Berkowitz & Padavic, 1999). At the implicit level, however, many African-American women may desire a Prince Charming (*see* Rudman & Heppen, 2003). The reconciling of these attitudes seemed most clear at the peak of the Obama campaign:

> President Barack Obama's name has become shorthand for a black man with integrity, character and spirituality, one who loves and values his wife and makes his family a priority—in other words, the kind of man that many black women had despaired of finding. (Scott, 2009)

In President Obama, many African-American women see the Ideal Black Man—one who has given them hope that they can, indeed, find a loving relationship with an African-American man. He makes "black love" seem attainable to African-American women. And although many African-American men aspire to find their Michelle Obama, many more African-American women seem to pin their hopes for love on the Obama marriage (Desmond-Harris, 2009; Flagenheimer, 2009; Scott, 2009). So at the explicit level, and quite possibly the implicit level, the Obamas have undermined the notion among many that "black love" and strong African-American families are impossible to attain.

As positive an effect the Obama marriage portends to have on African-American romantic relationships, it may also add complexity to these relationships. For, in the emerging dialogue about what their marriage means to African-Americans, there seems to be a perceived essentialism to their marriage (*see* Tucker, 1997). That being, for example, desirable and acceptable African-American romantic relationships are intraracial, heterosexual, and intrafaith (and possibly just among Christians). Even more, the quest among some to become part of a African-American "power couple" may be more than just a notion.

In her work on African-American women's attitudes about African-American and White, heterosexual inter-racial relationships, Childs (2005) conducted focus groups with African-American college women and in-depth interviews with inter-racially married African-American women. Childs' research revealed that many African-American women were opposed to romantic relationships between African-American men and White women not simply out of jealousy and anger toward White women. Rather, African-American women's opposition was based on White racism, African-American internalization of racism, and what inter-racial relationships represented to them and signified about their worth. Ultimately, their opposition flowed from their experience of racism and sexism, their devaluation by White beauty standards, and the shortage of potential African-American male partners and a lack of "substantive opportunities" to date interracially. And it is reassuring to African-American women that President Obama has an African-American wife (Scott, 2009).

At the implicit level, individuals tend to harbor a pro-heterosexual, anti-homosexual attitude. For example, individuals seem, at least, indirectly disgusted by gay men kissing in public and not disgusted by heterosexual kissing. Furthermore, the more disgust sensitive such individuals are, the more they demonstrate implicit, unfavorable associations with gay people as opposed to heterosexuals (Inbar, Pizarro, Knobe, Bloom, 2009). The implicit bias literature does not tie race to attitudes about homosexuals; however, research on blacks' explicit attitudes suggests that they harbor stronger anti-gay attitudes vis-à-vis whites (DeSantis & Coleman, 2009). And though there is no reason to suspect that African-American women would harbor stronger explicit or implicit anti-gay attitudes, African-American women have tended to express, at least, concern about African-American gay relationships, as they serve to diminish the pool of eligible African-American bachelors (Robinson, 2009).

Another aspect of President Obama that may be appealing to African-American women is that he is remarkably well educated, has dual Ivy League degrees, and has had a successful career since law school with a steep trajectory. This is no surprise given that a man's social status is an appealing quality to women but in more complex ways than traditionally thought. For example, Millar (2009) studied how a man's relationship involvement influences women's implicit response to low- and high-status professions. When a high-involvement (i.e., male interested in long-term relationship) context was subliminally primed, women implicitly associated more positive responses with high-status occupations than with low-status occupations. Conversely, when a low-involvement (i.e., male interested in short-term relationship) context was subliminally primed, this difference disappeared. Arguably, these changes in trait desirability are what cause women to seek higher status mates in high-involvement relationships.

Finally, and this may be equally salient for African-American men and women alike, Barack and Michelle's marriage coupled with their religious faith may be suggestive of being "equally yoked." Research suggests that African-Americans strongly value the role that religion plays in solidifying their romantic relationships—particularly with a partner of the same faith

(Marks, Hopkins, Chaney, Monroe, Nesteruk, & Sasser, 2008). This may be especially so among African-American Christians. This can be explained by people's implicit ingroup (Dasgupta, 2004) and Christian preferences (Rowatt, Franklin, & Cotton, 2005) as well as African-Americans' higher religiosity when compared to Whites (Taylor, Chatters, Jayakody, & Levin, 1996).

To reiterate, the Obama marriage would seem to undermine the explicit and implicit cynicism some African-Americans feel about their prospects for finding a suitable partner. But by the same token, the Obama marriage may also establish essential features of "Black love" in the minds of African-Americans. This essentialization may do two things to hamstring their efforts to find suitable partners. First, it may cause them to place more blame on various factors—for example, inter-racial dating, gay relationships, absence of appropriate education or financial resources—than may be warranted. Second, it may cause them not to look beyond their comfort zone—for example, with respect to race, religion, and socioeconomic status—for a partner. If there is one lesson that should be gleaned from the Obama marriage and one that should hopefully shape both explicit and implicit attitudes about "Black love," it is that Barack and Michelle's relationship should not be encapsulated in its current form. Their relationship and what they both bring to the table set a remarkably high standard (*see* Swerdlick, 2009). Looking back, they are a couple who met each other when there was little to no fame and glory surrounding them. They endured incredible sacrifices for each other and difficulties in their marriage to be at the pinnacle of world leadership, influence, and symbolism.

NOTES

1 Coltrane, J. (1965). *A Love Supreme*.
2 These statistics, which were reported by Chapman, were taken from a report from the U.S. Bureau of the Census titled *Marriage and Household Statistics*. Washington, DC: Government Printing Office, 1992.
3 This explanation comes from the article "Love in the time of hooking up" published in *The Times* on December 10, 2009. *The Times* is an online periodical that can be accessed at http://www.theweek.com/article/index/103947/Love_in_the_time_of_hooking_up#. Read the full article for a more comprehensive discussion of hooking up, including its prevalence and its consequences for young adults.

REFERENCES

Ackman, D. (2003). The richest U.S. presidents. *Forbes Magazine* (February 14, 2003). Accessed online at http://www.forbes.com/2003/02/14/cx_da_0214pres.html, last accessed July 29, 2010.

Amott, T., & Matthaei, J. (1996). *Race, Gender, and Work: A Multi-Cultural Economic History of Women in the United States*. Boston, MA: South End Press.

Anderson, C. (2009). *Barack and Michelle: Portrait of an American Marriage*. New York, NY: HarperCollins.

Baumrind, D. (1973). Authoritarian versus authoritative parental control. In M. Scarr-Salapatek & P. Salapatek (Eds.), *Socialization*. Columbus, OH: Charles E. Merrill.

Berkowitz, A. & Padavic, I. (1999). Getting a man or getting ahead: A comparison of white and black sororities. *Journal of Contemporary Ethnography, 27*, 530–557.

Bernard, J. (1966). *Marriage and Family among Negroes*. Englewood Cliffs, NJ: Prentice-Hall, Inc.

Billingsley, A. (1968). *Black Families in White America*. Englewood Cliffs, NJ: Prentice Hall.

Billingsley, A. (1974). *Black Families and the Struggle for Survival: Teaching our Children to Walk Tall*. New York, NY: Friendship Press.

Billingsley, A. (1992). *Climbing Jacob's Ladder*. New York, NY: Simon and Schuster.

Bramlett, M. D., & Mosher, W. D. (2001). *First marriage dissolution, divorce, and remarriage: United States* (Advanced Data from Vital and Health Statistics No. 323). Hyattsville, MD: National Center for Health Statistics.

Burton, L. M., & Tucker, M. B. (2009). Romantic unions in an era of uncertainty: A post-Moynihan perspective on African American women and marriage. *The Annals, 621*, 132–148.

Cannon, K. G. (1988). *Black Womanist Ethics*. Atlanta, GA: Scholars Press.

Canton, D. (2010). *Raymond Pace Alexander: A New Negro Lawyer Fights for Civil Rights in Philadelphia*. Jackson, MS: University Press of Mississippi.

Cash, F. B. (2001). *African American Women and Social Action: The Clubwomen and Volunteerism from Jim Crow to the New Deal 1896-1936*. Westport, CT: Greenwood Press.

Cate, K. L., Bassett, J. F. & Dabbs, Jr., J M. (2003). Fear primes may not affect women's explicit and implicit mate preferences. *Journal of Articles in Support of the Null Hypothesis, 1*, 49–56.

Chapman, A. (2006). The Black search for love and devotion: Facing the future against all odds. In H. P. McAdoo (Ed.), *Black Families* (pp. 285–296). Thousand Oaks, CA: Sage Publications.

Childs, E. C. (2005). Looking behind the stereotypes of the "angry black woman": An exploration of black women's responses to interracial relationships. *Gender & Society, 19*, 544–561.

Collins, P. H. (1990). *Black Feminist Thought: Knowledge, Consciousness, and the Politics of Empowerment*. Boston, MA: Unwin Hyman.

Collins, S. (1997). Black mobility in White corporations: Up the corporate ladder but out on a limb. *Social Problems, 44*, 55–67.

Czopp, A. M., Monteith, M. J., Zimmerman, R.S., & Lynam, D. R. (2004). Implicit attitudes as potential protection from risky sex: Predicting condom use with the IAT. *Basic and Applied Social Psychology, 26*, 227–236.

Dasgupta, N. (2004). Implicit ingroup favoritism, outgroup favoritism, and their behavioral manifestations. *Social Justice Research, 17*, 143–169.

DeSantis, A. & Coleman, M. (2009). Not on my line: Attitudes about homosexuality in black fraternities, in *Black Greek-letter Organizations in the 21st Century: Our Fight Has Just Begun*, edited by G. S. Parks. Lexington: University Press of Kentucky.

Desmond-Harris, J. (June 8, 2009). What single women can learn from Michelle: Would most Type A, professional women have dated Barack when he was a broke, big-eared organizer with a funny name? *The Root*. http://www.theroot.com/views/what-single-women-can-learn-michelle?page=0,0. Last accessed January 2, 2010.

Dixon, P. (2007). *African American Relationships, Marriages, and Families*. New York, NY: Routledge.

DuBois, W. E. B. (1969). *The Negro American Family*. New York, NY: New American Library.

Flagenheimer, M. (July 9, 2009). Oh, for their own Barack. *The Philadelphia Inquirer*, E01.

Frazier, E. F. (1966). *The Negro Family in the United States*. Chicago, IL: University of Chicago Press.

Giddings, P. (1984). *When and Where I Enter: The Impact of Black Women on Race and Sex in America*. New York, NY: Bantam.

Goldfarb, Z. A. (2007). Measuring wealth in the'08 candidates. *Washington Post*. The article, dated March 24, 2007, can be accessed online at http://www.washingtonpost.com/wp-dyn/content/article/2007/03/24/AR2007032400305.html, last accessed July 29, 2010.

Goodwin, P. Y. (2003). African American and European American women's marital well-being. *Journal of Marriage and Family, 65*, 550–560.

Harris, S. (1992). Black male masculinity and same sex relationships. *Western Journal of Black Studies, 16(2)*, 74–81.

Harris, W. (1992). *The Harder We Run: Black Workers Since the Civil War*. New York, NY: Oxford University Press.

Herskovitz, M. J. (1958). *The Myth of the Negro Past*. Boston, MA: Beacon.

Inbar, Y., Pizarro, D. A., Knobe, J., Bloom, P. (2009). Disgust sensitivity predicts intuitive disapproval of gays. *Emotion, 9*, 435–439.

Inniss, L.B. & Feagin, J. R. (1995). The Cosby Show: The view from the black middle class. *Journal of Black Studies, 25*, 692–711.

Jewell, K. S. (1993). *From Mammy to Miss American and Beyond: Cultural Images and the Shaping of U.S. Social Policy*. London: Routledge.

Jones, J. (1985). *Labor of Love, Labor of Sorrow: Black Women, Work, and the Family from Slavery to the Present*. New York, NY: Basic Books.

Kantor, J. (2009). The Obamas' marriage. *New York Times*. The full article, dated October 26, 2009, can be accessed online at http://www.nytimes.com/2009/11/01/magazine/01Obama-t.html?pagewanted=1&_r=1, last accessed July 29, 2010.

Kay, J. (2008). The Clintons cash in: Wealth and American politics. *World Socialist Web Site*. The full article, dated April 8, 2008, can be accessed online at http://www.wsws.org/articles/2008/apr2008/clin-a08.shtml, last accessed July 29, 2010.

Mack, K. (2002). A Social History of Everyday Practice: Sadie T.M. Alexander and the Incorporation of Women in the American Legal profession, 1925-60. *Cornell Law Review, 87*, 1405–1473.

Marable, M. (1984). The Black male: Searching beyond stereotypes. *National Scene, 53(6)*, 5–6, 26-30.

Marks, L. D., Hopkins, K., Chaney, C., Monroe, P. A., Nesteruk, O., & Sasser, D. D. (2008). "Together, we are strong": A qualitative study of happy, enduring African American marriages. *Family Relations, 57*, 172–185.

Matthaei, J. (1982). *An Economic History of Women in America: Women's Work, the Sexual Division of Labor, and the Development of Capitalism*. New York, NY: Schocken Books.

McAdoo, J. (1997). The roles of African American fathers in the socializtion of their children. In H. P. McAdoo (Ed.), *Black Families* (pp. 183–197). Thousand Oaks, CA: Sage Publications.

Millar, M. G. (2009). Implicit associations with social status: the effects of relationship involvement. *Evolution and Human Behavior, 30*, 356–362.

Mullings, L. (1996). *On Our Own Terms: Race, Class, and Gender in the Lives of African American Women*. New York, NY: Routledge.

Nevergold, B., & Brooks-Bertram, P. (2009). *Go Tell Michelle: African American Women Write to the New First Lady*. Albany, NY: State University of New York Press.

Nier, C. L. (1998). Sweet Are the Uses of Adversity: The Civil Rights Activism of Sadie Tanner Mossell Alexander, *Temple Political and Civil Rights Law Review, 8*, 59–86.

Olsson, A., Ebert, J. P., Banaji, M. R., & Phelps, E. A. (July 29, 2005). The role of social groups in the persistence of learned fear. *Science, 309*, 785–787.

Payne, M. A. (1994). The "ideal" black family?: A Caribbean view of The Cosby Show. *Journal of Black Studies, 25*, 231–249.

Porter, S. C. & Parks, G.S. (2010). Michelle Obama: Redefining images of Black women. *The Obamas and a (Post) Racial America*, edited by G. S. Parks & M. W. Hughey. NY: Oxford University Press.

Purdie-Vaughns, V. & Sumner, R. (2010). Sasha and Malia: Re-Envisioning Black Youth. *The Obamas and a (Post) Racial America*, edited by G. S. Parks & M. W. Hughey. NY: Oxford University Press.

Reiff, J., Dahlin, M., & Smith, D. (1993). Rural push and urban pull: Work and family experiences of older Black women in southern cities, 1880-1900. *Journal of Social History, 16*, 35–44.

Robinson, R. K. (2009). Racing the closet. *Stanford Law Review, 61*, 1463–1533.

Rojahn, J., Komelasky, K. G., & Man, M. (2008). Implicit attitudes and explicit ratings of romantic attraction of college students toward opposite-sex peers with physical disabilities. *Journal of Developmental and Physical Disabilities, 20*, 389–397.

Rowatt, W. C., Franklin, L. M., Cotton, M. (2005). Patterns and personality correlates of implicit and explicit attitudes toward Christians and Muslims. *Journal for the Scientific Study of Religion, 44*, 29–43.

Rudman, L. A. & Heppen, J. B. (2003). Implicit romantic fantasies and women's interest in personal power: A glass slipper effect?. *Personality and Social Psychology Bulletin, 29*, 1357–1370.

Scott, M. K. (June 18, 2009). "Looking for my Barack": He's hope for single black women. *The Commercial Appeal*, A6.

Shimkin, D. B., & Uchendu, V. (1978). Persistence, borrowing, and adaptive changes in Black kinship systems: Some issues and their significance. In D. B. Shimkin, E. M. Shimkin, & D. A. Frate (Eds.), *The Extended Family in Black Societies*. The Hague: Mouton Press.

Staples, R. (1978), *The Black Family: Essays and Studies*. Belmont, CA: Wadsworth Publishing Company.

Sudarkasa, N. (2006). Interpreting the African heritage in African American family organization. In H. P. McAdoo (Ed.), *Black Families* (pp. 29–47). Thousand Oaks, CA: Sage Publications.

Swerdlick, D. (June 16, 2009). What single women can't learn from Michelle: Five things to consider before the next man passes you by. *The Root*. http://www.theroot.com/views/what-single-women-can-t-learn-michelle. Accessed January 2, 2010.

Taylor, R. J., Chatters, L. M., Jayakody, R., Levin, J. S. (1996). Black and White differences in religious participation: A multisample comparison. *Journal for the Scientific Study of Religion, 35*, 403–410.

Thomson, J. W., Patel, S., Platek, S. M. & Shackelford, T.K. (2007). Sex differences in implicit association and attentional demands for information about infidelity. *Evolutionary Psychology, 5*, 569–583.

Tucker, L. R. (1997). Was the revolution televised?: Professional criticism about The Cosby Show and the essentialization of Black cultural expression. *Journal of Broadcasting & Electronic Media, 41*, 90–108.

University of Pennsylvania (2010a). Guide to the Alexander family collection. http://www.archives.upenn.edu/faids/upt/upt50/alexander_rpa.html. Accessed January 2, 2009.

University of Pennvania (2010b). Guide to the Alexander family collection. http://www.archives.upenn.edu/faids/upt/upt50/alexander_stma.html. Accessed January 2, 2009.

U.S. Census (n.d.). *Families and Living Arrangements*. Accessed online at http://www.census.gov/population/www/socdemo/hh-fam.html, last accessed July 29, 2010.

Weiner, L. (1985). *From Working Girl to Working Mother: The Female Labor force in the United States, 1820-1980.* Chapel Hill, NC: University of North Carolina Press.

White, D. G., (1985). *Ar'n't I a Woman?: Female Slaves in the Plantation South.* New York, NY: Schenkman Publishing.

Wilson, G. (1997). Pathways to power: Racial differences in the determinants of job authority. *Social Problems, 44,* 38–54.

The Obamas: Beyond Troubled Love

Jenée Desmond-Harris

Just two blocks from the White House, the greeting card section of a Washington, D.C. drugstore is a mass of red and pink clutter in a too-narrow aisle. Valentine's Day is near in Obama's America.

I need a card for my mother (touching). One for my grandmother (large print). A couple to lift the spirits of friends in dating dry spells (funny). There are headings for every brand of love: *Wife. Child. Someone Special.* And for every way to express it: *Humor. Religious. From Both of Us.*

And one I haven't seen before: *Troubled Love.*

It's in the Mahogany section—a bright corner of the store where, amidst the reds and pinks are browns, bold fonts, and prints meant to suggest African tapestries. Where the words "Blessings," "Rejoice," and "Pride" are dominant and the cards are addressed to "Momma" instead of "Mom" and "Girlfriend" instead of "Friend." It's the sub-brand Hallmark describes as having "cards to help African-Americans honor their relationships in innovative, compelling, and culturally relevant ways."

Troubled Love?

This heading is only available in the Mahogany section. (Yes, I checked). The lonely card in the category contains a tepid suggestion to push forward in an ailing relationship. Troubled, I suppose the consumer is to understand, is a brand of love that is "culturally relevant" for people who resemble the brown-skinned and curly-haired cartoon figures depicted on these specially tailored greetings.

No real surprise. Black love—love between African-Americans—is persistently characterized this way. Its image has been troubled by history, by misunderstandings, and by racist images and stereotypes. Perhaps most painfully, it has been troubled by the way the Black community has "consciously or subconsciously colluded with these myths," as the authors of this chapter put it.

With good reason, Black America has looked expectantly at Barack and Michelle Obama to put an end to all the trouble. Happy, attractive, successful, and loving, they provide validation to those who see an image of what they already knew existed (like Doris Green, quoted in this chapter, who says, "For Black people of my generation, it was all about family. The Black family was the norm, not the exception") and inspire those who only hoped such a relationship was possible.

This chapter is an acknowledgment of that potential for validation and inspiration and recognition of the psychic healing that the image of the Obamas has already provided. Throughout the campaign and long after inauguration, my friends and I posted pictures of the two them together on our facebook profiles. The caption, without being typed, was obvious: *This can happen. This makes me proud. This is what I see for myself.*

But in this chapter, there's an important caution, too. It's about a misguided interpretation of the Obamas. What the authors warn against, and what I'm afraid of, is embodied by another Mahogany card. This one has the image of a smirking, stylish Black woman. Hands on hips, with hoop earrings, against a magenta background, she says, "I'm looking for a man like Obama, but all I've been able to find is mo' drama!"

The card is clever, and it's in good fun (I admit, I picked up two that day in the drugstore for the dating dry spell contingent). But it's also a "culturally relevant" warning against the insecurity, cynicism, and judgment that have given the "troubled love" label the fuel it needs to survive for so long within the Black community. These issues have the power to color our view of Barack and Michelle in the same way they influenced our understanding of Black love, pre-Obama.

This chapter concludes that we must not characterize the Obamas' relationship so narrowly that they represent an unattainable goal. African-Americans are not monolithic, and healthy Black love does not have to mirror the Obamas' in style, religion, socio-economic status, and a place in the spotlight. As this chapter points out, it is important that the surface characteristics of their marriage don't "establish essential features of Black love" in our minds. We should focus instead on the core qualities of their relationship: Respect. Mutual support. Ambition. Affection. There's also a risk that we'll "encapsulate it in its current form," instead of emulating the behaviors and priorities it took to get there: real-life financial struggles, negotiation of relationship roles, hard work, and, yes, a car with a hole in the bottom.

The lesson? Although we can and should be comforted and inspired, we should not see the final, polished picture of American's first family as the only acceptable outcome for Black Americans. We should resist the urge to create a false dichotomy, with "Just like the Obamas" on one hand, and "mo drama" on the other.

This is the chapter's most important point. Amidst the celebration, relief, and pride associated with the Obamas and all they represent about the potential of relationships between African-Americans, we must be very deliberate about how we choose to make sense of them. Understood in proper perspective, the image of their marriage can be one important—and yes, "culturally relevant" step on the journey beyond troubled love.

CHAPTER 8

Sasha and Malia: Re-Envisioning African-American Youth

Valerie Purdie-Vaughns, Rachel Sumner, and Geoffrey L. Cohen

> When I take that oath of office, there will be kids all over this country who don't really think that all paths are open to them, who will believe that they can be anything they want to be.
>
> —*Barack Obama, quoted in Kantor (2009)*

> Barack has shown no matter what color you are you can be anything you want to be.
>
> —*African-American sixth-grade student, November 2008 in response to the question, "Is it important to you who won the United States presidential election?"*

Sasha and Malia Obama are arguably the most famous Black children in the United States today. Having been launched to national prominence during their father's campaign for the presidency, these girls are part of a family that has defied the odds all the way to the White House. Just before his inauguration as the first U.S. African-American president, Barack Obama published an open letter to his daughters in *Parade* magazine, writing "I want every child to have the same chances to learn and dream and grow and thrive that you girls have. That's why I've taken our family on this great adventure" (Obama, 2009, Jan. 18).

How much can Barack Obama, as a charismatic and counterstereotypical role model, actually affect youth, especially African-American youth, nationwide? From how well one performs on a quiz to which careers one perceives as being available, role models lay the framework for one's future possibilities. Barack Obama is the first enormously popular, nationally vindicated, African-American role model in many children's lives. Moreover, he has excelled in a role not stereotypically associated with African-Americans, succeeding in politics rather than sports or entertainment. The aftermath of Barack Obama's election, therefore, offers an opportune moment to explore the function and power of a role model for minority students.

Political pundits heavily discussed the first 100 days of his presidency, going back and forth about the economy and foreign policy; in this chapter, we will examine the time following the election and the first months of Obama's presidency through the eyes of a psychologist, exploring how media and the changing political climate may affect self-perception and achievement for middle school students.

One of the consequences of Barack Obama's "Yes, we can" presidential campaign and the symbolic significance of his becoming America's first African-American president has been a refocusing of the nation's attention on race and achievement. Numerous media reports, for example, have asked African-American and Latino students, who are often academically at risk, to assess the impact of Obama's success on their own motivation and achievement (Stannard, 2008; *New Haven Register,* p. 1). As evidenced by student responses in the news and the quote above from a middle school student who participated in the present research, Obama is clearly seen as a source of inspiration. Yet, whether Obama's achievements affect students' psychological functioning and achievement in school remains unclear.

This refocusing on race and achievement is evident in schools nationwide. Innovative educators have integrated Obama into their pedagogy to an extent unmatched by previous presidential elections (Dyson, 2008). Such transformations range from the informal (Obama posters in the classroom) to more substantive changes in the curriculum (Lewis, 2008). Underlying these grassroots changes to the classroom are the interlinked presumptions that students see Obama as a role model and that his achievements will enhance their own. Despite these changes, empirically driven science about how situational factors that transcend the classroom—in this case Barack Obama's ascendancy to the presidency—can have a proximal affect on student's psychological functioning remains nascent. This exemplifies what Bronfenbrenner called the macrosystem or sociocultural context in which child development occurs (Brofenbrenner, 1979).

This chapter will advance a psychological analysis of President Obama's election affecting the academic achievement of academically at-risk ethnic minority students. Much work has shown that affirming personal or group values can have positive effects on the school achievement of academically at-risk ethnic minorities—for example, having students reflect on the importance of their social relationships or their racial identity (Cohen, Garcia, Purdie-Vaughns, Apfel, & Brusztowski, 2009, This work is based on the notion that the interaction of situational factors in the environment and students' psychological state is a fundamental determinant of motivation and performance (Purdie-Vaughns et al., 2008). We have shown that changing the psychological climate in the classroom by introducing a new situational element—such as an affirmation intervention—can improve performance and positively change perceptions of the environment for minority students. If the election of Barack Obama acts as an affirmation for minority students, then we would expect to see similar improvements in academic performance when his success is made salient in a given environment.

Using data collected immediately following the 2008 presidential election and throughout Obama's first 9 months in office, we will advance an analysis of his impact on the academic achievement of minority students nationwide. First, we will discuss which facets of Barack Obama's identity and success might make him a particularly effective role model for minority youth. This will be followed by a description of our empirical work exploring the potential impact of Obama's election on students' psychological experience and academic performance. Finally, we will consider how best to maximize the potentially inspiring effect of Obama's success on African-American youth, presenting empirically supported suggestions gleaned from previous psychological research on role models.

WHAT MAKES OBAMA DIFFERENT FROM OTHER AFRICAN-AMERICAN ROLE MODELS?

Barack Obama is one of many successful African-Americans who may serve as a role model—family members, athletes, community leaders, musicians, and many other individuals inspire minority youth every day. Yet the impact of Barack Obama may be unique because he succeeded in a domain not stereotypically associated with African-Americans and was *elected* to his position by a majority of American voters. These characteristics of his success might make him an especially effective role model, particularly for young African-Americans.

African-American athletes, such as LeBron James or Venus and Serena Williams, and musicians, like Beyoncé or Jay-Z, have used their skills and dedication to become prominent, successful individuals whom many young children admire. Role models can profoundly influence their admirers by helping young people identify goals and strategies for achieving them (Lockwood & Kunda, 1997) and highlighting possible future selves (Lockwood, 2006). Among African-American youth, having a role model is associated with fewer aggressive behaviors and fewer symptoms of depression and anxiety (McMahon, Singh, Garner, & Benhorin, 2004). Additionally, because people are more likely to be influenced by someone who is similar to them (Bandura, 1968; Mussweiler, 2003), it is especially important for African-American youth to have same-race role models.

Obama as a counterstereotypical role model. Children may constrain their own aspirations to the domains in which they find their role models succeeding.

Role models not only inspire but also provide people with important information about their *own* abilities and possible future selves (Lockwood, 2006). Therefore, minority youth who are coming of age during the Obama presidency may very well use his example as a point of reference when forming their own aspirations. The success of Barack Obama in the realm of politics means that young African-Americans can have not only famous athletes and musicians as role models, but also the President of the United States, increasing the likelihood that they will imagine themselves pursuing and succeeding in a political career.

Studies in psychology have shown that having a role model from one's ingroup (e.g., ethnicity, gender, alma mater) might defend one against the negative effects of stereotype threat *if* one attends to the role model's counterstereotypical behaviors (Marx & Goff, 2005). For example, if an African-American student sits down in his classroom to take a math test and pauses to think about his role model Barack Obama, he will be less likely to do poorly on that test (as a result of the deleterious effects of stereotype threat) if he thinks about Obama's counterstereotypical behaviors (e.g., running for the presidency) rather than his stereotype-consistent behaviors (such as playing basketball) (Wout et al., 2009). Barack Obama's success is replete with counterstereotypical behavior, meaning that students will have plenty of examples to draw from when trying to focus on this role model's stereotype-inconsistent actions. This may make him a more potentially beneficial role model than other successful African-Americans whose track records, although impressive, are more consistent with existing stereotypes.

Obama as a role model with widely publicized achievements. Another factor that might distinguish Obama as a particularly effective role model is the widely publicized nature of his accomplishments: His life's journey from a single-parent family in Hawaii to an Ivy League education and then on to politics was a national topic of discussion both during and after the 2008 presidential election, meaning that many Americans are familiar with the narrative details of the 44th president's success. For a role model to be effective, the details of his or her success must be readily accessible for admirers: Buunk, Peiro, and Griffioen (2007) found that a role model can be inspiring even if one has never had direct contact with one's role model, so long as one is familiar with this person's record of success and can easily bring this success to mind. The fact that Barack Obama's counterstereotypical life and success are so widely known makes it more likely that he will be a role model capable of inspiring others, even those with whom he has not had direct contact.

Although Obama is not the first African-American to succeed in the domain of politics, he is the first to be elected to the presidency of the United States. His political success took place on a national scale and resulted in his holding the highest office, making Barack Obama a household name. Importantly, Barack Obama was elected to his position by a majority of American voters—including 9% of registered Republicans—meaning that his success can be seen as reflecting the nation's attitudes about race and achievement (FEC, 2009). If millions of voters would choose an African-American man to run the country, then America is a place where a majority (of voters, at least) believes in the capability of a minority leader. The scale and prominence of his achievement may serve as a societal-level disconfirmation of previous stereotypes related to minorities and achievement, and therein lies the distinct potential for Barack Obama to be an especially effective role model for minority youth.

Political figures such as Colin Powell and Condoleezza Rice held prominent positions in the presidential cabinet before Barack Obama arrived at the White House, but they were appointed to their positions by one individual and confirmed by dozens of others. This distinguishes their political success from Obama's in an important way: Relatively few individuals partook in the process that led to Condoleezza Rice and Colin Powell becoming Secretary of State. More than 131 million Americans voted in the 2008 presidential election, however, and almost 70 million of them cast ballots for Obama/Biden (FEC, 2009). Although these three African-Americans have all succeeded in politics, securing important positions in the American government, the extent to which the American public participated in their success varies greatly. The degree of public participation may correlate with the degree to which each of these individuals will positively impact minority youth, as greater public involvement may be reflective of broader societal attitudes.

Other African-American politicians besides Barack Obama have been elected to their positions, such as Newark's mayor Cory Booker or Deval Patrick, the governor of Massachusetts. The scale of their success in city and state elections, respectively, however, pales in comparison to the national election that was won by Barack Obama. Neither the election of Cory Booker nor Deval Patrick was hailed as a national referendum on race, whereas the election of Barack Obama was expected to "usher in a new era of race relations" (Kaufman & Fields, 2008) and change the way Americans feel about themselves and each other. Large-scale public expectation and affirmation may impact individual students more powerfully than these local politicians.

Almost 70 million Americans sent Barack Obama to the White House, believing that an African-American man should be president of the United States (FEC, 2009). Experiencing the 2008 presidential election could potentially change the way one thinks about America and Americans, attitudes and achievement, and race and racism, even if one was too young to vote.

A PSYCHOLOGICAL APPROACH TO OBAMA AS A ROLE MODEL AND EFFECTS ON AFRICAN-AMERICAN STUDENT ACHIEVEMENT

Although the election of Barack Obama generated much excitement among adults, with 69,456,897 voters casting ballots for Obama (FEC, 2009) and more than 71 million North American viewers tuning in to televised election night coverage (Neilsen, 2008), the extent to which children attended to the election's issues and outcome was less clear. Historically, children are not usually counted among those who are expected to know or care about politics. But the unprecedented level of media coverage coupled with the historic outcome of this particular election led many to assume that American youth, particularly minorities, would be profoundly affected by the election of Barack Obama.

The Obama Effect refers to the notion that ethnic minorities who reflect on Obama's achievements can experience positive outcomes in domains where they often contend with negative stereotypes, such as education. The explanation for this posited effect is that the symbolic significance of Obama can buffer students against the detrimental effects of psychological threat in their proximal environment (Marx, Ko, & Friedman, 2009; Aronson, Jannone, McGlone, & Johnson-Campbell, 2009). This threat arises from concerns about confirming negative stereotypes about the intellectual ability connected with one's racial group (Aronson, 2002; Aronson, Fried, & Good, 2002; Steele, 1997; Steele, Spencer, & Aronson, 2002; *see also* Cohen & Garcia, 2005). It is now well-established that such stereotype threat, a form of social identity threat, causes stress and cognitive impairment (Branscombe, Schmitt, & Harvey, 1999, Blascovich, Spencer, Quinn, & Steele, 2001; Schmader & Johns, 2003; Steele & Aronson, 1995), undermines academic belonging and school performance (Cook et al., 2009; Walton & Spencer, 2009; Cohen et al., 2006; Aronson et al., 2002), and can also undermine performance in test-taking situations. The significance of Obama's achievements could serve as a societal-level disconfirmation of stereotypes about minorities' ability to succeed in mainstream institutions and relieve threats to social identity.

Currently, not enough research exists to draw conclusions about the "Obama Effect." Yet, the possibility that Obama's highly publicized achievements could alleviate psychological threat and boost performance is suggested by experiments showing the positive effects of salient role models on test performance. Studies show that role models can have positive effects on motivation (Lockwood & Kunda, 1999) and that students contending with negative stereotypes perform better on challenging tests in the presence of role models who share their group identity (Marx & Roman, 2002; McIntyer, Paulson, & Lord, 2003; McGlone, Aronson, & Kobrynowicz, 2006). Individuals are buffered against the effects of social identity threat when role models share their group membership and are perceived as highly competent in the domain (Marx & Roman, 2002). To have positive effects, however, role models' achievements need to be perceived as relevant and personally attainable in the future (Lockwood & Kunda, 1997). Although the office of the Presidency of the United States may not be perceived as personally attainable when minority students think about Barack Obama, the prominence of his achievement may elucidate related academic and career goals for students who admire him.

THREE POSSIBLE HYPOTHESES ON OBAMA'S EFFECT

In addition to the research on role models mentioned above, studies showing that reflecting on important *group* identities, such as one's racial group, also suggest that Obama's achievements could improve students' own psychological functioning and achievement (Sherman et al., 2007). For stereotyped students, Obama's achievements could serve as a group affirmation (Sherman et al., 2007), which may reduce stress and improve performance. Taken together, the above research leads to the hypothesis that Obama's achievements may uniquely diminish threat and boost performance among ethnic minority students.

However, other psychological processes could offset these potential positive effects. Role models can fail to improve motivation or can even undermine it under certain circumstances. For example, this can occur if most of the role model's achievements seem beyond one's grasp (Lockwood & Kunda, 1997; Lockwood & Kunda, 1999). Moreover, subtyping, the tendency to see positive exemplars as exceptions to the rule (Brewer et al., 1981; Fiske et al., 2002), might lead students to see Obama as a unique exception and thus doubt his relevance to their lives. This research could lead us to hypothesize that Barack Obama's achievements would have a null or even negative impact on threat and performance not only among ethnic majority students but also among ethnic minority students.

A third plausible outcome is that *both* students who contend with negative stereotypes and students who do not may be positively affected by the significance of Obama's achievements. Irrespective of his political platform, Obama's election as the first African-American president of the United States is seen as a singular event that may carry a host of positive consequences. Obama's life story could be perceived as an example of someone who succeeds despite adversity and thus could be inspirational to students in general. People might admire and identify with Obama for reasons beyond race, which could make him inspirational to children regardless of their race, especially those individuals who perceive themselves and Obama as psychologically close or similar (Lockwood & Kunda, 1997; 1999; Tesser, 1988; Tesser & Campbell, 1983).

THE FIRST 100 DAYS: TESTING THE OBAMA EFFECT

In the study we report in this chapter, we examined whether the psychological salience of the first African-American to the U.S. presidency mitigates threat in middle school students and affects academic achievement. Our sample was comprised of sixth-grade students from middle to lower socioeconomic class families in a suburban Northeastern middle school where the student body was approximately half African-American and half White. We exploited social-psychological processes related to priming and affirmation effects (Bargh & Chartrand, 1999; Sherman & Cohen, 2006). This research shows that simply making salient a personally relevant target person or mental construct affects people's behavior and performance.

Accordingly, we experimentally manipulated the psychological salience of Barack Obama by having students reflect on the presidential election and their political beliefs using a brief questionnaire, approximately 1 week following the 2008 presidential election. A random half of students completed this questionnaire and the remaining students completed a filler questionnaire related to daily habits in school. Immediately following the prime, all students completed measures of psychological threat and political attitudes. Our primary focus was on students' sense of threat over the course of a calendar year. To explore such longitudinal effects, students' perceived threat was again assessed at the end of sixth grade and the beginning of seventh grade. We also collected school records over the course of this experiment to assess the effect of a brief Obama prime, if any, on academic achievement over the same time period.

Our previous research suggests that an affirmation intervention can improve performance and change perceptions of the environment for minority students (Cohen, Garcia, Apfel, & Master, 2006; Cohen, Garcia, Purdie-Vaughns, Apfel, & Brzustoski, 2009). Thus, we expected that Obama's achievements would affect students' psychological threat and performance in response to their school environment. The positive effects of Obama's election and presidency may be confined to African-American students. His election, however, may convey a more general message of mobility for ethnic minorities—the notion that their efforts can translate into advancement. If this is the case, similar effects should be found for both African-Americans and Latino Americans. Still another possibility is that Obama's election acts as an even more global source of inspiration. It could reinforce individuals' pride in being an American, in which case White students could benefit as well.

Set-up for the Study. We decided to test the effects of thinking about Obama on academic performance using a diverse sample of sixth-grade students attending a suburban middle school in the Northeastern United States that primarily served lower- to middle-class families. Just over half of the students who took part in the study were African-American or Latino, with both genders represented in our sample about equally.

We administered the experimental manipulation approximately 1 week after Obama won the presidential election. Experimenters unaware of student condition and hypotheses presented students with a packet containing study materials, explaining that the study was "to get an idea of what students your age think about and things that are going on in the world." Students were not told that there were multiple conditions and were asked to follow all instructions in their study packets and to not skip pages.

Half of the students in our sample answered 12 questions designed to subtly increase the salience of Obama and the presidential election. Students first responded to an open-ended question: *"Is it important to you who won the United States presidential election? If so, why?"* and were presented with two lines to write their responses. Next, students were asked to indicate the winner of the election by circling the appropriate name from a list of the presidential and vice presidential candidates. They were also asked to select one or more choices from a list of ethnicities that described President Obama. Another item assessed students' attitudes toward Obama (i.e., *"Obama is a person I respect"*) using a four-point scale ranging from 1 (*strongly disagree*) to 4 (*strongly agree*).

To further increase the salience of Obama's election and to assess students' political attitudes, an additional set of measures was included in the Obama salience condition. One measure assessed students' perceived *political engagement* using a scale adapted from the International Civic Education Study (ICES) (Baldi et al., 2001). This scale included three items (e.g., *"How often do you talk about the United States presidential election in your classroom?"*) that students responded to on a four-point scale ranging from 1 (*never*) to 4 (*very often*). Another measure assessed *identification with the election*. This scale consisted of two items (e.g., *"I am happy with who won the United States presidential election"*) that students responded to using a four-point scale ranging from 1 (*strongly disagree*) to 4 (*strongly agree*). The final measure assessed students' *national identification* (Baldi et al., 2001). The scale included three items (e.g., *"I have a great love of the United States"*) that students responded to using a four-point scale ranging from 1 (*strongly disagree*) to 4 (*strongly agree*). In sum, the questions we asked participants in the Obama prime condition were designed to have them think about the president, the election, and their relationship to both.

Students in the control condition, like their classmates in the Obama prime condition, answered a free-response question and 11 forced-choice items. However, instead of soliciting students' thoughts on the election and the president-elect, we asked about things that students might put in their locker, followed by a series of items asking about health and exercise (e.g., *"I don't really care what I eat as long as it tastes good"*) that students responded to using a 6-point scale ranging from 1 (*strongly disagree*) to 6 (*strongly agree*). The final series of questions asked about the number of hours they engaged in specific activities each day (e.g., *"I spend ___hour/s talking with my friends on the Internet each day"*). These questions were not expected to influence students' responses on the subsequent survey.

Our key outcome measures tried to capture both quantitative academic achievement and qualitative evaluations of the school environment. We will first present the results of the qualitative analysis, followed by the quantitative performance evaluation. We first coded student responses about the importance of Obama. To ascertain students' subjective experiences, we used a measure of social identity threat adapted from Cohen and Garcia (2005). This scale consists of 10 items regarding students' concerns with how they are perceived socially and academically (e.g., *"In school, I worry that people will think I am dumb if I do badly," "In school, I worry that people will judge me because of what they think about my racial group"*). Students responded to each item using a six-point scale ranging from 1 (*strongly disagree*) to 6 (*strongly agree*). Finally, we measured students' Grade Point Averages from school transcripts in core subjects: math, science, social studies, reading, and English/language arts.

THEMES ABOUT OBAMA AS ROLE MODEL FROM THE STUDENTS

Students in the Obama prime condition first responded to an open-ended question: *"Is it important to you who won the United States presidential election? If so, why?"* and were presented with two lines to write their responses. Answering this question 1 week after the election of Barack Obama, students were overwhelmingly positive about the president-elect and mentioned prominent campaign issues, such as taxes and the ongoing wars in Iraq and Afghanistan, with surprising frequency.

Overall, students thought that the 2008 presidential election was important. The vast majority of our respondents said that the outcome of the election was important to them, with very few students writing that the outcome of the election was *not* important to them. "Wanting to know who runs the country" was frequently cited as a reason for the personal importance of the election's outcome, perhaps reflecting a latent civic curiosity amongst our nation's youth.

Seeking to identify other recurring themes in the student responses, two coders were asked to read all of the student responses and indicate which topics were frequently mentioned. We found that both African-American and White students identified with Barack Obama, emphasizing similarity to the president-elect in their responses. In addition to this widespread identification, themes of race and change arose among many African-American students.

Although the racial component of Barack Obama's identity received much attention throughout the entire campaign and in the days following his election, this is only one facet of his identity, and there were many other dimensions on which students likened themselves to the president-elect. Some students did mention racial similarity when writing about the personal importance of his election ("Yes because he is the same race as us."), but other students, both minority and nonminority, chose to write about their *ideological* similarity to Barack Obama. In response to our question about the importance of the 2008 presidential election, an African-American student wrote, "I want a president that shares my opoin [sic]," and a White student wrote, "I think that having an African-American brings great change. I also stand with him on his issues." Students are clearly incorporating dimensions of similarity beyond race in their responses, finding ideological common ground with Obama independent of his status as the first African-American president. One student even used a partisan label in her response, writing that the 2008 election was important to her "because Barack Obama is a Democrat and so am I and he is going to help the economy." Although it is anyone's guess what one does to be a Democrat at the age of 12 years, it is apparent that students from various racial backgrounds were able to find commonality with America's first African-American president.

The fact that nonminority students identified with Barack Obama speaks to his remarkable potential as a role model who may inspire all children to strive for success. This is not to say, however, that his historic achievements do not make him a particularly powerful role model for minority youth: Obama's success challenges many existing negative stereotypes about African-Americans and achievement, and research has shown that comparing oneself to a more successful member of one's ingroup (e.g., African-Americans) when a negative group stereotype is salient can have positive effects on self-esteem (Blanton, Crocker, & Miller, 2000).

Although the overwhelming majority of students answered the questions, "Is it important to you who won the United States presidential election? If so, why?" by identifying with Obama, a subset of the students we surveyed focused on Barack Obama's being the first African-American president of the United States, writing things such as "Yes because we finially [sic] got a black man whose [sic] president," and "Yes it is very important who won the election because Barack Obama is the first African American president." Recognizing the historic significance of this election, some students even wrote about themselves reflecting on the event in the future (e.g., "Yes, because if I have children I could say, 'He is the first black president.'").

Consistent with previous research, White students were much less likely than their African-American peers to mention race in their response (Apfelbaum, Sommers, & Norton, 2008). To avoid seeming biased, many Whites adopt a strategy of "strategic colorblindness," which entails not mentioning race or racial difference. Studies have shown that this strategy is even utilized in situations where race is a salient and relevant topic (Apfelbaum, Sommers, & Norton, 2008), so it is not very surprising that White students would be less likely than African-American students to mention race when discussing the election of the first African-American president of the United States.

Change is another theme that emerged in students' responses. Mentioned as frequently in students' responses as the president-elect's race, this theme probably results in some part from Obama's popular "Change we can believe in" slogan. Some students linked the themes of change and race ("Yes, because he made a change on him being the first African-American"), whereas many students wrote more generally about change: "Yes because Obama is giving change to the USA. And all of those changes are that I like"; "Yes, because we need change in the United States." It is unclear whether the frequent mentions of change represent a simple repetition of a campaign slogan, a reaction to personal or familial distrust of President Bush, whose popularity waned over his presidency, or a grasp of the potential of democracy to bring about change and the demonstration of certain American ideals that are too often limited to discussion in social studies class and not a national stage. For whatever reason, students were thinking about change as an important part of the 2008 presidential election.

Change [in GPA and Identity Threat] We Can Believe in? If students worry that they might confirm negative intellectual stereotypes attached to their racial group, having them reflect on the recent election of Barack Obama should mitigate this worry, suggesting that success is attainable and that stereotypes might be changing. Consequently, we expected a reduction in threat only for negatively stereotyped students in the Obama salience condition. To test this prediction, we constructed a statistical model to determine what effects the Obama prime had over time in our students. We first examine cross-sectional differences in threat, as a function of stereotyped group and condition, immediately after the experimental manipulation. Our primary hypothesis predicts a significant stereotype group by condition interaction, with minority students who were prompted to think about Obama before reflecting on their own school environment expected to report less perceived threat than their minority peers who were in the control condition.

We first tested whether there were differences in threat by group and condition in November 2008, shortly after the presidential election and immediately after the Obama salience manipulation. As expected, results revealed a significant stereotype group by condition interaction, indicating that stereotyped (African-American and Latino) students in the Obama salience condition reported significantly less threat than those in the daily habits control condition. In other words, students who belonged to groups that experience identity and stereotype threat had this threat attenuated simply by being reminded about the president-elect.

Next, we examined the trajectory of social identity threat over time. In the control conditions, we found that stereotyped students' levels of identity threat stayed stable over time, whereas White students' threat declined. This suggests that although White students become socially acclimated and gain a sense of comfort in their school, minority students might not attain this level of belonging. Although the Obama prime did not change this pattern, it shifted the trajectory of belongingness for minority students such that they experienced a lower level of identity threat over the time-period of the study. This effect began to diminish by the fall of seventh grade. Follow-up tests revealed that although negatively stereotyped students in the Obama salience condition continued to have lower threat 6 months later in sixth grade (T2) than their peers in the control condition, this difference disappeared by the fall of seventh grade (T3). Nonstereotyped students did not differ by condition at any measurement occasion.

Results from the political measures and student responses suggested that students of all racial backgrounds identified with Barack Obama, leading us to contemplate whether this identification would boost academic performance across all racial groups when students thought about the president. To test whether the Obama salience manipulation affected academic performance in the quarter after the intervention, we ran a statistical model on students' second quarter GPA to determine whether, controlling for their GPA in the first semester, students in the Obama prime condition would perform better than students who wrote about their fitness habits, regardless of their racial background. As we predicted, our results revealed a significant effect of condition, but no effect of gender or stereotype group—that is, for any given level of pre-intervention quarter 1 GPA, stereotyped and nonstereotyped students in the intervention condition had slightly higher post-intervention quarter 2 GPA than those in the control condition. This effect was large enough that if a student was on the border between two grades, then being asked to think about Barack Obama was enough to boost them to the higher of the two. Given the brevity of the prime and the length of time between the prime exercise and the end of the quarter (approximately 7 weeks) this finding, although modest, is quite remarkable.

To summarize, in this experiment, we capitalized on a significant moment in American history. One week after the 2008 presidential election, we experimentally increased the salience of Obama among stereotyped and nonstereotyped sixth-grade students in middle school. Social identity threat and performance (GPA) were then tracked through the fall of seventh grade, a full calendar year after the election. Both African-American and Latino students reported experiencing less threat when Obama was made salient to them, an effect that persisted over an entire school year, even among the latter group, whose ethnicity differs from Obama's. Increasing the salience of Obama provided a small but significant boost to GPA at the end of the quarter in which the Obama-salience manipulation was conducted (controlling for previous quarter's GPA) for both stereotyped and nonstereotyped students. Taken together, this experiment demonstrates that subtly reflecting on Barack Obama's achievements can powerfully reduce stereotyped students' sense of threat and boost achievement for all students, even in a chronically evaluative setting such as school.

For students who contend with negative stereotypes, the significance of Obama's achievements may have been a powerful stereotype-disconfirming event. Making Obama salient may have lessened students' sense that race is a contingency affecting how others perceive them in school. This is important because, over time, threat may undermine students' abilities to foster cross-race relationships (McKown & Strambler, 2009) and stay engaged in school (Steele, 1997; Osborne & Walker, 2006), ultimately increasing the likelihood of lower performance. Because nonstereotyped students do not contend with these same stereotypes in school, their sense of threat was unaffected by the prime and declined over time.

These findings provide evidence that Obama's achievements could confer role model effects. First, regardless of ethnicity, Obama-primed students' end of quarter GPAs improved relative to students in the control condition. Second, although politics and the election were made salient to students across conditions, only Obama-primed students' performances improved, suggesting that reflecting about *Obama* was critical to the prime's effectiveness. Finally, among Obama-primed students, regardless of ethnicity, respect and admiration for Obama was high, an important condition for role model effects to occur.

Bringing Obama into the Classroom to Inspire without Intimidation.
Feeling admiration toward another person has been found to increase individuals' desires to improve themselves and achieve their goals (Algoe &
Haidt, 2009), so students simply admiring Barack Obama as a high-achieving
individual could lead to improvements in their personal motivation. In an
effort to capitalize on this potential role model and inspire students even
more, it may be tempting to say something like, "Look, Barack Obama did
well in school—you're just like him, so you can too." This, however, has the
potential to backfire, leading not to inspiration but demoralization. Research
in psychology has explored the nuanced relationship between individuals
and their role models, and to maximize the positive potential of a role model,
it is important to recognize one's similarity without diminishing the perceived
attainability of the role model's achievement (Lockwood & Kunda, 1997).

Not surprisingly, people are most likely to engage in social comparison
with someone who is similar to them on some dimension (Bandura, 1968;
Mussweiler, 2003; Lockwood & Kunda, 1997). There are many dimensions on
which people can be similar to Barack Obama, such as race, ethnicity, gender,
nationality, hobbies, ideology, religion, vocation, alma mater, and age, just to
name a few. Researchers have found that exposure to high-achieving individuals who are relevant to the self (e.g., are pursuing the same career) results
in participants rating themselves more positively on traits associated with
success, whereas exposure to a high-achieving individual who is not relevant
to the self has no effect on participants' self-ratings (Lockwood & Kunda,
1997). Research has also found positive effects for individuals who are part of
a minority group comparing themselves to another, more successful, member
of their ingroup (Brewer & Weber, 1994), indicating that Barack Obama might
be most effective as a role model for minority youth. If young African-
Americans can find a dimension on which they are similar to Barack Obama—
be it their family structure, political aspirations, ethnicity, or some other
characteristic—then they will be more likely to see him as relevant and therefore a potentially inspiring role model.

Following their experiment on role model relevance, Lockwood and
Kunda (1997) explored the impact of perceived attainability of role models'
success, and these findings are equally—if not more—important to include in
this discussion of Barack Obama as a potential role model. In this study, participants were first- and fourth-year accounting students who read a fictitious
newspaper article about a high achieving fourth-year accounting student. One
might expect that this potential role model would be most inspiring to the
fourth-year accounting students participating in the study, seeing how they
are similar to this individual in both intended vocation and age. In fact,
researchers found the exact opposite: First-year accounting students who read

about the successful fourth-year student rated themselves significantly more positively than first-year students who were not exposed to the role model. Fourth-year students, however, were more likely to rate themselves *less* positively than their peers who did not read about the successful student. Although the effect for fourth-year participants was not statistically significant, it does suggest that comparing oneself to someone who is similar and successful can have negative consequences for the self.

What might lead students to be adversely affected by exposure to a potential role model? Lockwood and Kunda suggest that the fourth-year students compared their own level of achievement to that of the outstanding fourth-year student presented in the newspaper article, and this comparison with someone who has achieved more at the same stage in their career was threatening to participants, resulting in their lower self-ratings on traits related to success. The first-year students, on the other hand, perceived the outstanding fourth-year student's success to be attainable: They still had 3 years to achieve what the student described in the newspaper had done, compared to the fourth-year participants, who did not have any more time to reach the same level of success as a fourth-year.

So, although African-American youth should be encouraged to find similarity between themselves and Barack Obama, they should be reminded of the time it took for him to get where he is today. Helping children think about Obama's achievements in politics, education, community organizing, or another domain in a way that makes them seem attainable will maximize the positive potential of their social comparisons. Emphasizing that Obama's success is the result of decades of hard work should help children perceive his level of accomplishment as something that they, too, could possibly achieve in the future, after they themselves have worked for that long.

Intuitively, positive expectations for students' performances in the classroom are beneficial and lead to a better scholastic experience. Again, however, there is empirical work demonstrating that the situation is often more nuanced than intuitions would allow. Some facets of social identity are associated with contradictory stereotypes—for example, an Asian woman contends with positive stereotypes about Asians' mathematical ability and negative stereotypes about women's math ability. One might expect that increasing the salience of an identity that is normally positively stereotyped would improve someone's performance on a stereotype-relevant task, but researchers have found the exact opposite. Work by Cheryan and Bodenhausen (2000) demonstrated that Asian-American women who were asked to think about their (positively stereotyped) ethnic identity before completing a math test performed *worse* than those who had been asked to think about their (negatively stereotyped) gender identity before the test. Although their findings are somewhat counterintuitive, they show that the "model minority" status associated with high expectations based on a social identity can impair performance much like negative expectations based on one's social identity.

Following the election of Barack Obama, there was much public discussion about expectations that the academic performance of African-American students would improve as a result of his being elected. Although the expectations themselves were positive in valence, minority students who are aware of the increased focus on their doing well in school may "choke under pressure" and end up performing worse than they would have without the elevated public expectations.

Negative consequences for African-American children could also stem from the fact that Barack Obama is an extreme example of a minority who has succeeded in mainstream institutions. People who compare themselves to an extremely successful individual, or exemplar, have been found to perceive themselves as being *less* like the exemplar than those who compare themselves to a moderately successful exemplar (Mussweiler, Ruter, & Epstude, 2004). When researchers asked participants to read about an extremely athletic person (such as Michael Jordan) or a moderately athletic person (like a former race car driver) and then rate their own level of athleticism, participants who read about Michael Jordan rated themselves as being significantly less athletic than those who had read about the race car driver (Mussweiler, Ruter, & Epstude, 2004).

Using social comparisons such as the one described above can be helpful, allowing situation-relevant information to be integrated into one's perceptions about one's relative attributes in a given setting. Imagine walking onto a basketball court knowing that you're about to face one of two opponents in a free-throw shooting contest: LeBron James or your grandmother. Your relative level of athleticism probably varies considerably depending on which of these two people you'll be playing against, and if asked to gauge your prospect of succeeding, it would be useful to compare your level of skill to that of your opponent. One would most likely anticipate success if facing grandma on the court, but defeat would be expected if asked to compete against an NBA player.

Social comparisons can be shaped by a focus on similarities or differences between the self and others. For young minorities who compare their own prospects for success against the extremely successful Barack Obama, inspiration will not be the most likely outcome if their comparison focuses on differences such as, "He went to private school and I go to public school" (Mussweiler, Ruter, & Epstude, 2004). To increase the likelihood that a comparison between oneself and Obama will lead to positive consequences like inspiration and improvements in motivation, one should instead focus on existing similarities (e.g., "Obama works hard and I work hard") (Mussweiler, Ruter, & Epstude, 2004; Lockwood & Kunda, 1997).

WHY DO ROLE MODEL EFFECTS FADE?

Notably, the positive effects of our Obama salience manipulation fade over time, with threat returning to its initial levels by the fall of seventh grade and the performance boost found in the second quarter wearing off in the course of the year. There is surprisingly little empirical research on actual role models and their long-term effect on students' psychological functioning and achievement in school settings. We can only speculate as to why role model effects such as ours faded. It is possible that role model effects are externally contingent, rising and falling with the role model's successes and difficulties. During the trajectory of the present study, President Obama's approval ratings suffered major declines (Pew Research Center, 2009). As the post-election elation wears off, perhaps Obama's potential to affect student achievement as a role model wanes as well.

Alternatively, as a role model becomes more commonplace, his/her ability to inspire fades (Campbell & Wolbrecht, 2006). Female political role models have been shown to exert their influence on young girls, primarily through their unique and *rare* status as *female* political figures (Campbell & Wolbrecht, 2006). Ironically, as the first African-American president in the history of the United States becomes old hat, students normalize his presence and his symbolic significance fades.

A third possibility is that students' own performance interacts with their perceptions of role models. Students' academic performance in middle school tends to decline (Eccles et al., 1991), so as students perceive Obama's achievements to be less attainable, they may become less inspired by them (Lockwood & Kunda 1997, 1999). Each of these explanations is important, providing ample opportunities for future research.

CONCLUDING THOUGHTS: RE-ENVISIONING AFRICAN-AMERICAN YOUTH

What does this mean for African-American children? Although Barack Obama's historic victory does not mean that we are now living in a post-racial America, it does mean that children are growing up in a country where a majority of voters chose a man of American and African descent to be their leader. Heralded as a pivotal event in American race relations, the election of Barack Obama instigated a national conversation about race and achievement, one that has the potential to reshape the content of racial stereotypes and the extent to which they are endorsed (both publicly and privately). Role models provide people with important information about their *own* abilities and possible future selves (Lockwood, 2006), so minority youth who are coming of age during the Obama presidency may very well use his example as a point of reference when forming their own aspirations.

Obama himself even explicitly outlines his route to success, sharing his story with American youth. In his back-to-school speech delivered in September 2009, the president likens his own struggles and successes to those being experienced by young students today:

> I get it. I know what it's like. My father left my mother when I was two years old, and I was raised by a single mother who struggled at times to pay the bills and wasn't always able to give us things the other kids had. There were times when I missed having a father in my life. There were times when I was lonely and felt like I didn't fit in. . .
>
> But at the end of the day, the circumstances of your life–what you look like, where you come from, how much money you have, what you've got going on at home–that's no excuse for talking back to your teacher or cutting class, or dropping out of school. That's no excuse for not trying.
>
> Where you are right now doesn't have to determine where you'll end up. No one's written your destiny for you. Here in America, you write your own destiny. You make your own future (Obama, 2009b).

Some facets of Barack Obama's achievement, such as the Ivy League education and personal financial success, are not unusual for a U.S. president. His struggles with issues surrounding race, family, and stability, however, closely resemble those experienced by many American youth today. By using his own story and consistently emphasizing the effort he exerted to overcome obstacles, Obama illustrates the opportunities and routes to success available to children of all backgrounds.

IMPROVING THE LIVES OF MINORITY YOUTH: YES WE CAN

The election of Barack Obama is by no means a panacea for the issues facing young African-Americans, but it does have the potential to positively affect them. Our research has shown that increasing the salience of Obama's victory shortly after the 2008 presidential election led to a slight boost in academic performance for students regardless of ethnicity. More importantly, this same brief manipulation reduced minority students' levels of self-reported social identity threat. Given that threat may undermine students' abilities to foster cross-race relationships (Strambler, 2009) and remain engaged in school (Steele, 1997; Osborne & Walker, 2006), the possibility that Obama's success would reduce this adverse consequence of belonging to a negatively stereotyped group is promising and should be considered further in research and the public discourse.

The American public's endorsement of Barack Obama may change the way young African-Americans think about the country they live in, their fellow citizens, and the content and validity of the stereotypes by which they might be judged. This is no small thing: Research on stereotype threat has demonstrated that an individual's concern related to confirming a negative stereotype about their group can seriously harm performance (Steele & Aronson, 1995), so if the election of Barack Obama leads African-American students to perceive those stereotypes as being less relevant (e.g., "People must not endorse the idea that African-American s are stupid if they would vote for Obama.") or their own performance as being less critical to others' judgment of their racial group (e.g., "Others will probably judge African Americans by Obama's success, not mine."), then stereotype threat may not inhibit performance to the same extent.

In this chapter, we explored a moment when a national election translated into higher achievement for individual students. These were promising, if fading, effects. The message is clear, however: Change is possible. Our educational system can shift the way students consider themselves and their own potential through smart interventions. In giving us a set of role models, our historic moment shapes us. We, in turn, must shape our history. What the media briefly did with Barack Obama's election (putting the glowing image of a smart African-American man into every living room), schools can do every day. The effects need not wane.

But this will take work. A reduction in students' perceptions of social identity threat, a tweaking of deeply entrenched stereotypes, and a prominent minority role model will not change the fact that minority students are still more likely to attend a school with teachers who are at the beginning of their careers or instructors who have less education and training in the subjects they are teaching, overcrowding and large class sizes (Edelman, 2004), just to name a few of the issues that continue to disproportionately affect minority students in America's public education system. Additionally, segregation by race and socio-economic status continues to rise in the United States (Bigg, 2009; Dewan, 2010). It will take much more than Obama's ascendancy to the White House to ameliorate the obstacles facing today's African-American youth. As President Barack Obama proclaimed during his inauguration (Obama, 2009c):

> Today I say to you that the challenges we face are real. They are serious and they are many. They will not be met easily or in a short span of time. But know this, America: They will be met. . .
>
> The time has come to reaffirm our enduring spirit; to choose our better history; to carry forward that precious gift, that noble idea, passed on from generation to generation: the God-given promise that all are equal, all are free, and all deserve a chance to pursue their full measure of happiness.

Whether or not Barack Obama is able to advance these ideals during his time as president, accomplishing the goals he outlined in his open letter to Sasha and Malia that all children are able "to learn and dream and grow and thrive" remains to be seen.

REFERENCES

Algoe, S., Haidt, J., (2009). Witnessing Excellence in Action: The other-praising emotions of elevation, admiration, and gratitude. *Journal of Positive Psychology, 4*, 105–127.

Apfelbaum, E. P., Sommers, S. R., & Norton, M. I. (2008). Seeing race and seeming racist? Evaluating strategic colorblindness in social interaction. *Journal of Personality and Social Psychology, 95*, 918–932.

Aronson, J. (2002). *Improving academic achievement: Impact of Psychological Factors on Education.* San Diego: Academic Press.

Aronson, J., Fried, C. & Good, C. (2002). Reducing the effects of stereotype threat on African American college students by shaping theories of intelligence. *Journal of Experimental Social Psychology, 38*, 113–125.

Aronson, J., Jannone, S., McGlone, M., & Johnson-Campbell T. (2009). The Obama effect: An experimental test. *Journal of Experimental Social Psychology, 45*, 957–960.

Baldi, S., Perie, M., Skidmore, D., Greenberg, E., & Hahn, C. (2001). What Democracy Means to Ninth-Graders: U.S. Results From the International IEA Civic Education Study (NCES 2001–096). U.S. Department of Education, National Center for Education Statistics. Washington, D.C.: U.S. Government Printing Office.

Bandura, A. (1968). Imitation. In D. L. Sills (Ed.), *International encyclopedia of the social sciences* (Vol. 7). New York: Macmillan.

Bargh, J. A., & Chartrand, T. L. (1999). The unbearable automaticity of being. *American Psychologist, 54*, 462–479.

Bigg, M. (January 14, 2009). U.S. school segregation on the rise: report. *Reuters.* Retrieved January 26, 2010 from http://www.reuters.com/article/idUSTRE50D7CY20090114

Blanton, H., Crocker, J., & Miller, D. T. (2000). The effects of in-group versus out-group social comparison on self-esteem in the context of a negative stereotype. *Journal of Experimental Social Psychology, 36*, 519–530.

Blascovich, J., Spencer, S. J., Quinn, D. M., & Steele, C. M. (2001). African-Americans and high blood pressure: The role of stereotype threat. *Psychological Science, 12*, 225–229.

Branscombe, N. R., Schmitt, M. T., & Harvey, R. D. (1999). Perceiving pervasive discrimination among African-Americans: Implications for group identification and well-being. *Journal of Personality and Social Psychology, 77*, 135–149.

Brewer, M. B., Dull, L., & Lui, L. (1981). Perceptions of the elderly: Stereotypes as prototypes. *Journal of Personality and Social Psychology, 41*, 656–670.

Brewer, M. B., & Weber, J. G. (1994). Self-evaluation effects on interpersonal versus intergroup social comparison. *Journal of Personality and Social Psychology, 71,* 83–93.

Bronfenbrenner, U. (1979). *The Ecology of Human Development: Experiments by Nature and Design.* Cambridge, MA: Harvard University Press.

Buunk, A. P., Peiro, J. M., & Griffioen, C. (2007). A positive role model may stimulate career-oriented behavior. *Journal of Applied Social Psychology, 37,* 1489–1500.

Campbell, D. E., & Wolbrecht, C. (2006). See Jane run: Women politicians as role models for adolescents. *The Journal of Politics, 68,* 233–247.

Cheryan, S., & Bodenhausen, G. V. (2000). When positive stereotypes threaten intellectual performance: The psychological hazards of "model minority" status. *Psychological Science, 11,* 399–402.

Cohen, G. L., & Garcia, J. (2005). "I am us": Negative stereotypes as collective threats. *Journal of Personality and Social Psychology, 89,* 566–582.

Cohen, G. L., Garcia, J., Apfel, N., & Master, A. (2006). Reducing the racial achievement gap: A social-psychological intervention. *Science, 313,* 1307–1310.

Cohen, G. L., Garcia, J., Purdie-Vaughns, V., Apfel, N., & Brzustoski, P. (2009). Raising minority performance with a values-affirmation intervention: A two-year follow-up. *Science, 324,* 400–403.

Cook, J. E., Purdie-Vaughns, V., Garcia, J., & Cohen, G. L. (2009). Do I or don't I, can I or can't I: The long-term impact of self-affirmation on perceptions of academic belonging. *Manuscript in preparation.*

Dewan, S. (2010, January 7). Southern schools mark two majorities. *The New York Times,* A20.

Dyson, M.E. (2008). Barack Obama's historic victory represents a quantum leap in the racial progress of the United States. Los Angeles Times (Nov. 5, 2008).

Eccles, J. S., Lord, S., & Midgley, C. (1991). What are we doing to early adolescents? The impact of educational contexts on early adolescents. *American Journal of Education, 99*(4), 521.

Edelman, M. W. "Written comments of Marian Wright Edelman for 'Educational Apartheid in the U.S.: Tracking Policies and Re-Segregation in America's Schools'." Congressional Black Caucus Foundation. 8 Sept. 2004. Retrieved January 5, 2010 from http://www.childrensdefense.org/child-research-data-publications/data/marian-wright-edelman-testimony-educational-apartheid-2004.html

Federal Election Commission (FEC). (2009). 2008 *Official presidential general election results.* Washington, DC. Retrieved January 15, 2010 from http://www.fec.gov/pubrec/fe2008/2008presgeresults.pdf

Fiske, S. T., Cuddy, A. J. C., Glick, P., & Xu, J. (2002). A model of (often mixed) stereotype content: Competence and warmth respectively follow from status and competition. *Journal of Personality and Social Psychology, 82,* 878–890.

Kantor, J. (2009). The Obamas' marriage. *The New York Times Magazine,* MM44.

Kaufman, J., & Fields, G. (2008, November 10). Election of Obama recasts national conversation on race. *The Wall Street Journal*, A8.

Lewis, S. (2008). Political Lesson: Schools find ways to integrate election into curriculum. Detroit News (Nov. 8, 2008).

Lockwood, P. (2006). "Someone like me can be successful": Do college students need same-gender role models? *Psychology of Women Quarterly, 30*, 36–46.

Lockwood, P., & Kunda, Z. (1997). Superstars and me: Predicting the impact of role models on the self. *Journal of Personality and Social Psychology, 73*, 91–103.

Lockwood, P., & Kunda, Z. (1999). Salience of best selves undermines inspiration by outstanding role models. *Journal of Personality and Social Psychology, 76*, 214–228.

Marx, D. M., & Goff, P. A. (2005). Clearing the air: The effect of experimenter race on targets' test performance and subjective experience. *British Journal of Social Psychology, 44*, 645–657.

Marx, D. M., Ko, S. J., & Friedman, R. A. (2009). The "Obama Effect": How a salient role model reduces race-based performance differences. *Journal of Experimental Social Psychology, 45*, 953–956.

Marx, D., & Roman, J. (2002). Female role models: Protecting women's math test performance. *Personality and Social Psychology Bulletin, 28*, 1183–1193.

McGlone, M.S., Aronson, J., & Kobrynowicz, D. (2006). Stereotype threat and the gender gap in political knowledge. *Psychology of Women Quarterly, 30*, 392–398.

McIntyre, R. B., Paulson, R., & Lord, C. (2003). Alleviating women's mathematics stereotype threat through salience of group achievements. *Journal of Experimental Social Psychology, 39*, 83–90.

McKown C., & Strambler M.J. (2009). Developmental antecedents and social and academic consequences of stereotype-consciousness in middle childhood. *Child Development, 80*, 1643–1659.

McMahon, S. D., Singh, J., Garner, L., & Benhorin, S. (2004). Taking advantage of opportunities: community involvement, well-Being, and urban youth. *Journal of Adolescent Health, 34*, 262–265.

Mussweiler, T. (2003). Comparison processes in social judgment: Mechanisms and consequences. *Psychological Review, 110*, 472–489.

Mussweiler, T., Rüter, K., & Epstude, K. (2004). The ups and downs of social comparison: Mechanisms of assimilation and contrast. *Journal of Personality and Social Psychology, 87*, 832–844.

Neilsen (2008, November 5). *National TV audience estimates for the election night 2008*. Retrieved January 5, 2010 fromhttp://blog.nielsen.com/nielsenwire/wp-content/uploads/2008/11/2008-election-night-w-20042000-final.pdf.

Obama, B. (January 18, 2009). What I want for you–and every child in America. *Parade*. Retrieved February 9, 2010 from http://www.parade.com/news/2009/01/barack-obama-letter-to-my-daughters.html.

Obama, B. "Prepared remarks of President Barack Obama: Back to school event." Arlington, VA. 8 Sept. 2009b. Retrieved January 5, 2010 from http://www.whitehouse.gov/mediaresources/PreparedSchoolRemarks.

Obama, B. "Inaugural address." Washington, DC. 20 Jan. 2009c. Retrieved February 9, 2010 from http://www.whitehouse.gov/the_press_office/President_Barack_Obamas_Inaugural_Address

Osborne, J. W., & Walker, C. (2006). Stereotype threat, identification with academics, and withdrawal from school: why the most successful students of colour might be most likely to withdraw. *Educational Psychology, 26*, 563–577.

Pew Research Center. (2008). *High marks for campaign, high bar for Obama.* Washington, D.C.: Kohut, A. Retrieved January 20, 2010 from http://people-press.org/reports/pdf/471.pdf.

President Obama. [Editorial]. (2008, November 5). *The Guardian*, 35.

Purdie-Vaughns, V., Steele, C.M., Davies, P., Ditlmann, R., Randall-Crosby, J. (2008). Identity contingency threat: How diversity cues signal threat or safety for African-Americans in mainstream settings. *Journal of Personality and Social Psychology, 94*, 615–630.

Schmader, T., & Johns, M. (2003). Converging evidence that stereotype threat reduces working memory capacity. *Journal of Personality and Social Psychology, 85*, 440–452.

Sherman, D. K., & Cohen, G. L. (2006). The psychology of self-defense: Self-affirmation theory. *Advances in Experimental Social Psychology, 38*, 183–242.

Sherman, D. K., Kinias, Z., Major, B., Kim, H.S., & Prenovost, M. A. (2007). The group as a resource: Reducing biased attributions for group success and failure via group-affirmation. *Personality and Social Psychology Bulletin, 33*, 1100–1112.

Stannard, E. (2008). Role Model: Young Black Men say Barack Obama an Inspiration. (2008, November 9). *The New Haven Register*, p. 1.

Steele, C. M. (1997). A threat in the air: How stereotypes shape intellectual identity and performance. *American Psychologist, 52*, 613–629.

Steele, C. M., & Aronson, J. (1995). Stereotype threat and the intellectual test performance of African Americans. *Journal of Personality & Social Psychology, 69*, 797–811.

Steele, C. M., Spencer, S. J., & Aronson, J. (2002). Contending with group image: The psychology of stereotype and social identity threat. In M.P. Zanna (Ed.), *Advances experimental social psychology* (Vol. 34, pp. 379–440). San Diego, CA: Academic Press.

Tesser, A. (1988). Toward a self-evaluation maintenance model of social behavior. In L. Berkowitz (Ed.), *Advances in experimental social psychology*, (pp. 181–227). New York: Academic Press.

Tesser, A., & Campbell, J. (1983). Self-definition and self-evaluation maintenance. In J. Suls & A. Greenwald (Eds.), *Social psychological perspectives on the self* (pp. 1–31). Hillsdale, NJ: Erlbaum.

U.S. Census Bureau (2009). *Voter turnout increases by 5 million in 2008 presidential election*. Washington, DC. Retrieved January 21, 2010 from http://www.census.gov/Press-Release/www/releases/archives/voting/013995.html

Walton, G. M. & Spencer, S. J. (2009). Latent ability: Grades and test scores systematically underestimate the intellectual ability of negatively stereotyped students. *Psychological Science, 20,* 1132–1139.

Wout, D. A., Shih, M. J., Jackson, J. S., & Sellers, R. M. (2009). Targets as perceivers: How people determine when they will be negatively stereotyped. *Journal of Personality and Social Psychology, 96,* 349–362.

Re-Envisioning Black Youth

Marc Lamont Hill

As we enter the early stages of the "Obama era," the plight of Black youth remains one of the most urgent social issues. In the educational realm, Black youth remain under-represented in post-secondary institutions and over-represented in special education classes, suspension lists, and dropout rolls. In other sectors of public life, such as public health, criminal justice, and the labor market, Black youth linger at the bottom of nearly all indices of social prosperity and remain firmly at the top of all indices of social misery. Within the public imagination, Black youth are perennially framed as dangerous social burdens, unworthy of the basic provisions, protections, and supports that are afforded to their White counterparts.

In the midst of these sobering circumstances, the authors of the preceding chapter force us beyond romantic and hortatory narratives about Barack Obama's historic victory. Instead, they force us to ask penetrating questions about the concrete benefits of such a victory, particularly as it relates to the self-perception and achievement of Black youth. Simply put, how does the ascendance of a Black president produce new sites of educational possibility for our children? Given Obama's early failure to substantively challenge free-market fundamentalism, corporate cronyism, environmental abuse, and imperialist aggression, such questions are not only legitimate but urgently necessary.

Through their empirical investigation, the authors offer a compelling and provocative set of claims about the value of the Obama Presidency for helping Black youth re-imagine the role of race and racism in American life. The authors suggest that Obama serves as a role model whose success within the racially treacherous realms of education and politics allows them to reassess their own life chances, rethink the viability of American democracy, and recommit themselves to academic excellence. Without question, such claims provide necessary help and hope as we attempt to reconcile the existence of a Black president with pervasive levels of Black suffering.

Although we can (and should) find comfort in these powerful and necessary insights, we must not allow them to seduce us into naïve or counterfactual optimism about the future of our youth. After all, as centuries of educational research has demonstrated, Black children have never been plagued by aspirational deficits. Even amidst the most oppressive social conditions in human history, Black youth have always aspired to be doctors, lawyers, engineers, and teachers at rates that surpass other racial and ethnic groups. Tragically, however, the road from aspiration to attainment for minority youth has always been plagued by resource gaps, structural inequality, and institutionalized forms of White supremacy. To ignore these material realities is to endorse a dangerous and dishonest gospel of individualism that traces educational success to the exclusive repositories of talent and desire.

To be clear, the authors of this chapter are not guilty of such a practice. On the contrary, they offer complex and subtle insights that enable us to find legitimate purpose, value, and hope in the Obama Presidency. Nevertheless, the full power of these insights can only be leveraged within a social context that closes the gap between aspiration and attainment, between merit and destiny. If we commit ourselves to producing such a world for our children, then, and only then, will Obama's Presidency realize its full potential for our children.

CHAPTER 9

Obama and Global Change in Perceptions of Group Status

George Ciccariello-Maher and Matthew W. Hughey

Within the American context, as articulated by other authors in this volume, the march toward racial equality remains a treacherous journey with mixed results: Research in the area of "system justification theory" provides one explanation for why and how racial progress has become stagnant in recent years. This approach identifies the existence of an ideological motivation to justify the existing social order. Such a motivation operates in part through implicit expressions of internalized inferiority by those most disadvantaged by the prevailing system. Given that people may be de-biased at the implicit level, the election of President Obama and the prominence of the Obama family portends an auspicious beginning for America and a possible move toward significant decreases in nonconscious racial bias.

But the prominence of Barack Obama and the Obama family could have just as significant an effect beyond the borders of the United States. In countries around the world, societies are often divided into privileged and disadvantaged groups, with the latter often viewed negatively, remaining marginalized and politically powerless in their countries. However, inasmuch as the dispossessed may be aware of America's racial history and the meteoric rise of President Obama, his election may very well serve to alter the modes of thinking about race, social class, and minority–majority status among people outside the United States. However, the Obama phenomenon also entails the serious risk, one borne out in system justification theory, of rapid reorientation in which nonconscious de-biasing may occur alongside a relative absence of systemic change. This danger also exists on the international level. This chapter employs system justification theory to address both the potential and the dangers of Obama's election vis-à-vis systems of inequality beyond the borders of the United States.

SYSTEM JUSTIFICATION THEORY

In an effort to explain the persistence of unjust structures of inequality despite the clear interests that many would have in seeing such structures transformed, some scholars have developed what they call "system justification theory." This approach sets out from the claim that such structures persist in part because "people are motivated to defend, justify, and rationalize the status quo" (Jost, Pietrzak, Liviatan, Mandisodza, & Napier, 2007 p. 592). Put briefly, system justification theory seeks to explain how and why people support the status quo even when it is against their interests to do so, which in turn sheds light on the intransigence of existing systems and the oft-noted difficulty of achieving substantive social change.

Research in this field has demonstrated that although those sectors privileged by the prevailing social system behave predictably to defend that system and those privileges, the less conventional and more counterintuitive side of the story is one in which those *lacking* privileges within, and disadvantaged by, the same system also exhibit similar behavior in support of the status quo. Hence, the disadvantaged are placed in conflict with both their individual and group interests (Jost, Banaji, & Nosek, 2004: 909). The effects of this conflict, too, are borne out in research, which both demonstrates *(1)* the internal conflict (as measured by self-esteem, depression, and neurotic tendencies) and *(2)* group conflict (as measured by attitudes toward membership) appear in exacerbated form in those individuals who throw in their lot with the status quo (Jost & Burgess, 2000). In an effort to compensate for the cognitive dissonance that such a position therefore entails, some such individuals emerge as even more fervent defenders of the system than those who reap its benefits. Because the gap between one's position and one's support for the system "cannot be resolved by rationalizing one's own behavior . . . a rationalization of the system is necessary to resolve emotional discomfort" (Jost et al., 2007, p. 593).

In a retrospective survey of the system justification literature, some authors associated with the approach summarize the claims it entails:

(1) there is a general ideological motive to justify the existing social order,

(2) this motive is at least partially responsible for the internalization of inferiority among members of disadvantaged groups,

(3) it is observed most readily at an implicit, nonconscious level of awareness, and

(4) paradoxically, it is sometimes strongest among those who are most harmed by the status quo. (Jost, Banaji, & Nosek, 2004: 881)

Put differently: a major part of what allows for the intransigence of the status quo is the internalization of inferiority (what we will call *outgroup favoritism*). The fact that outgroup favoritism manifests *implicitly* is no surprise, because the pressures of individual and group interest are such that *explicit* self-hatred or self-denigration is often difficult to plausibly maintain in a society structured by political correctness and a commitment to being supposedly "post-racial" (Hughey, 2010, 2007). Key, however, are the implications of this implicit inferiority, as its subterraneous character allows it to function unperceived, as a sort of invisible support buttressing systems of privilege and inequality.

Further, these same inertial dynamics have serious implications for those instances where change *does* indeed occur through a terminal crisis in the legitimacy of the prevailing social system. The general motive to support the status quo and derive security from identifying with it leads—in situations where that status quo has become wholly untenable—to a peculiar phenomenon: the rapid reorientation of allegiance and transference of loyalty to the new status quo as a substitute source of security and psychic stability, a process that occurs to some degree regardless of the new system's particular characteristics (Jost et al., 2007, p. 592). Here, the implications are clear. System justification logically favors a minimization of change and a bias toward symbolic or cosmetic changes that leave structures of inequality substantively intact, and this process is "certainly germane for those concerned with its ability to obfuscate the material realities of racial inequality" (Hughey, 2010, p. 19).

Although it is still too early to tell, this phenomenon shows the degree to which Obama's election might serve as a double-edged sword vis-à-vis the legitimation of systems of inequality in the United States, undermining internalized inferiority among the disadvantaged while allowing those same groups to identify more easily with a new status quo, to some degree irrespective of the substantive changes it has undergone. As we will see, this domestic danger that system justification theory illumines, is reproduced internationally in two ways. First—and in the vein of Tocqueville—a new "American Exceptionalism" threatens to misrepresent the United States abroad, and second, domestically within individual countries, which are undergoing processes of social transformation. As we move forward in a discussion of the international implications of the Obama phenomenon, we will maintain this two-pronged focus: first, on the potential for implicit racial debiasing and undermining of outgroup favoritism that Obama's election would seem to promise and, second, on the risk posed by the tendency toward rapid reorientation of system justification in the absence of significant structural change.

Before moving to a discussion of the international context, however, we must first address some initial challenges left unanswered in the system justification literature. Central among these is the fact that as a mode of diagnosing the counterintuitive stability of systems of social inequality, system justification theory, strictly understood, does not offer a theory of social transformation, of rupture with the status quo. However, some clues to such rupture are nevertheless available in inverted form, and for the sake of brevity, we focus here on outgroup favoritism or implicit, nonconscious feelings of inferiority.

System justification theory posits such outgroup favoritism as central to those processes that function to uphold and justify the status quo. Internalized inferiority on the part of the disadvantaged is, in other words, the glue that holds the system together. This glue operates in turn by undermining both individual identification and interest as well as group identification and interest insofar as either of these challenge identification with the system. Hence, undermining outgroup identification as well as fostering individual self-esteem and group identity among disadvantaged populations might feasibly serve to undermine the effects of system justification. Furthermore, as these processes tend to manifest primarily on the implicit level and remain largely untenable on the explicit level (Jost, Banaji, & Nosek, 2004, p. 893), one might also reasonably expect the process of making explicit the operations of systemic inequality (e.g., in racism, social class, etc.) to similarly undermine the centripetal and inertial effects of system justification. In sum, the undermining of outgroup favoritism can occur through two simultaneous and inter-related processes: facilitating individual and group identification and making implicit racism and outgroup favoritism explicit (and thereby untenable).

As we have seen in the other chapters that comprise this volume, the so-called "Obama effect" bears significant promise in undermining these individual and group manifestations of system justification, with specific reference to African-Americans, who can to some degree be expected to find both individual self-worth and group identification bolstered by the existence of a Black president. However, with regard to prevailing structures of inequality, system justification theory also alerts us to the potential ambiguities of the Obama phenomenon. In what follows, we will turn to a discussion of the international impact of Obama's election, with a particular emphasis on both its potential to counteract outgroup favoritism and the danger of systemic reorientation.

COUNTERACTING OUTGROUP FAVORITISM

The global face of Obama's election remains marked by similar ambiguities, contributing simultaneously to an undermining of outgroup favoritism among members of disadvantaged groups (expressed primarily through new candidacies) while in the same gesture facilitating a new American Exceptionalism that threatens to conceal the persistence of global structures of inequality. If anything, the double-edged sword that is the Obama phenomenon becomes even *more* acute in an international setting, as we must wonder *which* system is being justified: the global economic structures of the world system? international structures of racialization? or local, domestic structures of inequality? And what difficulty is entailed when justification of the status quo on one level coincides with rupture on another level? Although our focus in this chapter is on systems of racialization, as will become clear, it is not possible to entirely parse these out from other moments of the prevailing status quo. But even a narrow focus on racism and racialization gives rise to complicated questions of particular, local histories, and the forms that race and racism have assumed in various parts of the globe (Hughey, 2010).

Although we must bear in mind the difficulty that such particularities entail both for our theoretical apparatus and discussion (systems justification research having been drawn largely from the U.S. context), and although we must not *assume* applicability elsewhere, the goal of this chapter is necessarily more modest. We attempt to tentatively assess the international impact of the Obama phenomenon vis-à-vis systems of racial oppression and the justification of the status quo that emerges from oppressed, disadvantaged, and racialized groups and individuals. Has Obama's election undermined tacit support for the status quo among groups racialized as "Black" worldwide? Has it facilitated either the development of individual self-worth or group identity? We recognize that our answers can only be partial and that in all likelihood they will only raise more questions than they answer.

Here, a specific difficulty emerges that must be noted at the outset: If system justification theory places great emphasis on the *implicit* level, then using intensive survey research to demonstrate the disconnect between what are frequently explicit critiques of the system by oppressed groups and individuals and underlying and implicit support for its structures (Jost, Banaji, & Nosek, 2004: 893) is a level of analysis that we cannot hope to reproduce here in the absence of survey data. But we *can* track—central to our claims below—the twofold movement whereby Obama's election contributes to undermining outgroup favoritism: first, in facilitating *identification* (as expressed primarily in new candidacies), and second, in contributing to the process of *revealing* underlying racist structures, rendering the implicit explicit, and thereby less plausibly tenable. The two gestures remain intertwined, and as we will see, the second is particularly important in the international context, where race and racism often assume nuanced forms.

Perhaps the best concrete measure we have of the effect of Obama's election on undermining outgroup favoritism internationally is the wave of candidacies that his victory immediately inspired, candidacies that sit at the intersection of individual and group identification. In one case, an African-born farmer in Russia named Joaquim Crima was inspired to run for local office in the notoriously racist nation (Ioffee, 2009). Although open expressions of racism are common in Russia, Crima's candidacy can be argued to have brought this debate to the surface. One respondent, for example, stated that she would not vote for him because she did not want to "live in Africa," whereas another simply refused to vote for Blacks in general. Interestingly, and perhaps given the openness of such expressions, Crima even attempted to tap into both a historical tradition of anti-Black racism alongside current deleterious framings of Obama (Parks & Heard, 2010) to gain attention for his campaign, advertising on billboards his campaign promise to "toil like a Negro" if elected. Although Crima lacked the political capital and connections necessary to be a serious contender, he hoped to stimulate debate and provoke discussion of race in Russia, while communicating to ruling elites that the times might have been changing. As Crima's campaign manager put it, he hoped Crima's candidacy would prove to be "an experiment that the Kremlin will be interested in supporting."

Another interesting case is that of Bolivia, in which recent reports have emphasized the importance of Obama's election to the Afro-Bolivian population. According to a recent article in the mainstream press:

> Obama stands as an example that we can follow," says Marfa Inofuentes, a leader of the Afro-Bolivian Center for Comprehensive Community Development in La Paz. "We, like him, want to have our own representative in Congress. And we dream than we can also have an Afro-Bolivian president some day. (Llana, 2009)

But although these hopes are real, and Afro-Bolivians see Obama as an example that bodes well for their own future, the article ignores the process of recognition for Afro-Bolivians that begin long before Obama and only briefly mentions the new Bolivian constitution, one that enshrines the rights of Afro-Bolivians for the first time in the nation's history. And it makes no mention of the fact that these transformations have occurred under the watch of Evo Morales—the country's first ever indigenous president—and the social movements that propelled him to power.

One could also cite the emblematic case of Black Iraqis in Basra, who are openly referred to as "slaves" (Dougherty, 2009; *see also* Salman & Susman, 2008). Jalal Thiyab Thijeel of the Movement of Free Iraqis described Obama's victory as "inspiring." As he put it:

> "We told our people, Inshalla [sic], God willing, Obama is going to win, and if he wins, it will be a victory for all black people in the world. . . We're going to make him a model to follow. Even our old women were praying for him to win." But as he continues to describe the significance of the shift in local consciousness that the election brought about, the ambiguities and even contradictions begin to become apparent: "Now we, the dark-skinned

people, feel even closer to the American people because Obama is one of us. . . There's a change in international politics. . . Obama won, and not that long ago, in his country, black people were marginalized, so this event has shattered all barriers." (Dougherty, 2009)

The irony should be immediately clear: this is a man speaking under a condition of military occupation. Although this does not negate entirely the potential impact of Obama's election, it should nevertheless alert us to both the dangers of exaggerating that impact and its complexity.

Specifically, one clear danger in such accounts is that they often say more about those writing them—about the demand within the United States for stories that reflect American optimism and self-righteousness after years of war—than they say about their purported subjects. Russia's Crima, for example, was clearly a marginal actor with little electoral potential, and the article contains no reference to his relationship to any kind of movement representing the interests of African immigrants. And a close read of the Bolivian article reveals that it is less identification with Obama than previous struggles that have allowed Afro-Bolivians to emerge as a social force capable of confronting entrenched racism (*see* below for clear parallels with the Venezuelan case). Given the war in Iraq and the pressing nature of cognitive dissonance in the United States, moreover, it should be no surprise that the mainstream media has only recently discovered "Black Iraqis."

Certainly, however, such accounts indicate that something important is occurring as a result of the reception of Obama's election across the globe. Specifically, individual candidacies here indicate to some degree (in some cases) a new willingness to express individual and group identification which conflicts with the prevailing structures of the system. Whereas these three cases indicate the potential for Obama's election to spur identification in a manner that could undercut outgroup favoritism, equally important in terms of outgroup favoritism, moreover, is the degree to which Obama's election, the candidacies he stimulates, and the conflicts these candidacies engender reveal on the explicit level something that had remained largely implicit: beliefs in racial inferiority either among those in power or internalized by the disadvantaged. Although we will look more closely at one such case below (China), the recent diplomatic fallout between the Obama administration and Honduran coup leaders and the new critiques of racial discrimination in socialist Cuba are both worth briefly mentioning.

In Honduras, where a recent coup against the popular leftist government of Manuel Zelaya place the government in the hands of business elites headed by Roberto Micheletti, a clear tension emerged between the coup regime's pro-Western stance and Obama's race. When it seemed as though there would

be little resistance to the coup in U.S. circles of power, there was little disconnect, but as soon as Obama voiced even his tepid opposition to the coup—
even when this fell short of a demand to return Zelaya to power—the response
by the coup regime was clear. Former foreign minister for the *de facto* regime,
Enrique Ortez Colindres, attacked the U.S. president as a "little black man" or
negrito, who "doesn't know anything" ("Colindres," 2009). Colindres apolo-
gized after a strenuous complaint by the U.S. ambassador and was promptly
removed from his position. But perhaps epitomizing the vagaries of the global
stage, the Obama Administration has nevertheless been accused of tacitly
supporting the coup.

Cuba, often seen as a sort of post-racial paradise, has come under fire
recently by various American intellectuals for the persistence of racial discrimination, and some have suggested that this is a partial result of the Obama
presidency (Fausset, 2010). A recent open letter signed by dozens of activists
and intellectuals has expressed support for jailed Black dissidents, and
although recognizing the gains of the Cuban Revolution in decreasing racism,
the letter demands that the government go further to address the needs of
Afro-Cubans. Here, Obama's impact is of a more complex and geopolitical
nature (of the sort we will discuss below with regard to Venezuela): it is arguably only under a liberal Democrat that such liberal critics would issue such a
statement, because to have done so under President Bush would have been to
run the risk of association with the anti-Cuban right.

THE NEW AMERICAN EXCEPTIONALISM

System justification theory assists us in recognizing this dual potential that
Obama's election promises internationally—namely, that of facilitating individual and group identification by disadvantaged and racialized groups and
that of revealing on an explicit level the often implicit functioning of that
racism. But if system justification theory helps us to see the positive, then it
also alerts us to the negative: the ever-present danger whereby the loyalties of
those suffering under the old system are rapidly transferred to a new and
reoriented status quo. On the international level, this danger emerges as a part
of the very same process, whereby Obama's election is televised and transmit-
ted across the globe in the guise of a new "American Exceptionalism," in
which the United States is portrayed as a country of almost unlimited upward
mobility for even the most disadvantaged groups.

In a recent article, Radhika Parameswaran (2009) skillfully dissects this
double-edged sword, this dual international effect of the Obama election.
Drawing parallels to the global solidarity expressed in the wake of the events
of September 11, 2001, Parameswaran demonstrates the ways in which

Obama's election "fueled neoliberal American exceptionalist discourse in the arenas of racial progress and equality . . . and Obama's own nationalist rhetoric bolstered this transnational investment American colorblind nationalism" (p. 202). This transformation, moreover, was all the more sudden and unexpected given the fact that previous reference points for racial politics in the United States—namely, Hurricane Katrina, whose imagery had decloaked U.S. racism and cultivated a degree of global solidarity from poor populations—were so diametrically opposed to this message (p. 198). For Parameswaran, this reality was undermined by the exceptionalist rhetoric surrounding Obama's historic ascent to power.

But Parameswaran is careful not to lay the blame entirely at Obama's own doorstep or to put forth too negative a view. Obama's election, she insists, does indeed portend the possibility of a loosening of racial categories that brings the African-American experience into dialogue with global patterns of racialization. The relationship between this potential effect and the new "exceptionalist" discourse is one that revolves around the paradox of the media, an irony that is all the more powerful and unavoidable in the international arena. It was the global media that made possible the positive effect of Obama's election in undermining outgroup favoritism globally, as "television, along with Obama, occupies the role of heroic protagonist, uniting global audiences. . . [and] project[ing] a discourse of global racial solidarity crossing the boundaries of class and nation" (p. 199). But it is this very same media that facilitates and fuels the new American Exceptionalism, smoothing the transition of system justification through "the selective repetition and amplification of particular rhetorical statements" (p. 202; *see also* Pinkney, 2009). We have already seen this amplification in the veritable explosion of articles on aspiring "Bolivian Obamas" or "Russian Obamas" discussed above and will need to bear such tensions in mind as we move forward. Further, we require attention not only to this exceptionalism as a reorientation of the global legitimacy and justification of the United States but also to the domestic systemic reorientations to which system justification theory correctly alerts our attention.

In what follows, we will first consider the Venezuelan example as one that both bears out and problematizes certain assumptions held by system justification theory, pointing toward the need for a more dynamic theory capable of charting the parameters of the conflict between advantaged and disadvantaged groups, the decline of and replacement of the status quo, and the reorientation of system justification tendencies toward this new system. We will then conclude with the case of China, where the response to Obama's election has revealed a number of other global dynamics that complicate our view in productive ways. In both cases, we will keep our sights trained on the simultaneous potential and danger of the Obama phenomenon: the former in undermining outgroup favoritism through both facilitating identification and making implicit structures and inferiority explicit, and the latter in facilitating systemic reorientation.

Venezuela in Latin American Context

Although there is a great deal of variation across countries, it is safe to say that racial divisions have never been as clear-cut in Latin America as in the United States, resulting from both the process and the ideological function of *mestizaje*, or ethnic mixing. As a result of this legacy and a history of U.S. imperialism, the response in the region to Obama's election has been a more complicated matter altogether. In brief, *mestizaje* as an actual process created a greater ethnic variation among the Latin American population, as did the fact that the combining elements were themselves multiple: Spanish-born Whites, locally born Whites (*criollos*), a large indigenous population, and African slaves. But this process of mixing has not prevented the operation of race according to a framework largely similar to that of the United States, in which those classified as "Black" or "Indian" occupy the lowest position while those classified as "White" (no matter how ethnically mixed) occupy a higher position, and in which this hierarchy is held together by a combination of racism in the latter and internalized outgroup favoritism in the latter (Ishibashi, 2003). The discourse of *mestizaje* then functions as a buttress to this system of racialization that operates by obscuring its functions: by identifying the nation as mixed and by insisting that "we are all mixed," the very real operations of racism and the correlation between race and poverty is thereby hidden from view (Ciccariello-Maher, 2007).

This situation presents a double-challenge from the perspective of system justification theory: not only does racial inequality thrive on implicitly internalized racism among the oppressed, but it also benefits from the explicit denial of even the existence of race as a category of social importance. At the same time, however, inequality in general and extreme poverty are more severe in Latin America than in the United States, as is the availability and prevalence of a variety of radical discourses—often rooted in their opposition to U.S. imperialism in the region—that undermine the status quo. As a result of this combination of factors, Latin American history, in general, has seen a multiplicity of breaks with the status quo, but these have rarely emerged with explicit reference to questions of race and racial oppression.

Venezuela stands as an opportune and exemplary case in which the radical rupture of the status quo coincided with, and was even *preceded* by, the emergence of mobilizations by Afro-Venezuelan organizations. The old status quo was many things at once: neoliberal; dominated by wealthy, White, and culturally Americanized elites; and perceived by many as complicit with

U.S. imperialism. As a result, although Afro-Venezuelan organizing had emerged prior to Hugo Chávez's failed coup attempt of 1992, and certainly prior to his 1998 election, challenging the invisibilization of both racial divisions and racial discrimination (Ciccariello-Maher, 2010), this mobilization soon came to be tightly bound up with opposition to the system as a whole, opposition for which Chávez stood as symbol and figurehead.

A combination of economic, political, and social factors made the collapse of the old Venezuelan system—and its justificatory processes—almost inevitable. The new Chávez regime that replaced it was thus already one assumed to represent the interests of Afro-Venezuelans (a fact facilitated by Chávez's open celebration of his own Afro-Indigenous heritage), and support quickly aligned in favor of this new status quo. Speaking in terms of the system justification paradigm, this was a situation in which the rupture with the status quo facilitated, and was in turn itself enabled by, the development of Afro-indigenous and Afro-Venezuelan identity. In other words, the undermining of the status quo was tightly bound up with those identification processes running counter to the outgroup favoritism that upholds systems of inequality more generally.

Further, if we have identified the potential benefit of making the implicit explicit, the potential for revealing racist structures in undermining the necessarily implicit functioning of internalized racism among members of oppressed communities, then this too played a role in the Venezuelan transformation. As system justification would predict, moreover, this shift from the implicit to the explicit emerged in the context of a crisis (Jost, Banaji, & Nosek, 2004: 890). In the early 1980s, and specifically beginning with the 1983 currency devaluation, the Venezuelan political system entered into a severe crisis of legitimacy, and as system justification theory would predict, this led to an increase in the deployment of stereotypes to justify that system and to seek scapegoats for its decline (Herrera Salas, 2004, pp. 117–118; Herrera Salas, 2005, p. 79). As a result, in the Venezuelan case, we can note the coincidence of two key steps in undermining the outgroup favoritism, the internalized racism, which system justification theory would see as crucial in upholding systems of racial oppression, and these operate as two sides of the same coin: the emergence of explicit racism on the part of (generally White) elites and of ethnic identification on the part of the (largely Afro-Indigenous) poor and oppressed classes.

But in this case, system justification theory, as a relatively static approach, lacks an understanding of the dynamic and dialectical relationship between the two, one that we see borne out in Venezuelan identity dynamics: the economic crisis provoked a resurgence of overt racism, which itself contributed to the emergence and fortification of Afro-Venezuelan identity, which in turn provoked further racism (Ciccariello-Maher, 2010). In other words, system justification theory identifies system legitimacy directly with outgroup favoritism among the oppressed, and so we might expect a loosening of the former to undermine the latter as well. But the undermining of outgroup favoritism, or what Venezuelans term *endo-racism* (Montañez, 1993; Mijares, 1997), was additionally stimulated by the resurgent racism that the crisis itself had prompted.

In turning to the danger of which the system justification framework warns us—the tendency toward rapid reorientation of legitimacy in the presence of merely cosmetic change—we again come up against the complication of multiple, overlapping systems of oppression and inequality and the question of *which* system is being justified, and this is a question that parallels the difficulties of the U.S. context, which many other authors in this volume address. In brief, Afro-Venezuelan identity was immediately upon Chávez's election, subsumed within the broader class-based and anti-imperialist identity posed by the Chavista coalition. As a result, transformative claims specific to Black Venezuelans have encountered resistance and accusations that Afro-Venezuelans are seeking "special" treatment, as well as a general insistence that what matters fundamentally is to support Chávez. In the context of Obama's election, this begins to sound familiar.

This is a question that can only be resolved in terms of actual social change, and by determining whether Afro-Venezuelan support for Chávez reflects the general dynamics of system justification, or whether the new status quo is substantively better than the old. For Afro-Venezuelans at the moment, the answer seems to be the latter, but this is not an unqualified answer. If, as we have seen, there is a tendency to mute demands from Afro-Venezuelan sectors, there have also been very real gains, both concrete and symbolic. As to the former, we could cite the development of Afro-Venezuelan cacao cooperatives, the reform of the education system to include Afro-Venezuelan history, and the establishment of an annual Afro-Venezuelan day (Harris, 2007). Although Indigenous Venezuelans currently enjoy a greater degree of formal recognition and autonomy than Afro-Venezuelans, a component of the narrowly defeated 2007 constitutional reform proposal would have contributed to correcting this imbalance. The latter have largely been addressed above in the question of undermining outgroup favoritism, but it is worth briefly indicating the dynamic interplay between these two aspects: Concrete gains have provided an institutional basis and social legitimacy for the expanding and deepening of Afro-Venezuelan organizing, which itself bodes well in terms of facilitating group and individual identification and undermining endo-racism. At the very least, we could say that both the actual changes and potential for undermining outgroup favoritism are currently more pronounced in Venezuela than domestically in the United States.

But to turn more directly to the subject of this volume as a whole, we must question the effect of Obama's election in Venezuela. Did it stimulate or encourage Black identity on either the individual or group level? Or, conversely, did it contribute to the uncritical reorientation toward the status quo discussed above? And speaking in terms of the peculiarly global face of this reorientation, did Obama's election contribute to what Parameswaran (2009) terms a new American Exceptionalism, whose function is a global reorientation of system justification that elides the history of U.S. imperialism and intervention while perpetuating the myth of upward mobility? Perhaps predictably, in light of the recent realignment of system justification in Venezuela and its particular parameters, Obama's election would be met with more ambivalence than elsewhere. And this ambivalence would be exacerbated by perceptions of the U.S. government—at the helm of which Obama now stood—as an oppressive, imperialist power.

Put simply, as a result of the close identification of Afro-Venezuelan movements with the Chávez regime and the tense relationship that has historically existed between that regime and the U.S. government—especially since the latter supported a 2002 coup that temporarily removed Chávez from power—any identification between Afro-Venezuelans and the African-American president are inevitably filtered and inflected through global geopolitics. We can see this in a sampling of documents from Afro-Venezuelan organizations and discussions of Obama that have appeared in Venezuela during the past year. In general, what we find in these documents is the fact that Obama's position as U.S. Head of State has created a complex and subtle debate in Venezuela over the meaning of his race and the importance of his election. Although many expressed a degree of hope that Obama's election would bode well for international affairs—here, Chávez's own 2009 speech to the U.N. General Assembly—a clear skepticism prevailed. This has manifested in everything from a subtle critique of Obama's own class privilege (Hernández, 2008) to the claim that he has been "whitened" by his position at the helm of an imperialist country (Echeverría, 2009). Such skepticism only deepened in the aftermath of the June 2009 Honduran coup, toward which the position of the Obama Administration was vague at best (Lares, 2009; Ciccariello-Maher, 2009).

This skeptical tenor is well-summarized by Jesús "Chucho" García, the founder of the Afro-Venezuelan Network and longtime activist on behalf of Afro-descended Venezuelans. In an article entitled "Beware of Obama-mania," García argues:

> If only he could support the Asian, Latino and African migrants who were unable to fulfill the American Dream. If only he were able to help countries in Africa, where his father was from, and eliminate militarist projects like

AFRICOM. . . As Afro-descendents, I don't believe it's a question of skin or
of an automatic pigmentary solidarity with the first Afro-descended president of the United States of the North (not the United States of America).
It's an essentially ideological question, and we will see after January 20th
2009, when he assumes the presidency, where the Audacity of Hope and
his "refoundation of the American Dream" will be headed. (García, 2008)

It is worth underlining García's explicit critique of the exceptionalist
paradigm of the "American Dream," which Obama's election has resuscitated.
If Obama still maintains "the ethic of the children of the African Diaspora,"
García adds, he will need "to learn with humility" from the transformative
processes underway in Latin America. It would not be long, however, before
García's minimal hope would dissipate: When the Obama Administration
decided to boycott the 3rd U.N. conference on racism, García would note the
bitter irony of such a position (García, 2009).

In sum, Venezuela's recent transformation of the status quo—both
racial and more generally—has created a situation in which the sort of Black
identification encouraged by Obama's election has *not* coincided, as in
Parameswaran's (2009) analysis, with a new American exceptionalism; rather,
it has been quite the opposite: a deeper and more subtle and nuanced understanding of the function of race vis-à-vis U.S. imperialism and a deep skepticism of precisely those dynamics of system reorientation to which system
justification theory would alert us. Hence, rather than offering a story of the
effect of Obama's election, the Venezuelan case is instead a *parallel* story in
which declining system legitimacy and the rejection of some aspects of the
status quo allowed for the election of an outside candidate who reflected personally a response to the racism prevalent in the society in question, thereby
potentially undermining outgroup favoritism. However, the Venezuelan case
(and system justification theory) also reflects the danger of reorientation that
Obama's election entails on the domestic level, entailing a centripetal effect
whereby oppressed sectors are expected to identify with the new system,
irrespective of what actual changes have occurred vis-à-vis the prevailing
inequality of the previous system.

POST-MAO CHINA AND GLOBAL SYSTEM JUSTIFICATION

As we have already seen, the reception and impact of Obama's election has
differed drastically from region to region and country to country, and if we
have seen the peculiar challenge posed by Latin American patterns of
racialization—in which race is ever-present but concealed—then we will see
something similar operating in the case of China, but to a very different effect.
In what follows, we will track the impact of Obama's election alongside a

parallel phenomenon that has attracted much attention of late: the experience of 20-year-old Chinese singer Lou Jing. But first, we must again speak in broad terms of the historical parameters of race and racism in China.

Like Venezuela and much of Latin America, China has a deep history of racism, one in which race both intersects with class and has been to some degree concealed, obscured, and explicitly denied. Although historical references to China and the Chinese have long corresponded to the adjective "yellow," it was not until the 19th century that such references would assume an explicitly biological character (Dikötter, 1994, p. 404). If this timing coincided with parallel developments in Europe and elsewhere, recent scholarship has gone to great lengths to deny two prevalent and complementary narratives: First, that racism has no roots indigenous to China, and second, that as a result, racial conceptions and discrimination were therefore imported from the West (p. 405). Current scholarship further insists that recent manifestations of racial resentment in China are not abstract xenophobia, as had been believed previously, but rather the very specific and local manifestations of Chinese racism (Sautman, 1994, pp. 413–425; Dikötter, 1994, p. 411). If there is admittedly no single overarching structure of Chinese racism, it is nevertheless possible and imperative to identify some contingent patterns that demonstrate some historical consistency.

One such pattern, and one of importance to our subject, is the traditional intermingling and intersection of race and class. Barry Sautman, for example, draws upon recent survey data to suggest that anti-Black racism in contemporary China draws upon "a recrudescence of elite values that link and denigrate those who are dark and those who are poor" (1994, p. 427). Traditionally, Chinese elites idealized light skin as an indication that one was not engaged in manual, peasant labor, and this beauty ideal would intersect comfortably with racism. However, during the 1950s to 1970s, Maoist ideology would subvert this equation from both sides, placing a new value on manual labor domestically and on Third World solidarity abroad (especially with African nations). As Sautman argues, however, this "ideological inversion" was but an intermission, and the post-Mao reform era would see a return to the race-class pairing, facilitated by both the weakening of ties to Africa and celebrations of individual entrepreneurial advancement (1994, p. 428). This "recrudescence" would manifest most starkly in a number of attacks and anti-African riots occurring in the 1970s and 1980s led predominantly by Chinese students.

This peculiar intersection of reform and racism sets the Chinese example apart in some ways from what we saw in the case of Venezuela. Whereas the latter would see a recrudescence of racism amid economic crisis—a pattern predicted by the system justification literature—Chinese racism would resurface with a vengeance amid unprecedented economic growth. As fashion publisher Hung Huang describes it: "The kind of prejudice you see now really happened with the economic growth" (Richburg, 2009). This fact, alongside the particularities of Chinese outgroup favoritism, reveal the specificity of the function of race in contemporary China, especially vis-à-vis the global economic system, the United States, and the Obama phenomenon.

Let us recall that Sautman and others have argued that Chinese racism is not merely abstract xenophobia. This is borne out in the survey data he discusses, which demonstrates not only a denigration of *both* Blacks and peasants but also a distinct valorization of Whites. Such a valorization of "hegemonic whiteness" manifests in diverse registers and often transcends overt political orientation and national context (Hughey, 2010, 2009a, 2009b). This valorization of whiteness extends to beauty standards and exceeds even that of fellow Asians, such that it cannot be explained by either traditional conceptions (in which Yellow and White are both valued equally) or economic concerns (in which Americans are equated with wealth) (Richberg 2009, pp. 424–433). (Here, it is worth recalling that skin-whitening creams, not to mention eye surgery, constitutes a $100-million-a-year industry in China.) As a result, if the anti-African student riots were often provoked by sexual relationships between African men and Chinese women, similar anxieties are not directed toward White men, who are often seen as a potential economic boon for the family in question.

Hence, if this outgroup favoritism cannot be explained in purely economic terms, it nevertheless has a very real economic component that sheds light into the way in which contemporary patterns of Chinese racism are transposed onto the geopolitical stage: whiteness and the West stand for economic growth and affluence, whereas blackness and Africa coincide with poverty, stagnation, and domestic conditions of manual labor. What is peculiar is that the Chinese "race" stands somewhere in-between, as a sort of racial semi-periphery that simultaneously denigrates those below while emulating those above. As a result, outgroup favoritism among Chinese coincides with racism against African immigrants, with both functioning to uphold and legitimize the hierarchical structure of the global capitalist system. In what follows, we will briefly discuss the implications of this global racial-economic hierarchy through a discussion of both Chinese pop singer Lou Jing and Obama's election and November 2009 visit to China.

In August 2009, Lou Jing garnered massive media attention in China following her appearance on a televised talent competition called "Let's Go! Oriental Angel." This attention, however, owed less to her actual performance than to her skin color: Lou was conceived during her mother's adulterous affair with an African-American man. As Frazier (2010) explains, the Chinese response to Lou's performance, especially in Internet chatrooms and discussion boards, was as visceral as it was complex:

> Some Chinese netizens labeled Lou Jing a disgrace to the Chinese nation and argued that her skin color prevents her being a "real" and "true" Chinese. Such denunciations of Lou Jing increased rapidly, to the degree that acclaimed writer Hung Huang came to Lou's defense and posted on her blog, "In the same year that Americans welcome Obama to the White House, we can't even accept this girl with a different skin color."

But despite a spate of stories in the U.S. press in which the response to Lou's appearance serves merely as a vehicle to put Chinese racism on display, Frazier sounds a note of caution, suggesting that such responses may have more to do with American Exceptionalism than on-the-ground facts.

First, he notes the significant lag that separated Lou's appearance (August 2009) and the vast bulk of the stories appearing in the U.S. press (November 2009), explaining that these were inspired more by Obama's November visit to China than a desire to understand local Chinese racial dynamics. Second, what analysis does appear in such articles is partial at best, presenting China as a static racist monolith characterized by inflexible identities, a view that conceals the "diversity and complexity of responses by Chinese citizens and Chinese enthusiasts that have emerged surrounding Lou Jing and issues of anti-Black racism in China." As Frazier insists, this diversity and complexity is not reducible to Lou supporters versus detractors but also cuts to the very heart of the "intersectionality" of race, class, and gender in China, and the specific divergence between how Africans and African-Americans are viewed.

Whereas continental Africans appear symbolically as impoverished beneficiaries threatening to drag China down, in opposition to wealthy Americans who promise to raise all boats, African-Americans stand to some degree between the two but are furthermore inflected through prevalent media imagery, both "positive" (sports, music) and "negative" (crime, poverty). In her "Oriental Angel" appearance, Lou (introduced suggestively as the "Halle Berry of the East") would performatively occupy this in-between-ness, deploying African-American imagery and tropes (by rapping) but doing so in a way which both reinscribed her native Chinese status while stretching what it meant to be Chinese (here, Frazier's account closely parallels Parameswaran's description of the global Obama effect). "Her rap," Frazier insists, "conveyed that race and nationality are socially constructed, lived, and performed, and deduced that Blackness and Chineseness are not mutually exclusive or incompatible spaces of identity." Although the tropes Lou performed were largely commercial creations and failed to reflect the actual living conditions of

Africans in China, Lou was nevertheless able to transform herself into a creative subject and to challenge Chinese racism through her performance.

It is this precise ambivalence surrounding Lou Jing that would provide the
context for Obama's November 2009 visit to China: As simultaneously African
(more literally so than Lou) and American (and thus Western), the response to
Obama would also be far from simplistic and monolithic. Interestingly, some
of Lou's detractors sought to attack her by calling her "the daughter of Obama"
(Frazier, 2010). This was not the first time that a visit from a U.S. official
would spark a racist response: Condoleezza Rice experienced the same during
a 2005 visit. But we might expect the fact that a Black man stands at the helm
of what is perceived by many Chinese as the flagship of economic progress,
development, and affluence, to offer a severe challenge to prevailing patterns
of racialization in which race and class are frequently bound together.
The degree to which this challenge has opened up a productive and occasion-
ally nuanced debate on race in China is evident even in mainstream press
reports (bearing in mind both Frazier's analysis and our concerns about
exceptionalism).

First, there are several reports of an Internet poll conducted in China, in
which one-third of the 3,581 respondents, when asked about Obama's most
attractive aspect, responded that it was his skin color (Krishnan, 2009). Second,
we could mention the seemingly innocuous case of an infamous T-shirt featuring Obama dressed as Mao, which read "Oba-Mao" and "Serve the People,"
and which serves to reinforce the historical association of Maoist China (in
contrast to contemporary China) with anti-racism and global Third World
solidarity (Chang, 2009). Finally, to complete the triangle, many Chinese-
American responses recognize the reality of a global economic inversion:
Whereas many once came to the United States in search of the "American
Dream," many are now looking back to see this dream becoming a reality in
their native home (Associated Press, 2009).

This brief sampling of press reports speaks volumes, indicating the loosening of the fundamental pair of associations underlying Chinese racism: the
association of the United States with wealth (economic crisis) and with whiteness (in Obama's election). Furthermore, in drawing Obama—however
symbolically—into the orbit of pre-reform Chinese Communism and ques-
tioning the relevance of "American Exceptionalism," Obama's election could
contribute to a resurgence of Chinese solidarity with the Third World. Finally,
in terms of the overt racism-classism expressed toward African immigrants as
well as the internalized racism and outgroup favoritism of even affluent
Chinese, one could hope that Obama's election might serve to break the linkage between blackness and poverty, one already challenged by the global

imagery of African-Americans, into which Lou Jing so effectively tapped (this, certainly, is the implication of the Internet poll cited above).

CONCLUSION

If our efforts to address the international implications of the Obama phenomenon through the optic of system justification theory requires that the latter be stretched and transformed, then we hope that this has been a fruitful process. System justification theory provides us a framework for understanding both the importance of outgroup favoritism in maintaining systems of inequality and the danger entailed by the rapid reorientation of said systems. In our effort to track the potential for Obama's election to undermine this outgroup favoritism, we have necessarily had to turn from system justification theory, strictly understood, to its more active implication, emphasizing the possibility of rupturing outgroup favoritism both by facilitating individual and group identification and by revealing as explicit the previously implicit presence of inequalities. But to do this, we have further needed to insist upon a more dynamic and dialectical view that tracks the interplay between, on the one hand, ethnic identification and, on the other, the appearance of explicit stereotyping in the process of systemic decline.

However, as is also the case within the United States, the danger of systemic realignment or reorientation is a very real one, and one that militates against substantive transformation of systems of inequality. One key element of this danger in the international arena is the resurgence of a new American Exceptionalism in which Obama's image washes away a century of crimes past and serves to justify new imperialism abroad. But rather than insisting that one or the other side of this phenomenon—optimism toward undermining internalized racism or pessimism toward the ruses of power—will necessarily predominate, it instead behooves us to look closely at the local contexts, social dynamics, and concrete conditions within which such a struggle will be played out.

REFERENCES

Associated Press (2009, November 15). Chinese-Americans reflect on Obama's trip. Retrieved from http://www.msnbc.msn.com/id/33951029, accessed January 4, 2010.

Chang, E. (2009, November 16). "Communist Obama" T-shirt Tussle. *In the Field: CNN Blogs*. Retrieved from http://inthefield.blogs.cnn.com/2009/11/16/obama-communist-t-shirt-tussle/, accessed January 4, 2010.

Ciccariello-Maher, G. (2007). Toward a Racial Geography of Caracas: Neoliberal Urbanism and the Fear of Penetration. *Qui Parle 16 (2)*, 39–72.

Ciccariello-Maher, G. (2009, July 3). The Counter-Revolution Will Not be Tweeted: The Honduran Coup and the Limits of Hope and Change. *Counterpunch*. Retrieved from http://www.counterpunch.org/maher07032009.html, accessed January 4, 2010.

Ciccariello-Maher, G. (2010). Jumpstarting the Decolonial Engine: Symbolic Violence from Fanon to Chávez. *Theory & Event 13* (1).

Colindres: Obama a "little black man." (2009, July 9). *Huffington Post*. Retrieved from http://www.huffingtonpost.com/2009/07/09/colindres-obama-a-little_n_228910.html, accessed January 4,2010.

Dikötter, F. (1994). Racial Identities in China: Context and Meaning. *The China Quarterly 138*, 404–412.

Dougherty, J. (2009, January 19). Black Iraqis make Obama a model to follow. *CNN*. Retrieved from http://www.cnn.com/2009/WORLD/meast/01/19/obama.black.iraqis/index.html, accessed January 4, 2010.

Evcheverría V. P. (2009, December 28). El negro Obama es blanqueado en EEUU por el gran imperio de los blancos (los clásicos yanquis). *Aporrea.org*. Retrieved from http://www.aporrea.org/tiburon/a92417.html, accessed January 4, 2010.

Fausset, R. (2010, January 3). Black activists launch rare attack on Cuba about racism. *Los Angeles Times*. Retrieved from http://www.latimes.com/news/nation-and-world/la-na-cuba-blacks3-2010jan03,0,5391302.story, accessed January 4, 2010.

Frazier, Robeson T. (2010, November 18–21). China's Chocolate Girl Wonder: Lou Jing and Anti-Black Racism. Conference Paper for panel, Si(gh)ting Female Bodies: Performing Nation, Race and Transnationalism on Stage and Screen, American Studies

Association Conference, San Antonio, TX.

García, J. (2008, October 28). Mosca con la Obamanía. *Aporrea.org*. Retrieved from http://www.aporrea.org/internacionales/a66256.html, accessed January 4, 2010.

García, J. (2009, March 23). De la abolición de la esclavitud al racismo. *Aporrea.org*. Retrieved from http://www.aporrea.org/ideologia/a74834.html

Harris, L.C. (2007, July 13). Real Rights and Recognition Replace Racism in Venezuela. *Green Left Weekly* (717). Retrieved from http://www.greenleft.org.au/2007/717/37209, accessed January 4, 2010.

Hernández, R. (2008, November 8). Obama: más de lo mismo en Estados Unidos (Parte I). *Aporrea.org*. Retrieved from http://www.aporrea.org/actualidad/a66832.html, accessed January 4, 2010.

Herrera Salas, J.M. (2004). Racismo y discurso político en Venezuela. *Revista Venezolana de Economía y Ciencias Sociales 10* (2), 111–128.

Herrera Salas, J.M. (2005). Ethnicity and Revolution: the Political Economy of Racism in Venezuela. *Latin American Perspectives 32* (2), 72–91.

Hughey, M. W. (2010). "Navigating the (Dis)similarities of White Racial Identities: The Conceptual Framework of "Hegemonic Whiteness." " *Ethnic & Racial*

Studies 99999(1): 1–21. iFirst article: URL: http://dx.doi.org/10.1080/01419870903125069, accessed January 4, 2010.

Hughey, M. W. (2009a). "Cinethetic Racism: White Redemption and Black Stereotypes in "Magical Negro" Films." *Social Problems 56(3)*. 543–577.

Hughey, M. W. (2009b). "The Janus Face of Whiteness: Toward a Cultural Sociology of White Nationalism and White Antiracism." *Sociology Compass 3(6)*, 920 – 936.

Hughey, M. W. (2007). "Racism with Antiracists: Color-Conscious Racism and the Unintentional Persistence of Inequality." *Social Thought and Research 28*, 67–108.

Ioffee, K. (2009, August 5). Joaquim Crima wants to be the Russian Obama. *HuffingtonPost.* Retrieved from http://www.huffingtonpost.com/2009/08/05/joaquim-crima-wants-to-be_n_251705.html, accessed January 4, 2010.

Ishibashi, J. (2003). Hacia una apertura del debate sobre el racismo en Venezuela: exclusión e inclusión estereotipada de personas "negras" en los medios de comunicación. In D. Mato (Ed.), *Políticas de identidades y diferencias sociales en tiempos de globalización* (33–61). Caracas: FACES-UCV.

Jost, J. T., Banaji, M.R., & Nosek, B.A. (2004). A Decade of System Justification Theory: Accumulated Evidence of Conscious and Unconscious Bolstering of the Status Quo. *Political Psychology 25 (6)*, 881–919.

Jost, J. T., & Burgess, D. (2000). Attitudinal ambivalence and the conflict between group and system justification motives in low status groups. *Personality and Social Psychology Bulletin 26*, 293–305.

Jost, J. T., Pietrzak, J., Liviatan, I., Mandisodza, A.N., & Napier, J.L. (2007). System Justification as Conscious and Nonconscious Goal Pursuit. In J. Shah & W. Gardner (Eds.), *Handbook of Motivation Science* (pp. 590–605). New York: Guilford.

Krishnan, A. (2009, November 16). In China, Obama's popularity challenges race stereotypes. *The Hindu*. Retrieved from http://www.hindu.com/2009/11/16/stories/2009111654071300.htm, accessed January 4, 2010.

Lares, J. J. (2009, July 2). Señor Obama, esta bajo golpe de estado usted también. *Aporrea.org*. Retrieved from http://www.aporrea.org/internacionales/a81336.html, accessed January 4, 2010.

Llana, S. M. (2009, February 1). Black Latin Americans dream Obama will mean better times. *Christian Science Monitor*. Retrieved from http://www.mcclatchydc.com/226/story/61246.html, accessed January 4, 2010.Mijares, M.M. (1997). *Racismo y endoracismo en Barlovento*. Caracas: Fundación Afroamérica.

Montañez, L. (1993). *El racismo oculto en una sociedad no racista*. Caracas: Tropykos.

Parks, G. S. and Heard, D.C. (2010). " "Assassinate the Nigger Ape": Obama, Implicit Imagry, and the Dire Consequences of Racist Jokes." *Rutgers Race & Law Review*.

Parameswaran, R. (2009). Facing Barack Hussein Obama: Race, Globalization, and Transnational America. *Journal of Communication Inquiry 33* (3), 195–205.

Pinkney, L. (2009, January 22). The Obama Spectacle: History, hypocrisy, and empire. Retrieved from http://www.blackcommentator.com, accessed January 4, 2010.

Richburg, K.B. (2009, November 14). Chinese talk about racism ahead of Obama trip: President shatters stereotype of the West being run by whites. *Washington Post*. Retrieved from http://www.msnbc.msn.com/id/33936653/ns/world_news-washington_post/, accessed January 4, 2010.

Salman, R., & Susman, T. (2008, August 14). IRAQ: Black Iraqis hoping for a Barack Obama win. *Los Angeles Times*. Retrieved from http://latimesblogs.latimes.com/babylonbeyond/2008/08/baghdad-black-i.html, accessed January 4, 2010.

Sautman, B. (1994). Anti-Black Racism in Post-Mao China. *The China Quarterly 138*, 413–437.

Obama and Group Change in Attitudes about Group Status

Michael C. Dawson

Does Barack Obama's election reinforce or undermine cognitive systems of racial and class domination outside of the United States? Further, does his election reinforce or undermine critiques of U. S. imperialism as particularly non-European peoples find hope and perhaps identification with Obama and his election? These are the central questions that motivate Ciccariello-Maher's and Hughey's chapter. Early survey evidence from the United States as well as events in the Middle East and elsewhere suggest that the euphoria generated by Obama's election is fragile. Although his election may not prompt the development of oppositional consciousness either within the United States or elsewhere, there is also little chance that his election will lead greater defense of the United States and its policies by disadvantaged populations around the globe.

The authors argue that some of the disadvantaged (whether by race, class, or both) "justify the existing social order" and "paradoxically, it is sometimes strongest among those who are most harmed by the status quo," thus "buttressing systems of privilege and inequality." Part and parcel of this process according to the "system justification theory" favored by the authors is the internalization of feelings of implicit inferiority, which they also refer to as *outgroup favoritism*. On the positive side, the authors hypothesize that Obama's election could undermine outgroup favoritism as the election of a Black president provides a strong symbolic example of non-European achievement of power and excellence. Indeed, they provide some anecdotal evidence from various parts of the world consistent with this more favorable result of Obama's election. The election of a Black president, the authors fear, however, could very well also lead to a diminishing of group solidarity among the disadvantaged. To use Debord's language, the *spectacle* of the election served both to mask the fact that basic structures of inequality have not fundamentally changed and, worse, lead to collective amnesia for what the authors term the *domestic and particularly international crimes* of the past and present (Debord, 1994).

Survey evidence from the United States provides consistent, if not conclu-
sive, evidence of the process that Ciccariello-Maher and Hughey describe.
Between the middle 1990s and 2005 African-Americans increasingly believed
that racial equality for Blacks would either not be achieved during their life-
times or, for some, not at all within the United States. By 2005, more than 80%
of African-Americans were this pessimistic. Yet by October 2008, the spectacle
of the presidential campaign had reduced this percentage to less than 50%—a
monumental shift toward optimism about race in the United States by a very
large segment of the Black population. Similarly, as noted, there was strong
evidence of a more positive attitude toward the United States evinced particularly by people of African descent from Iraq to Russia.

Ciccariello-Maher and Hughey use the examples of Venezuela and China
to show how both at least a partially antagonistic relationship with the United
States combined with the workings of racism within both societies worked to
attenuate feelings of goodwill toward either the president or the United States.
There is also domestic and international evidence to suggest that the Obama
effect that worries the authors and Radhika Parameswaran (whose work the
authors report argues that Obama's election facilitated the American neoliberal economic and foreign policy agenda) is very fragile. Survey evidence
from the United States shows that Black pessimism about the prospects of
racial equality (as measured above) increased by 10% in a *6-month* period
between 2009 and 2010. Blacks are *rapidly* becoming pessimistic again. The
effect of the spectacle has worn off in the face of unchanging underlying
conditions in disadvantaged communities in the United States, a presidential
agenda more conservative than that favored by the mainstream of African-
American public opinion, and the growing virulence of racism within the
country. One can also speculate that we see a similar fragility in international
optimism as Obama Administration policies ranging from Middle East and
Latin American policy to the refusal to attend the international anti-racism
conference rapidly disappointed those who were looking for a major progressive and more egalitarian foreign policy from the United States with the
election of Obama. Unfortunately, one of the more durable racial effects of the
president's election has been the mobilization of racism from leaders in countries such as Honduras and Italy as well as within the not-so-extreme right
within the United States at any sign that there might be even the mildest of
progressive aspects to the President's domestic and foreign policy agendas.
Ciccariello-Maher and Hughey are absolutely correct to caution us that the
reaction to the first Black president of the United States will be conditioned on
local contexts and the relations these localities have with the United States.
It is also more globally probable that whatever optimism was generated by
the transition to the Obama Administration is fragile to the degree it remains

at all and that the complicated politics of race both domestically and internationally is both more contentious and more visible than it was before the election of Barack Obama.

REFERENCE

Debord, G. (1994). *The Society of the Spectacle*. New York: Zone Books.

CHAPTER 10

The Role of Race in American Politics: Lessons Learned from the 2008 Presidential Election

Thierry Devos

Does the election of Barack Obama as President of the United States of America mean that race is no longer a factor in American politics? Some commentators have suggested that the outcome of the 2008 presidential election was evidence that we are living in a "post-racial America" or at least that we are rapidly moving in that direction. In a nutshell, the assumption is that the racial and cultural prejudices and stereotypes of prior eras no longer play a critical role in determining the electability of minority candidates. At the same time, the picture emerging from contemporary research on prejudice and stereotyping stresses the pervasiveness of these phenomena. Although the more overt and blatant forms of racial prejudice are fading, covert forms of prejudice and stereotyping remain prevalent in many settings. In the present chapter, we focus on the role that subtle, unconscious biases play in the political arena. During political campaigns, overt racism is rarely expressed, and racially charged incidents are less frequent than they used to be. At the same time, however, analyses of recent political elections continue to document the role that racial attitudes play in American politics. To examine this issue, we ground our analysis in social-psychological research. Our goal is to examine the various ways in which race and racial attitudes remain potent sources of influence, shaping how political candidates are perceived and the extent to which people are likely to vote for them. To increase understanding of the role of race in American politics, we capitalize on a series of prominent theoretical models and on a flurry of research conducted in the context of the 2008 presidential election.

The election of Barack Obama to the nation's highest office was an unprecedented event. More than 69 million voters (53% of the popular vote; 365 Electoral College votes; 28 states and the District of Columbia) expressed their support for Senator Obama, which was 9 million votes more than the Republican candidate, Senator McCain received (46% of the popular vote; 173 Electoral College votes; 22 states) (Federal Election Commission Report, 2009).

Without a doubt, the candidate of the Democratic Party won the election by a comfortable margin. The significance and implications of his victory for ethnic relations in the United States have been much debated, and diverging opinions have been articulated. These alternative viewpoints cannot be reduced to divisions across party lines or demographic criteria. Instead, these perspectives convey the complexity and multidimensionality of this historic moment. On one hand, Obama's election could be seen as the emergence of a post-racial era, a striking symbolic success that could lead to more steps toward racial equality. On the other hand, there are concerns that his election will overshadow the continued existence of covert racist attitudes and undermine efforts to address pervasive pockets of racial inequalities. When it comes to the role of race in the electoral process, commentators, analysts, social scientists, and laypersons have voiced quite different opinions. Before discussing theoretical accounts relevant to these issues and considering the available empirical evidence, let us quickly review potential arguments that race was or was not a factor in the 2008 presidential election.

Skepticism regarding the potential role of race in American politics has existed for quite some time. The argument is not that racism is no longer an issue in the United States, but that its impact tends to be overstated. In the realm of political matters, this viewpoint posits that racial prejudice plays a fairly minimal role and does not account for resistance to policies aimed at remedying to racial disparities and inequalities (Sniderman & Carmines, 1997). Considering the way the presidential campaign unfolded, it could be argued that Democrats made a concerted effort not to frame central issues in racial terms. To the extent that racism was not a very salient or debated issue during the campaign, it seems unlikely that race or racial attitudes shaped support for the protagonists. In addition, and despite the fact that Obama identifies as an African-American, his mixed racial background may have minimized the propensity to appraise his positions through racial lenses or to direct prejudicial reactions toward him.

Counterarguments that point to the role of race in the election are not in short supply. In contrast to the assumption that racism is no longer a central issue in the United States, one could argue that racial prejudice and discrimination, although perhaps less blatant, remain of paramount importance in this country (Wise, 2009). For example, opinions about a variety of policies continue to be anchored in racial attitudes (Sears, Sidanius, & Bobo, 2000). If the barriers that would have made Obama's candidacy impossible a few decades ago are mostly dissipated, subtle forms of prejudices and stereotypes linger. Many Americans still harbor negative attitudes toward ethnic minorities, and it might be expected that these attitudes would dampen support for a candidate who is perceived as African-American.

Instead of speculating about the respective merits of these viewpoints, we will examine them in light of research conducted at the crossroads of social psychology, political psychology, and political science.

CONTEMPORARY RACISM IN THE CONTEXT OF POLITICAL ELECTIONS

When and Why People Vote across Racial Lines

Exit poll data provide a simple yet telling way of examining the role that race may have played in the 2008 presidential election. The breakdown of votes as a function of self-reported racial identity indicates that a minority of Whites voted for Senator Obama (43%) and a majority voted for Senator McCain (55%), whereas an overwhelming majority of African-Americans voted for Obama (95% vs. 4%) and he also gained support from a majority of Latinos (67% vs. 31%), Asians (62% vs. 35%), and other racial groups (66% vs. 31%; CNN, 2008). Racial identity is confounded with many factors that could partially account for this pattern, political orientation being one of them. In addition, the picture becomes more complex when regional differences are examined. It is worth stressing that Obama received an extraordinarily low percentage of the White vote in the Deep South: Southern Whites were much more likely to vote for the Republican candidate in 2008 (McCain vs. Obama) than in 2004 (Bush vs. Kerry) (Jenkins, 2009). It is hard to conclude based on these numbers that race was not a factor in the election (Bobo & Dawson, 2009).

Overall, these figures are very much in line with a common observation: In biracial elections, Black and White voters are more likely to vote for candidates of their own race. There are many ways to explain this relationship. Not surprisingly, people are more likely to vote for candidates who are similar to them. It is worth noting that this similarity-attraction principle in electoral settings plays a more potent role for groups defined on the basis of race than gender (Sigelman & Sigelman, 1982). The pattern will not surprise readers familiar with research on ingroup favoritism (e.g., Brewer, 1999; Messick & Mackie, 1989): The tendency to evaluate more favorably and to allocate more resources or power to ingroup members than to outgroup members is one of the most replicable and robust effects in the social-psychological literature.

Racially determined voting partially explains why Black candidates rarely win elections in jurisdictions where they represent a minority of the electorate (Cameron & Epstein, 1996; Epstein & O'Halloran, 1999). As an example of the underrepresentation of African-Americans in elected bodies, only four African-Americans had served in the entire history of the U.S. Senate until Obama became a Senator in 2005 (two of them were elected during

Reconstruction), and Obama was the only Black Senator when he announced that he was running for president in 2007.

However, exit polls of the last presidential election also document that a substantial portion of the electorate voted across racial lines. A long tradition of research in political science has identified various factors that influence cross-racial voting (Bullock, 1984; Parks & Rachlinski, 2008). For example, the proportion of African-Americans at the county or state level has a negative effect on cross-racial voting among White voters, meaning that they are less likely to vote for a Black candidate (Huckfeldt & Kohfeld, 1989). In contrast, when the density of African-Americans is assessed at a more local level (e.g., precinct or borough), this effect reverses: as density increases, Whites in that district are more likely to vote for Black candidates (Carsey, 1995). One explanation for these opposing effects of racial composition of a population is that a growing proportion of Black voters might be seen as a threat to White dominance at the state level but that daily interracial interactions might foster the adoption, among Whites, of political views similar to those predominant in the local context. In other words, racial composition is a measure of the relative power of two distinct interest groups at the state level and a measure of integration within a community at more microlevel. These effects can also be explained without a direct reference to racial hostility or tolerance. When the density of the Black population makes it very likely that a Black candidate will be elected, White voters may prefer to vote for the Black candidate who is most favorable to their interests than for a White candidate who is not very likely to be elected (Liu, 2001). What would appear to be racial tolerance would, in fact, be a strategic adjustment that protects Whites' interests.

It could be argued that the notion of threat to Whites' interests is less relevant today than it was decades ago. For example, a recent analysis of House elections failed to provide evidence for the hypothesis that White voters discriminate against Black candidates (Highton, 2004). Based on the outcome of congressional elections in 1996 and 1998, White voters were not less likely to vote for a Black candidate regardless of the candidate's party affiliation. However, given that this study relied on self-reports of voting behavior, the pattern obtained may stem, to some extent, from voters underreporting their reluctance to vote for a Black candidate. Even if these issues are less potent than they used to be, lingering feelings of fear, resentment, and hostility still affect electoral contests. Appeals to Whites' racial concerns may have become more insidious, rather than completely disappearing from political campaigns (Mendelberg, 2001; Rachlinski & Parks, 2009).

Race-based considerations continue to shape the outcome of electoral contests. For example, they appear to have played a significant role in Asian-Americans' overwhelming support for Senator Hillary Clinton over Senator

Barack Obama in the Democratic primaries. When Obama lost the primaries in California and New Jersey, some pundits contended that he had a difficulty connecting with Asian-Americans. Analysis of a large-scale telephone survey of Asian-American voters confirmed that respondents who did not see political commonalities between Asian-Americans and African-Americans were less likely to vote for Obama in the primaries (Ramakrishnan, Wong, Lee, & Junn, 2009).

Social Desirability and the Expression of Political Attitudes

White respondents' increasing willingness to vote for a hypothetical qualified Black candidate for president is indicative of a shift in racial attitudes (Schuman, Steeh, Bobo, & Krysan, 1997). Polls conducted at the onset of the 2008 campaign are consistent with this assessment: An overwhelming majority of respondents indicated that race would not be a factor in their choice (Alter, 2006). However, discrepancies between the explicit endorsement of a color-blind ideology and actual behavior are not uncommon. Ideals embraced publicly may not translate to support for minority candidates in the privacy of the voting booth. From this perspective, voting intentions reported to pollsters may be seen as a representation of strong norms against the public expression of racial prejudices.

This idea garnered some attention in academic settings and in the media during the 2008 presidential campaign. It was frequently discussed in reference to the so-called "Bradley effect." The term was coined to capture the fact that Los Angeles Mayor Thomas Bradley, a Black Democrat, lost the 1982 California gubernatorial election to Attorney General George Deukmejian, a White Republican, despite having a substantial lead in pre-election preference polls. The election was close, and many factors played a role in the outcome, but exit polls revealed that a portion of Democrat and Independent voters decided to support the White Republican candidate because they believed that the government was doing too much for Blacks and other minorities. If a small proportion of the electorate openly admitted that race played a role in their political behavior, it is likely that the outcome of the election was also driven by an unwillingness of a significant fraction of the electorate to openly express a racial preference that contributed to their voting behavior. In other words, some voters might have lied to pollsters. There are a number of alternative explanations for the gap between polling data and actual voting, including methodological shortcomings of polling techniques and last-minute change of mind on the part of some voters. Nonetheless, the possibility that Whites are not being honest when they express their support for a Black candidate or that they may have a hard time translating their intention in actual behavior struck a chord among political analysts and scientists.

Analyses of the 1992 National Election Survey and of the 1989 New York City mayoral (Dinkins vs. Giuliani) election provide fairly direct evidence for the idea that voters are reluctant to state their opinion on racially polarizing issues for fear of appearing racist (Berinsky, 1999). Voters who privately opposed school integration or were reluctant to vote for a Black candidate were not willing to express those opinions publicly. Instead, these individuals were more likely to report that they did not know where they stand on the issue or were undecided. These response options provided a way out that appeared racially neutral. Social desirability effects in polling situations were also documented in the context of the 1989 Virginia gubernatorial (Wilder vs. Coleman) election (Finkel, Guterbock, & Borg, 1991). White voters were more likely to express an intention to vote for the Black candidate, Douglas Wilder, when the interviewer was Black. This effect was more pronounced among Democrats and among individuals who were relatively uncertain about their intentions. Wilder ended up winning the election by a margin of less than half a percent and after a recount. He became the first African-American elected governor of a state.

During the primaries and the election, commentators and analysts speculated about the specter of a similar phenomenon: Would a Bradley effect hurt the Obama candidacy? Obama's victory seems to refute this possibility, but the final outcome of the election is not incompatible with the notion that a reluctance to vote for a Black candidate somewhat reduced his margin of victory. Some analysts concluded that public opinion polls during the 2008 election were extremely accurate and relatively immune to social desirability biases. For example, an analysis of six Pew Research surveys conducted from September through the weekend before the November election showed little evidence of racial sensitivity in the patterns of responses based on the race of respondents and the race of the interviewers (Keeter, Kiley, Christian, & Dimock, 2009). Additional analyses indicated that respondents who declined to participate in the polling were more likely to be racially conservative, but the magnitude of this effect was quite small.

Analyses conducted in the context of the Democratic primaries revealed a more complex picture (Greenwald & Albertson, 2008). Comparing data from pre-election polls with actual voting patterns during the primaries, Greenwald and Albertson discovered that the tendency to overpredict or underpredict support for Obama in polls was a function of the percentage of African-Americans in the state population. More precisely, a pattern consistent with the Bradley effect (overprediction of support for Obama) emerged in some states with relatively low African-American populations (e.g., New Hampshire, California, and Massachusetts), but an opposite effect (under-prediction of support for Obama) occurred in states with relatively large African-American populations (e.g., South Carolina, Alabama, and Georgia). Given that caucuses require a public vote, the fact that Obama did better among White voters in caucuses than in primaries could also be taken as evidence for the idea that social desirability biases shaped the expression of political preferences (Rachlinski & Parks, 2009).

Taken together, these data are just one illustration of the potential impact of social desirability and self-presentational concerns on political judgments and preferences. Analysts typically emphasize that insidious and lingering racial prejudices persist but are not likely to be stated publicly. It is not socially acceptable to voice a reluctance to vote for a candidate based on racial, ethnic, or cultural background or, for that matter, any other demographic characteristic (gender, age, sexual orientation, or religion). Yet what is publicly unacceptable does not always correspond with behavioral responses, particularly in the privacy of the voting booth. The analyses conducted by Greenwald and Albertson (2008) broaden the issue and reveal that what individuals state publicly or in a polling situation is not just a reflection of egalitarian or anti-prejudice attitudes. It may also incorporate assumptions about the political beliefs predominant in a particular state. In addition, concerns about appearing prejudiced cannot be reduced to deliberate attempts to hide one's true feelings. Research on the motivation to control prejudice not only accounts for the fact that people differ in the extent to which they seek to control the expression of prejudice but also makes a clear distinction between two sources of this motivation (Plant & Devine, 1998). Some individuals are externally motivated and attempt to control their responses because of social pressures or impression management; they try to appear unprejudiced because they are cognizant of today's political correctness. Others may be internally motivated; they act in unprejudiced ways because such behavior is consistent with their internal values and beliefs. Differences in responding between public and private contexts are typically found among individuals who are externally motivated (Plant & Devine, 1998). Individuals who are internally motivated will exert efforts to control prejudicial responses even in the privacy of the voting booth.

Whether social desirability pressures are sufficient to produce the kind of mispredictions that capture media attention depends on a plethora of contextual factors. The important point is that racial issues continue to shape attitudes and behaviors despite strong norms against the expression of judgments based on group membership.

Symbolic Racism and Opposition to Black Candidates

As mentioned earlier, opposition to Black candidates in political elections may no longer be grounded in perceived threat to Whites' interests (e.g., competition for material resources including jobs or education, concerns for personal safety, etc.; Kinder & Sears, 1981). Instead, opposition to minority candidates may arise from the meaning attached to their potential election. The concept of symbolic racism captures the idea that opinions and attitudes that are racially biased are often expressed symbolically as support for core American values or opposition to policies aimed at overcoming racial injustices (Sears & Henry, 2005). Contemporary racial biases combine a lingering dislike for Blacks and beliefs about Blacks' lack of effort and undeserved benefits (Sears, van Laar, Carillo, & Kosterman, 1997).

Most tests of symbolic racism have been conducted in local or state elections. The 2008 presidential campaign provided a first opportunity to examine the impact of symbolic racism in a national election. Taking this perspective, Obama's candidacy may have been appraised as an attempt to promote policies or actions that would change race relations in this country and be a step further in the direction of undeserved benefits. His candidacy could also be dismissed as a reflection of affirmative action based advantages that Obama had received during his education and career.

Dwyer, Stevens, Sullivan, and Allen (2009) examined the extent to which symbolic racism (Sears et al., 1997) and modern sexism (Swim, Aikin, Hall, & Hunter, 1995) influenced affective reactions to Barack Obama and Sarah Palin. Data from a national survey conducted in October 2008 indicated that symbolic racism had a significant impact on candidate evaluations, whereas modern sexism did not. More precisely, symbolic racism predicted the extent to which respondents displayed negative attitudes toward Obama and positive attitudes toward Palin. Interestingly, this pattern held across party affiliation. Modern sexism did not significantly influence evaluations of either Palin or Obama. In sum, racial attitudes dampened positive feelings for Obama, but sexist beliefs did not lessen positive feelings for Palin. However, one should not conclude, based on these findings, that sexism did not play a role in the presidential election: Some responses to the candidacy of Hillary Clinton were very much in line with current conceptualizations of sexism (Sykes, 2008).

Variations in affective responses to political candidates stem not only from party identification or political orientation, but also from racial attitudes. A debated issue is whether the impact of racial attitudes is relatively systematic or context-dependent. One approach posits that the influence of racial attitudes on voting decisions of Whites is moderated by a number of factors (Citrin, Green, & Sears, 1990). Attributes of the candidates and the electoral context determine the extent to which anti-Black attitudes shape voting behavior. For example, anti-Black attitudes were a stronger predictor of candidate choice in a nonpartisan election for state superintendent of schools compared with a partisan gubernatorial election. Other data suggest that racial prejudice has a more profound and pervasive impact on cognitive and affective responses to Black candidates. Even when the campaign focuses on ostensibly nonracial and mainstream issues such as clean air legislation or job safety, racial prejudice produces perceptual distortions of a Black candidate's message (Moskowitz & Stroh, 1994).

IMPLICIT ATTITUDES AND BEHAVIOR IN THE POLITICAL ARENA

Automatic Affective Responses to Political Candidates

Although political decision-making has often been conceptualized as a rational process determined by maximization of expected utility (Lau, 2003), scholars have stressed the need to incorporate affective responses into models of political behavior (Abelson, Kinder, Peters, & Fiske, 1982). Support for or opposition to political candidates is rooted in emotional responses elicited by candidates or by issues relevant to the election (Christ, 1985; Westen, 2007). In addition, a growing body of research documents that affective or evaluative responses often operate outside of conscious awareness or control (Devos, 2008; Petty, Fazio, & Briñol, 2009; Wittenbrink & Schwarz, 2007). Affective responses may be automatically activated when an attitude object is made salient. However, because they are relatively unconscious, individuals may not be able to report them accurately.

In this section, we focus on the implications of research on implicit (automatic or unconscious) biases for political attitudes and behavior (Burdein, Lodge, & Taber, 2006). Conceptual and methodological developments in this domain have had a profound impact on the study of racial biases (see Chapter 2). It is now well-established that attitudes toward politicians can be measured using techniques developed to assess associations that are not consciously controllable. For example, the Implicit Association Test (IAT, Greenwald, McGhee, & Schwartz, 1998) can be employed to determine whether people hold an implicit preference for one candidate over another (Nosek, Banaji, & Greenwald, 2002; Nosek et al., 2007). The ease with which pleasant or unpleasant words can be associated with one or another of two opposing candidates allows researchers to infer implicit attitudes toward those two politicians.

Implicit Attitudes and Voting Behavior

Do implicit attitudes influence voting behavior? It is often assumed that voting is a deliberative behavior involving conscious and controlled processes. However, experimental research has challenged this assumption and demonstrates that feelings and thoughts that are not accessible to introspection or that cannot be consciously controlled account for voting behavior. Fazio and Williams (1986) provided an initial demonstration of the impact of spontaneous affective responses on voting behavior during the 1984 presidential election. The faster participants expressed their opinion about the suitability for office of Reagan or Mondale, the more the expressed attitude accounted for subsequent voting behavior.

Additional evidence for the influence of automatic and nonconscious processes on political decision making has been obtained since that initial study. A large-scale Internet study conducted during a parliamentary election in Germany showed that implicit attitudes toward five major political parties explained voting behavior over and above explicit self-report measures (Friese, Bluemke, & Wänke, 2007). A study conducted in another national context (Italy) established the predictive validity of implicit attitudes toward political candidates (Arcuri, Castelli, Galdi, Zogmaister, & Amadori, 2008). The researchers examined whether the relative implicit attitudes toward Silvio Berlusconi (leader of the right-wing coalition) or Francesco Rutelli (leader of the left-wing coalition) measured 1 month before the election accounted for voting behavior reported by participants immediately after the election. In line with the findings reported earlier, implicit political attitudes were consistent with voting behavior among a sample of voters who clearly sided with one or the other of the opposing parties. More surprising, however, was the finding that implicit political preferences of self-described undecided voters also predicted their subsequent voting behavior. These findings suggest the presence of embryonic attitudes even among voters who are not aware of their preference for one of the two opposing candidates. In contrast to verbal reports of uncertainty, undecided electors showed an implicit preference for one of the political candidates, and these automatic or spontaneous affective responses predicted future voting behavior (*see also* Galdi, Arcuri, & Gawronski, 2008).

Implicit Racial Attitudes and the 2008 Election

Studies reviewed in the previous section focused on the predictive validity of implicit *political* attitudes, but they do not speak to the role of implicit *racial* attitudes. According to a recent meta-analysis, implicit racial attitudes, measured using the IAT, predict behavior more effectively than parallel explicit (self-report) measures of attitudes (Greenwald, Poehlman, Uhlmann, & Banaji, 2009).

Data collected through Project Implicit (a research and educational website available at https://implicit.harvard.edu) provide a test of the predictive validity of racial attitudes in the context of the 2008 presidential election (Greenwald, Smith, Sriram, Bar-Anan, & Nosek, 2009). The week before election day, approximately 1,000 registered voters reported their choice between the principal contenders (John McCain & Barack Obama) and completed several measures that might predict their candidate preference, including two implicit measures of racial attitudes (the Brief IAT, Sriram & Greenwald, 2009, and the Affect Misattribution Procedure [AMP], Payne, Cheng, Govorun, & Stewart, 2005), two self-report measures of racial preference for European-Americans (Whites) relative to African-Americans (Blacks), the symbolic racism scale (Henry & Sears, 2002), and a measure of political liberalism-conservatism. Although each of the four racial attitude measures were correlated with intention to vote for McCain rather than for Obama, the implicit racial attitude measures predicted voting intention independently of the self-report racial attitude measures, and also independently of political conservatism and symbolic racism. These data demonstrate the predictive validity of implicit racial attitudes in the political domain. This study also showed that implicit racial attitudes were linked to symbolic racism. The pattern of correlations was consistent with the notion that symbolic racism is a blend of lingering negative feelings and an endorsement of conservative traditional values (Sears & Henry, 2005).

A limitation of this data collection is that the sample was not representative of the U.S. population. Indeed, more than 80% of the sample reported an intention to vote for Barack Obama. Three other surveys conducted using representative samples of American adults yielded very similar results (Payne et al., 2010). Explicit and implicit prejudices were measured during the months preceding the election. In this case, only the AMP was used to measure implicit prejudice. Consistently, explicit and implicit prejudices were significant predictors of later vote choice. Both levels of response make unique contributions to voting behavior. Interestingly, explicit and implicit prejudices accounted for slightly different behavioral responses: Respondents higher in explicit prejudice were more likely to vote for McCain rather than for Obama. However, respondents higher in implicit prejudice, although less likely to vote for Obama, were not more likely to vote for McCain; instead, they were more inclined to either abstain or to vote for a third-party candidate.

The impact of implicit racial attitudes on voting behavior might be context-dependent. A recent study has shown that the presence of party cues limited the effect of group attitude on the willingness to vote for a Hispanic candidate (Kam, 2007). In the absence of a party cue, the more participants held positive implicit or explicit attitudes toward Hispanics, the more they were likely to support a Hispanic candidate. The presence of party cues, however, eliminated the impact of attitudes toward Hispanics on political choice. These findings are consistent with prior research on the role of party cues

(Sigelman & Sigelman, 1982). Race or ethnicity plays a role, but it may at times be overridden by other relevant pieces of information.

As a whole, these studies demonstrate the importance of implicit racial biases in explaining political behavior. Research on implicit prejudices and stereotyping suggests that feelings and thoughts about social groups function often at a relatively automatic or unconscious level. Although these responses are not consciously controllable and are not necessarily available to introspection, they do appear to play a role in determining behavioral responses. Even among voters who strongly subscribe to egalitarian principles, and who consider that race should not play a role in voting decisions, thoughts and feelings that reside outside of conscious awareness shape political preferences. These voters may be unaware that their behavior is racially motivated and may genuinely believe that race was not a factor in their decision to vote for a White candidate rather than for a Black candidate, as they are not aware of the unconscious factors that may have played a role in that choice.

COMPLEXITIES OF RACIAL CATEGORIZATIONS

Defying Simplistic Racial Stereotypes

The 2008 presidential election also brought to the fore the complexity of cognitive and affective responses that may come into play in political contests. Barack Obama defied simple-minded stereotypes. At least among supporters of his candidacy, Obama was ascribed many positive characteristics: he was depicted as charismatic, well-educated, bright, and inspiring. These traits may be assigned to him based on his personal accomplishments and credentials. They can also be a function of group memberships that define important facets of his social self. For example, he was a relatively young candidate to the presidency, a Harvard graduate, and a community organizer in Chicago. At the same time, these characterizations might not be unrelated to changes in the content and valence of stereotypes about ethnic groups. Overall, negative traits are now less often ascribed to African-Americans. Adjectives that used to be included in the stereotype of Blacks (such as lazy, ignorant, or stupid) are no longer among the most frequently associated with this ethnic group (Fiske, Bergsieker, Russell, & Williams, 2009). At least under some circumstances, these negative traits continue to be implied. For example, describing Obama as "articulate" and "bright" is implicitly endorsing old-fashioned stereotypes ("most Blacks are stupid and ignorant") by highlighting that this particular Black man is different.

More important, a simplistic application of a unidimensional affective model may not be appropriate to capture how people respond to political candidates and social groups. The stereotype content model provides a useful framework to make sense of the increasing complexity of these images (Fiske, Cuddy, & Glick, 2007; Fiske, Cuddy, Glick, & Xu, 2002). The model posits that stereotypes of groups can be organized according to two fundamental dimensions: warmth-morality and competence-agency. Fiske and her collaborators (2009) employed this conceptual model to examine the role of racial stereotypes and perceptions of Barack Obama in the 2008 election. Generic stereotypes of Black Americans, at least among relatively egalitarian undergraduates, emphasize warmth-related traits (e.g., passionate, gregarious, loyal to family ties, talkative, musical, very religious, or sportsmanlike). According to Fiske et al. (2009), such images of Black Americans can be understood as a form of negative stereotyping by omission. Although these qualities are all positive, they refer primarily to the warmth-morality dimension. The failure to include qualities of competence implies their absence. In addition, Black Americans are often subdivided according to social class: Black professionals are differentiated from low-income working class Blacks. The Black professional subtype is characterized as highly competent and moderately warm, fitting the image associated with Barack Obama. During the campaign, he used a calm and measured tone, rarely smiling in pictures, stressing his competence. His warmth was rarely highlighted except in representations of him as a family man. He could not easily be cast as incompetent based on his credentials, although attacks on his alleged inexperience can be understood as attempts to move him down the competence dimension.

Categorizations of Multiracial Individuals

In the case of Barack Obama, the complexity of cognitive and affective responses may also stem from his mixed ethnic and cultural background. President Obama has defined himself as a Black man with mixed racial heritage. His father was from Kenya, whereas his mother was White and originally from Kansas.

Recent research on how people categorize multiracial individuals speaks directly to responses elicited by Obama's racial identity (Peery & Bodenhausen, 2009). Peery and Bodenhausen (2008) examined how racially ambiguous persons are categorized. In their study, participants first were presented with racially ambiguous (i.e., morphed combinations of White and Black faces) photographs of a number of persons. To determine automatic reactions based on a person's physical features, participants completed a speeded categorization task requiring rapid judgments about whether each target was Black or not Black and also whether each target was White or not White. In the absence of any information about parentage, monoracial categorization patterns were the most common for the racially ambiguous targets, and the percentage categorized as Black and not White (32%) was comparable to the percentage categorized as White and not Black (30%). However, when photographs of the target's parents were included, the categorization pattern shifted markedly toward categorizing the targets as Black and not White (44%) rather than White and not Black (20%) when the person was characterized as having one Black parent and one White parent. This demonstrates that automatic categorizations tend to follow the principle of hypodescent: Having one Black parent resulted in disproportionally assigning a person to the category "Black and not White." Immediately after this task, participants were asked to describe the race of the racially ambiguous targets, in a non-speeded, reflective questionnaire format. In contrast to the automatic categorizations, these more deliberative responses showed that having known mixed-race parentage resulted in a stronger likelihood of categorizing a person as multiracial.

Once again, this points to potential discrepancies between responses that are based on relatively automatic processes and responses reflecting more deliberative processes. Rapid racial categorizations reflect a legacy of rigid and pervasive notions of racial identity that are not consistent with a society increasing in diversity and complexity. At the same time, a more complex and multicultural conception of racial identities emerges from more deliberative categorizations.

Despite the fact that some wondered whether Barack Obama was too White to be considered Black (Coates, 2007), this research suggests that he was probably automatically categorized by most people as Black and not White. This being said, deliberative racial categorizations also matter and have implications for judgment and behavior. In light of research showing that prejudicial reactions are more likely to be directed toward African-Americans who are strongly identified with their racial group (Kaiser & Pratt-Hyatt, 2009) or who have Afrocentric phenotypical characteristics (Maddox, 2004), Barack Obama was wise not to overemphasize his racial identity over the course of the campaign, and his physical appearance may have dampened negative racially based affective responses.

Some White voters may have considered Barack Obama acceptable and likable because he was perceived as different from most African-Americans. He defied traditional ethnic stereotypes and defined a new model of acceptable Blackness (Wise, 2009). Although Senator Obama embraced the fact that he is a Black man, he avoided stressing his racial identity in a way that might concern or threaten White Americans. In fact, the support he enjoyed among White Americans was not unrelated to the fact that issues of racial inequalities and tensions were not playing a prominent role in his campaign. A portion of the electorate may have supported his candidacy precisely because he was portrayed in a de-racialized way. Some part of the White electorate may have voted for him because he *was* Black, and his success was consistent with their beliefs.

From the perspective of Black voters, the tendency to minimize race and focus on issues that reach across ethnic divisions may have elicited more ambivalent responses. Despite marrying a Black woman, living in a predominantly Black neighborhood, attending a predominantly Black church, his racial authenticity was questioned within African-American communities. Obama was born in Hawaii and spent a portion of his childhood in Jakarta. Thus, some Black voters were somewhat unsure that he could relate to their daily experiences. Suspicions about his candidacy and loyalty may also have arisen because he seemed to be respected by the predominantly White elite.

In sum, winning the election probably required an ability to navigate issues of race and ethnicity that are more complex and nuanced than they were a few decades ago. Racial distinctions elicit less polarized responses and can no longer be appraised along a simplistic dualist model. However, this does not signify that race is irrelevant. Instead, it points to new challenges. Obama had to be Black enough to be embraced by Black voters yet de-racialized enough to gain support within other ethnic groups. Had he presented himself as a candidate driven by the interest of the Black community, there is little doubt that he would not have gained the momentum that allowed his ascendance on the national stage.

When Racial Identity Makes You Less American

Another deep-seated bias that Obama had to contend with was the difficulty to grant the American identity to non-White Americans. Over the course of the campaign his patriotism, allegiance to U. S. interests and even his citizenship were questioned. For example, the facts that he declined to wear a flag pin and failed to salute the flag on one occasion were highlighted. Some opponents put an undue emphasis on his foreign-sounding middle name (Hussein). The "Birthers" argued that he was ineligible to be president because of questions surrounding his birth status. Even more perplexing, Michelle Obama was castigated for stating she had only recently felt proud of the United States. The message is clear: "The Obamas are not authentic Americans." These are illustrations of a more general propensity to view members of ethnic minority groups as perpetual foreigners. Contrary to core values of equality and freedom, the American identity is more strongly associated with people of European descent than with other ethnic groups (Devos & Banaji, 2005; *see also* Chapter 4). The linkage between being White and being American can be conceptualized as a form of exclusionary patriotism (Sidanius & Petrocik, 2001): National attachment becomes inextricably linked to prejudice toward subgroups that do not embody the dominant definition of the national identity.

Consistent with this hypothesis, survey data showed that the more White respondents—particularly those belonging to the working class—expressed an attachment to U.S. national symbols, the less likely they were to vote for Obama (Parker, Sawyer, & Towler, 2009). This symbolic patriotism can be used to justify Whites' dominance and to dampen support for a non-White president.

In this vein, a series of experiments conducted during the presidential campaign demonstrated that the ability to associate the American identity with Barack Obama was clearly a function of the extent to which he was seen as a Black person (Devos & Ma, 2010). Obama was, at an implicit level, viewed as less American than Hillary Clinton, John McCain, or even Tony Blair (then British Prime Minister) when race was made focal. This bias was attenuated, although not always completely eliminated, when the politicians were categorized based on their personal identity (first and last names). Moreover, the extent to which individuals implicitly linked the American identity to politicians predicted their willingness to support them; those who had difficulty seeing Obama as an American were less likely to support him. This effect held even after controlling for explicitly measured prejudice and political orientation.

EQUALITY AND THE PERVASIVENESS OF RACIAL DIVISIONS

The election of Barack Obama has stimulated much discussion about progress toward racial equality in the United States. The presence of a Black family in the White House will mark a shift in the way Americans think about race, but will it also be a milestone toward achieving greater equality and harmony between groups defined on the basis of race, ethnicity, or cultural backgrounds, or will racial divisions and structural racial inequalities remain?

Maintaining Group-Based Hierarchy

A recent longitudinal study exploring the idea that support or opposition to Obama might be grounded in motivation to maintain group-based hierarchy revealed two interesting findings (Knowles, Lowery, & Schaumberg, 2009). The first is relatively straightforward and consistent with the previous section: Anti-egalitarian voters opposed Obama because of his perceived foreignness. The second is more intriguing: Obama found support among some individuals who aspire to maintain racial inequalities. More precisely, anti-egalitarianism was associated with an increased tendency to vote for Obama among individuals who claimed that his victory signals the end of racism. In this case, support for Obama was anchored in a motive to promote the idea that racism has been eliminated. In line with social dominance theory

(Sidanius & Pratto, 1999), the endorsement of anti-egalitarian views is anchored in beliefs rationalizing intergroup inequalities.

Individuals interested in maintaining the current social hierarchy may have been motivated to oppose Obama's candidacy because it represented a symbolic and substantive challenge to that order. The election of an African-American president may threaten White dominance. Anxiety over minority gains in political power and support for conservative political candidates has been linked to social dominance motives (Pratto, Sidanius, Stallworth, & Malle, 1994). At the same time, Obama's victory could be construed as evidence that racism has been eliminated and racial equity has been achieved in the United States. Asserting Obama's election as a sign that we are living in a post-racial era might, indirectly, undermine efforts to increase equality by denying that such efforts are necessary. Thus, depending on expectations about the consequences of Obama's election, the motive to maintain the current hierarchical nature of race relations may go hand-in-hand either with opposition to or support for the candidacy of an African-American.

Paradoxical Effects on Support for Social Policies

The election of Barack Obama might have beneficial consequences for race relations and might help reduce both explicit and implicit levels of racial prejudice. At the level of relatively automatic or unconscious responses, several lines of research and theoretical models suggest that the election of an African-American to the nation's highest office should decrease stereotyped beliefs and responses (Gawronski & Bodenhausen, 2006). For example, the accessibility of positive Black exemplars and the association of government-related words (e.g., president, leader) with the concept "Black" has been found to decrease implicit racial prejudice and stereotyping (Plant et al., 2009).

At the same time, the election of Barack Obama may be accompanied by counterintuitive or ironic effects. Kaiser, Drury, Spalding, Cheryan, and O'Brien (2009) provide a striking illustration of this possibility. They found that after the election, participants were more likely to endorse the idea that racism was less of a problem in the United States today than in the past and less likely to support policies aimed at addressing racial inequalities and remedying racial injustices (e.g., affirmative action, desegregation programs, efforts to promote diversity, etc.). Given the continued prevalence of racial disparities in virtually all aspects of American society, these results have important implications. If it is construed as evidence for undeniable racial progress and validation for a meritocratic system, Obama's election could, ironically, decrease support for policies aimed at mitigating racial injustice.

Such ironic effects are consistent with research on moral credentials (Monin & Miller, 2001). When individuals have an opportunity to express their egalitarian values and, as a result, establish their moral credentials, they are more prone to transgress those values. Directly relevant to the last presidential election, Effron, Cameron, and Monin (2009) conducted three studies demonstrating that the opportunity to endorse Barack Obama subsequently made individuals more prone to favor Whites over Blacks: expressing support for Obama made participants more willing to describe a job in the police force as better suited for Whites than for Blacks; for participants who scored high on a measure of racial prejudice, endorsing Obama increased intentions to allocate money to an organization serving Whites at the expense of an organization serving Blacks. In sum, voting for Barack Obama may give some White voters the moral capital that affords them the opportunity to be less concerned about racial biases in other contexts, perhaps even including future elections.

Diverging Views on the Meaning of the Election

Another element contributing to the pervasiveness of racial divisions and the difficulty of overcoming racial inequalities lies in the existence of different perspectives on these issues. For example, African-Americans, Hispanics, and Whites clearly differ in their beliefs about the meaning of an Obama victory (Hunt & Wilson, 2009). Specifically, data from a June/July 2008 Gallup-USA Today survey showed that African-Americans, relative to Whites and Hispanics, were more likely to appraise an Obama victory as important and meaningful in terms of racial change. In contrast, Hispanics were more prone than African-Americans and Whites to endorse the idea that Obama's victory would translate into concrete societal changes, including expanded opportunities for Blacks in politics. Thus, for African-Americans, the election of Obama had a symbolic significance, but they did not anticipate that it would necessarily translate in substantive racial progress. This illustrates that race or ethnicity shapes respondents' outlooks on the meaning of Obama's presidency.

In the same vein, opinion surveys document that Whites reliably perceive a greater rate of progress toward racial equality than do African-Americans. Eibach and Purdie-Vaughns (2009) discussed two psychological factors that contribute to these diverging perceptions. First, Whites and African-Americans tend to adopt different reference points to assess racial progress. More precisely, perceptions of progress toward racial equality are anchored in comparisons with the past for Whites and in comparisons with ideal standards for members of ethnic minorities (Eibach & Ehrlinger, 2006). Second, there is a general tendency to frame social change as a zero-sum game in which Blacks' gains entail losses for Whites (Eibach & Keegan, 2006). These two factors foster a racial polarization on the topic of racial equality. As Eibach and Purdie-Vaughns (2009) note, a challenge for the Obama presidency is to frame the issue of progress toward racial equality in a way that bridges these divisions.

CONCLUSION

Despite the outcome of the 2008 presidential election, the empirical evidence presented in this chapter emphasizes the pervasive impact of race on the perception of political candidates, which has broad implications for American politics. There are multiple ways in which racial attitudes and identity continue to play a ubiquitous role in politics. Having narrowed our discussion to affective and cognitive reactions to political candidates and the likelihood of supporting or opposing them, we can draw a number of straightforward lessons from the 2008 election. First, despite the prevalence of egalitarian principles, a nontrivial segment of the electorate might have been influenced by race when choosing their candidate. Second, although there were no substantial discrepancies between polling data and actual voting behavior at the national level, there is still some evidence that social desirability and impression management concerns affect the extent to which individuals express their political preferences. These effects cannot be reduced to attempts to conceal a reluctance to vote for a Black candidate and must be better understood. What is expressed in a polling situation or a voting booth is the result of a complex interplay of social influences. Third, opposition to minority candidates may arise from the meaning attached to their potential election. Blatant expressions of resentments, fears, or concerns for the interests or position of one's group in society have declined, but research on symbolic racism suggests that lingering racial biases continue to influence affective and cognitive responses to political candidates and social issues. Fourth, unconscious or automatic prejudices and stereotypes have an impact on how political candidates are viewed and thus shape voting decisions. Research on implicit racial biases offers some insights on the contexts and experiences that are most likely to produce an alignment between unconscious or automatic associations and egalitarian ideals endorsed at a more conscious or deliberate level. Fifth, recent models or conceptualizations of racial biases allow us to comprehend the ways in which stereotypical beliefs and racial categorizations continue to operate in a societal context that is becoming increasingly diverse and multicultural. Finally, despite the enthusiasm surrounding the election of Barack Obama and the striking symbolic success that it represents for racial progress, analysts and scientists have started to document paradoxical or unintended consequences of his presidency that underscore the challenges of overcoming racial divisions and traces of a long history of oppression.

The election of Barack Obama prompted some commentators to proclaim that we have now moved to a "post-racial United States," or defeated racism. These statements contrast with the picture that emerges from the literature reviewed in the present chapter. By most accounts, it is premature to announce the end of racial biases in the political arena. Many factors contribute independently or interactively to political attitudes and behaviors. Our discussion has concentrated on the impact of race and racial attitudes, focusing to a large extent on covert biases against Black Americans. Despite the pervasive public endorsement of principles of racial equality, inclusion, and anti-discrimination, issues related to racial attitudes need to stay on the radar of analysts and social scientists interested in the complexities of political processes and relations between groups defined in terms of race, ethnicity, or cultural background. The hidden obstacles that some candidates have to navigate may explain why some groups continue to hold little political power. On a more optimistic note, the election of Barack Obama holds the promise of a renewed and constructive dialogue on race relations. Instead of prematurely concluding that we are now free of racial prejudices, the current state of affairs should be viewed as an opportunity to increase awareness of subtle racial biases that may affect the fairness and equity of the political system.

NOTE

The author thanks Jeff Bryson and Que-Lam Huynh for their valuable comments on a previous draft.

REFERENCES

Abelson, R. P., Kinder, D. R., Peters, M. D., & Fiske, S. T. (1982). Affective and semantic components in political person perception. *Journal of Personality and Social Psychology, 42*(4), 619–630.

Alter, J. (2006, December 25). The race is on. *Newsweek.*

Arcuri, L., Castelli, L., Galdi, S., Zogmaister, C., & Amadori, A. (2008). Predicting the vote: Implicit attitudes as predictors of the future behavior of decided and undecided voters. *Political Psychology, 29*(3), 369–387.

Berinsky, A. J. (1999). The two faces of public opinion. *American Journal of Political Science, 43*(4), 1209–1230.

Bobo, L. D., & Dawson, M. C. (2009). A change has come. *Du Bois Review: Social Science Research on Race, 6*(1), 1–14.

Brewer, M. B. (1999). The psychology of prejudice: Ingroup love or outgroup hate? *Journal of Social Issues, 55*(3), 429–444.

Bullock, C. S. (1984). Racial crossover voting and the election of black officials. *Journal of Politics, 46*(1), 238.

Burdein, I., Lodge, M., & Taber, C. (2006). Experiments on the automaticity of political beliefs and attitudes. *Political Psychology, 27*(3), 359–371.

Cameron, C., & Epstein, D. (1996). Do majority-minority districts maximize substantive black representation in Congress? *American Political Science Review, 90*(4), 794–812.

Carsey, T. M. (1995). The contextual effects of race on white voter behavior: The 1989 New York city mayoral election. *Journal of Politics, 57*(1), 221–228.

Christ, W. G. (1985). Voter preference and emotion: Using emotional response to classify decided and undecided voters. *Journal of Applied Social Psychology, 15*(3), 237–254.

Citrin, J., Green, D. P., & Sears, D. O. (1990). White reactions to black candidates. *Public Opinion Quarterly, 54*, 74–96.

CNN (2008). *Local exit polls - election center 2008 - elections & politics from CNN.com.* Retrieved December 23, 2009, from http://www.cnn.com/ELECTION/2008/results/polls/val=USP00p1

Coates, T. P. (2007, February 1). Is Obama black enough? *Time Magazine.*

Devos, T. (2008). Implicit attitudes 101: Theoretical and empirical insights. In W. D. Crano, & R. Prislin (Eds.), *Attitudes and attitude change* (pp. 61–84). New York, NY: Psychology Press.

Devos, T., & Banaji, M. R. (2005). American = white? *Journal of Personality and Social Psychology, 88*(3), 447–466.

Devos, T., & Ma, D. S. (2010). *How "American" is Barack Obama? The role of national identity in a historic bid for the White House.* Manuscript submitted for publication.

Dwyer, C. E., Stevens, D., Sullivan, J. L., & Allen, B. (2009). Racism, sexism, and candidate evaluations in the 2008 U.S. presidential election. *Analyses of Social Issues and Public Policy, 9*(1), 223–240.

Effron, D. A., Cameron, J. S., & Monin, B. (2009). Endorsing Obama licenses favoring whites. *Journal of Experimental Social Psychology, 45*(3), 590–593.

Eibach, R. P., & Ehrlinger, J. (2006). "Keep your eyes on the prize": Reference points and racial differences in assessing progress toward equality. *Personality and Social Psychology Bulletin, 32*(1), 66–77.

Eibach, R. P., & Keegan, T. (2006). Free at last? Social dominance, loss aversion, and white and black Americans' differing assessments of racial progress. *Journal of Personality and Social Psychology, 90*(3), 453–467.

Eibach, R. P., & Purdie-Vaughns, V. (2009). Change we can believe in? Barack Obama's framing strategies for bridging racial divisions. *Du Bois Review: Social Science Research on Race, 6*(1), 137–151.

Epstein, D., & O'Halloran, S. (1999). Measuring the electoral and policy impact of majority voting districts. *American Journal of Political Science, 43*(2), 367–395.

Fazio, R. H., & Williams, C. J. (1986). Attitude accessibility as a moderator of the attitude–perception and attitude–behavior relations: An investigation of the 1984 presidential election. *Journal of Personality and Social Psychology, 51*(3), 505–514.

Federal Election Commission Report. (2009). *2008 official presidential general election results.* Retrieved December 23, 2009, from http://www.fec.gov/pubrec/fe2008/2008presgeresults.pdf

Finkel, S. E., Guterbock, T. M., & Borg, M. J. (1991). Race-of-interviewer effects in a preelection poll: Virginia 1989. *Public Opinion Quarterly, 55*(3), 313–330.

Fiske, S. T., Bergsieker, H. B., Russell, A. M., & Williams, L. (2009). Images of black Americans. *Du Bois Review: Social Science Research on Race, 6*(1), 83–101.

Fiske, S. T., Cuddy, A. J., Glick, P., & Xu, J. (2002). A model of (often mixed) stereotype content: Competence and warmth respectively follow from perceived status and competition. *Journal of Personality and Social Psychology, 82*(6), 878–902.

Fiske, S. T., Cuddy, A. J. C., & Glick, P. (2007). Universal dimensions of social cognition: Warmth and competence. *Trends in Cognitive Sciences, 11*(2), 77–83.

Friese, M., Bluemke, M., & Wänke, M. (2007). Predicting voting behavior with implicit attitude measures: The 2002 German parliamentary election. *Experimental Psychology, 54*(4), 247–255.

Galdi, S., Arcuri, L., & Gawronski, B. (2008). Automatic mental associations predict future choices of undecided decision-makers. *Science, 321*(5892), 1100–1102.

Gawronski, B., & Bodenhausen, G. V. (2006). Associative and propositional processes in evaluation: An integrative review of implicit and explicit attitude change. *Psychological Bulletin, 132*(5), 692–731.

Greenwald, A. G., & Albertson, B. (2008). *Tracking the race factor - Pew research center.* Retrieved December 23, 2009, from http://pewresearch.org/pubs/755/tracking-the-race-factor

Greenwald, A. G., McGhee, D. E., & Schwartz, J. L. K. (1998). Measuring individual differences in implicit cognition: The implicit association test. *Journal of Personality and Social Psychology, 74*(6), 1464–1480.

Greenwald, A. G., Poehlman, T. A., Uhlmann, E. L., & Banaji, M. R. (2009). Understanding and using the implicit association test: III. meta-analysis of predictive validity. *Journal of Personality and Social Psychology, 97*(1), 17–41.

Greenwald, A. G., Smith, C. T., Sriram, N., Bar-Anan, Y., & Nosek, B. A. (2009). Implicit race attitudes predicted vote in the 2008 U.S. presidential election. *Analyses of Social Issues and Public Policy, 9*(1), 241–253.

Henry, P. J., & Sears, D. O. (2002). The symbolic racism 2000 scale. *Political Psychology, 23*(2), 253–283.

Highton, B. (2004). White voters and African American candidates for Congress. *Political Behavior, 26*(1), 1–25.

Huckfeldt, R. R., & Kohfeld, C. W. (1989). *Race and the decline of class in American politics.* Urbana: University of Illinois Press.

Hunt, M. O., & Wilson, D. C. (2009). Race/ethnicity, perceived discrimination, and beliefs about the meaning of an Obama presidency. *Du Bois Review: Social Science Research on Race, 6*(1), 173–191.

Jenkins, P. (2009). *Holder, race and Obama's 10% of the white Alabama vote.* Retrieved December 23, 2009, from http://www.huffingtonpost.com/paul-jenkins/holder-race-and-obamas-10_b_168852.html

Kaiser, C. R., Drury, B. J., Spalding, K. E., Cheryan, S., & O'Brien, L. T. (2009). The ironic consequences of Obama's election: Decreased support for social justice. *Journal of Experimental Social Psychology, 45*(3), 556–559.

Kaiser, C. R., & Pratt-Hyatt, J. (2009). Distributing prejudice unequally: Do whites direct their prejudice toward strongly identified minorities? *Journal of Personality and Social Psychology, 96*(2), 432–445.

Kam, C. D. (2007). Implicit attitudes, explicit choices: When subliminal priming predicts candidate preference. *Political Behavior, 29*(3), 343–367.

Keeter, S., Kiley, J., Christian, L., & Dimock, M. (2009). *Perils of polling in election '08 - Pew research center.* Retrieved December 23, 2009, from http://pewresearch. org/pubs/1266/polling-challenges-election-08-success-in-dealing-with

Kinder, D. R., & Sears, D. O. (1981). Prejudice and politics: Symbolic racism versus racial threats to the good life. *Journal of Personality and Social Psychology, 40*(3), 414–431.

Knowles, E. D., Lowery, B. S., & Schaumberg, R. L. (2009). Anti-egalitarians for Obama? Group-dominance motivation and the Obama vote. *Journal of Experimental Social Psychology, 45*(4), 965–969.

Lau, R. R. (2003). Models of decision-making. In D. O. Sears, L. Huddy, & R. Jervis (Eds.), *Oxford handbook of political psychology* (pp. 19–59). New York: Oxford University Press.

Liu, B. (2001). Racial contexts and white interests: Beyond black threat and racial tolerance. *Political Behavior, 23*(2), 157–180.

Maddox, K. B. (2004). Perspectives on racial phenotypicality bias. *Personality and Social Psychology Review, 8*(4), 383–401.

Mendelberg, T. (2001). *The race card: Campaign strategy, implicit messages, and the norm of equality.* Princeton, N.J.: Princeton University Press.

Messick, D. M., & Mackie, D. M. (1989). Intergroup relations. *Annual review of psychology, 40*, 45–81.

Monin, B., & Miller, D. T. (2001). Moral credentials and the expression of prejudice. *Journal of Personality and Social Psychology, 81*(1), 33–43.

Moskowitz, D., & Stroh, P. (1994). Psychological sources of electoral racism. *Political Psychology, 15*(2), 307–329.

Nosek, B. A., Banaji, M. R., & Greenwald, A. G. (2002). Harvesting implicit group attitudes and beliefs from a demonstration website. *Group Dynamics, 6*(1), 101–115.

Nosek, B. A., Greenwald, A. G., & Banaji, M. R. (2007). The implicit association test at age 7: A methodological and conceptual review. In J. A. Bargh (Ed.), *Social psychology and the unconscious: The automaticity of higher mental processes* (pp. 265–292). New York: Psychology Press.

Nosek, B. A., Smyth, F. L., Hansen, J. J., Devos, T., Lindner, N. M., Ranganath, K. A., et al. (2007). Pervasiveness and correlates of implicit attitudes and stereotypes. *European Review of Social Psychology, 18*, 36–88.

Parker, C. S., Sawyer, M. Q., & Towler, C. (2009). A black man in the White House? *Du Bois Review: Social Science Research on Race, 6*(1), 193–217.

Parks, G. S., & Rachlinski, J. J. (2008). A better metric: The role of unconscious race and gender bias in the 2008 presidential race. *Cornell Legal Studies Research Paper no. 08-007.*

Payne, B. K., Krosnick, J. A., Pasek, J., Lelkes, Y., Akhtar, O., & Tompson, T. (2010). Implicit and explicit prejudice in the 2008 American presidential election. *Journal of Experimental Social Psychology, 46,* 377–374.

Payne, B. K., Cheng, C. M., Govorun, O., & Stewart, B. D. (2005). An inkblot for attitudes: Affect misattribution as implicit measurement. *Journal of Personality and Social Psychology, 89*(3), 277–293.

Peery, D., & Bodenhausen, G. V. (2008). Black + white = black: Hypodescent in reflexive categorization of racially ambiguous faces. *Psychological Science, 19*(10), 973–977.

Peery, D., & Bodenhausen, G. V. (2009). Ambiguity and ambivalence in the voting booth and beyond. *Du Bois Review: Social Science Research on Race, 6*(01), 71.

Petty, R. E., Fazio, R. H., & Briñol, P. (Eds.). (2009). *Attitudes: Insights from the new implicit measures.* New York: Psychology Press, Taylor & Francis.

Plant, E. A., Devine, P. G., Cox, W. T. L., Columb, C., Miller, S. L., Goplen, J., et al. (2009). The Obama effect: Decreasing implicit prejudice and stereotyping. *Journal of Experimental Social Psychology, 45*(4), 961–964.

Plant, E. A., & Devine, P. G. (1998). Internal and external motivation to respond without prejudice. *Journal of Personality and Social Psychology, 75*(3), 811–832.

Pratto, F., Sidanius, J., Stallworth, L. M., & Malle, B. F. (1994). Social dominance orientation: A personality variable predicting social and political attitudes. *Journal of Personality and Social Psychology, 67*(4), 741–763.

Rachlinski, J. J., & Parks, G. S. (2009). *Implicit bias, election '08, and the myth of a post-racial America.* Retrieved December 18, 2009, from http://ssrn.com/abstract=1456509

Ramakrishnan, S. K., Wong, J., Lee, T., & Junn, J. (2009). Race-based considerations and the Obama vote. *Du Bois Review: Social Science Research on Race, 6*(1), 219–238.

Schuman, H., Steeh, C., Bobo, L., & Krysan, M. (1997). *Racial attitudes in America: Trends and interpretation.* Cambridge, MA: Harvard University Press.

Sears, D. O., van Laar, C., Carillo, M., & Kosterman, R. (1997). The origins of white Americans opposition to race-targeted policies. *Public Opinion Quarterly, 61,* 16–53.

Sears, D. O., & Henry, P. J. (2005). Over thirty years later: A contemporary look at symbolic racism. *Advances in Experimental Social Psychology, 37,* 95–150.

Sears, D. O., Sidanius, J., & Bobo, L. (Eds.). (2000). *Racialized politics: The debate about racism in America.* Chicago: University of Chicago Press.

Sidanius, J., & Petrocik, J. R. (2001). Communal and national identity in a multiethnic state: A comparison of three perspectives. In R. D. Ashmore, L. Jussim & D. Wilder (Eds.), *Social identity, intergroup conflict, and conflict resolution* (pp. 101–129). Oxford, U.K.: Oxford University Press.

Sidanius, J., & Pratto, F. (1999). *Social dominance: An intergroup theory of social hierarchy and oppression.* Cambridge, MA: Cambridge University Press.

Sigelman, L., & Sigelman, C. K. (1982). Sexism, racism, and ageism in voting behavior: An experimental analysis. *Social Psychology Quarterly, 45*(4), 263–269.

Sniderman, P. M., & Carmines, E. G. (1997). *Reaching beyond race*. Cambridge, MA: Harvard University Press.

Sriram, N., & Greenwald, A. G. (2009). The brief implicit association test. *Experimental Psychology, 56*(4), 283–294.

Swim, J. K., Aikin, K. J., Hall, W. S., & Hunter, B. A. (1995). Sexism and racism: Old-fashioned and modern prejudices. *Journal of Personality and Social Psychology, 68*(2), 199–214.

Sykes, P. L. (2008). Gender in the 2008 presidential election: Two types of time collide. *PS, Political Science and Politics, 41*, 761–764.

Westen, D. (2007). *The political brain: The role of emotion in deciding the fate of the nation*. New York: Public Affairs.

Wise, T. (2009). *Between Barack and a hard place: Racism and white denial in the age of Obama*. San Francisco, CA: City Lights Books.

Wittenbrink, B., & Schwarz, N. (Eds.). (2007). *Implicit measures of attitudes*. New York: Guilford Press.

The State of the Post-Racial Union

Farai Chideya

In his subsequent essay on "The Role of Race in American Politics," Thierry Devos offers us a portrait of how the election of Barack Obama both conformed to and deviated from existing patterns of race and voting. The picture that emerges is nuanced and complex—of an America that has made some significant strides in dealing with racial bias in voter preference but hardly escaped it. Still, in the face of clear data that race does matter, can we talk about either the election or the groundbreaking Presidency it produced as "post-racial?"

"Post-racial" was the most popular phrase in the 2008 election after "hope" and "change." It was usually applied to the candidate, Barack Obama, himself, and sometimes to the nature of his followers. Hold that thought. Now flash-forward to January 2010, a year after the inauguration, when President Barack Obama took the podium to deliver the State of the Union Address. He talked about jobs (23 mentions), the economy (15 mentions), and energy (15 mentions). He did not mention the words "race" or "racial," and the only time he mentioned the word "Black" was in the phrase "Black Tuesday," referring to the stock market crash of 1929.

After the State of the Union, the MSNBC cable channel host Chris Matthews made this comment about the President: "He is post-racial, by all appearances. I forgot he was black tonight for an hour. You know, he's gone a long way to become a leader of this country, and past so much history, in just a year or two. I mean, it's something we don't even think about."

The essayist and memoirist Ta-Nehisi Coates responded this way in an online essay for The Atlantic: "Chris Matthews didn't forget Barack Obama was black. Chris Matthews forgot that Chris Matthews was white. . . . This is why Obama will never be postracial—he can't make white people face the lie of their ignorance, anymore than Jimmy Baldwin could make black people face the lie of our homophobia. It's white people's responsibility to make themselves postracial, not the president's."

There is a distinct sense that the "post-racial" meme is about absolution, specifically about White voters seeking absolution from the legacy of race by voting for a Black man who won't demand that Americans address issues of racial equality. This aspect of the "post-racial" dream has a lot to do with the fear of payback. Andrew Hacker, the author of books including 1992's *Two Nations: Black and White, Separate, Hostile, Unequal,* wrote about race and voters in the New York Review of Books shortly before the 2008 election:

> Resentment of perceived black privilege is also involved, as we have seen with respect to affirmative action, and even fear of some kind of racial payback. Over half of a largely white sample told a Rasmussen poll that they feel Obama continues to share at least some of Reverend Jeremiah Wright's positions on America.

The fear of Black payback goes back as far as fear of slave rebellions. In modern politics, it means that some voters fear that Black politicians will favor Black interests, just as White politicians have often favored White interests. In fact, if you look at the history of American government, there has been a far greater transfer of Black wealth to White Americans and skewing of public funds toward non-Blacks than the reverse.

Instead of a payback mentality, the Obama Administration seems to deliberately be hands-off on dealing with problems facing Black America. Last month, there was a spat between the Congressional Black Caucus and the Administration over whether the Administration was doing enough for African-Americans. (According to economist and Bennett College president Dr. Julianne Malveaux, the real non-employment rate among African-Americans may be 27%.) The tussle between the President and the Congressional Black Caucus is worth keeping an eye on, because it begs the question: Is the only way to be a post-racial president to ignore the specific structural inequities of race, and if so, at what cost to the nation?

CHAPTER 11

Obama's Potential to Transform the Racial Attitudes of White Americans

John F. Dovidio, Samuel L. Gaertner, Tamar Saguy, and Eric Hehman

The election of Barack Obama as President of the United States is a truly historic event that, beyond its political implications, can have deep and lasting significance on the internalized racial attitudes of Whites in the United States. For the past 60 years, intergroup contact has represented the most potent intervention for improving Whites' attitudes toward Blacks (Allport, 1954; Dovidio, Gaertner, & Kawakami, 2003). Work in the area of Contact Theory has demonstrated that inter-racial contact involving a positive personal connection and cooperative interaction is particularly effective for improving intergroup attitudes generally. However, today, as in the past, residential and occupational forms of segregation in America limit this type of intergroup contact. Nevertheless, recent developments in social psychology have revealed that contact does not have to be direct and personal to be effective. "Virtual" contact or indirect forms of contact in which people learn of the positive intergroup orientations of other Whites can also significantly reduce prejudice. Thus, in this chapter, we describe how the election of President Obama has the potential to transform race relations in the United States because of the unprecedented inter-racial contact it provides for White Americans.

We begin this chapter by reviewing historical trends and contemporary aspects of racial attitudes and race in the United States. Then we consider the current psychological nature of racial bias in America, explaining why progress toward equality is increasingly difficult to achieve. We next describe evidence that intergroup contact, direct or indirect, can improve intergroup attitudes and apply these principles to understand how the presidency of Barack Obama can transform Whites' racial attitudes at a fundamental level. After that, we consider circumstances and processes that can promote or limit President Obama's effectiveness and positive impact on race relations.

TRENDS IN RACIAL ATTITUDES AND RACIAL DISPARITIES

Since the passage of the Civil Rights legislation in the mid 1960s, norms of egalitarianism have grown stronger, whereas expressed racial prejudice and negative stereotypes among White Americans have declined dramatically. National representative surveys (General Social Survey, 2009) reveal that in 1973, 37% of White Americans felt there should be laws prohibiting interracial marriage, but by 2002 that figure declined to 10%. In 1972, approximately 40% of Whites believed that Whites had the right to keep Blacks out of their neighborhoods, whereas by 1996, only 11% supported this view. In 1977, more than one-fourth of White Americans attributed Blacks' lower socioeconomic status than Whites to their "inborn disability"; in 2006, only 8% expressed this opinion. As Bobo (2001) concluded in his review of trends in racial attitudes, "The single clearest trend in studies of racial attitudes has involved a steady and sweeping movement toward general endorsement of the principles of racial equality and integration" (p. 269). In fact, Barack Obama's candidacy for president likely benefited substantially from this trend away from blatant racism. In 1958, the majority of White Americans said that they would *not* vote for a well-qualified presidential candidate if that candidate was Black; by 2007 about 95% said they would (General Social Survey, 2009; Pollster.com, 2009).

However, in recent years, change toward the complete acceptance of Blacks by White Americans has slowed in many areas. For example, the percentage of Whites who reported feeling "close" to Blacks was only slightly higher (69.7%) in 2006 than what it was 10 years earlier (67.2%; General Social Survey, 2009). Although disparities can have causes other than discrimination, economic indices show consistent differences in status based on race. The median family income for Blacks is less than two-thirds that of Whites, a differential that has widened over the past two decades (Blank, 2001). In 2007, the percentage of Blacks living in poverty (24.5%) was almost three times the rate for Whites (DeNavas-Walt, Proctor, & Smith, 2008). The gap between the rich (in which Whites are overrepresented) and the poor (in which Blacks are overrepresented) has widened in recent years (Roberts, 2004).

Moreover, structural changes in the United States are limiting the opportunities for direct inter-racial contact, particularly of the forms that are most effective for reducing bias. Steady trends toward residential integration that were observed from 1950 to 1970 have slowed in the South and stagnated in the North (Massey, 2001). Massey (2001) observed, "Either in absolute terms or in comparison to other groups, Blacks remain a very residentially segregated and spatially isolated people" (p. 403). Politically, recent Supreme Court decisions restricting the positive role of racial consideration in admissions to college (*Gratz and Hamacher v. Bollinger*, 2003) and professional school

(*Grutter v. Bollinger*, 2003) have limited programs that increase the likelihood of intergroup contact in schools, one of the most important opportunities for contact given prevailing residential segregation in America. Supreme Court decisions have also undermined race-based school desegregation plans for primary and secondary school districts (*Parents Involved in Community Schools v. Seattle School District No. 1*, 2007). For many, the recent *Ricci v. DeStefano* (2009) Supreme Court decision, concerning promotions within the fire department in New Haven, Connecticut, signals the erosion of support by the courts for affirmative action in the workplace and can ultimately increase employment segregation. Taken together, this series of decisions by the highest court in the land limits the kinds of personal inter-racial contact that frequently occur at school and at work and is so valuable for improving intergroup attitudes.

The election of Barack Obama is thus extremely fortuitous given the current political and social climate relating to race in contemporary U.S. society. Despite earlier enormous strides benefiting Blacks, progress toward true racial equality has generally slowed and, some would argue, has stalled or reversed itself in some areas. What can explain these recent trends, particularly in a society in which blatant prejudice is now relatively rare? In the next section, we discuss the impact of subtle racism on race relations in America.

The Subtlety of Contemporary Racism

Even while overt racism has declined significantly, Whites' racial prejudice still exerts a pervasive negative influence on the lives of Blacks. This effect is less direct and is fueled by new, more subtle forms of prejudice, such as aversive racism (Dovidio & Gaertner, 2004; Gaertner & Dovidio, 1986; Pearson, Dovidio, & Gaertner, 2009). Aversive racism rests on an inherent contradiction: That is, many Whites who consciously, explicitly, and sincerely support egalitarian principles and believe themselves to be nonprejudiced also harbor, without full awareness, negative feelings and beliefs about Blacks and other historically disadvantaged groups. Whereas the vast majority of White Americans appear to endorse nonprejudiced principles, a substantial majority of Whites also have automatically activated, often unconscious biases against Blacks (Nosek, Banaji, & Greenwald, 2002). These unconscious negative feelings and beliefs develop as a consequence of normal, almost unavoidable, and frequently functional cognitive, motivational, and social-cultural process. The existence of both the conscious endorsement of egalitarian values and unconscious negative feelings toward Blacks makes aversive racists' attitudes complex and produces a distinct pattern of discriminatory behavior. Aversive racists exhibit subtle discrimination, which is expressed in indirect, rationalizable ways.

People generally approach social situations with either a "promotion" or "prevention" regulatory orientation (Higgins, 1999). A promotion focus directs attention to potential positive outcomes and benefits, elicits positive emotions associated with making progress, and generates an approach orientation. By contrast, a prevention focus involves a sensitivity to negative outcomes, arouses negative emotions such as guilt and anxiety, and produces an avoidance motivation. The core motivation underlying aversive racism reflects a prevention focus. In inter-racial interactions, aversive racists concentrate on avoiding appearing biased. They try to suppress negative racial feelings or beliefs, but often these efforts to control bias deplete their cognitive resources, and biased thoughts "rebound" and influence their behavior. Because they are more focused on avoiding "doing wrong" than on "doing right," aversive racists avoid inter-racial interactions when possible. This avoidance motivation leads aversive racists to be systematically less helpful to Blacks than to Whites, and although guarded about behaving in an anti-Black way, they more freely engage in pro-White behavior, which ultimately advantages Whites as a group over Blacks (Gaertner et al., 1997).

One of the practical challenges posed by aversive racism involves the question of how to change the racial attitudes among Whites who already believe that they are nonprejudiced but who harbor their biases unconsciously, discriminate primarily in ways that can be justified on the basis of some factor other than race, and are motivated to avoid exposure to information that would suggest that they might be racially biased. Traditional anti-bias education interventions that emphasize that racism is bad and the people should not be prejudiced are ineffective for aversive racists. Aversive racists are convinced they are not prejudiced; they see themselves as part of the solution, not part of the problem. Thus, interventions to improve the attitudes of aversive racists need to be directed at their unconscious negative feelings and beliefs. Intergroup contact is uniquely promising in this respect.

INTERGROUP CONTACT THEORY

Intergroup contact has long been considered to be one of psychology's most effective strategies for improving intergroup relations. Research in this area has built a solid and substantial foundation of empirical evidence and theoretical formulations that specify when and how intergroup contact can reduce prejudice. For more than 60 years, the "Contact Hypothesis" (Allport, 1954; Pettigrew, 1998) has represented a promising and popular strategy for reducing intergroup bias and conflict. This hypothesis proposes that simple contact between groups is not automatically sufficient to improve intergroup relations.

In his highly influential version of the Contact Hypothesis, Allport (1954) hypothesized:

> To be maximally effective, contact and acquaintance programs should lead to a sense of equality in social status, should occur in ordinary purposeful pursuits, avoid artificiality, and if possible enjoy the sanction of the community in which they occur. The deeper and more genuine the association, the greater its effect. While it may help somewhat to place members of different ethnic groups side by side on a job, the gain is greater if these members regard themselves as part of a *team*. (Allport, 1954 p. 489, original italics)

Allport's identified four prerequisite features for contact to be successful at reducing intergroup conflict and achieving intergroup harmony. These four features are *(1)* equal status within the contact situation; *(2)* intergroup cooperation; *(3)* common goals; and *(4)* support of authorities, law, or custom (*see* Pettigrew, 1998). Since then, two other critical features have been identified: personalized interaction and friendships. Personalized interactions in which information about each other's unique qualities is exchanged reduce prejudice and stereotyping by undermining the validity of the outgroup stereotypes with conflicting immediate and concrete experience (Brewer & Miller, 1984; Miller, 2002). Intergroup friendships are also particularly important, in part because they incorporate aspects of the other five basic features (Pettigrew, 1998).

Since Allport's (1954) formulation, the Contact Hypothesis has received extensive empirical attention over the years, and the accumulated evidence strongly supports it. Pettigrew and Tropp (2006, 2008), in their meta-analyses of more than 750 studies, demonstrated that intergroup contact indeed reduces intergroup prejudice, and the beneficial effect of contact is greater when Allport's optimal conditions are present in the contact situation than when they are not. In recognition of the substantial empirical evidence in support of the benefits of contact on intergroup attitudes and the conceptual elaboration of the underlying processes, the framework is currently termed *Contact Theory*.

Indirect Forms of Contact. What makes Obama's presidency so promising for improving race relations is that contact does not have to be direct and personal to improve intergroup attitudes. Intergroup contact over the Internet can also improve Whites' attitudes toward Blacks (Yablon & Katz, 2001). Symbolic contact, in terms of positive exposure to Blacks in the media (Mutz & Goldman, 2010), can also exert a significant influence in reducing Whites' prejudice toward Blacks. More frequent contact of this type promotes a more positive attitude. In addition, because individuals are generally motivated to identify with high-status and powerful people, exposure to a Black president can be a particularly potent form of media influence. In our own research (Hehman, Gaertner & Dovidio, 2009), for example, we found that White college students expressed more favorable attitudes toward Blacks 1 month after Obama was elected president, compared to a comparable sample who reported their attitudes within 1 month prior to election day.

Because of humans' unique cognitive capacities, imagery can also play an important role in changing attitudes. For example, work on eliminating phobias through systematic desensitization often asks people to imagine themselves in a variety of ways in relation to stimuli that arouse fear, disgust, or anxiety. Crisp and Turner (2009) have recently demonstrated that mental simulation of contact can similarly reduce prejudice toward an outgroup. Moreover, they argue that "unlike actual contact . . . the imagined contact effect seems unfettered by a raft of necessary conditions, other than the two core principles" (p. 234). The first principle is that it is critical to run through a mental script of the interaction (vs. imagining an outgroup member in the absence of contact); the second principle is that the imagined contact must be positive (see Turner, Crisp, & Lambert, 2007). Thus, to the extent that Whites admire President Obama and can imagine positive interaction with him (e.g., related to agreement with his position on particular issues), they are likely to show improvement in their attitudes toward Blacks generally.

Even in the absence of personal imagined positive contact with President Obama, Whites may develop more favorable attitudes toward Blacks through another form of vicarious experience—learning that people they know have positive attitudes toward him (Wright, Aron, McLaughlin-Volpe, & Ropp, 1997). The extended contact effect, in which people learn that a member of their group is friends with an outgroup member, has been demonstrated to reduce biases in a variety of intergroup contexts, such as between Catholic and Protestants in Northern Ireland (Paolini, Hewstone, Cairns, & Voci, 2004), between White and South Asian students in the United Kingdom (Turner, Hewstone, Voci, & Vonofakou, 2008), and even among children as young as 5 years old (Cameron, Rutland, Brown, & Douch, 2006).

In an era of the 24-hour news cycle, in which press coverage of the president is ubiquitous, Obama's presidency and the virtual contact of White Americans with him can also directly address the key element of racial bias among aversive racists: the automatically activated, and typically unconscious, negative associations with Blacks. Previous research has shown that calling to mind examples of admired Blacks (e.g., Denzel Washington) can inhibit the normally spontaneous activation of negative racial stereotypes among Whites (Dasgupta & Greenwald, 2001). Directly investigating the impact of Barack Obama's national prominence, Plant et al. (2009) found that implicit anti-Black prejudice and stereotyping among White college students was significantly lower during Obama's presidential campaign than it was for prior samples at the same institution. Moreover, in a second study, Plant et al. demonstrated that implicit prejudice was lower among Whites who more strongly associated characteristics of Obama with Blacks generally. For young children, their frequent contact with President Obama through the media can insulate them from internalizing traditional negative stereotypes of Blacks and the kinds of socialized negative affective associations that form a foundation for the development of unconscious bias (Rudman, 2004). Given the limited personal contact that Whites have with Blacks, continued residential segregation in the United States, and the dismantling of race-based school desegregation plans, Whites' contact with President Obama is a particularly important force for promoting positive intergroup relations.

A critical element in the effectiveness of intergroup contact for reducing bias is not just the frequency of contact but also the nature of the contact. If, in addition to changing the affective aspect of bias (i.e., feelings), the goal is to alter group stereotypes (i.e., beliefs that are widely shared about the characteristics associated with a group), then the degree to which contact involves typical members of the outgroup is important (Brown & Hewstone, 2005). The more typical an outgroup member is of the outgroup as a whole, the more likely any counterstereotypical characteristics of that person would be generalized to the group, thus undermining traditional stereotypes.

The problem here is that Barack Obama, who is biracial, may not be regarded as a typical Black American. Physically, he does not have "prototypically" Black features or skin color. Although prior to his election, many Whites feared that he was too Black, almost a year after his election, White students who were presented with a series of photographs that systematically varied Obama's skin color from very light to very dark chose a picture of him that was lighter than his actual skin color (Hehman & Gaertner, 2009). Barack Obama's background (e.g., raised by a White family) and his "elite" educational experiences may also lead Whites to see him as atypical of Blacks generally. Whites' perceptions of Obama as more "White" and less typical of Blacks, which can contribute to their acceptance and support of him, may thus limit his impact for changing the ways Whites perceive Blacks overall.

OBAMA'S RHETORIC AND THE FRAMING OF RACE RELATIONS

Beyond the issues of whether the quality of contact is positive and outgroup members are typical of their group, which are indeed critical elements of the effectiveness of intergroup contact for reducing prejudice and stereotyping (Tausch & Hewstone, 2010), the ways race relations are framed is key in transforming racial attitudes. In his campaign speeches and his presidential rhetoric, Barack Obama has emphasized America's capacity to change generally and articulated a vision of intergroup relations in which members of different races share identity and purpose. Obama's impact on Whites' racial attitudes is therefore critically influenced not only by how he is perceived by Whites but also by how he actively shapes the perceptions of Whites toward members of other groups.

Change we can believe in. One of the most prominent messages of Barack Obama's presidential campaign involved the promise of change: change in American foreign policy, in America's image in the eyes of the international community, and in health care and the economy. To the extent that Obama increased confidence in the possibility for change generally, his message may have had positive effects on Whites' racial perceptions more specifically. People whose worldview embraces change (an incremental view) are more reluctant to use group stereotypes (Chiu, Hong & Dweck, 1997), and they provide more help to stigmatized outgroups than do those whose worldview is more static (Levy, Chiu, & Hong, 2006). Therefore, Obama's slogan, "Change we can believe in," may have altered people's worldviews about the possibility and desirability of change, facilitating a positive shift in Whites' attitudes toward and stereotypes of Blacks.

From Prevention to Promotion: The Role of Common Identity. Whereas previous efforts to achieve equality have focused on *preventing* bias, the presidency of Barack Obama can have a critical influence for *promoting* equality. The symbolism of having a Black man representing the United States—at the center rather than at the historic periphery—conveys a powerful message about the inclusion of Blacks in America. Beyond the impact of his mere presence in the media, President Obama has framed intergroup relations in America in a way that enhances the impact of contact.

Research on the Common Ingroup Identity Model (Gaertner & Dovidio, 2000, 2009) reveals that one important way that contact operates psychologically to reduce intergroup bias is by changing the way people think of group membership. Race represents an important, "default" form of social categorization in the United States. People spontaneously use perceptions of race to categorize others as ingroup or outgroup members. Categorization of a person as an ingroup member rather than as an outgroup member, in turn, has been demonstrated to produce more positive evaluations and stronger affective connections and to influence how information about people is processed. Upon mere categorization, people value ingroup members more than outgroup members. With respect to affective responses, ingroup categorization facilitates greater empathy in response to others' needs. In terms of information processing, people retain information in a more detailed fashion for ingroup members than for outgroup members, have better memory for information about ways ingroup members are similar and outgroup members are dissimilar to the self, and remember more positive information about ingroup than outgroup members (*see* Gaertner & Dovidio, 2000).

The effects on information processing further reinforce pro-ingroup biases in evaluations. For example, perhaps as a consequence of the development of these different schemas, people are more generous and forgiving in their explanations for the behaviors of ingroup relative to outgroup members. Cognitive and affective pro-ingroup biases can also promote more positive behaviors. Identifying others as ingroup members elicits greater helping and cooperation. Thus, changing the basis of categorization from race to an alternative dimension can alter who is a "we" and who is a "they," undermining a contributing force to contemporary forms of racism, such as aversive racism (*see* Gaertner & Dovidio, 2000, 2009).

Although Whites' preconceptions exert an important influence on how they categorize Blacks and Whites, perceptions of commonality can be substantially shaped by the actions of Blacks in these interactions. For example, we found that a brief statement by a Black person at the beginning of contact situation wherein he saw himself primarily as a member of the campus community produced a significantly more positive response to him and to Blacks generally by Whites, compared to situations in which he mentioned his race as central in his primary identity (Dovidio et al., 2010). The more Blacks emphasize their separate racial identity, the more bias they arouse in Whites (Kaiser & Pratt-Hyatt, 2009).

Barack Obama, both while campaigning and after the election, explicitly embraced the commonality. Crocker and Hughes (2009) noted his emphasis on "self-transcendent goals" that focus on what is needed for the larger whole and "sense of common purpose. . . . The promise of a democracy where we can find the strength and grace to bridge divides and unite in common effort" (Obama, August 28, 2008). For example, on the eve of election day, Obama stated, "We have never been just a collection of individuals or a collection of red states and blue states, we are and always will be the United States of America." (Obama, Nov. 4, 2008). In his Inauguration Address, he reinforced this message:

> We are a nation of Christians and Muslims, Jews and Hindus, and nonbelievers. We are shaped by every language and culture, drawn from every end of this Earth. . . . America, in the face of our common dangers, . . . with eyes fixed on the horizon and God's grace upon us, we carried forth that great gift of freedom and delivered it safely to future generations. (Obama, Jan. 20, 2009)

In speeches such as these, Obama's emphasis is on "we" and on the importance of cooperation and solidarity. Thus, although his presence itself represents a positive form of intergroup contact for most Whites, his words, which speak to a common ingroup identity among all Americans regardless of racial or ethnic group membership, directly invoke the psychological mechanism that underlies effective contact. Messages such as these can powerfully reorient the focus of intergroup relations from a focus on preventing discrimination to one of promoting equality and the common welfare of all Americans.

One of the potential dangers of focusing solely on common group identity, however, is that when a common identity dominates, differences and disparities between the separate groups—the majority and minority group—become less salient. Distinctions are ignored and disparities between the groups are obscured by a focus on commonality. Consequently, members of advantaged groups, who would be likely to support practices promoting social change if they perceived their advantaged position as illegitimate, may be less likely to endorse these initiatives when group-based disparities are masked by a focus on superordinate group identity and commonality.

Consistent with this reasoning, Saguy, Tausch, Dovidio, and Pratto (2009) found that a commonality-focused encounter produced more positive attitudes among members of a high-power group toward members of a low-power group than did a difference-focused interaction, but it did not translate into action to benefit the other group (*see also* Dixon, Durrheim, & Tredoux, 2005). In particular, the commonality-focused interaction led members of the high-power group to attend less to the other group's disadvantage and to feel that intergroup relations were already stable and satisfactory, which reduced their motivation to act to create actual equality in resources.

Creating a common group identity in a way that obscures subgroup memberships can also lead minority group members to relax their motivation for change through collective action (Saguy et al., 2009; Wright & Lubensky, 2009). Collective action among minority group members is facilitated by having a salient separate identity and perceptions of illegitimate differences in resources between the majority and minority group—both of which can be obscured by sole focus on common identity. Saguy, Tausch, Dovidio, Pratto, and Singh (2010) have shown, for example, that when intergroup relations are positive in ways that induce members of minority groups (including Arabs in Israel and Muslims in India) to pay less attention to resource disparities between groups, have more positive attitudes toward the majority group, and see the majority group as more benevolent, they are less motivated to engage in or support collective action to benefit their group.

Taken together, these findings converge to suggest that a focus on cross-group commonalities can ultimately work to reinforce existing social inequalities. Social change toward more justice and equality between groups is unlikely to come about when people are less aware of social injustice and of the need to change unfair social practices. When aiming for social change, the challenge is to find ways of raising awareness and mobilizing people toward action, while still maintaining a sense of commitment to a common goal and common identity. By delivering the message that people from different racial and ethnic groups can all benefit from a more just and equal society, Obama managed to meet this challenge by emphasizing both commonalities and separate group identities that operate in a system of inequality that requires change. This emphasis is reflected in his address delivered after the Reverend Wright controversy (Obama, March 18, 2008):

> Race is an issue that I believe this nation cannot afford to ignore right now . . . The fact is that the comments that have been made and the issues that have surfaced over the last few weeks reflect the complexities of race in this country that we've never really worked through - a part of our union that we have yet to perfect. And if we walk away now, if we simply retreat into our respective corners, we will never be able to come together and solve challenges like health care, or education, or the need to find good jobs for every American. . . . your dreams do not have to come at the expense of my dreams; investing in the health, welfare, and education of black and brown and white children will ultimately help all of America prosper.

This focus on commonalities of fates and goals simultaneously operating alongside separate group identities fits with the theoretical advancement of the Common Ingroup Identity Model to encompass a dual identity (Gaertner & Dovidio, 2000). The development of a common ingroup identity does not necessarily require each group to forsake its less inclusive group identity. Indeed, demands to forsake these group identities or to adopt a color-blind ideology would likely arouse strong reactance and exacerbate intergroup bias. In addition, and as mentioned earlier, forsaking these subgroup identities might also direct attention away from group-based disparities, leading to the reinforcement of existing inequalities.

According to the dual-identity perspective, it is possible to promote recognition of both common superordinate group and subgroup identities. Promoting the recognition of these "dual identities" among Whites can have a positive influence on their intergroup orientations. Common identity creates a sense of moral inclusion and sensitizes people to injustices within the group, and acknowledging racial differences increases recognition of unfair group-based disparities (Dovidio, Gaertner, & Saguy, 2009). For example, Smith and Tyler (1996) found that, regardless of whether they strongly identified with being White, those respondents with a strong inclusive American identity were more likely to base their support for affirmative action policies that would benefit Blacks and other minorities more on concerns about fairness than about their own self-interest. However, respondents who identified themselves primarily as being White rather than as being American focused more on the negative impact of affirmative action on them and their racial group (Whites). This pattern of findings suggests that a strong superordinate identity (such as being American) encourages support of policies that would benefit members of other racial subgroups without giving primary consideration to their own instrumental needs.

During his campaign and during his presidency, President Obama has explicitly recognized the many groups represented within the overarching common American identity but primarily while emphasizing their cooperative interdependence and the critical contributions of each for a truly united America. He describes America as "a country that has made it possible for one of its own members to run for the highest office in the land and build a coalition of white and black, Latino and Asian, rich and poor, young and old" (Obama, March 18, 2008). Even when he speaks of a past that was divided by race, he directs attention to a primary vision of unity:

> Contrary to the claims of some of my critics, black and white, I have never been so naïve to believe that we can get beyond our racial divisions in a single election cycle or with a single candidacy. . . . But I have asserted a firm conviction . . . that working together we can move beyond some of our racial wounds, and that in fact we have no choice if we are to continue on the path to a more perfect union. (Obama, March 18, 2008)

Thus, maintaining the salience of different racial and ethnic groups within a strong superordinate American identity is critical for mobilizing Whites to recognize the need to work harder to achieve racial and ethnic equality in the United States (*see also* Eibach & Purdie-Vaughns, 2009).

CONCLUSION

The United States, in its founding documents, promised "equality and justice for all." Nevertheless, it has historically been a nation characterized by racial *in*equality. Myrdal (1944), for example, identified the paradox between historical egalitarian values and racist traditions in the United States, describing the "American dilemma." According to Myrdal, the dilemma is that "on the one hand . . . the American thinks, talks, and acts under the influence of high national and Christian precepts and, on the other hand . . . group prejudice against particular persons or types of people . . . dominate his outlook (p. xliii). Today, America remains divided economically, residentially, and socially by race.

The election of Barack Obama as President of the United States, however, represents an unprecedented opportunity to change race relations in America psychologically as well as politically. Although many have argued that Obama's election itself is evidence that racism is "a thing of the past" and that America is currently a "post-racial" society, race still matters. Whether acknowledged or not and regardless of whether other common identities are prominent in consciousness, racial categories are automatically activated to some degree. White Americans cannot be truly color-blind.

Subtle forms of prejudice, such as aversive racism, will likely influence Whites' perceptions of President Obama and his policies. Knight, Hebl, Foster, and Mannix (2003) found that even innocuous mistakes of Black leaders are commonly used by Whites to justify negative evaluations of them. Unconscious negative racial attitudes can operate indirectly by narrowing the notions used to define competence, patriotism, or other important qualities of a Black political leader (Parker, Sawyer, & Towler, 2009). A highly admired Black man, like Barack Obama, thus walks a psychological tightrope in the eyes of White Americans, with much less latitude for error than for a White person. Former President Jimmy Carter recently attracted considerable attention and stimulated controversy in the public discourse with his comments about the role of race in reactions to President Obama. Carter stated,

> I think an overwhelming portion of the intensely demonstrated animosity toward President Barack Obama is based on the fact that he is a Black man, that he's African American . . . that racism inclination still exists. And I think it has bubbled up to the surface because of the belief among many White people, not just in the South but around the country, that African Americans are not qualified to lead this great country. (Franke-Ruta, 2009)

Carter's interpretation is consistent with aversive racism.

Nevertheless, even at a time of continued segregation and erosion of laws and policies designed to promote integration, the election of Barack Obama provides significant new opportunities for "virtual" interracial contact for Whites. Regular exposure to Obama through the media in a distinctively counterstereotypical role will change the way that millions of White Americans will think about race. Although the impact for some will be limited by perceptions of Obama as an exceptional case, Contact Theory suggests that the quantity and quality of intergroup contact afforded by Obama's presidency can have significant impact for reducing Whites' prejudice. This repeated exposure can also combat implicit prejudice, which forms the foundation for aversive racism.

The potential of President Obama for reducing Whites' racial prejudice resides not simply in how he is viewed by Whites but also in how he shapes

Whites' views of race relations through his rhetoric. He articulates an overall vision of commonality and unity, while acknowledging racial and ethnic difference, disparity, and injustice. Obama's speeches urge Americans of all races and ethnicities to move beyond the intergroup tensions and narrow interests that have dominated race relations in the past to recognize mutual interdependence and common goals to take responsibility for *promoting* the welfare of all.

In conclusion, the presidency of Barack Obama brings America to a critical juncture—one that can take White Americans from the limitations of being motivated primarily by a fear of doing wrong to a genuine motivation to promote a truly fair and just multicultural society. Daily exposure to him can change the way Whites feel about Blacks generally, as well as undermine the uncertainty, anxiety, and fear that inhibit more future interracial contact and interfere with constructive intergroup relations (Shelton & Richeson, 2005). Racism cannot be eliminated by ignoring race; the legacy of past discrimination and the existence of contemporary subtle discrimination would perpetuate inequity into the future. Thus, the election of Barack Obama is a fortuitous event for race relations in America. It brings race to the forefront of America's consciousness in a way that provides Whites unprecedented opportunities for the type of inter-racial contact that can reduce their prejudice and leads members of all groups to recognize their interdependence, accept responsibility for promoting equality, and embrace fundamental changes in intergroup relations that will benefit America collectively.

NOTE

Preparation of this chapter was supported by NSF Grant # BCS-0613218 awarded to the first two authors and Spencer Grant #200900193 awarded to the first author.

REFERENCES

Allport, G. W. (1954). *The nature of prejudice.* New York: Addison-Wesley.

Blank, R. M. (2001). An overview of trends in social and economic well-being, by race. In N. J. Smelser, W. J. Wilson, & F. Mitchell, F. (Eds.), *Racial trends and their consequences* (Vol. 1, pp. 21–39). Washington, D.C.: National Academy Press.

Bobo, L. (2001). Racial attitudes and relations at the close of the twentieth century. In N. J. Smelser, W. J. Wilson, & F. Mitchell, F. (Eds.), *Racial trends and their consequences* (Vol. 1, pp. 264–301). Washington, D.C.: National Academy Press.

Brewer, M. B., & Miller, N. (1984). Beyond the contact hypothesis: Theoretical perspectives on desegregation. In N. Miller & M. B. Brewer (Eds.), *Groups in contact: The psychology of desegregation* (pp. 281–302). Orlando, FL: Academic Press.

Brown, R., & Hewstone, M. (2005). An integrative theory of intergroup contact. In M. P. Zanna (Ed.), *Advances in experimental social psychology* (vol. 37, pp. 255–343). San Diego, CA: Academic Press.

Cameron, L., Rutland, A., Brown, R., & Douch, R. (2006). Changing children's intergroup attitudes toward refugees: Testing different models of extended contact. *Child Development, 77*, 1208–1219.

Chiu, C., Hong, Y., & Dweck, C. S. (1997). Lay dispositionism and implicit theories of personality. *Journal of Personality and Social Psychology, 73*, 19–30.

Crisp, R. J., & Turner, R. N. (2009). Can imagined interactions produce positive perceptions? Reducing prejudice through simulated social contact. *American Psychologist, 64*, 231–240.

Crocker, J., & Hughes, S. B. (2009). Ecosystem perspective and Barack Obama's campaign for the presidency. *Du Bois Review, 6*, 125–136.

Dasgupta, N., & Greenwald, A. G. (2001). On the malleability of automatic attitudes: Combating automatic prejudice with images of admired and disliked individuals. *Journal of Personality and Social Psychology, 81*, 800–814.

DeNavas-Walt, C., Proctor, B. D., & Smith, J. C. (2008). *Income, poverty, and health insurance coverage in the United States, 2007.* Washington, DC: U.S. Government Printing Office. Retrieved on July 22, 2010, from http://www.census.gov/prod/2008pubs/p60-235.pdf.

Dixon, J. A., Durrheim, K. & Tredoux, C. (2005). Beyond the optimal strategy: A "reality check" for the contact hypothesis. *American Psychologist, 60*, 697–711.

Dovidio, J. F., & Gaertner, S. L. (2004). Aversive racism. In M. P. Zanna (Ed.), *Advances in experimental social psychology* (vol. 36, pp. 1–51). San Diego, CA: Academic Press.

Dovidio, J. F., Johnson, J. D., Gaertner, S. L., Pearson, A. R., Saguy, T., & Ashburn-Nardo, L. (2010). Empathy and intergroup relations. In M. Mikulincer & P. Shaver (Eds.), *Prosocial motives, emotion, and behavior: The better angels of our nature* (pp. 393–408). Washington, D.C.: APA Press.

Dovidio, J. F., Gaertner, S. L., & Kawakami, K. (2003). The Contact Hypothesis: The past, present, and the future. *Group Processes and Intergroup Relations, 6*, 5–21.

Dovidio, J. F., Gaertner, S. L., & Saguy, T. (2009). Commonality and the complexity of "we": Social attitudes and social change. *Personality and Social Psychology Review, 13*, 3–20.

Eibach, R. P., & Purdie-Vaughns, V. (2009). Change we can believe in? Barack Obama's framing strategies for bridging racial divisions. *Du Bois Review, 6*, 137–151.

Franke-Ruta, G. (2009, September 16). Carter cites "racism inclination" in animosity toward Obama. *Washington Post*, Retrieved September 17, 2009, from http://voices.washingtonpost.com/44/2009/09/15/carter_cites_racism_inclinatio.html

Gaertner, S. L., & Dovidio, J. F. (1986). The aversive form of racism. In J. F. Dovidio & S. L. Gaertner (Eds.), *Prejudice, discrimination, and racism* (pp. 61–89). Orlando, FL: Academic Press.

Gaertner, S. L., & Dovidio, J. F. (2000). *Reducing intergroup bias: The Common Ingroup Identity Model.* Philadelphia, PA: The Psychology Press.

Gaertner, S. L., & Dovidio, J. F. (2009). A Common Ingroup Identity: A categorization-based approach for reducing intergroup bias. In. T. Nelson (Ed.), *Handbook of prejudice.* (pp. 489–506). Philadelphia, PA: Taylor & Francis.

Gaertner, S. L., Dovidio, J. F., Banker, B. et al. (1997). Does racism necessarily mean anti-Blackness? Aversive racism and pro-Whiteness. In M. Fine, L. Powell, L. Weis, & M. Wong (Eds.), *Off white* (pp. 167–178). London: Routledge.

General Social Survey (2009). Retrieved September 1, 2009, from http://www.norc.org/GSS+Website/

Gratz and Hamacher v. Bollinger (2003). 123 U.S. 2411.

Grutter v. Bollinger (2003). Certiorari to the United States Court of Appeals for the Sixth Circuit, No. 02—241. Argued April 1, 2003—Decided June 23, 2003.

Hehman, E. & Gaertner, S. L. (2009). *Tracking support for President Obama's national policies and racial attitudes of Whites.* Unpublished data. Department of Psychology, University of Delaware, Newark.

Hehman, E., Gaertner, S. L. & Dovidio, J. F. (2009). *Racial attitudes before and after the election of President Obama.* Unpublished data. Department of Psychology, University of Delaware, Newark.

Higgins, E. T. (1999). Promotion and prevention as motivational duality: Implications for evaluative processes. In S. Chaiken & Y. Trope (Eds.), *Dual-process theories in social psychology* (pp. 503–525). New York: Guilford Press.

Kaiser, C., R., & Pratt-Hyatt, J. S. (2009). Distributing prejudice unequally: Do Whites direct their prejudice toward strongly identified minorities? *Journal of Personality and Social Psychology, 96,* 432–445.

Knight, J. L., Hebl, M. R., Foster, J. B., & Mannix, L. M. (2003). Out of role? Out of luck: The influence of race and leadership status on performance appraisals. *The Journal of Leadership and Organizational Studies, 9,* 85–94.

Levy, S. R., Chiu, C., & Hong, Y. (2006). Lay theories and intergroup relations. *Group Processes & Intergroup Relations, 9,* 5–24.

Massey, D. S. (2001). Residential segregation and neighborhood conditions in U. S. metropolitan areas. In N. J. Smelser, W. J. Wilson, & F. Mitchell, F. (Eds.), *Racial trends and their consequences* (Vol. 1, pp. 391–434). Washington, D.C.: National Academy Press.

Miller, N. (2002). Personalization and the promise of contact theory. *Journal of Social Issues, 58,* 387–410.

Mutz, D. C., & Goldman, S. K. (2010). Effects of mass media on stereotyping and prejudice. In J. F. Dovidio, M. Hewstone, P. Glick, & V. M. Esses (Eds.), *Handbook of prejudice, stereotyping, and discrimination* (pp. 241–257). Thousand Oaks, CA: Sage.

Myrdal, G. (1944). *An American dilemma: The Negro problem and modern democracy.* New York: Harper.

Nosek, B. A., Banaji, M. R, & Greenwald, A. G. (2002). Harvesting implicit group attitudes and beliefs from a demonstration website. *Group Dynamics: Theory, Research, and Practice, 6,* 101–115.

Obama, B. (2008, March 18). Retrieved on November 21, 2009, from http://www.msnbc.msn.com/id/23690567/page/2/

Obama, B. (2008, August 28). Retrieved on November 21, 2009, from http://www.notable-quotes.com/o/obama_barack_vi.html

Obama, B. (2008, Nov. 4). Retrieved November 21, 2009, from http://www.cnn.com/2008/POLITICS/11/04/obama.transcript/

Obama, B. (2009, Jan. 20). Retrieved on November 21, 2009 from http://www.whitehouse.gov/blog/inaugural-address/

Paolini, S., Hewstone, M., Cairns, E., & Voci, A. (2004). Effects of direct and indirect cross-group friendships on judgments of Catholics and Protestants in Northern Ireland: The mediating role of an anxiety-reduction mechanism. *Personality and Social Psychology Bulletin, 30,* 770–786.

Parents Involved in Community Schools v. Seattle School District No. 1 (2007). Certiorari to the United States Court of Appeals for the Ninth Circuit, No. 05—98. Argued December 4, 2006—Decided June 28, 2007.

Pearson, A. R., Dovidio, J. F., & Gaertner, S. L. (2009). The nature of contemporary prejudice: Insights from aversive racism. *Social and Personality Psychology Compass, 3,* 10-.1111/1-25.

Parker, C. S., Sawyer, M. Q., & Towler, C. (2009). A Black man in the house? The role of racism and patriotism in the 2008 presidential election. *Du Bois Review, 6,* 193–217.

Pettigrew, T. F., & Tropp, L. R. (2006). A meta-analytic test of intergroup contact theory. *Journal of Personality and Social Psychology, 90,* 751–783.

Pettigrew, T. F., & Tropp, L. R. (2008). How does intergroup contact reduce prejudice? Meta-analytic tests of three mediators. *European Journal of Social Psychology, 38,* 922–934.

Pettigrew, T. F. (1998). Intergroup Contact Theory. *Annual Review of Psychology, 49,* 65–85.

Plant, E. A., Devine, P. G., Cox, W. T. L., Columb, C., Miller, S. L., Goplen, J., Peruche, B. M. (2009). The Obama effect: Decreasing implicit prejudice and stereotyping. *Journal of Experimental Social Psychology, 45,* 961–964.

Pollster.com, (2009). Retrieved November 21, 2009, from http://www.pollster.com/

Ricci v. DeStephano (2009). Certiorari to the United States Court of Appeals for the Second Circuit, No. 0—1428. Argued April 22, 2009—Decided June 29, 2009.

Roberts, J. (2004, Aug. 16). Income gap of poor, rich, widens. Retrieved on November 21, 2009 from http://www.cbsnews.com/stories/2004/08/13/national/main635936.shtml.

Rudman, L. A. (2004). Sources of implicit attitudes. *Current Directions in Psychological Science, 13*, 79–82.

Saguy, T., Tausch, N., Dovidio, J. F., & Pratto, F. (2009). The irony of harmony: Intergroup contact can produce false expectations for equality. *Psychological Science, 29*, 114–121.

Saguy, T., Tausch, N., Dovidio, J. F., Pratto, F, & Singh, P. (2010). Tension and harmony in intergroup relations. In M. Mikulincer & P.R., Shaver (Eds.). *Understanding and reducing aggression, violence, and their consequences.* Washington, D.C.: American Psychological Association. (in press)

Shelton, J. N., & Richeson, J. A. (2005). Intergroup contact and pluralistic ignorance. *Journal of Personality and Social Psychology, 88*, 91–107.

Smith, H. J., & Tyler, T. R. (1996). Justice and power: When will justice concerns encourage the advantaged to support policies which redistribute economic resources and the disadvantaged to willingly obey the law? *European Journal of Social Psychology, 26*, 171–200.

Tausch, N., & Hewstone, M. (2010). Intergroup contact. In J. F. Dovidio, M. Hewstone, P. Glick, & V. M. Esses (2010). *Handbook of prejudice, stereotyping, and discrimination* (pp. 544–560). Thousand Oaks, CA: Sage.

Turner, R. N., Crisp, R. J., & Lambert, E. (2007). Imagining intergroup contact can improve intergroup attitudes. *Group Processes and Intergroup Relations, 10*, 427–441.

Turner, R. N., Hewstone, M., Voci, A., & Vonofakou, C. (2008). A test of the extended intergroup contact hypothesis: The mediating role of perceived ingroup and outgroup norms, intergroup anxiety and inclusion of the outgroup in the self. *Journal of Personality and Social Psychology, 95*, 843–860.

Wright, S. C., & Lubensky, M. E. (2009). The struggle for social equality: Collective action versus prejudice reduction. In S. Demoulin, J-P Leyens, & J. F. Dovidio (Eds.), *Intergroup misunderstandings: Impact of divergent social realities* (pp. 291–310). New York: Psychology Press.

Wright, S. C., Aron, A., McLaughlin-Volpe, T., & Ropp, S. A. (1997). The extended contact effect: Knowledge of cross-group friendships and prejudice. *Journal of Personality and Social Psychology, 73*, 73–90.

Yablon, Y. B. & Katz, Y. J (2001). Internet-based group relations: A high school peace education project in Israel. *Education Media International, 38*, 175–182.

Black Behavior and Moral Dissonance: Missing Mechanisms in Theorizing the Obama Effect

Richard O. Lempert

By coincidence, my last reading before I sat down to write this was a *Washington Post* feature on how Obama's campaign, election, and "Kick Off the School Year" speech has inspired black youth in and around Washington, D.C. One young man who dropped out of school in the sixth grade thanks Obama for his newfound dedication to securing a GED. A seemingly nerdy 11-year-old was inspired by Obama to set his sights on his school class presidency. He ran and won. Bright high school students who, before they heard Obama talk, were content to get by on native ability report reworking their essays before turning them in and in other ways performing to higher standards.

Students of prejudice and intergroup relations have typically been far more concerned with understanding and changing the behavior and attitudes of dominant, discriminating majorities than they have with understanding and changing the attitudes and behavior of discriminated-against minorities. But the two are interrelated. If the Obama Presidency works to reduce prejudice and improve Black–White relationships, then it is likely that some of this effect will be attributable to changing Black attitudes and behavior rather than to the kinds of direct effects on Whites, or on White–Black cooperation, that the chapter has as its focus. Indeed, if Black–White relationships improve markedly in the coming half decade, then it may be hard to prove empirically the importance of the election. Obama was elected in the midst of trends that by themselves may be reducing White racial hostility. The generations frightened by the race riots of the 1960s are aging or dying out, crime rates have dropped substantially for almost all major crimes, teenage pregnancies (including black teenage pregnancies) have fallen dramatically, and cross-racial marriage rates have greatly risen. Moreover, 40 years of affirmative action has helped create a vastly expanded black middle class and means that many of today's white elites and opinion leaders have gone to school with Blacks and/or interacted with talented Blacks on their jobs.

In thinking about the implications of Obama's election and of the school and workplace integration attributable to affirmative action, I am reminded of a concept I introduced long ago in a brief article that appeared in an obscure, largely unavailable and short-lived journal (Lempert, 1974): the concept I called *moral dissonance*. I used it to explain how crimes become decriminalized, citing the demise of the Salem witch hunts after the governor's wife was accused and reductions in the opprobrium and penalties that attached to marijuana use after its use spread beyond Blacks and jazz musicians to otherwise mainstream white college students. Reflecting on cognitive dissonance theory, I argued that there was a similar drive to consistency across moral evaluations. If, for example, a white college student (especially one's own) is regarded as morally upright and marijuana use is regarded as morally bad, one or the other evaluation is likely to change. The child may be disowned if he doesn't stop smoking, or the notion that smoking marijuana is evil may give way to the idea that it is benign or that it is just a stage kids pass through.

Moral dissonance may be a mechanism that explains one of the best established findings recounted in this chapter—namely, that in many settings, contact reduces prejudice and that its effects are greatest when people of different races depend on each other to reach a common goal. Given what we now know about the powerful effects of emotion on cognition, I would argue that it is cognitively easy for Whites, without realizing it, to regard black skin and stereotypically black facial features as *morally* suspect. If a White unconsciously associates Blacks with immorality (crime, riots, illegitimacy), then working with a black companion toward a common goal or perceiving a black candidate's policies as more desirable than the white candidate's will create the drive state of moral dissonance. One way to resolve this is to relax or even drop the unconscious link between black skin and immorality. If the Obama presidency has a long-term prejudice-reducing effect, I think this is a (not "the") likely reason why.

Moral dissonance may, however, be reduced in another way. Consistency can be achieved not just by abandoning prejudiced attitudes. It can also be achieved by changing moral evaluations of an otherwise seemingly good person. This, I suggest, is why so many attacks against Obama have been characterized by extreme vitriol and why attacks that have involved obvious untruths (e.g., the birther conspiracy) have had such staying power despite overwhelming evidence to the contrary. By dominating cognition, hidden prejudice leads some Americans honestly to perceive Obama as evil.

Although the Obama Presidency may seem like it cannot help but reduce prejudice and improve race relations, this happy outcome is not guaranteed. The fact of a black president does not tell us how moral dissonance will be resolved. Dissonance resolution will turn in some measure on Obama's behavior as president. But it will also turn on how attempts to discredit Obama resonate with most people (the right, finding itself unable to deny Obama's persuasive rhetoric, is now trying to turn it against him by labeling him an "empty shirt"), which is, in turn, likely to depend on how successful Obama's presidency appears. As president, Obama can control his speech and behavior, but he cannot control how others speak of him. Nor, despite a strong tendency to credit or blame whoever is president for the nation's strengths or woes, can a president quickly turn economic disaster on its head or prevent all terrorist attacks from succeeding. Thus, if my suggestions are correct, the long-term implications of the Obama presidency for race relations in this United States may in some measure be determined by forces beyond any person's control.

New Bottle, Same Old Wine: The GOP and Race in the Age of Obama

Russell J. Webster, Donald A. Saucier, and Gregory S. Parks

Since the rise of Barack Obama on the national, political landscape, his presence and prominence has caused the Republican Party and far right great consternation. Their concern has been about Obama's overwhelming popularity with certain demographic groups, especially minorities. And this concern may have been most evident after the long, 2008 primary season—when Obama won the nomination of the Democratic Party over Hillary Clinton. It was during that period when many female Democrats were outraged at what they perceived to be sexism in the media's coverage of then Senator Clinton and their party's nomination process (Parks & Roberson, in press; Zernike, 2008). Accordingly, Republican presidential nominee, Senator John McCain, "rolled the dice" and picked then Alaskan Governor Sarah Palin as his running mate. His gamble was that his pick of a relatively unknown woman as his running mate would woo disaffected women who had supported Clinton (Dunham, 2008). Critics of McCain's tactic highlighted the irony of his selection, given the Republican's history of opposition to measures such as the Equal Rights Amendment and legislation requiring equal pay for women. In essence, they felt that McCain was pandering to female voters (Martin & Ratcliffe, 2008; Mauriello, 2008).

Despite the Republican's concerns about female voters during the 2008 election, their concerns about minority voters were and have been just as palpable. Long branded "the party of old, White men," the GOP earned the reputation of racial exclusiveness and ignoring minority issues (Fauntroy, 2007; Mendelberg, 2001; Topping, 2008). Accordingly, their concerns about garnering minority voters are most evident in the rise of Louisiana Governor Bobby Jindal and Republican National Committee chairman Michael Steele. Jindal has been heralded as the Republican's "Obama" in that Jindal is a racial minority, young, handsome, and bright, as well as coming from an attractive family and humble beginnings. Jindal is also considered a strong GOP contender for the presidency in 2012 (Dewan, 2009). In fact, during President

Obama's first speech to a joint session of Congress, Jindal was selected to provide the GOP's counter-response (Issenberg, 2009).

Michael Steele, on the other hand, was elected the RNC's first Black chairman, and from the very start of his chairmanship, he vowed to bring all racial and ethnic groups, along with the hip-hop generation, into the GOP's fold. He also painted himself as Obama's fiercest critic, employing a rapper's "How Ya like me now?"[1] (Williams, 2009). Steele's strategy consisted of informing local GOP chairmen that if they did not want to build coalitions within minority communities, then those chairmen had to step aside for chairmen who would (Simon, 2009). But Steele's attempt to remake the GOP went beyond expectations about what GOP leadership, at every level, must do. His makeover strategy also consisted of projecting his own image and rhetoric of diversity. For example, he offered some "slum love"[2] to Bobby Jindal and promised to extend the GOP's reach to "urban-suburban hip-hop settings" as part of his "off the hook" party-building efforts (Milbank, 2009). Even President Obama recognized Steele's overt, and sometimes over-the-top and stereotypic, appeal to Black voters. For example, at the 2009 Correspondents' Dinner, Obama said, "Michael Steele is in the house tonight. Or as he would say, 'in the heezy.' Wassup?" (Schwab & Bedard, 2009).

In this chapter, we evaluate the degree to which the attempts by the GOP to recast itself among racial minorities—largely by catapulting Republican politicians to the heights of the national scene—are likely to work in the absence of fundamental changes in racial imagery, rhetoric, and attitudes. Generally, we argue that the GOP's racial politics cannot and should not be fully interpreted when unmoored from its historical and contemporary context. Further, we posit that modern advances in measuring racial attitudes, coupled with specific imagery and rhetoric both during and after the 2008 presidential election, highlight why the GOP's efforts to racially recast itself are and will likely be futile.

Since the election of Barack Obama to the United States Presidency in November of 2008, there have been many comments made and imagery used by members of the political right that expressed negativity toward both President Obama himself and minority groups in general. Some of these comments and imagery have been overtly racist, whereas some have been more ambiguous. The literature investigating the relationships between political orientation and racial bias, both in recent history and in the context of contemporary theories of racial prejudice, suggests that these comments and imagery may be at least partially attributable to explicit and implicit prejudice that (predominantly White) conservatives harbor toward minority groups. We will examine these comments and imagery, as well as the often passive reactions to them by other conservatives, within the framework of this research on racial bias. Further, we will examine the efforts made by the Republican Party to demonstrate their egalitarian values, such as by promoting women and minorities to high positions within the Party, against their efforts to discount and devalue minorities of the Democratic Party along arguably racial lines.

Race and the GOP: A Perspective from Recent History

Once, a long time ago, Blacks were deeply invested in and appreciative of the Republican Party. Today, it is difficult to imagine that this was once so. Some have even argued that "The GOP's lack of Black support should be an embarrassment to a party, that, during Reconstruction, enjoyed more African American support than Democrats do now" (Fauntroy, 2007, p. 1; *see also* Mendelberg, 2001; Topping, 2008). What happened to the Republican Party being the Party of Lincoln? The history of Blacks defecting from the Republican Party to the Democratic Party was protracted and complex (Topping, 2008).

In 1854, a coalition of anti-slavery party members (e.g., American, Free Soil) and Northern Democrats founded the Republican Party. This new party's primary mission was to restrict the expansion of slavery. Amazingly, their success was immediate in that only 6 years later, Abraham Lincoln was elected president. Soon, the Republican Party overtook the Whig Party and has since become one of the major two voting parties in the United States (Fauntroy, 2007). However, after a post-Reconstruction resurgence among Democrats, the Republican Party sought to be a truly National Party by wooing moderate Democrats in the South. In trying to woo these Democrats, the Republican Party's pro-Black stances began to erode, laying the foundation for Blacks' transition to the Democratic Party (Fauntroy, 2007).

Racial equality slowly became a predominant social norm as Blacks made advances in social, economic, and political circles in the early twentieth century, especially with the founding of the National Association for the Advancement of Colored People (NAACP) in the 1930s. From the 1930s to the 1950s, Blacks—in particular, the NAACP—and Democrats progressively forged a deep alliance. In this time, Republican President Herbert Hoover (elected in 1929) grew increasingly disinterested in racial issues during the Great Depression (Topping, 2008). After Hoover, Democratic President Franklin Roosevelt (elected 1933) made minor strides in promoting racial equality but was generally popular among Blacks because of his economic policies (i.e., the New Deal; Fauntroy, 2007). More importantly, during Hoover's and Roosevelt's terms, millions of Blacks migrated from the South to Northern urban centers (e.g., New York, Philadelphia, Chicago), and these urban centers increasingly became a key demographic among Democrats (Fauntroy, 2007; Topping, 2008). Hoover was also unsuccessful at managing the chaos of replacing millions of lost Black workers; Whites had to start doing

"Negro jobs," which perpetuated negativity toward Blacks among White Southerners (Fauntroy, 2007, p. 45).

Harry Truman (elected in 1945)—also a Democrat—became the most outspoken champion of racial equality in the twentieth century (until the election of John F. Kennedy in 1961; Mendelberg, 2001; Topping, 2008). Indeed, White social conservatives (termed "Dixiecrats") walked out of the 1948 Democratic Convention to protest Truman's efforts to promote racial equality. Truman won re-election (barely), which further validated Democrats' pro-Black tendencies. Strikingly, in 1948, the majority of Blacks for the first time self-identified as Democrats. *The* turning point came in 1964 with the election of Lyndon Johnson, another strong supporter of pro-Black policies, in which Blacks overwhelmingly voted Democratic (94%; Fauntroy, 1997). Concurrently, Dixiecrats and other White social conservatives (mainly from the South) increasingly flooded the Republican Party ranks and continued to promote overtly racist arguments supporting racial inequality through the 1970s (Mendelberg, 2001; Philpot, 2007).

Consequently, since the middle of the twentieth century, the GOP has generally been perceived as insensitive toward and uninterested in advancing issues that benefit racial minorities. Most evident, Republicans have not garnered more than 18% of the Black vote since Lyndon Johnson's election. Moreover, some evidence has shown a noticeable influx of White Democrats into the Republican party in the North, partly because of lingering resentment toward Blacks for receiving "special privileges" (e.g., perceptions that Affirmative Action placed unqualified Blacks in White jobs; Greenberg, 1987). Recently, however, Republicans have attempted to change their image on race issues.

Tasha Philpot, in her recent book, *Race, Republicans, and the Return of the Party of Lincoln* (2007), discusses the attempts that the Republican Party has made to improve people's perceptions of the Party's views on race in the 2000, 2002, and 2004 election cycles. To improve these perceptions successfully, Philpot has argued the GOP must do two things. First, they must portray a consistent change in their views on race. Second, they must make others see these changed views as a relevant factor in evaluating the GOP. In attempting to fulfill these objectives, the GOP sought to demonstrate their more egalitarian views on race by incorporating a more diverse body of people into the Party. Further, the GOP made concerted efforts to verbalize a more "compassionate conservatism." Unfortunately, these GOP efforts appeared to come without any meaningful proposed or actual policy changes that would serve to advantage minority groups. Philpot examined whether superficial elements to demonstrate more egalitarian views on race without more substantial efforts at policy advancement were enough to change perceptions of the Republican Party and their views on race.

In the 2000 election cycle, the GOP's efforts resulted in some improvement in how people perceived the GOP's views on race, particularly by Whites who viewed the Republican Party's convention coverage without seeing subsequent critical media coverage. Blacks' perceptions of the GOP's views on race were unchanged. Two key hurdles were faced by the GOP. First, as discussed, the GOP has a long and well-documented history of being unsupportive of, and in many cases actively resistant to, advancing race issues. Second, critical media coverage that highlighted inconsistencies in the GOP's treatment of race issues (e.g., George W. Bush addressed the NAACP, but Trent Lott stated the United States would be better off if Strom Thurmond had been elected in 1948) hindered GOP efforts to promote a more race sensitive image. In the 2002 and 2004 election cycles, the GOP had more success in improving people's perceptions of the Party's views on race. By then, the inconsistencies in the GOP's messages regarding their views on race were reduced, and the greater consistency in their rhetoric of more racial positivity yielded some dividends. Blacks' attitudes toward the Republican position on race issues improved slightly. Further, and ultimately more importantly, slightly more Black voters voted Republican. But again, these mildly successful efforts to improve perceptions of the GOP's views on race came without changes in actual or proposed policy changes (Philpot, 2007).

The incorporation of a more diverse populace into the GOP as a strategy to demonstrate their forward thinking on race and gender issues continued in the 2008 election cycle. The GOP's recent advancement of individuals like Michael Steele, Bobby Jindal, and Sarah Palin may be seen as attempts to counter, or mirror, the Democratic Party's demonstration of inclusiveness in the high levels of their Party's ranks. Ultimately, when the GOP advances individuals to represent specific demographic group like Blacks or women without such individuals being perceived as being highly qualified for the positions they are given, the transparency of the attempt to "look better" without acting better will be unlikely to change perceptions of the GOP.

Further hindering the GOP's efforts to improve perceptions of their views on race have been the historical use of implicit messages that denigrate Blacks and other racial minority groups. In her book *The Race Card: Campaign Strategy, Implicit Messages, and the Norm of Equality*, Tali Mendelberg (2001) described the use and effects of several implicit racial messages in Republican political campaigns from the the Civil War to the present, highlighting instances from the 1964, 1988, and 2000 presidential campaigns. These examples included Republicans' use of accounts of crimes committed by Blacks as evidence of their Democratic opponents being soft on crime, use of ads deriding welfare showing only Blacks as welfare recipients, and arguments for racially insensitive measures using seemingly nonracial rationalizations, such as support for the flying of Confederate flags to memorialize Southern heritage and for building walls on the Mexican–American border to decrease crime and welfare dependency. Mendelberg discussed how Democrats accused Republicans of using the messages as implicit racial statements, and how these accusations may have hurt the GOP consequently in terms of how they were viewed on race issues. Nonetheless, Mendelberg also discussed how some White voters may then downplay how much their support of the GOP and Republican candidates is related to views on racial issues, rather than lessen their support of the GOP. In any case, the past (and present) inclusion of racially laden messages by the GOP in political campaigns has earned the perception that Republicans are not progressive in their racial policies. And, as stated earlier, without proposing, supporting, or implementing more progressive policies for racial minorities, these perceptions are likely to be slow in changing.

RACE AND THE GOP: AN EMPIRICAL PERSPECTIVE

Political ideology has been traditionally characterized as a left–right distinction. Researchers have argued and found empirical support for the notion that the differences between those on the left and right wings of the political spectrum differ in several meaningful psychological ways. Chief among these are two aspects: the support for (vs. resistance to) social change and the rejection (vs. acceptance) of inequality. Simply put, liberals tend to support social change and reject inequality, whereas conservatives tend to resist social change and accept inequality (Jost, Nosek, & Gosling, 2008). Accordingly, research has shown that as a result of these fundamental differences in ideology, conservatives are more likely than liberals to prefer stability over flexibility and tradition over progress (Jost et al., 2008).

It may also be the conservatives and liberals are simply different in who they are in terms of their underlying dispositions. Evidence shows that conservatives show greater support than liberals toward things representing "conventionalism, traditionalism, and adherence to social norms" and show less support than liberals toward things representing "openness, tolerance, and sensation-seeking" (Jost et al., 2008). This may result from personality dispositions that conservatives are more orderly, conventional, and better organized than are liberals, who are more curious, creative, and open-minded (Carney, Jost, Gosling, & Potter, 2008). Thus, conservatives may just be oriented in a manner that makes the advancement of minority groups, as well as the legislative and social change that would accompany that progress, inconsistent with their dispositional tendencies and preferences.

Furthering this conjecture, it may be the case that political ideology in general, and conservatism in particular, is a motivated belief system that stresses and justifies resistance to change and justification of inequality (Jost, Glaser, Kruglanski, & Sulloway, 2003). These motives may then mediate the connections between political conservatism and perceptions of threat and uncertainty (Jost, Napier, Thorisdottir, Gosling, Palfai, & Ostafin, 2007). In essence, conservatives may more strongly advocate an adherence to the status quo by justifying the existing social order and hierarchy, via a phenomenon known as system justification (Jost, Banaji, & Nosek, 2004). According to this theory, individuals may be motivated to see the existing social hierarchy in way that makes it legitimate, such that the social ordering of demographic groups (e.g., Whites occupying a higher social status than racial minority groups) will be maintained (*see also* social dominance orientation; e.g., Pratto, Sidanius, Stallworth, & Malle, 1994). Indeed, researchers have shown that system justification is a perspective more strongly held by conservatives than liberals and is associated with more negative attitudes toward racial minority groups (Jost et al., 2004). Thus, conservatives may be motivated to advocate belief systems that preserve the existing social order and resist improving the situations for racial minority groups socially and legislatively.

Our own recent data demonstrate the connection of political orientation and racial attitudes. We have found that not only are White conservatives more likely to show affective prejudice toward socio-economically competitive outgroups (e.g., Blacks) than are liberals, but these differences appear to be attributable to conservatives' higher levels of right-wing authoritarianism and lower levels of internal motivation to control prejudice (Webster, Burns, Pickering, & Saucier, 2009). In another study, we found that White conservatives harbored more prejudice toward "progressive" groups (e.g., liberals, environmentalists, feminists) than did liberals and that these differences were partially mediated by conservatives' higher levels of belief that these groups violated their worldviews and lower levels of internal motivation to control prejudice (Webster & Saucier, 2010). Overall, our studies suggest that White conservatives have less internal motivation to be unprejudiced—that is, it is less a part of their self-concepts to be egalitarian, especially toward groups with which they may be in competition.

In summary, a plethora of research has shown that higher degrees of political conservatism are associated with higher levels of prejudice toward traditionally disadvantaged and minority groups. Although this relationship is by no means perfect, it does provide a compelling theoretical and empirical position from which to examine, and possibly at least partially explain, the use of racial imagery and rhetoric by the GOP about Obama and other minorities.

THE RIGHT'S RACIAL IMAGERY AND RHETORIC ABOUT OBAMA

Recent history has been littered with racially loaded comments made and imagery created by members of the GOP and their conservative supporters. These comments and imagery have promoted stereotypic depictions of prominent minorities in the Democratic Party. Some have demonstrated levels of negativity that border on hatred. These comments and imagery have been about race in general, but also has targeted specific individuals.

In response to comments made by the GOP members and other conservatives, accusations have been leveled that members of the GOP and other conservatives have focused on race and race issues in inappropriate and potentially antisocial ways. For example, Jeremy Levitt, a law professor at Florida A&M University, accused Fox News, Glenn Beck, and Bill O'Reilly of instigating racial tensions by having "a race deck, and they play the ace of spades every day" (Graham, 2009). These allegations have also targeted former Republican media consultant Roger Ailes, who has been accused of using his position at Fox News to play on racial animosity and fears to incite opposition to President Obama's administration. Evidence offered for these allegations include chronic comments make by Fox News commentators Glenn Beck, Bill O'Reilly, and Sean Hannity. For example, Glenn Beck claimed that President Obama "has a deep-seated hatred for White people or the White culture" and "is, I believe, a racist," and accused Sonia Sotomayor of having made "one of the most outrageous racist remarks I've heard" regarding her comment about what her experience as a Latina woman would bring to her perspective on the Supreme Court, cementing his point by stating that "she sure sounds like a racist here" (Media Matters for America, 2009).

There is really no shortage of comments made by GOP members and conservatives that are racially biased. Joshua Trevino, in an endorsement of racial profiling at the United States–Mexico border, wrote on Twitter that "my red hair and pale skin IS my passport" (Weiner, 2009). Trevino is a former speechwriter for the Bush Administration. Lynn Jenkins, a GOP member of the House of Representatives, claimed that the GOP needed to find a "great White hope" to challenge President Obama in 2012 (Stein, 2009). Brian Kilmeade insinuated that Americans have less "pure genes" because Americans "keep marrying other species and ethnicities" on a July episode of "Fox and Friends" (Drivas, 2009). RNC Chairman Michael Steele made a comment the 2009 Young Republicans Meeting that he would attract young Blacks to the GOP by offering "fried chicken and potato salad" (Browning, 2009). David Vitter, a GOP Senator, stated that he was not sure if a Supreme Court decision that declared state laws that banned interracial marriage to be unconstitutional was correctly decided (Stark, 2009). In July 2009, Audrey Shay, then the leading candidate to be elected chairman of the Young Republicans, allegedly supported a comment made by a friend on her Facebook page that stated, "Obama Bin Lauden [*sic*] is the new terrorist . . . Muslim is on there side [*sic*] . . . need to take this country back from all these mad coons . . . and illegals," with the reply, "You tell em Eric! lol!," although she claimed to be replying to an earlier comment (Avlon, 2009). Despite this debacle, Shay was ultimately elected chairman that same month.

Moreover, it appears that the GOP's racial bias influences policy decisions and enforcement. According to a report released by the Government Accountability Office in December 2009, when compared to the Clinton Administration, there was a significant drop in the enforcement of major anti-discrimination and voting rights laws (Savage, 2009).

Perhaps most interesting in investigating the possibility that the GOP has pervasive race-related negativity among its member ranks, Michael Steele himself recently made comments during a television interview about how White members of the GOP are afraid of Blacks and that he has felt that type of negative emotionality directed toward him (News One, 2009). As the ranking Republican in the RNC—a handpicked leader of the GOP—it is telling that Steele has experienced this sentiment (and admitted as much), and aids in our understanding of the relationship of the GOP with race issues.

Probably no one has endured more personal attacks related to race than President Obama himself. Trent Franks, a Republican member of the House of Representatives, called Obama "an enemy of humanity" in discussing Obama's position on abortion (Stein, 2009). Racially based attacks on President Obama have targeted him as an individual as well as his political agenda, but also his accomplishments. Regarding his winning the Nobel Peace Prize, Rush Limbaugh claimed the win "fully exposes the illusion that is Barack Obama" as a symbol of a "weakened, neutered U.S." Erick Erickson of the site RedState. com wrote, "I did not realize the Nobel Peace Prize had an affirmative action quota" (Stein, 2009). Further attacks have even centered on President Obama's constitutional eligibility to be President of the United States in terms of his place of birth. Trent Franks demanded that President Obama produce a birth certificate to demonstrate that he was born in the United States (Stein, 2009).

The members of President Obama's family have also been vulnerable to race-related criticism. Posts on Free Republic, a conservative blog, described Malia Obama, the President's daughter as "a typical street whore" and "ghetto street trash," with another post stating "wonder when she will get her first abortion." Michelle Obama, the President's wife, was pictured on the same blog with caption, "To entertain her daughter, Michelle Obama loves to make monkey sounds" (Parry, 2009).

It is important to note that we have not provided a comprehensive or exhaustive listing of the recent racially insensitive comments made and images used by GOP members and conservatives. We have merely taken note of and gathered examples as we noticed them, and as such, these should be taken as a sampling for illustrative purposes. Promotion of, and even passive tolerance of, such inflammatory racial imagery and rhetoric may lead to important negative social consequences (Mendelberg, 2001; Philpot, 2007). Few overt statements of disapproval of such imagery and rhetoric have been made by prominent Republicans (in a prominent exception, GOP Senator Lindsey Graham of South Carolina commented that the birther movement challenging President Obama's place of birth were "crazy" and also attempted to dispel myths that President Obama is a closet Muslim; Stein, 2009). At relatively low levels, there is perpetuation of inappropriate racial stereotypes and prejudice toward minorities. At more extreme high levels, it may seem to condone more overt animosity or even aggression. The Secret Service's investigation of a Facebook poll that asked, "Should Obama be killed?" with the choice options consisting of "No," "Maybe," "Yes," and "Yes if he cuts my health care" (huffingtonpost.com; theplumline.whorunsgov.org) provides a chilling example of how far racial bias may extend.

IMPLICIT RACE BIAS AND THE POLITICAL RIGHT

Racial bias has been re-conceptualized by researchers. Although historically examined as a blatant, overt negativity that prejudiced individuals would harbor and express toward outgroups, contemporary researchers have instead investigated racial bias as it exists in more subtle and possibly unconscious ways. This shift from examining "old-fashioned" conceptualizations of racial bias began in the late 1970s and early 1980s, when it was shown that despite individuals' claims to be egalitarian and consequent decreases in levels of expressed overt racial prejudice (e.g., Dovidio & Gaertner, 1991), their discriminatory behavior still showed evidence of negative attitudes toward outgroups. Theorists have conceptualized this more modern form of racial bias as emerging in less obvious and more socially acceptable ways that are less easily recognized as being racially biased (McConahay, Hardee, & Batts, 1981), such as toward social and political policies that would affect minority groups rather than toward the specific minority group members (McConahay & Hough, 1976). This may come under the guise of widely shared moral value orientations (e.g., the Protestant ethic; Katz & Hass, 1988) or in the form of passive behaviors like avoidance produced by feelings of aversion toward minority groups (Gaertner & Dovidio, 1986).

The shift in the expression of racial bias from overt to more subtle forms appeared because of individuals' general recognition that prejudice and discrimination are socially undesirable. As such, individuals are often motivated to inhibit behavioral expressions of prejudice to avoid both the internal feelings of guilt they may feel (e.g., Fazio & Hilden, 2001; Monteith, 1993) and the social sanctions they may receive as consequences (e.g., Dunton & Fazio, 1997; Plant & Devine, 1998). However, prejudice may still emerge in behavior when situational ambiguity allows the behavior to be perceived and defended by actors as being motivated by something other than prejudice. That is, when discriminatory behavior can be justified as something else, and when there is little internal or external pressure to suppress the behavior, then discrimination is likely to occur (Crandall & Eshleman, 2003; Crandall, Eshleman, & O'Brien, 2002).

Measures of racial bias have evolved to assess both the automatic and controlled components of prejudice (Devine, 1989), with a focus on examining the levels of racial bias that individuals possess that would emerge through less conspicuous behaviors despite their efforts to suppress it, including how individuals describe stereotypical and counterstereotypical events (von Hippel, Sekaquaptewa, & Vargas, 1997) and evaluate the merits of racially biased arguments (Saucier & Miller, 2003). Further, measures of how quickly individuals make stereotypical associations at an implicit level have emerged to show racial bias at an automatic cognitive level (Fazio, Jackson, Dunton, & Williams, 1995; Greenwald, McGhee, & Schwartz, 1998).

Automatic and controlled components of prejudice are predictive of different behaviors. Automatic components of prejudice best predict automated types of behaviors, particularly nonverbal cues (e.g., eye contact, gesturing, sitting position). The relationship between implicit bias and automated discriminatory behavior is best exemplified in studies examining inter-racial interactions in social (Dovidio, Kawakami, & Gaertner, 2002; Plant & Devine, 2003; Rudman & Ashmore, 2007), medical (Bach, Kramer, Warren, & Berg, 1999; Melancon et al., 2009; Schulman et al., 1999), and clinical (Sue et al., 2007) settings. A key finding from these studies is that although White participants may not say anything overtly racist in inter-racial interactions, Black participants are perceptive enough to notice White participants' discomfort or aversion in the interaction via Whites' nonverbal cues. Further, even subtle forms of prejudice in the media can have an enormous impact on the behaviors and attitudes of its viewers. Parks and Heard (2009) have relayed how implicit racist imagery and jokes that dehumanize Obama may facilitate or condone death threats on President Obama. Further, as discussed earlier, Mendelberg (2001) highlighted how ambiguously racist media articles and images (but not overtly racist media) have helped conservative candidates gain support in elections for decades. Thus, despite being less obvious, implicit racial bias has important behavioral consequences.

Conversely, controlled components of prejudice are best predictive of discriminatory behaviors that involve conscious, thoughtful judgment, including discrimination in helping situations (Saucier, Miller, & Doucet, 2005), in the evaluation of job applicants (Dovidio & Gaertner, 2000), and on race-relevant policy (e.g., support for budget cuts for minority organizations; Rudman & Ashmore, 2007). Illustrating this behavioral domain, following the slow and insufficient federal response to help the victims of Hurricane Katrina in New Orleans, social psychologists examined the situation from contemporary theories of racial bias and argued that racial bias toward the victims, many of whom were Black, was likely a factor (Henkel, Dovidio, & Gaertner, 2006; Napier, Mandisodza, Anderson, & Jost, 2006; Saucier, McManus, & Smith, 2009; Saucier, Smith, & McManus, 2007).

Although political conservatism is highly related to negative explicit prejudice toward minority groups (including Blacks), research has similarly shown that conservatives exhibit higher levels of racial bias at implicit levels as well. Specifically, conservatives exhibit more negative attitudes toward Blacks, less egalitarian ideology, and stronger preferences for higher status groups than do liberals at implicit levels (e.g., Cunningham, Nezlek, & Banaji, 2004; Jost, Banaji, & Nosek, 2004; Jost et al., 2008; *see also* Ashburn-Nardo & Livingston, this volume).

Two recent papers have further probed the relationships between conservatism and implicit and explicit forms of prejudice. Son Hing, Chung-Yan, Zanna, and Hamilton (2008) developed a two-dimensional model of prejudice based upon participants' scores on implicit and explicit measures of racial bias (in this case the target of prejudice was Asians). Scores on each measure categorized people into one of four quadrants: truly low-prejudiced (those scoring low on both implicit and explicit prejudice), aversive racists (those scoring high on implicit and low on explicit prejudice), principled conservatives (those scoring high on explicit but low on implicit), and modern racists (those scoring high on both implicit and explicit prejudice).

The political ideologies of these four groups importantly differed: truly low-prejudiced and aversive racists more greatly endorsed egalitarian and humanistic values, whereas principled conservatives and modern racists more greatly identified as conservative and capitalist. Further, modern racists scored highest on a measure of right-wing authoritarianism and exhibited the most discrimination when asked to recommend a racial minority group member for employment, especially when the individual had ambiguous qualifications. Although the targets of prejudice in these studies were Asian, theoretical models of modern racism would predict that Son Hing et al.'s model should hold when the targets of prejudice are Blacks.

A dissertation completed by Inna Burdein (2007) also delineated two "sub-types" of conservatives ("sophisticated" vs. "non-sophisticated") in trying to assess whether conservatives support or oppose certain racial policies because of their ideology (e.g., Protestant work ethic) or because they want to ensure a negative outcome for minorities. Burdein found that despite conservatives' assertions that their race-based policy decisions are based on ideological concerns and *not* specifically on racial concerns, at the implicit level racial policies activated racial, but *not* ideological, concepts. Further, conservative ideology is more strongly linked to racial concepts (stereotype accessibility) among more "sophisticated" conservatives—that is, those conservatives with more elaborate and detailed conservative ideologies.

In sum, the research on the relationships between political orientation and explicit and implicit racial prejudice shows that conservative ideology is related to greater endorsement of Black stereotypes, anti-Black sentiment, and anti-Black legislation both at explicit and implicit levels. Conservatives appear to be less intrinsically motivated to inhibit their prejudices and more likely to justify their policy decisions based on ideological or, even more blatantly, racial considerations depending on the sophistication of their conservative ideology. The more adept political conservatives who are trying to promote greater diversity in the GOP likely are more "sophisticated" and make ideological rather than race-based appeals to justify their discriminatory policy decisions. Sophisticated or principled conservatives may then be more likely to blame unprincipled conservatives (the "fringe") for the multitude of racist imagery and rhetoric appearing during the Obama campaign and presidency.

It appears then that conservatives will only try to suppress their prejudices when external forces compel them to do so, typically either to avoid conflict with racial minorities or to bolster the image of the GOP. However, racial bias may emerge even when individuals attempt to suppress it, as evidenced by the many examples of conservatives' racist imagery and rhetoric during Obama's campaign and presidency. It is important to consider that individuals may not always want to suppress their prejudices. Instead, individuals may attempt to seek methods by which they may behave in discriminatory ways to further a social agenda (Sinclair & Kunda, 2000). One way to attempt to rationalize discriminatory behavior as something less prejudiced is to provide an alternative nonprejudiced rationale for the behavior, such as when Whites discriminate against Blacks in employment only when Whites can provide reasons to justify such discrimination (e.g., Dovidio & Gaertner, 2000; *see also* Son Hing et al., 2008). More importantly, another way to rationalize discriminatory behavior is to defend oneself as being generally non-prejudiced with evidence of one's own tolerant and egalitarian values. This may be attempted by showing one's support for carefully selected minority group members or policies that would aid minority groups. This display of moral credentials or legitimacy credits may "cover" the behavior in much the same way a person who makes a racist statement may claim the statement is not racist because he or she "has Black friends." The selection of Palin as McCain's running partner and Steele's selection as the ranking Republican in the Party may have been attempts to use this strategy to demonstrate the GOP's egalitarian perspective despite their recent and long-term history of failing to demonstrate that egalitarian perspective.

To further attempt to show how sensitive the GOP is to minority interests, the Republican National Committee posted a website that contained the names of 16 famous Republican "Heroes." The list included only 4 White men. The remaining 12 individuals included 7 Blacks, 1 Latino/a, and 4 women. One noteworthy inclusion was Jackie Robinson, who was the first Black baseball player in the major leagues, who asserted in his autobiography that he considered himself an independent, not a Republican (Stein, 2009). This appears to be an obvious attempt for the GOP to associate itself with a famous and revered champion for civil rights to insinuate that they uphold and support those same ideals. Doing so when the individual himself distanced himself from the GOP is a questionable tactic.

CONCLUSION

Overall, given the research showing conservatives' implicit and explicit levels of racial bias in addition to the many behavioral examples of this bias found in the media during Barack Obama's campaign and presidency, we argue that there is likely some element of the GOP that harbors negativity toward Obama and his administration in particular—precisely because he is Black—and toward ethnic and gender minorities in general. This negativity may be unconscious, or it may be conscious and because of racial, rather than ideological, considerations—whether or not conservatives are willing to admit it. Second, we argue that the selection of Palin as McCain's running partner, Steele's selection as the ranking Republican in the Party, and Bobby Jindal's early push to the presidency, are superficial attempts to demonstrate the GOP's egalitarian perspective despite their recent and long-term history of failing to demonstrate that egalitarian perspective. Republicans may be superficially promoting diversity by "propping up" minority group members to prominent positions in the GOP in lieu of making substantial changes in their policies to be more supportive of minority groups, especially toward Blacks.

Without policy change, it is unlikely that these superficial efforts will be successful in reviving perceptions of the GOP as supporting the egalitarian ideals that formerly made it the Party of Lincoln.

NOTES

1 See Kool Moe Dee (1990). *How Ya Like Me Now.* Jive Records.
2 See "Slumdog Millionaire" (2008). Twentieth Century Fox.

REFERENCES

Avlon, John (July 6, 2009). New GOP "Racist" Headache. Retrieved July 6, 2009 from http://www.thedailybeast.com/blogs-and-stories/2009-07-06/new-gop-racist-headache/p/.

Bach, P. B., Cramer, L. D., Warren, J. L., & Begg, C. B. (1999). Racial differences in the treatment of early-stage lung cancer. *New England Journal of Medicine, 34,* 1198–1205.

Browning, Bil (July 14, 2009). Steele: I'll Woo Blacks to GOP with "Fried Chicken and Potato Salad." Retrieved on July 16, 2009 from http://www.huffingtonpost.com/bil-browning/steele-gop-woos-blacks-wi_b_231534.html.

Burdein, I. (2007). *Principled conservatives or covert racists: Disentangling racism and ideology through implicit measures.* Unpublished doctoral dissertation, Stony Brook University.

Carney, D. R., Jost, J. T., Gosling, S. D., & Potter, J. (2008). The secret lives of liberals and conservatives: Personality profiles, interaction styles, and the things they leave behind. *Political Psychology, 29* (6), 807–840.

Crandall, C. S., & Eshleman, A. (2003). A justification-suppression model of the expression and experience of prejudice. *Psychological Bulletin, 129,* 414–446.

Crandall, C. S., Eshleman, A., & O'Brien, L. (2002). Social norms and the expression and suppression of prejudice: The struggle for internalization. *Journal of Personality and Social Psychology, 82* (3), 359–378.

Cunningham, W. A., Nezlek, J. B., & Banaji, M. R. (2004). Implicit and explicit ethnocentrism: Revisiting the ideologies of prejudice. *Personality & Social Psychology Bulletin, 30,* 1332–1346.

Devine, P. G. (1989). Stereotypes and prejudice: Their automatic and controlled components. *Journal of Personality and Social Psychology, 56* (1), 5–18.

Dewan, Shaila (February 26, 2009). Gov. Jindal, Rising Star, Plummets after Speech. *The New York Times,* 20.

Dovidio, J. F., & Gaertner, S. L. (1991). Changes in the expression of racial prejudice. In H. J. Knopke, R. J. Norrell, & R. W. Rogers (Eds.), *Opening doors: Perspectives on race relations in contemporary America* (pp. 119–148). Tuscaloosa: University of Alabama Press.

Dovidio, J. F., & Gaertner, S. L. (1986). Prejudice, discrimination, and racism: Historical trends and contemporary approaches. In J. F. Dovidio &

S. L. Gaertner (Eds.), *Prejudice, discrimination, and racism* (pp. 1–34). Orlando, FL: Academic Press.

Dovidio, J. F., & Gaertner, S. L. (2000). Aversive racism and selection decisions: 1989 and 1999. *Psychological Science, 11* (4), 315–319.

Dovidio, J. F., Kawakami, K., & Gaertner, S. L. (2002). Implicit and explicit prejudice and interracial interaction. *Journal of Personality and Social Psychology, 82,* 62–28.

Drivas, Peter (July 20, 2009). Brian Kilmeade Apologizes for Racist "Pure Species" Comment. Retrieved July 20, 2009 from http://www.huffingtonpost.com/2009/07/20/brian-kilmeade-apologizes_n_241135.html.

Dunham, Richard (August 31, 2008). McCain Rolls Dice with VP Choice: Palin Brings Payoff Potential, but also Risks. *The Houston Chronicle,* A1

Dunton, B. C., & Fazio, R. H. (1997). An individual difference measure of motivation to control prejudiced reactions. *Personality and Social Psychology Bulletin, 23* (3), 316–326.

Fauntroy, M. K. (2007). *Republicans and the Black vote.* Boulder, CO: Lynne Rienner.

Fazio, R. H., & Hilden, L. E. (2001). Emotional responses to a seemingly prejudiced response: The role of automatically activated racial attitudes and motivation and control prejudiced reactions. *Personality and Social Psychology Bulletin, 27* (5), 538–549.

Fazio, R. H., Jackson, J. R., Dunton, B. C., & Williams, C. J. (1995). Variability in automatic activation as an unobtrusive measure of racial attitudes: A bona fide pipeline? *Journal of Personality and Social Psychology, 69,* 1013–1027.

Graham, Nick (September 24, 2009). Law Professor Confronts O'Reilly Over Fox News and the Far Right: "Fox News, Far Right Have a Race Deck, and They Play the Ace of Spades Every Day. Retrieved November 6, 2009 from http://www.huffingtonpost.com/2009/09/24/law-professor-confronts- o_n_299350.html.

Greenberg, S. B. (1987). *Democratic defection revisited.* Retrieved December 15, 2009 from http://www.gqrr.com/articles/1952/3314_r_democraticdefection_040187.pdf.

Greenwald, A. G., McGhee, D. E., & Schwartz, J. L. K. (1998). Measuring individual differences in implicit cognition: The implicit association test. *Journal of Personality and Social Psychology, 74* (6), 1464–1480.

Henkel, K. E., Dovidio, J. F., & Gaertner, S. L. (2006). Institutional discrimination, individual racism, and Hurricane Katrina. *Analyses of Social Issues and Public Policy, 6,* 99–124.

Issenberg, Sasha (February 25, 2009). Governor Jindal: Restore GOP Ideals. *The Boston Globe,* 11A.

Jost, J. T., Banaji, M.R., & Nosek, B.A. (2004). A decade of system justification theory: Accumulated evidence of conscious and unconscious bolstering of the status quo. *Political Psychology, 25,* 881–919.

Jost, J. T., Glaser, J., Kruglanski, A. W., & Sulloway, F. J. (2003). Political conservatism as motivated social cognition. *Psychological Bulletin, 129* (3), 339–375.

Jost, J. T., Napier, J. L., Thorisdottir, H., Gosling, S. D., Palfai, T. P., & Ostafin, B. (2007). Are needs to manage uncertainty and threat associated with political conservatism or ideological extremity? *Personality and Social Psychology Bulletin, 33* (7), 989–1007.

Jost, J. T., Nosek, B. A., & Gosling, S. D. (2008). Ideology: Its resurgence in social, personality, and political psychology. *Perspectives on Psychological Science, 3* (2), 126–136.

Katz, I., & Hass, R. G. (1988). Racial ambivalence and American value conflict: Correlational and priming studies of dual cognitive structures. *Journal of Personality and Social Psychology, 55* (6), 893–905.

Martin, Gary, & R.G. Ratcliffe (August 30, 2008). Reaction is Mixed as Democrats depart Denver. *The San Antonio Express-News,* 17A.

Mauriello, Tracie (September 5, 2008). No Single, Simple Answer on How Women See Palin. *The Pittsburgh Post-Gazette,* A1.

Media Matters for America (October 30, 2009). Ailes Brings History of Race-Baiting to Fox. Retrieved November 6, 2009 from http://mediamatters.org/press/releases/475746.

McConahay, J. B., Hardee, B. B., & Batts, V. (1981). Has racism declined in America? It depends on who is asking and what is asked. *Journal of Conflict Resolution, 25,* 563–579.

McConahay, J. B., & Hough, J. C., Jr. (1976). Symbolic racism. *Journal of Social Issues, 32,* 23–45.

Melancon, J. K., Kucirka, L. M., Boulware, L. E., Powe, N. R., Locke, J. E., Montgomery, R. A., & Segev, D. L. (2009). Impact of medicare coverage on disparities in access to simultaneous pancreas and kidney transplantation. *American Journal of Transplantation, 9,* 1–7.

Mendelberg, T. (2001). *The race card: Campaign strategy, implicit messages, and the norm of equality.* Princeton University Press: Princeton, NJ.

Milbank, Dana (May 20, 2009). Steele Speaks and, to Quote Reagan, the Bombing Starts. *The Washington Post,* A2.

Monteith, M. J. (1993). Self-regulation of prejudiced responses: Implications for progress in prejudice-reduction efforts. *Journal of Personality and Social Psychology, 65,* 469–485.

Napier, J. L., Mandisodza, A. N., Anderson, S. M., & Jost, J. T. (2006). System justification in responding to the poor and displaced in the aftermath of Hurricane Katrina. *Analyses of Social Issues and Public Policy, 6* (1), 57–73.

News One (November 9, 2009). Steele: White Republicans Are Scared of Me. Retrieved November 19, 2009 from http://newsone.com/nation/steele-white-republicans-are-scared-of-me/.

Parks, G. S. and Roberson, Q. M. (in press). "Eighteen Million Cracks": Gender's Role in the 2008 Presidential Campaign. *William & Mary Journal of Women & the Law.*

Parks, G. S., & Heard, D. C. (2009). "Assassinate the nigger ape": Obama, implicit imagery, and the dire consequences of racist jokes. Retrieved December 7, 2009 from *http://scholarship.law.cornell.edu/cgi/viewcontent.cgi?article=1063&context= clsops_papers.*

Parry, Chris (July 14, 2009). Conservative Free Republic Blog in Free Speech Flap After Racial Slurs Directed at Obama Children. Retrieved July 16, 2009 from http://www.vancouversun.com/story_print.html?id=1782375&sponsor=.

Philpot, T. S. (2007). *Race, Republicans, and return of the party of Lincoln.* Ann Arbor, MI: University of Michigan Press.

Plant, E. A., & Devine, P. G. (1998). Internal and external motivation to respond without prejudice. *Journal of Personality and Social Psychology, 75* (3), 811–832.

Plant, E. A., & Devine, P. G. (2003). The antecedents and implications of interracial anxiety. *Personality and Social Psychology Bulletin, 29* (6), 790–801.

Pratto, F., Sidanius, J., Stallworth, L .M., & Malle, B. F. (1994). Social dominance orientation: A personality variable predicting social and political attitudes. *Journal of Personality and Social Psychology, 67*, 741–763.

Rudman, L. A., & Ashmore, R. D. (2007). Discrimination and the implicit association test. *Group Processes and Intergroup Relations, 10* (3), 359–372.

Saucier, D. A., McManus, J. L., & Smith, S. J. (2009). Discrimination against out-groupmembers in helping situations. In S. Stürmer & M. Snyder (Eds.), *The psychology of prosocial behavior: Group processes, intergroup relations, and helping* (pp. 103–120). Oxford, UK: Wiley-Blackwell.

Saucier, D. A., & Miller, C. T. (2003). The persuasiveness of racial arguments as a subtle measure of racism. *Personality and Social Psychology Bulletin, 29* (10), 1303–1315.

Saucier, D. A., Miller, C. T., & Doucet, N. (2005). Differences in helping Whites and Blacks: A meta-analysis. *Personality and Social Psychology Review, 9*, 2–16.

Saucier, D. A., Smith, S. J., & McManus, J. L. (2007). The possible role of discrimination in the rescue response after Hurricane Katrina. *Journal of Race and Policy, 3* (1), 113–121.

Savage, C. (2009). Report examines civil rights during Bush years. Retrieved December 7, 2009 from http://www.nytimes.com/2009/12/03/us/politics/ 03rights.html?_r=2&ref=todayspaper.

Schwab, Nikki and Paul Bedard (May 11, 2009). Correspondents' Dinner Party Notes: Steele Call's Obama's "Wassup" Brotherly Love. *U.S. News & World Report*, __.

Schulman, K. A., Berlin, J. A., Harless, W., Kerner, J. F., Sistrunk, S., Gersh, B. J et al. (1999). The effect of race and sex on physicians' recommendations for cardiac catheterization. *New England Journal of Medicine, 34*, 618-626.

Simon, Roger (March 8, 2009). Steele Has No Idea What He's Gotten Himself Into. *Chicago Sun-Times*, A19.

Sinclair, L., & Kunda, Z. (2000). Motivated stereotyping of women: She's fine if she praised me but incompetent if she criticized me. *Personality and Social Psychology Bulletin, 26* (11), 1329–1342.

Son Hing, L. S., Chung-Yan, G. A., Zanna, M. P., & Hamilton, L. K. (2008). A two-dimensional model that employs explicit and implicit attitudes to characterize prejudice. *Journal of Personality and Social Psychology, 94*, 971–987.

Stark, Mike (November 18, 2009). Senator Vitter on Video: I Don't Know if Loving Was Correctly Decided. Retrieved November 19, 2009 from http://www.huffingtonpost.com/mike-stark/senator-vitter-on-video- i_b_362379.html.

Stein, Sam (August 31, 2009). GOP Rep. Behind "Great White Hope" Remark Voted For Bill With Same Phrase. Retrieved August 31, 2009 from http://www.huffingtonpost.com/2009-08-31/gop-rep-behind-whit_n_272589.html.

Stein, Sam (September 29, 2009). GOP Rep. Trent Franks Calls Obama "An Enemy ofHumanity. Retrieved September 29, 2009 from http://www.huffingtonpost.com/2009/09/29/gop-rep-trent-franks-call_n_302713.html.

Stein, Sam (October 1, 2009). Sen. Graham Calls Beck "A Cynic" and Birthers "Crazy." Retrieved October 1, 2009 from http://www.huffingtonpost.com/2009/10/01/sen-graham-calls-beck-a-c_n_306434.html.

Stein, Sam (October 9, 2009). Obama's Nobel Prize Inspires Conservative Outrage and Confusion. Retrieved October 9, 2009 from http://www.huffingtonpost.com/2009/10/09/obamas-nobel-prize- inspir_n_315167.html.

Stein, Sam (October 13, 2009). RNC: Jackie Robinson Was A Republican. Retrieved October 19, 2009 from http://www.huffingtonpost.com/2009/10/13rnc-jackie-robinson-was-a_n_318618.html.

Sue, D. W., Capodilupo, C. M., Torino, G. C., Bucceri, J. M., Holder, A. M. B., Nadal, K. L., & Esquilin, M. (2007). Racial microaggressions in everyday life: Implications for clinical practice. *American Psychologist, 62* (4), 271–286.

Topping, S. (2008). *Lincoln's lost legacy.* Gainsville, FL: University Press of Florida.

von Hippel, W., Sekaquaptewa, D., & Vargas, P. (1997). The Linguistic Intergroup Bias as an implicit indicator of prejudice. *Journal of Experimental Social Psychology, 33*, 490-509.

Webster, R. J., Burns, M., Pickering, M., & Saucier, D. A. (2009). *The regulation and expression of prejudice as a function of political orientation.* Unpublished manuscript, Kansas State University.

Webster, R. J., & Saucier, D. A. (2010). *Spanning the political divide: Why are liberals and conservatives prejudiced toward different groups?* Manuscript submitted for publication.

Weiner, Rachel (September 21, 2009). Josh Trevino, GOP Consultant: "My Red Hair and Pale Skin IS My Passport. Retrieved September 23, 2009 from http://www.huffingtonpost.com/2009/09/21/joshua-trevio-gop- consult_n_293938.html.

Williams, Joseph (March 1, 2009). RNC Chairman Plans Turnaround for Battered Party. *The Boston Globe*, 8.

Zernike, Kate (August 31, 2008). Can You Cross Out "Hillary" and Write "Sarah"? *The New York Times*, 1.

New Bottle, Same Old Wine: A Response

Melissa Harris-Lacewell

If we are in a post-racial age, then why do so many choices of the Republican Party seem transparently motivated by race? This is the question posed by the authors of this chapter.

The authors assert that the GOP remains bound to issues of race in three ways. First, Republicans have highlighted and elevated people of color to prominent, national positions within the party to gain favor with minority voters. Second, they have openly contested the Obama Administration using racist imagery and tactics. Finally, the authors contend that Republican voters are more prone to racial prejudice than their Democratic counterparts.

These are valuable observations, but I want to challenge the authors to think somewhat differently about these conclusions.

This chapter overstates the implausibility of African-American voters considering the GOP as a viable alternative. The authors accurately point to the sweeping historical shift that moved African-American voters out of the Republican Party and into the Democratic Party during the mid-twentieth century. However, they overstate the strength of the contemporary attachment between Black Americans and the Democratic Party. Beginning with Jesse Jackson's presidential primary bids in the 1980s, African-Americans have vigorously questioned whether Democrats take Black voters for granted.

African-Americans consistently give more than 85% of their vote to Democratic candidates, but throughout the past two decades, Black respondents in public opinion surveys reported that they did not perceive meaningful differences between the political parties. Therefore, although they may not yet be ready to realign their basic partisan attachment, Black voters are not always enthusiastic Democrats. In fact, African-Americans showed some willingness to support a GOP presidential candidate when George W. Bush doubled his vote share among Black voters in his 2004 re-election.

Admittedly, it seems the GOP has lost its toehold with Black voters during the past 5 years. President Bush's approval ratings sank to the low single digits among African-Americans after he failed to respond promptly to the devastation of New Orleans following Hurricane Katrina. Two years later, black Democratic registration increased dramatically when Barack Obama emerged as viable contender for the Democratic nomination. Although Black Democratic partisanship is currently quite strong, the Republican Party is not entirely misguided in their efforts to cast the party as a viable alternative for minority voters.

Still, I doubt the high visibility of Black and Brown officials in the Republican Party is primarily an effort to diversify supporters. Michael Steele, Bobby Jindal, Condi Rice, and other highly visible Republicans-of-color are more important for securing a broad base of White voters than for attracting new Black voters. Open racial hostility is considered an inappropriate expression in contemporary American politics. Most White voters are uncomfortable with supporting a political party that utterly lacks racial diversity. The appointment of highly visible Black, Latino, and Asian Republicans was a key strategy during President Bush's Administration. It remains part of the strategy for the contemporary Republican Party, but it is a strategy aimed at soothing and solidifying support among White voters, rather than significantly increasing Black and Latino support.

I also think the authors overstate the extent to which racial animus is constitutive of conservative political beliefs. They offer evidence that Republican discourse is infused with racist language and imagery; they further argue that conservative voters harbor more prejudicial dispositions. This analysis has two dangers. First, it assumes that there is no principled opposition to President Obama's policies that is not steeped in racism. Second, it implies that liberals and Democrats are free of meaningful racial bias. Both conclusions are troubling.

The Sotomayor confirmation hearings and health-care discourse during 2009 made obvious that some members of the GOP were willing to counter White House actions by using strategies, language, and images meant to stoke racial fear and anxiety. But these tactics do not preclude the possibility of principled conservative opposition. By arguing that racism is constitutive of Conservatism, the authors unfairly limit the range of legitimate political worldviews within the American system.

This argument also fails to acknowledge that racial animus is not the sole domain of Republicans and Conservatives. Members of the Democratic Party and of the American progressive left are also guilty of racial insensitivity and of supporting policies with racially disparate impact. Any attempt to locate racism solely on one side of the political spectrum undoubtedly serves to obscure the meaningful ways that race and racism influence partisan choices in both parties.

Republicans are no longer the party of Lincoln, but similarly, Democrats are no longer the party of Lyndon Johnson. The post-racial hypothesis fails on both sides of the aisle.

About the Editors

Gregory S. Parks, J.D., Ph.D., is a Visiting Fellow at Cornell Law School. He has served as a law clerk on the United States Court of Appeals for the Fourth Circuit and the District of Columbia Court of Appeals. He earned his B.S. from Howard University, his M.S. from the City University of New York, his Ph.D. from the University of Kentucky, and his J.D. from Cornell Law School.

Dr. Parks' scholarly articles have appeared in such journals as: *University of Pennsylvania Law Review PENNumbra; Florida State Law Review; Cornell Journal of Law & Public Policy; Journal of Criminal Law & Criminology; William and Mary Journal of Women and the Law; Rutgers Race & Law Review; Hastings Women's Law Journal; Psychology, Public Policy & Law.* He has also published numerous scholarly books, among them *Critical Race Realism: Intersections of Psychology, Race, and Law* (2008) and *12 Angry Men: True Stories of Being a Black Man in America Today* (forthcoming in 2011). Dr. Parks' other scholarship focuses on African-American fraternities and sororities.

Matthew W. Hughey, Ph.D., is an Assistant Professor of Sociology and an Affiliate Faculty member with the program of African-American Studies and the program of Gender Studies at Mississippi State University. He earned his B.A. from the University of North Carolina at Greensboro, his M.Ed. from Ohio University, and his Ph.D. from the University of Virginia.

Dr. Hughey has published his scholastic work in top peer-reviewed journals: *Social Problems; Ethnic and Racial Studies; Journal of Contemporary Ethnography; Critical Sociology; Journal of African American Studies; Western Journal of Black Studies; Sociology Compass;* and *Humanity and Society.* He has also co-edited two scholarly books entitled *Black Greek-Letter Organizations, 2.0: New Directions in the Study of African American Fraternities and Sororities* (forthcoming from University Press of Mississippi, 2011) and *12 Angry Men: True Stories of Being a Black Man in America* (forthcoming from The New Press, 2011).

About the Contributors

Leslie Ashburn-Nardo, Ph.D., is an Associate Professor of Psychology at Indiana University–Purdue University Indianapolis. She earned her B.A. in psychology from Wake Forest University, her M.A. in psychology from the University of North Carolina at Wilmington, and her Ph.D. in experimental (social) psychology from the University of Kentucky. Dr. Ashburn-Nardo's research focuses on prejudice, prejudice reduction, stigma, and implicit social cognition. Her work has been published in social psychology journals such as *Journal of Personality and Social Psychology, Journal of Experimental Social Psychology, Personality and Social Psychology Bulletin, Group Processes and Intergroup Relations,* and *Social Cognition.* Dr. Ashburn-Nardo's teaching was also recognized with a 2009 Society for the Teaching of Psychology Honorary Membership for Infusing Diversity into Teaching.

Meghan G. Bean is a Ph.D. Candidate in the Department of Psychology at Northwestern University. She received a B.S. from Tufts University and M.S. in Social Psychology from Northwestern University. Her research has examined whether intersecting social identities, such as age and occupation, can attenuate the stereotype that Black men are dangerous. She is also pursuing research examining the development, maintenance, and perception of trust within and across group boundaries.

Tamara L. Brown, Ph.D. is an Associate Professor of Psychology at the University of Kentucky, a Licensed Clinical Psychologist. She earned her Ph.D. from the University of Illinois at Urbana-Champaign. Co-editor of *African American Fraternities and Sororities: The Legacy and the Vision,* Dr. Brown is a public scholar of the psychology of the African American experience.

George Ciccariello-Maher received his Ph.D. in political theory from the University of California, Berkeley, and is an Assistant Professor of Politics at Drexel University. He is currently completing a people's history of Venezuela's Bolivarian Revolution, entitled *We Created Him* (under contract with Duke University Press). A frequent press commentator on Latin American and

U.S. politics and social movements, his dispatches have appeared in *Counterpunch, MR Zine, ZNet, Venezuela Analysis, Alternet, MediaLeft, The SF Bayview,* and *Wiretap Magazine.* His articles have appeared in *Theory & Event, Qui Parle, Monthly Review, Radical Philosophy Review, Listening, Journal of Black Studies, Human Architecture,* and *The Commoner.* He has also translated books by Enrique Dussel and Immanuel Wallerstein.

Geoffrey L. Cohen, Ph.D. is the James G. March Professor of Organizational Studies in Education and Business and Professor of Psychology at Stanford University. He earned his Ph.D. from Stanford University in psychology. Dr. Cohen's work focuses on identity, stigma, and psychological intervention. His work has been published widely in journals such as *Science, Journal of Personality and Social Psychology,* and *Child Development.*

Nilanjana Dasgupta, Ph.D., is an Associate Professor of Psychology at the University of Massachusetts, Amherst. She received an A.B. from Smith College, a Ph.D. in Psychology from Yale University, and completed a post-doctoral fellowship at the University of Washington, Seattle. Her research finds that the local cultural milieu in which individuals are immersed have profound effects on their implicit attitudes and behavior toward members of outgroups, ingroups, and the self. Although stereotypes are known to bias individuals' judgments and behaviors implicitly despite their explicit egalitarian beliefs, she finds that implicit bias is not immutable. Under some conditions, immersion in local environments that highlight admired members of stereotyped groups significantly attenuates implicit bias in thought and action. Dr. Dasgupta has published widely in leading psychology journals. Through collaborations with lawyers, legal scholars, teachers, and other social scientists, she applies her research findings to law, politics, and K-12 teacher education. Dr. Dasgupta's research is funded by the National Science Foundation and the National Institutes of Health.

Thierry Devos, Ph.D., is an Associate Professor in the Department of Psychology at San Diego State University. He received his Ph.D. in social sciences from the University of Lausanne, Switzerland. His research focuses on how social identities operate outside of conscious awareness and control. Specifically, he is interested in the implicit interconnections between ethnic and national identities, and in factors affecting the implicit academic self-concept of under-represented groups. He has published more than 30 articles in academic journals and more than a dozen contributions to edited volumes. His research has been funded by the National Institute of Mental Health and the Swiss National Science Foundation.

John F. Dovidio, Ph.D., earned his B.A. from Dartmouth College and M.A. and Ph.D. from the University of Delaware. He is currently Professor of Psychology at Yale University. Before that, he was a professor at the University of Connecticut and at Colgate University. He has served as president of the Society for Personality and Social Psychology, the Society of Experimental Social Psychology, and Society for the Psychological Study of Social Issues. He has been editor of the *Journal of Personality and Social Psychology–Interpersonal Relations and Group Processes*, *Personality and Social Psychology Bulletin*, and *Social Issues and Policy Review*. His research interests are in stereotyping, prejudice, and discrimination; social power and nonverbal communication; and altruism and helping.

Samuel L. Gaertner, Ph.D., is a Professor of Psychology at the University of Delaware. He received a B.A. (1964) from Brooklyn College, Ph.D., and a Ph.D. in Psychology (1970) from The City University of New York: Graduate Center. Professor Gaertner's research has been supported by grants from the Office of Naval Research, the National Institutes of Mental Health and currently, the National Science Foundation. Together with John Dovidio, he has shared the Gordon Allport Intergroup Relations Prize, the Kurt Lewin Memorial Award (a career award) from the Society for the Psychological Study of Social Issues, Division 9 of the American Psychological Association.

Eric Hehman is a graduate student in social psychology at the University of Delaware. He received his B.A. from the University of Massachusetts, Dartmouth, in 2001. His research interests include intergroup dynamics and the resolution of intergroup conflict.

John T. Jost is Professor of Social Psychology at New York University. He received his Ph.D. from Yale University in 1995 and has taught at the University of California at Santa Barbara and Stanford University. Jost has published over 90 scientific articles and book chapters as well as four edited volumes, including *Social and Psychological Bases of Ideology and System Justification*. In 2007, he was named one of the five most highly cited social-personality psychologists in the world at the rank of Associate Professor. Other awards and honors include the Gordon Allport Intergroup Relations Prize, the Society for Personality and Social Psychology Theoretical Innovation Prize, the Erik Erikson Early Career Award for Research Achievement in Political Psychology, the International Society for Self & Identity Early Career Award, and the Morton Deutsch Award for Distinguished Scholarly and Practical Contributions to Social Justice. Jost was Editor-in-Chief of *Social Justice Research* (2003–2007) and has served on several editorial boards and executive committees of professional societies. He is a Fellow of the Association for Psychological Science and is Editor of the Oxford University book series on Political Psychology.

Kristin A. Lane is an Assistant Professor in the Psychology Program at Bard College. Her current research focuses on implicit bias, or attitudes and stereotypes that exist at a relatively less conscious level. Her work investigates the origins of such biases and their consequences in both laboratory and field set-tings. She has particular interests in the extent to which implicit attitudes and stereotypes can help account for in participation in academic domains (includ-ing the gender disparity in the sciences), and the application of the work to public policy and law. Kristin received her Ph.D. (Social Psychology) from Harvard University, her M.S. (Psychology) from Yale University, and her B.A. (Psychology and Mathematics) from the University of Virginia. Prior to arriv-ing at Bard, she was the Cabot Postdoctoral Fellow for Innovation in Teaching at the Derek Bok Center for Teaching and Learning at Harvard University.

Robert W. Livingston is an Assistant Professor at the Kellogg School of Management at Northwestern University. He received a B.A. from Tulane University, an M.A. from UCLA, and a Ph.D. in Social Psychology from The Ohio State University. Livingston's research investigates topics related to prejudice, inequality, status, and leadership. His work has been published in numerous top-tiered journals of social psychology including *Psychological Science, Journal of Personality and Social Psychology, Personality and Social Psychology Bulletin,* and *Journal of Experimental Social Psychology.*

Clarenda M. Phillips, Ph.D. is an Associate Professor of Sociology and Department Chair at Morehead State University. With a specialization in race, ethnicity, class, and gender, Dr. Phillips earned her Ph.D. from the University of Illinois at Urbana-Champaign and her B.A. from DePauw University. Co-editor of *African American Fraternities and Sororities: The Legacy and the Vision,* Dr. Phillips is a community-engaged scholar focusing on African American families, mental health, and coping.

Shanette C. Porter, Ph.D. is a Postdoctoral Fellow at Northwestern University. Dr. Porter's research focuses on social cognition and, more specifically, goals, attitudes, and intergroup processes. She has collaborated with multiple authors on topics ranging from automatic attitudes to linguistic influences on diverse teams.

Valerie Purdie-Vaughns, Ph.D. is an Assistant Professor of Psychology at Columbia University. Professor Purdie-Vaughns' primary area of research is stigma and intergroup processes. Given the pervasiveness of stigma in inter-personal, intergroup, and international contexts, her research projects include the exploration of: *(1)* contextual cues and reduction of threat in mainstream intellectual settings and *(2)* whether crime and mental illness have a face. Her articles have appeared in *Journal of Personality and Social Psychology, Child Maltreatment: Journal of American Professional Society on the Abuse of Children,* and *Journal of Marriage and the Family.*

Jennifer A. Richeson, Ph.D. is Professor of Psychology and African-American Studies and Faculty Fellow at the Institute for Policy Research at Northwestern University. Professor Richeson's research on interracial contact and perceptions of Black men has been published in various scholarly journals including, *Psychological Science*, the *Journal of Personality and Social Psychology*, *Nature Neuroscience*, and the *Journal of Experimental Social Psychology*. She recently won the 2009 Distinguished Scientific Award for Early Career Contribution to Psychology (Social Psychology) from the American Psychological Association and in 2006, she was named one of 25 MacArthur Foundation Fellows for her research "highlighting and analyzing major challenges facing all races in America and in the continuing role played by prejudice and stereotyping in our lives."

Tamar Saguy, Ph.D., is an Assistant Professor of psychology at the Interdisciplinary Center (IDC) Herzliya. Her research centers on the role of relative group power in intergroup processes. She received her Ph.D. in social psychology from the University of Connecticut in 2008 and was subsequently a postdoctoral associate at Yale University. She was born and raised in Israel and received a B.A. in Psychology and Communication in 2000 and an M.A. in Social Psychology in 2003 from Tel-Aviv University.

Donald A. Saucier, Ph.D., is Associate Professor and Director of Undergraduate Studies in the Psychology Department at Kansas State University. He received his B.A. in Psychology and Classical Civilization from Colby College and his M.A. and Ph.D. in Experimental Social Psychology from the University of Vermont. His research focuses on the measurement and expression of prejudice, in particular as it emerges in support of and opposition to various social and political policies and in helping situations. His scholarly work has been published in such journals as *Personality and Social Psychology Review*, *Personality and Social Psychology Bulletin*, the *Journal of Race and Policy*, and the *Journal of Interpersonal Violence*.

Rachel Sumner graduated from William Smith College, after which she worked with Drs. Valerie Purdie-Vaughns, Geoffrey Cohen, and Julio Garcia on a longitudinal study aimed at reducing the racial achievement gap in middle school. She has presented her research at the conferences of the Society for Personality and Social Psychology and the Association for Psychological Science and is currently pursuing her doctoral studies at Cornell University.

Joshua Waytz graduated from Northwestern University, where he majored in Psychology and Economics. At Northwestern, he was an honors student, was named to the Dean's List quarterly, and participated in efforts to improve socio-economic and racial diversity in admissions. His research interests include: stereotyping and prejudice, behavioral economics, and communication technology. Waytz's honors thesis investigated the impact of Barack Obama's presidency on race relations.

Russell J. Webster is a doctoral student in social/personality psychology at Kansas State University. Russell earned his B.A. in psychology at North Central College and his M.A. in social and cognitive processes at Ball State University. His primary research interests are in the study of the etiology, expression, and regulation of prejudice, stereotyping, and discrimination, with a special focus on the justification-suppression model of prejudice and terror management theory. Russell also studies the history of prejudice research in the behavioral sciences.

Kumar Yogeeswaran is a Ph.D. student in the Department of Psychology at the University of Massachusetts, Amherst. He received his B.A. from Ithaca College where he majored in Psychology and minored in Mathematics, and an M.S. in Social Psychology from the University of Massachusetts, Amherst. Kumar's research focuses on intergroup relations with an eye toward understanding how factors like perceived threat, emotion, and motivation increase versus decrease intergroup bias and how such biases impact human behavior. He is particularly interested in the nexus between national and ethnic identity. His recent projects focus on the tension between multiculturalism and assimilation as competing political ideologies in pluralistic nations and the role of negative emotions and threat on intergroup relations.

About the Commentators

Ian Ayres, J.D., Ph.D., is the William K. Townsend Professor of Law and Anne Urowsky Professorial Fellow in Law at Yale Law School and a Professor at the Yale School of Management.

Lawrence D. Bobo, Ph.D., is the W.E.B. Du Bois Professor of the Social Sciences at Harvard University.

Farai Chideya is a multimedia journalist and radio host who has written a novel and three books on race, politics, and media.

Michael C. Dawson, Ph.D., is the John D. MacArthur Professor of Political Science and the College at the University of Chicago.

Jenée Desmond-Harris, J.D., is an attorney and writer.

Eddie Glaude, Jr., Ph.D., is the William S. Tod Professor of Religion and African-American Studies, Department of Religion, and Chair, Center for African-American Studies at Princeton University.

Melissa Harris-Lacewell, Ph.D., is an Associate Professor of Politics and African-American Studies at Princeton University.

Marc Lamont Hill, Ph.D., is an Associate Professor of Education and Anthropology at Columbia University's Teachers College as well as an affiliate faculty member in African-American Studies at Columbia University.

Richard O. Lempert, J.D., Ph.D., is the Eric Stein Distinguished University Professor of Law and Sociology, *Emeritus* at the University of Michigan.

Kenneth W. Mack, J.D, Ph.D., is a Professor of Law at Harvard Law School.

Julianne Malveaux, Ph.D., is the President of Bennett College.

Marc H. Morial, J.D., is the President and CEO of the National Urban League.

Index